Modern Music and After

Modern Music and After

Paul Griffiths

OXFORD
UNIVERSITY PRESS

OXFORD
UNIVERSITY PRESS

Oxford University Press, Inc., publishes works that
Further Oxford University's objective of excellence
in research, scholarship, and education.

Oxford   New York
Auckland   Cape Town   Dar es Salaam   Hong Kong   Karachi
Kuala Lumpur   Madrid   Melbourne   Mexico City   Nairobi
New Delhi   Shanghai   Taipei   Toronto

With offices in
Argentina   Austria   Brazil   Chile   Czech Republic   France   Greece
Guatemala   Hungary   Italy   Japan   Poland   Portugal   Singapore
South Korea   Switzerland   Thailand   Turkey   Ukraine   Vietnam

Published by Oxford University Press, Inc.
198 Madison Avenue, New York, New York 10016

www.oup.com

Oxford is a registered trademark of Oxford University Press

Library of Congress Cataloging-in-Publication Data
Griffiths, Paul, 1947 Nov. 24–
Modern music and after / Paul Griffiths.—3rd ed.
p.   cm.
Includes bibliographical references and index.
ISBN 978-0-19-974050-5
1. Music–20th century–History and criticism.
I. Title.
ML197.G76 2010
780.9′04–dc22   2009047959

for Edmund

Music Acknowledgments

Examples are reproduced by kind permission of copyright holders or their agents as indicated. All rights are reserved by those copyright holders, and international copyright secured.

Ex. 1   Pierre Boulez, Sonatina for flute and piano (1946) © Amphion Editions Musicales; by permission of Les Editions Durand

Ex. 2   Pierre Boulez, Piano Sonata No. 2 (1946–48): I © Editions Heugel

Ex. 3   Luigi Nono, *Variazioni canoniche* for orchestra (1950) © Ricordi (Milan)

Ex. 4   John Cage, *Sonatas and Interludes* for prepared piano (1946–48): I © Henmar Press Inc., New York; by permission of Peters Edition London Ltd.

Ex. 5   John Cage, *Music of Changes* for piano (1951): I © Henmar Press Inc., New York; by permission of Peters Edition London Ltd.

Ex. 6   Morton Feldman, *Projection II* for five players (1951) © C. F. Peters Corporation, New York; by permission of Peters Edition Ltd.

Ex. 7   Earle Brown, *December 1952* © 1961 (renewed) Associated Music Publishers, Inc. (BMI)

Ex. 8   Olivier Messiaen, *Mode de valeurs et d'intensités* for piano (1949–50) © 1950 Editions Durand

Ex. 9   Karlheinz Stockhausen, *Kreuzspiel* for six players (1951)
          © Universal Edition
Ex. 10   Pierre Boulez, *Structures Ib* for two pianos (1951–52)
          © Universal Edition
Ex. 11   Luigi Nono, *Y su sangre ya viene cantando* for flute and
          chamber orchestra (1952) © Schott Music
Ex. 12   Karlheinz Stockhausen, *Studie II* in electronic sounds
          (1954) © Stockhausen Verlag
Ex. 13   Jean Barraqué, Piano Sonata (1950–52) © 1993
          Bärenreiter-Verlag Karl Vötterle GmbH & Co. KG,
          Kassel
Ex. 14   Elliott Carter, String Quartet No. 1 (1950–51): II © 1995
          G. Schirmer, Inc. (ASCAP)
Ex. 15   Milton Babbitt, *Three Compositions for Piano* (1947): I
          © Boelke-Bomart/Alfred A. Kalmus
Ex. 16   Conlon Nancarrow, Study No. 5 for player piano (early
          1950s) © Schott Music
Ex. 17   Stefan Wolpe, Oboe Quartet (1955): IV © 1976 Josef
          Marx Music Company
Ex. 18   György Ligeti, *Musica ricercata* for piano (1951–53): III
          © Schott Music
Ex. 19   Karlheinz Stockhausen, *Kontra-Punkte* for ten players
          (1952–53) © Universal Edition
Ex. 20   Karlheinz Stockhausen, *Klavierstück III* (1952) © Universal
          Edition
Ex. 21   Pierre Boulez, *Le Marteau sans maître* for contralto and six
          players (1953–55): I © Universal Edition
Ex. 22   Luigi Nono: *Il canto sospeso* for solo singers, choir, and
          orchestra (1955–56): II © Schott Music
Ex. 23   Karlheinz Stockhausen, *Zeitmasze* for woodwind quintet
          (1955–56) © Universal Edition
Ex. 24   John Cage, *Concert for Piano and Orchestra* (1957–58)
          © Henmar Press Inc., New York; by permission of Peters
          Edition London Ltd.
Ex. 25   Pierre Boulez, Piano Sonata No. 3 (1956–57): *Trope*
          © Universal Edition
Ex. 26   Luciano Berio, *Circles* for female singer, harpist, and two
          percussionists (1960) © Universal Edition
Ex. 27   Jean Barraqué: . . . *au delà du hasard* for five groups
          (1958–59) © 1993 Bärenreiter-Verlag Karl Vötterle GmbH
          & Co. KG, Kassel
Ex. 28   Igor Stravinsky, *Movements* for piano and orchestra
          (1958–59) © 1960 Hawkes & Son (London) Ltd.
Ex. 29   Olivier Messiaen, *Réveil des oiseaux* for piano and orchestra
          (1953) © 1955 Editions Durand

Ex. 30   Olivier Messiaen, *Sept Haïkaï* for piano and small orchestra (1962) © Editions Leduc

Ex. 31   Giacinto Scelsi, String Quartet No. 4 (1964) © 1984 Editions Salabert

Ex. 32   Sylvano Bussotti, *Per tre sul piano* (1959) © Universal Edition

Ex. 33   Mauricio Kagel, *Anagrama* for solo singers, speaking choir, and ensemble (1957–58) © Universal Edition

Ex. 34   György Kurtág, *The Sayings of Péter Bornemisza* for soprano and piano (1963–68) © Universal Edition

Ex. 35   Karlheinz Stockhausen, *Kontakte* for piano, percussion, and electronic sounds (1958–60) © Stockhausen Verlag

Ex. 36   Peter Maxwell Davies, *Taverner*, opera (1962–70): final scene © 1972 Boosey & Hawkes Music Publishers Ltd.

Ex. 37   Bernd Alois Zimmermann, *Monologe* for two pianos (1960–64) © Schott Music

Ex. 38   Luciano Berio, *Sinfonia* for eight voices and orchestra (1968–69): III © Universal Edition

Ex. 39   Harrison Birtwistle, *Verses for Ensembles* (1969) © Universal Edition

Ex. 40   Mauricio Kagel, *Match* for two cellos and percussion (1964) © Universal Edition

Ex. 41   Cornelius Cardew, *Treatise* (1963–67) © Hinrichsen Edition; by permission of Peters Edition London Ltd.

Ex. 42   Cornelius Cardew, 'Soon' (1971) © Estate of Cornelius Cardew

Ex. 43   Luciano Berio, *Sequenza III* for female voice (1965–66) © Universal Edition

Ex. 44   Heinz Holliger, *Siebengesang* for oboe and orchestra (1966–67): opening oboe solo © Schott Music

Ex. 45   Helmut Lachenmann, *Pression* for cello (1969–70) © 1972 Musikverlage Hans Gerig, Köln, assigned 1980 to Breitkopf & Härtel, Wiesbaden

Ex. 46   Iannis Xenakis, *Evryali* for piano (1974) © 1973 Editions Salabert

Ex. 47   Milton Babbitt, *Post-Partitions* for piano (1966) © C. F. Peters Corporation, New York; by permission of Peters Edition Ltd.

Ex. 48   La Monte Young, *The Well-Tuned Piano* (1964–), reproduced from an article by Kyle Gann in *Perspectives of New Music* by permission of author and editor

Ex. 49   Steve Reich, *Violin Phase* for four violins (1967) © Universal Edition

Ex. 50   Howard Skempton, *One for Martha* for piano (1974) from *Collected Piano Pieces* © Oxford University Press

Ex. 51   Pierre Boulez, *Rituel* for orchestra (1974–75) © Universal
          Edition
Ex. 52   György Ligeti, *Bewegung* for two pianos (1976) © Schott
          Music
Ex. 53   Harrison Birtwistle, *Melencolia I* for clarinet and orchestra
          (1976) © Universal Edition
Ex. 54   Karlheinz Stockhausen, *Mantra* for two pianos and
          electronics (1970) © Stockhausen Verlag
Ex. 55   Bill Hopkins, *Pendant* for violin (1968–69, rev. 1973)
          © Universal Edition
Ex. 56   Arvo Pärt, *Für Alina* for piano (1976) © Universal Edition
Ex. 57   Galina Ustvolskaya, Piano Sonata No. 5 (1986) © Inter-
          nationale Musikverlage Hans Sikorski
Ex. 58   Wolfgang Rihm, *Kein Firmament* for ensemble (1988)
          © Universal Edition
Ex. 59   Alfred Schnittke, String Quartet No. 3 (1983): II © Uni-
          versal Edition
Ex. 60   Valentyn Silvestrov, *Quiet Songs* for baritone and piano
          (1974–77): 'Shto v imeni tebe moem' © Musikverlag M. P.
          Belaieff
Ex. 61   Morton Feldman, *Three Voices* (1982) © Universal Edition
Ex. 62   Helmut Lachenmann, *Allegro sostenuto* for clarinet, cello,
          and piano (1987–88) © 2003 Breitkopf & Härtel,
          Wiesbaden
Ex. 63   John Cage, *Two* for flute and piano (1988): flute part
          © Henmar Press Inc., New York; by permission of Peters
          Edition London Ltd.
Ex. 64a   György Kurtág, *Twelve Microludes* for string quartet
          (1977–78): V © Editio Musica Budapest
Ex. 64b   György Kurtág, . . . *quasi una fantasia* . . . for piano and
          ensembles (1987–88): IV © Editio Musica Budapest
Ex. 65   Heinz Holliger, *Scardanelli-Zyklus* (1975–79): 'Der Sommer
          (III)' © Schott Music
Ex. 66   Salvatore Sciarrino, *Sei capricci* for violin (1975–76): II
          © Ricordi (Milan)
Ex. 67   Brian Ferneyhough, *Unity Capsule* for flute (1975–76)
          © Hinrichsen Edition; by permission of Peters Edition
          London Ltd.
Ex. 68   Brian Ferneyhough, *Etudes transcendentales* for soprano
          and four instruments (1982–85): II © Hinrichsen Edition;
          by permission of Peters Edition London Ltd.
Ex. 69   Michael Finnissy, *English Country-Tunes* for piano (1977):
          © United Music Publishers
Ex. 70   Elliott Carter, *Night Fantasies* for piano (1978–80) © 1982
          Associated Music Publishers, Inc. (BMI)

Ex. 71   Iannis Xenakis, *Tetora* for string quartet (1990) © Editions Salabert

Ex. 72   Luigi Nono, *La lontananza nostalgica utopica futura* for violin (1988) © Ricordi (Milan)

Ex. 73*a*   Karlheinz Stockhausen, nuclear formula for Eva © Stockhausen Verlag

Ex. 73*b*   Karlheinz Stockhausen, *Pietà* for soprano and flugelhorn (1990) © Stockhausen Verlag

Ex. 74   Harrison Birtwistle, *Ritual Fragment* for fourteen players (1990) © Universal Edition

Ex. 75   Luciano Berio, *Formazioni* for orchestra (1985–87) © Universal Edition

Ex. 76   George Benjamin, *Antara* for sixteen players (1985–87) © 1993 Faber Music Ltd.

Ex. 77   Horatiu Radulescu, *Das Andere* for viola (1984) © Lucero Print

Ex. 78   Gérard Grisey, *Périodes* for seven players (1976) © Ricordi (Milan)

Ex. 79   Claude Vivier, *Lonely Child* for soprano and orchestra (1980) © Boosey & Hawkes, Inc.

Ex. 80   Steve Reich, *Different Trains* for string quartet and recording (1988) © Hendon Music, Inc.

Ex. 81   Louis Andriessen, *De Staat* for ensemble and voices (1972–76) © 1994 Boosey & Hawkes Music Publishers Ltd.

Ex. 82   Franco Donatoni, *Still* for soprano and ensemble (1985) © Ricordi (Milan)

Ex. 83   John Adams, *Nixon in China*, opera (1985–87): final scene © 1987 Hendon Music, Inc.

Ex. 84   György Ligeti, Etude 1 'Désordre' for piano (1985) © Schott Music

Ex. 85   Kaija Saariaho, *Graal théâtre* (1994) © 1998 Chester Music Ltd.

Ex. 86   György Ligeti, Etude 17 'À bout de souffle' for piano (1997) © Schott Music

Ex. 87   Thomas Adès, *Arcadiana* for string quartet (1994): I © 1995 Faber Music Ltd.

Ex. 88   George Benjamin, *Viola, Viola* for two violas (1997) © 1998 Faber Music Ltd.

Ex. 89   John Zorn, *Shibboleth* for string trio, clavichord, and percussion (1997) © 2002 Hips Road Edition

Ex. 90   Heinz Holliger, *Schneewittchen*, opera (1997–98) © Schott Music

Ex. 91   Salvatore Sciarrino, *Luci mie traditrici*, opera (1996–98) © Ricordi (Milan)

Contents

2001

Prelude

This is not a history of music since 1945. It is not even a history of Western classical music—to use two epithets as loaded as they are slippery
—since 1945. It is, rather, an account of a musical movement that
gained huge momentum after 1945 (though of course its origins went
back further): a movement of radical renewal. To the composers of the
immediate postwar years, music seemed to have stalled. The great innovations of a generation before—those of *The Rite of Spring*, of Schoenberg's early atonal works, of Debussy's perpetual flux, of Varèse's ram-
pant percussion, of Ives's polyphony of styles—had not been followed
up. They had also been largely ignored by the world of musical performance. Modernism was always concerned with both these things, with
maintaining music's progress and with installing progressive music
within the general repertory.

Now, more than sixty years later, it would be easy to conclude that
the first of these tasks has been taken to the limit (if the second has
barely been begun), and the structure of this book reflects an uncertainty within the modernist project since the 1970s. Yet as long as
musical society largely ignores the changes (and the nonchanges) that
human mentality has accommodated or striven to accommodate in recent decades—the shifts and stabilities explored in the music under
discussion—the 'after' in this book's title is only a prospect and modern
music remains unfinished.

1945

No other date has left such a mark. The capitulation of
Germany in early May and of Japan in the summer brought
the Second World War to an end, and seems to have closed
the era of massive combat by which empires exerted their
supremacy. However, these events were accompanied by
others whose effects have not ended or even been diminished. The liberation of Nazi concentration camps revealed
that murder and suffering on an immense scale could be
perpetrated at the hands of quite ordinary people; the dropping of the first atomic bombs showed that these minor
agents were no longer necessary. People who survived the
war, and who came after, have had to live with a darker
awareness of what is humanly possible.

It can be no surprise that 1945 represents a shift in music.
The destruction, havoc, grief, and misery felt across the world
—and the widespread hopes for a new social order, and therefore a new culture—demanded not just reconstruction but
an alternative paradigm. Among composers, few were not
moved to make a fresh start, as we can see in the cases of Igor
Stravinsky, Olivier Messiaen, Elliott Carter, and many others.
The instigators of change, though, were not these mature
figures but the young: people just coming to adulthood in a
shattered world.

To the extent that this shattered or disordered world is still recognizably our own, a world of lost certainties and uncertain gains, so is its music—what we still, two-thirds of a century later, want to call 'modern music', because it feels as new now as it did then, and because everything that has happened in music since hinges, whether in extension or retraction, on that post–1945 moment.

1

Rational and Irrational

Western Europe, 1945–50

Paris, 1945–48

Nothing is ever quite new. Efforts to remake music after 1945 always appealed to the renewal of earlier in the century; indeed, the new phase was regularly justified as continuing what had been started at that time and left in abeyance for two decades. Similarly, nothing is ever totally localized. New beginnings soon after 1945 can be traced in the United States, Japan, central Europe, and other regions. Nevertheless, Paris in the immediate postwar years was an unusually active focus of innovation.

Though musical life had continued during the German occupation, the ending of the war was an incentive to breathe again, and then to change the world. In Paris, as throughout the previous Nazi empire, liberation made it possible to perform, discuss, and hear music that had been banned for being adventurous or Jewish or, to take the prominent case of Schoenberg, both. The moment, then, was right. And there were the right people to take possession of the moment. Olivier Messiaen (1908–92) during these years was composing his largest and most elaborate work so far, the *Turangalîla* symphony, a composition to crown his earlier achievements and at the same time display new concerns he shared with the young students who had gathered around him at the Paris Conservatoire. Pierre Boulez (b. 1925), the most gifted of them, was taking off from Messiaen and Schoenberg in a bold new direction, and Pierre Schaeffer (1910–95), in the studios of Radiodiffusion-

Télévision Française, was working towards the first examples of musique concrète, music made by transforming recorded sounds and
composed not onto paper but onto the heavy black discs of the contemporary gramophone.

The Young Boulez

Scattered across Europe in 1945 were students who, though unaware
of each other, shared many of the same convictions. Hans Werner
Henze (b. 1926), in Heidelberg, was rapidly assimilating music that had
been proscribed since his early childhood: Schoenberg, Berg, Stravinsky, and jazz. In Budapest and Milan, György Ligeti (1923–2006) and
Luciano Berio (1925–2003) were beginning to explore new avenues.
At the same time, in the United States, slightly older composers—Elliott
Carter (b. 1908), John Cage (1912–92), Conlon Nancarrow (1912–97),
Milton Babbitt (b. 1916)—were starting afresh. Of course, this is the
view of hindsight. Nancarrow's work was almost unknown until the
1970s, which is when Ligeti and Berio began to publish their early
compositions. But in the quasi-omniscience of retrospect, all these
composers and more (Messiaen notably) were going, if not in the same
direction, at least away from the same source, seeking alternatives to
some or all of the old musical certainties: metrical rhythm and consecutive form, tonal harmony and consistency of voice, standard genres
and regular groupings. Boulez was by no means prominent yet: no
composition of his was heard in a large forum until 1948 or published
until 1950. But in his music, right from 1945, he was unique in his
determination.

He was set on his path by the year he spent, that of 1944–45, in
Messiaen's class, as he later recalled: 'Names that were all but forbidden, and works of which we knew nothing, were held up for our admiration and were to arouse our intellectual curiosity. . . . Africa and
Asia showed us that the prerogatives of "tradition" were not confined
to any one part of the world, and in our enthusiasm we came to regard
music as a way of life rather than an art: we were marked for life.'[1]

In Boulez's case the admiration and the curiosity did not wash
away—rather they intensified—a need to challenge, even to reject.
Hence his equivocal relationship with his principal teacher. Though he
eagerly followed rehearsals for the first performance of Messiaen's *Trois
Petites Liturgies* in April 1945, in his later career as a conductor he has
never touched the score, nor that of the complete *Turangalîla* (1946–
48), preferring the works Messiaen wrote in the 1950s and 1960s—
scores arguably influenced by his own music. At the time, the echo of

---

1. Pierre Boulez, 'A Class and Its Fantasies', *Orientations* (London, 1986),
404; the piece was originally published as a tribute to Messiaen on his fiftieth
birthday. See also 'In Retrospect', in ibid., 405–6.

Messiaen's symmetrical modes (such as the octatonic scale) remained detectable in his compositions only because those modes were being so punishingly negated, and for several years the pupil was expressly hostile to his erstwhile master. In a critical paragraph from one of his earliest essays, published in 1948, he concluded that Messiaen 'does not compose—he juxtaposes.'[2]

To some extent, the hostility was the display of a delayed adolescence; it was also a necessary fuel for the young composer's creative zeal. Boulez formed himself in explosive reaction against what he found around him—not just the dusty Conservatoire but Messiaen, Schoenberg, Berg, Bartók, Stravinsky, all of whom were furiously taken to task in the polemical articles he wrote during his twenties, just as they were being implicitly taken to task in his compositions of those years. His most typical way of arguing on behalf of his music was to show how it realized potentialities that had been glimpsed by his predecessors but fudged by them for want of perspicacity or intellectual bravery. For example, the same essay that criticizes Messiaen the 'juxtaposer'— an essay devoted to finding a way forward for rhythm—admonishes Bartók for having a rhythmic style 'much simpler and more traditional' than that of *The Rite of Spring*, Jolivet because 'his empirical technique has prevented him from going very far', Messiaen for failing to integrate rhythm and harmony, Schoenberg and Berg because they 'remain attached to the classical bar and the old idea of rhythm', and Varèse 'for spiriting away the whole problem of technique . . .[:] a facile solution which solves nothing'. Even Webern—whom the young Boulez took as a touchstone of unflinching modernism, and whom he was at pains to isolate from other members of that crucial grandfatherly generation as the only exemplar[3]—even Webern is glancingly, parenthetically chided for 'his attachment to rhythmic tradition'.

Messiaen recalled that during this period Boulez 'was in revolt against everything';[4] Boulez himself remembers that 'it was our privilege to make the discoveries and also to find ourselves faced with nothing'.[5] The artist who is 'against everything' can, by virtue of that, look around him and find 'nothing'. Boulez's iconoclasm was perhaps extreme, but not exceptional for a self-confident young man in his late teens and early twenties, especially in a world that had lost its bearings. What was exceptional was the fact that musical history yielded itself to iconoclasm—that a composer in these years could set himself against

2. Pierre Boulez, 'Proposals', *Stocktakings from an Apprenticeship* (Oxford, 1991), 49.

3. See, for example, his 1952 essay 'Possibly . . . ', in ibid., 114, and the conclusion of his 1961 encyclopedia entry on Webern, in ibid., 303.

4. Claude Samuel, *Olivier Messiaen: Music and Color* (Portland, Oreg., 1994), 199.

5. Boulez, *Orientations*, 445.

not only the Milhauds and Poulencs but also the Messiaens and Schoen-
bergs, and could find, in his contrariety, the spur to creating works that
have come to be regarded as signals of their epoch.

There were perhaps several reasons, quite beyond anything in
Boulez's psychology, why that could happen, and why the same rebel-
lious spirit could be found in many of his contemporaries. One was the
need, after the war, to rebuild, and the feeling that the future lay with
a new generation—a generation unsullied by the compromises that
had been forced on people during the 1930s and then during the war.
Another, more particularly concerned with music, was the evident fact
that a period of artistic upheaval had been followed by two decades
during which the clock of progress had slowed, or even reversed. Yet
another factor would have been the philosophical movement, centred
in Paris, which viewed the individual as self-created. References to
Jean-Paul Sartre in Boulez's writings and lectures are rare, but many of
his statements ring out with a cold, clear bravery as those of a solitary
hero: 'There is no such thing as historical inevitability. History is what
one makes it. I hold very firmly to this principle.'[6]

Boulez wholeheartedly endorsed the view—voiced by a century of
avant-gardes as well as by Schoenberg and Adorno—that there is an
arrow in history. But it was up to the individual to seize that arrow and
run with it, or not. There could be no going back; hence his impatience
with neoclassicism. The way forward he soon found. René Leibowitz
(1913–72), a Polish-born musician who had studied with Webern in
the early 1930s, came to Paris in 1945 and in February of that year
conducted (presumably this was then necessary) a recording of Schoenberg's Wind Quintet that was broadcast immediately after the liberation of France. It is not clear whether what Boulez heard was the original performance or the broadcast, but in either event the piece seemed
to answer all his dissatisfactions. 'It was a revelation to me. It obeyed
no tonal laws, and I found in it a harmonic and contrapuntal richness,
and a consequent ability to develop, extend and vary ideas, that I had
not found anywhere else. I wanted, above all, to know how it was
written, so I went to Leibowitz and took with me other students from
Messiaen's harmony class'.[7]

In retrospect, it is ironic that Schoenberg's Op. 26 should have been
the work to provide this determining experience, for while Schoenberg's atonal works (Opp. 11–22) were to remain part of that select
repertory Boulez deemed beyond reproach, he was soon to criticize the
adherence to classical models of form in the serial pieces that followed,
just as, with even more inevitability, he was to turn his pen against

6. Pierre Boulez, *Conversations with Célestin Deliège* (London, 1977), 33.
7. Quoted in Joan Peyser, *Boulez: Composer, Conductor, Enigma* (London,
1977), 32–33.

Leibowitz in 'Proposals'.[8] The bombshell might be more easily understood if this had been Boulez's first encounter with anything by Schoenberg, as it just about could have been: the Nazi ban had put the seal on
the prewar Parisian antipathy to *dodécaphonie*—though it is hard to believe he had heard nothing of the twelve-note master from Messiaen.
Perhaps the crucial matter was being introduced to Schoenberg and to
serialism as sound, for almost nothing by Schoenberg or his pupils had
yet been commercially recorded. It had been the sound of Stravinsky's
Chant du rossignol, heard over the radio, that had first opened his ears
to 'modern music';[9] it was now the sound of the Schoenberg Wind
Quintet that pointed him in a new direction. Perhaps in both cases the
unexpectedness was decisive. Boulez's language in speaking of his formative experiences is almost that of religious conversion: the 'brand-
ing', the 'revelation'. Schoenberg's Op. 26 provided a road-to-Damascus
experience.

A few published excerpts from Boulez's early compositions[10] hint
at what happened. A Toccata—one of five piano pieces written in December 1944 and January 1945, and therefore before the confrontation with serialism—seems to be attempting to create a totally chromatic world by rapidly piling up motifs characteristic of Messiaen's
modes. Particularly prominent are motifs including a tritone and a perfect fifth, whose diminishing echoes go on at least as far as the cantata
Le Soleil des eaux (1948). Also striking is the adumbration of two kinds
of music on which Boulez was to base his First Piano Sonata, a long
seventeen months later: relatively slow music that includes rapid grup-
petti, and so displays a simultaneity of tempos more characteristic of
extra-European traditions (as, for instance, in the nimble ornaments
an Indian musician might introduce into preludial material, or in the
overtone-related speeds of Indonesian percussion orchestras); and extremely fast music in which all qualities of harmony and contrapuntal
relation are hammered towards uniform pulsation (here again the goal
seems to be non-Western, though this time Boulez had clear pointers
available, especially in the toccata-style piano music of Messiaen—
such as the 'chord theme' in the *Vingt Regards sur l'Enfant-Jésus*, which
Messiaen was completing when Boulez joined his class—and Bartók).

After the experience of Schoenberg's Op. 26, in the Theme and
Variations for piano left hand (June 1945) and the first two movements of a Quartet for ondes martenot (August–September 1945), we

8. For a study of the conflict, written from a viewpoint sympathetic to
Leibowitz, see Reinhard Kapp, 'Shades of the Double's Original: René Leibowitz's Dispute with Boulez', *Tempo*, 165 (1988), 2–16.

9. New Yorker profile of Boulez by Peter Heyworth, reprinted in William
Glock, ed., *Pierre Boulez: a Symposium* (London, 1986), 5.

10. Accompanying Gerald Bennett's article, ibid., 44–52.

find a Boulez who has mastered Schoenbergian serialism, and added to it a quite non-Schoenbergian and already non-Leibowitzian rhythmic irregularity based on cells rather than metres, thereby attempting some union of Schoenberg and Messiaen (the flavour of Messiaen's harmony is perhaps more a residue than an attempt). The next step, which could have followed the discovery of Webern, was a sudden reduction of scale, in the *Notations* of December 1945, to flash views of musical worlds, worlds that again include interminglings of speed and slowness (No. 1) and a hectic toccata (No. 6), besides varieties of trapped ostinato.

This collection's abstract title alone made it a trace of the future. It had, however, very little place in the present, as it was lost until the late 1970s. Many of Boulez's other early pieces, too, were lost or withdrawn, others not performed or published until several years after they were written. The history being considered here is that of a composer who, as yet, was little known beyond a small coterie. That, however, was to change. As music director for the theatre company run by Jean-Louis Barrault and Madeleine Renaud, a post he took up in 1945, Boulez gained access to literary and social circles in Paris that would respond to an eruptive force.

Boulez dedicated *Notations* to Serge Nigg (1924–2008), who it seems was the liveliest of the bunch of contemporaries to have come with him through Messiaen to Leibowitz, and whose career arrestingly points up something that Boulez was not: political. Boulez's political indifference—perhaps his political atheism—is all the more remarkable given how the vocabulary of his reminiscences suggests not only Pauline conversion but revolutionary activism. To many of his contemporaries the connections were inescapable: the connections between rethinking music and rethinking society, both activities to be done on the basis of rational, egalitarian principles in determined opposition to the philosophical floundering that had gone before. In these few years before the full freeze of the Cold War, it was not disingenuous or merely idealistic to see the possibility of revolution spreading across Europe, and thereby providing the home for a new musical order. Soon, though, the happy alliance of socialism and serialism was to wither as a dream, and Nigg's political commitment—fully formed by the time of his four Eluard songs (1948) and cantata *Le Fusillé inconnu* (1949)—led him along a familiar path towards musical conservatism in the interests of mass appeal. Nor was he by any means alone among Western Europeans in reliving what had been the tensions of Soviet cultural policy in the first two decades after 1917: his exact contemporary Luigi Nono (1924–90) fought that fight.

To Boulez it might have appeared that abstention from politics was necessary in order to focus on bringing about the musical revolution. (It could also be that his refusal of political engagement was allied with his rejection of Leibowitz.) Quite what he hoped for after the revolution is unclear, and perhaps was so then. The effort to generalize serialism—to apply twelve-note principles to domains other than pitch, such as duration, instrumentation, dynamic or, for the piano, mode of attack—was not explicitly voiced in his compositions or writings until 1951, by which time Messiaen had pointed the way in his *Mode de valeurs et d'intensités*. Before then his expressed theoretical endeavour was rather more limited: to ensure—quoting again from the 1948 essay in which he had briskly surveyed his predecessors' contributions to rhythm—'that techniques as varied as those of dodecaphony can be balanced by a rhythmic element itself perfectly "atonal"'.[11]

The fact that Babbitt had devised a kind of rhythmic serialism just the year before, quite independently, might seem to justify Boulez's Schoenbergian and Adornoesque belief in a historical imperative within music. Yet the two composers had little to say to one another when opportunity arose: Babbitt was to express his disappointment with European serialism,[12] and Boulez's only evidence of reciprocal interest was a single performance (of Babbitt's *Correspondences* for string orchestra and tape in 1973) when he was at the head of the New York Philharmonic. Besides, there is the testimony of the pieces they were writing during this period, for Babbitt's graceful and witty lucidity could hardly be further from Boulezian attitudes of vehemence, in music as in words.

Creative violence in Boulez's first published works is associated, on one level, with the presence in all of them of the piano, since to the examples he had drawn from Messiaen and Bartók he could add those of Schoenberg's Op. 11 pieces and *Pierrot lunaire*, in which he admired 'a kind of piano writing . . . with considerable density of texture and a violence of expression because the piano is treated . . . as a percussive piano which is at the same time remarkably prone to frenzy'.[13] He also accepted Schoenberg as an ideal of form in what was for a long time his earliest composition in print, his Sonatina for flute and piano (1946), jamming four movement-types—the specific model was Schoenberg's Chamber Symphony Op. 9—into a continuous structure. One can understand why he might have been attracted by this idea. It offered a double-layered form to equal in complexity his treatment of pitch and rhythm as separate but joinable parameters. It enabled him to return, after the unusual brevity of *Notations*, to the expansiveness and dynamism of his earlier music. And it set him, at a time when he was still a member of Leibowitz's group, in the line of the master.

But the piece is contra-Schoenberg too, inevitably. At the opening of the 'first movement' the flute makes a rare complete linear statement of the row, which in this form contains a restricted variety of intervals

11. Boulez, 'Proposals', 54.
12. See below, pp. 90–91.
13. Boulez, *Conversations with Célestin Deliège*, 30.

Example 1   Pierre Boulez, Sonatina

(see example 1): major sevenths, major thirds (plus one major tenth),
tritones, and fifths, including two expressions of the tritone-fifth motif,
as B♭–E–A and D–A♭–E♭. These limitations, and the explicit division of
the series into groups of five, five, and two notes, may indicate a wish
to profit from Webern's example of using serialism as a control on interval content while avoiding Webern's symmetry. The piano accompanies and echoes with a sequence of row forms in which the same
five-five-two partition often obtains; in bar 37, for example, the left
hand's five-note set is an inversion of the flute's. Also to be noted, in
bars 34 and 38, is Boulez's use of row fragments as harmonic units, a
technique he would have found in Schoenberg and Webern, and was
to make central to his musical practice. However, the glimmering or
racing stasis of his subsequent works is here a long way off. So, indeed,
is the regular movement of Schoenberg's or Webern's serial works. Instead, metre and beat are in a turmoil of change, and progress is maintained, powerfully, by the dynamic level and the impetus of the gestures,
right from the opening insistence (the first hexachord of a row form is
read forwards, the second simultaneously backwards) on the B♭ – B cell
that is the piano's focus in this passage. Webern's straight-line geometries are shattered and distorted over curves. The whole Western ideal
of music to be apprehended moment by moment, as purposeful growth,
is countered, and the writing for both instruments—the suggestions of

drums, xylophones, and vibraphones in the piano, the use of the flute's extreme high register, with its inevitable breakdown of tone—points as much to traditions from beyond Europe. In that is perhaps the Sonatina's most radical departure: to be open to non-European music without recourse to any kind of exoticism.

What also contributes to the Asian or African quality of the piece is Boulez's understanding of theme as ostinato. Where the Sonatina is most thematic, in the quite unusually symmetrical and playful scherzo, it sounds drilled to be so, and the initial five-note idea in the flute part of example 1, though a recurrent gesture, functions less as a theme than as a periodic signal. And while the whole row does appear again in the slow movement, it is buried as a trilling cantus firmus, overlaid by elements that seem unrelated to it and purely decorative: the texture now is distinctly predictive of Boulez's later music. At other points, as in the section beginning at bar 296, Boulez destroys the series wilfully and utterly, splitting it into dyads he engages in a purely rhythmic development without reference to the pitch orderings in the series. This is typical of a work whose intensiveness comes partly from the antagonism between serial repetition and the perpetual quest for ways of transforming and disintegrating the series beyond recognition, and partly from those harsh metrical dislocations that derive from the kind of cellular rhythm inherited from Messiaen and *The Rite of Spring*. Boulez's achievement here, in combining the lessons of his predecessors, in looking out from Europe, in expanding serial technique, and in conveying an unmistakeable determination all his own, is extraordinary for a composer of twenty-one.

Boulez's Second Piano Sonata

Boulez's position as the leader of the young Parisian serialists appears in retrospect to have been definitively established by 1948, the year in which he not only completed his Second Piano Sonata but also had a score performed on French radio (his music for René Char's *Le Soleil des eaux*) and published two articles in the new journal *Polyphonie*. This was to be the pattern of his activity for the next several years—producing music, and arguments in support of that music—and it testifies to his chosen role as the head of a revolutionary phalanx. In 'The Current Impact of Berg',[14] prompted by a series of performances in Paris, he attacked the 'Romanticism' and 'attachment to tradition' he found in various works by the composer, his attack being stimulated particularly by a tendency to praise Berg at the expense of Schoenberg and Webern as the master of atonality with a human face. The other essay was the already invoked 'Proposals', in which he not only called his predecessors to task but offered indications of the path forward with reference to his

14. Boulez, *Stocktakings*, 183–87.

own recent works: the Sonatina, the Char cantata *Le Visage nuptial*, a lost symphony, and the Second Piano Sonata.

The Second Sonata, a much weightier work than the Sonatina or the slim, two-movement First Sonata, is a half-hour piece in four movements, and shows, besides an extension of Boulez's diversifying serial technique, a deeper involvement of rhythm as a functional participant. Comparison of the sonata with Beethoven's 'Hammerklavier' has long been commonplace, and seems to have been invited by the composer in creating music of Beethovenian weight, density, and texture (this is a far more continuous, propelled piece than the Sonatina, as well as a heavier one), and in providing strong intimations of sonata form in the first movement and of fugue in the finale. Given that Boulez, when he wrote the work, was still in his early twenties and unknown outside a small Paris circle, his appeal to Beethoven bespeaks a certainty in his historical position that the piece has justified in itself and in its career. It was the first of his works to be published, editions appearing not only in Paris but also in New York, thanks to Boulez's friendship with Cage, who also arranged a performance in the city, by David Tudor. In the 1970s it was taken up by Maurizio Pollini. The work is also one of the few that Boulez has not suppressed or revised. Where the chronological places of, for example, *Le Soleil des eaux* and *Le Visage nuptial* have been confused by repeated recastings, the Second Sonata persists as a means of direct access to the young Boulez in the heat of creation—of creation by destruction. As he was to recall: 'I tried to destroy the first-movement sonata form, to disintegrate slow movement form by the use of the trope, and repetitive scherzo form by the use of variation form, and finally, in the fourth movement, to demolish fugal and canonic form. Perhaps I am using too many negative terms, but the Second Sonata does have this explosive, disintegrating and dispersive character, and in spite of its own very restricting form the destruction of all these classical moulds was quite deliberate.'[15]

Since Boulez was here speaking a quarter of a century after the event, he could have been influenced by how his work had come to be regarded in the interim. However, his already mentioned creative violence is strikingly expressed in the music's markings, especially in the last movement. Having asked, in his opening remarks, that the player should 'avoid absolutely, above all in slow tempos, what are customarily called "expressive nuances"', Boulez repeatedly requires in the finale that the sound be 'percussive','strident', 'exasperated', arriving near the end at the instruction to 'pulverize the sound'. Destructiveness is at least implicit, too, in what he wrote at the time in 'Proposals': the destructiveness of one whose only response to his musical forefathers was antagonistic, and the destructiveness of one whose ideal was ceaseless change. If there were to be a coherent relationship between

15. Boulez, *Conversations with Célestin Deliège*, 41–42.

Example 2a   Pierre Boulez, Piano Sonata No. 2, opening

Example 2b   Pierre Boulez, Piano Sonata No. 2, later in first movement

pitch and rhythm, then, as he saw it, rhythm had to obey similar laws of instability and non-repetition to those obtaining in his serial universe; as he wrote in 'Proposals', 'the principle of variation and constant renewal will guide us remorselessly'.[16]

The most usual result of this principle in the Second Sonata is a tangled counterpoint of cells, frequently in three or four parts, perpetually reinterpreting the proportions of a few basic motifs. Example 2a shows the initial two bars of the sonata and example 2b a passage from later in the first movement, the latter redrawn in order to show the polyphony more clearly (the division into parts here is arbitrary). Among other correspondences, the semiquaver repeated-note motif of example 2a appears in example 2b in units of semiquavers, triplet quavers, quavers and triplet crotchets, each time to a different transformation of the same intervals. The patterning, however, is in tension with the music's density and speed, to create an alarming sense of music going too fast, hurtling out of control.

16. Boulez, *Stocktakings*, 57.

Cellular counterpoint of this kind is alternated in the first movement with vigorous chordal charges (Tempo II) that serve to reinject
the music with energy whenever it shows signs of flagging or of coming to a dead end, and that themselves strive towards an even quaver
motion that, once achieved, is suddenly galloped into triplets before
the counterpoint returns 'rapide et violent'. A second opposition is created between passages in which the twelve notes are fixed in register,
creating a feeling of obsessiveness or frustration, and others in which
they are free; in example 2b the C♯, D and G♯/A♭ are so fixed (constitut-
ing an instance of the tritone-fifth motif). Out of these two kinds of
dialectic Boulez generates the impression of a classical sonata allegro,
but since the movement is at the same time constantly redrawing its
basic thematic material, it manifests too a headlong rush away from
any kind of formal definition.

The other movements are as described in the above quotation from
the composer (only the third uses the same series as the first, the second and fourth having their own). The second movement, like the
slow section of the Sonatina, looks towards the later Boulez, but now
in terms more of form than texture. A relatively simple first part is,
though with considerable variation, repeated in retrograde and interrupted by musical parentheses in faster or slower tempos: this is what
Boulez meant by referring to the medieval practice of troping. Contrasting with this elaborate structure, the third movement is straightforwardly a scherzo with three trios,[17] though passed through the filter
of variation form (the four scherzo sections are related as original, retrograde inversion, inversion, and retrograde): the relatively simple style
of this movement perhaps reflects its early date, for it was finished in
May 1946, which might suggest that it was originally planned not for
the Second Sonata but for the First. The finale is again a highly ramified construction. Starting with three and a half pages of desperate
suggestion around the basic ideas, it plunges into the extreme bass for
an ominous serial statement that gives rise to a quasi-fugal development in two phases, the themes being defined more by rhythm than
by pitch.

In most of this movement, as throughout those before, Boulez
works with concatenations of cells, but in one section (defined by the
tempo of quaver note=126 and beginning at the bottom of page 34 in
the Heugel edition) he seems to be trying out a new arithmetical approach to rhythm—one that Messiaen had introduced in the movements
'Turangalîla II' and 'Turangalîla III' of his *Turangalîla* symphony.[18] Both
composers used rhythmic values that are all multiples of a semiquaver;

---

17. See Boulez, *Conversations with Célestin Deliège*, 41. However, the original title was 'Variations-Rondeau'; see Jean-Jacques Nattiez, ed., *The Boulez-
Cage Correspondence* (Cambridge, 1993), 77.

18. See Robert Sherlaw Johnson, *Olivier Messiaen* (London, 1977), 92–93.

the Boulez passage has values between two and nine semiquavers, with some relationships between successions of values in different polyphonic lines. At one point, for example, the sequence 2-7-3-7-4-9-2 coincides with its retrograde, and though the moment is too brief for any firm conclusions to be drawn, the way is opened here towards the serial durations found in the musical manifesto of total serialism (i.e., serial organization of all parameters) that Boulez would provide four years later in the first book of his *Structures* for two pianos. It is noteworthy, and similarly significant in the light of Boulez's future development, that the pitch lines here do not show the same retrograde relationship. Following Messiaen's example, Boulez treats rhythm and pitch as separately composable elements, and as elements whose structures may even be placed in open conflict, provided there is the notional coherence of both having the same abundant freedom.

Example 2*b* has already suggested both the separateness and the intensiveness of Boulez's rhythmic development, but there are other places in the work, especially in the finale, where the rhythmic counterpoint is more orderly, at least in how it is notated. (In much of the music Boulez wrote in his twenties the notation serves to reveal aspects of compositional technique that a more practical orthography might obliterate, as if the music were intended not only to be played and heard but to give lessons to junior composers, and perhaps even to be discussed in histories of music.) At one point, for instance, a rhythmic canon is projected by lines made up of variants of two cells: one is distinguished by having two equal values plus a third that is dissimilar (e.g., dotted semiquaver—dotted semiquaver—semiquaver), the other by symmetry (e.g., semiquaver—semiquaver triplets—semiquaver: in Messiaen's terms such rhythms are 'nonretrogradable'). The modifications of these motifs are easy to follow, but the ties—not to mention the low dynamic level of this section, the speed, the density, and the absence of any parallel cross-references on the pitch level—thoroughly obscure what is going on. The highly evolved construction is obliterated as it is established.

Such negativity, as has already been indicated, is characteristic of Boulez's early music, and in particular of this sonata. The violence of the work is not just superficial rhetoric but symptomatic of a whole aesthetic of annihilation, and especially of a need to demolish what had gone before. To quote Boulez again on this: 'History as it is made by great composers is not a history of conservation but of destruction— even while cherishing what has been destroyed.'[19] The massively powered developments of the sonata's outer movements bring an autodestructive impetus to the classical moulds of sonata allegro and fugue in what is at the same time a determined refutation of Schoenberg's conservative practice with regard to form. Simultaneously, Boulez effaces

19. Boulez, *Conversations with Célestin Deliège*, 21.

his own constructive means (while leaving traces for readers of the printed music), not only by piling up rhythmic cells so that they obliterate one another, as in example 2, but also by pressing his proliferating serial method so hard that any unifying power in the basic interval shapes is threatened.

Other Stories

Nothing could better illustrate the gap—but also the underlying alliance—between master and pupil than to place Boulez's Second Piano Sonata alongside Messiaen's precisely contemporary *Turangalîla* symphony. Boulez's ardour is dynamic, Messiaen's static. The one is all becoming (and not becoming), the other all being. Boulez detonates traditional forms; Messiaen accepts elementary schemes of repetition and alternation. Where Boulez negates, Messiaen affirms. The symphony is a ten-movement cycle of celebration: a celebration of exhilarating pulsation, of radiant harmony, of the rich colours to be found in a large orchestra augmented by ondes martenot and by a solo piano at the head of a tuned percussion group also including glockenspiel, celesta, and vibraphone.

The similarities between the sonata and the symphony would have to include intermittent high speed, cellular rhythm (though of course regular pulse is the exception in Boulez), and perhaps also erotic impulse. In almost everything Boulez has said and written about his own music, the interlacing of creation and destruction is seen in quite abstract terms. However, of the two vocal works he produced during this period, both to words by René Char, the larger, *Le Visage nuptial*, sets poems of intense sexual imagery, while the other, *Le Soleil des eaux*, begins, in its definitive form, with a song of sensual longing. According to his own account, he was drawn to Char's poetry because of 'the clipped violence of his style, the unequalled paroxysm, the purity'[20]— ideals that accorded with his musical project. As to his expressive affiliations, in works of clamorous intensity and occasional languor, he has had little to say. He also moderated both cantatas' immoderacy—to which they owed part of their obstinate power—in later revisions. *Le Visage nuptial*, originally set out in 1946–47 for soloists with two ondes martenot, piano, and percussion, was subsequently orchestrated and then substantially revised in the late 1980s. *Le Soleil des eaux* was reinterpreted in three successive cantata versions in 1950, 1958, and 1965.

Insisting on musical revolution, Boulez's writings of the period only rarely mention expressive purpose, which makes such breaks all the more telling. Somewhat later he recalled how he had been 'struck in a very violent way' by the beauty of African and Far Eastern music

20. Antoine Goléa: *Rencontres avec Pierre Boulez* (Paris, 1958), 99.

(the music that Messiaen had taught him to admire), 'a beauty so far removed from our own culture and so close to my own temperament',[21] but most striking and most immediate is the revelation at the end of 'Proposals', with reference to another French artist who had been 'struck in a very violent way' by extra-European cultures. 'I think', he wrote, 'that music should be collective hysteria and magic, violently modern—along the lines of Antonin Artaud.' But then immediately comes the recoil: 'I have a horror of discussing verbally what is so smugly called the problem of aesthetics . . . I prefer to return to my lined paper.'[22]

The work he returned to his lined paper to write was the *Livre pour quatuor* (1948–49), his first instrumental work without piano. The medium of the string quartet inevitably imposed, as he has said, 'a certain reticence',[23] but it also made available a wide variety of tone colour, for he took up effects to be found in the quartets of Debussy, Bartók, Berg, and Webern. Of the six projected movements, the even-numbered ones (except perhaps for IV, which has been neither published nor performed) are those in which attention is fixed most firmly on the development of rhythmic cells in an intensive manner proceeding from the Second Sonata. The odd-numbered movements are freer in feeling and motion, and often touch an abstracted sensuousness that also marks the opening song of *Le Soleil des eaux*. But rhythmic complexity is a feature throughout, and no doubt accounted for the delayed and piecemeal première of the work: movements I and II were not heard until 1955, and III, V, and VI followed only in the early 1960s. Partial performances are not, however, in contradiction with the nature of the *Livre*, for the players are invited to choose and order movements as they will.

With this project delayed, the Char cantatas revised and other pieces suppressed, the history of Boulez's works of the late 1940s is complex. His statements about history, such as have been quoted here, suggest a single march of events, into which he strode, and whose tempo he made his own (or vice versa). Later explanations, such as emerge from his interviews with Deliège, emphasizing the Sonatina and the sonatas as way stations towards the first book of *Structures*, ratify that view, which became part of the ideology of new music. And so other achievements of his passionately creative early twenties, such as the Char cantatas, the *Livre pour cordes*, and the long withdrawn Sonata for two pianos, were relegated to the margins. What thereby emerged as a zealous pursuit of historical necessity is only a part of the truth of the young Boulez's artistic behaviour. It is no less remarkable for that.

21. 'Sonate, que me veux-tu?', *Perspectives of New Music*, i/2 (1963), 34.
22. Boulez, *Stocktakings*, 54.
23. Boulez, *Conversations with Célestin Deliège*, 53.

Musique Concrète

The presence of the ondes martenot in the music that Boulez and Messiaen were writing at this time—Boulez's Quartet and *Le Visage nuptial*, Messiaen's *Turangalîla*—can be understood in various ways: Boulez was a performer on the instrument, and Messiaen used its capacity to suggest a voice unearthly in its range, power, and wordlessness. Whether at the time they were also concerned with electronic music as a goal is unclear; Boulez's early writings suggest that the problems consuming him were those of *écriture*. However, there were others who were eager to explore new sound resources, and in May 1948, Pierre Schaeffer created the first example of what became known as 'musique concrète': *Etude aux chemins de fer*, a three-minute piece made by manipulating recordings of railway trains.[24]

Experiments with discs had been conducted before the war, notably (and independently) by Milhaud, Hindemith, and Varèse, but it remained to Schaeffer to discover and use the basic techniques of sound transformation: reversing a sound by playing its recording backwards, altering it in pitch, speed, and timbre by changing the velocity of playback, isolating elements from it, and superimposing one sound on another. Just as important as these possibilities was the change to the art of composition. Every example of musique concrète was an improvisation created by the composer working directly with the sounds available: notation and performance were bypassed, and many traditional compositorial skills—those of imagining sounds and shapes, and setting them down precisely enough for the needs of performers—were irrelevant. Perhaps for those very reasons, electronic music was soon set on a path apart from other music, to become a sphere (too often regarded as a secondary sphere) with its own institutions and proponents.

At the time, though, Schaeffer's hopes, like Boulez's, would seem to have been more utopian. Both men were convinced that their innovations—techniques of sound transformation for the one, principles of rhythm and form adequate to serialism for the other—were historically inevitable and would provide a way towards the musical future. Schaeffer's aim was to use his techniques in order to free his material from its native associations, so that an event could become not just an evocative symbol but a pure 'sound object' amenable to compositional treatment. To have depended on the original associations would have been, in his terms, to create not music but literature, to make a drama of sound effects rather than a musical composition of rhythms and timbres. An important discovery was made when he remarked that the removal of the opening instants of a sound, the 'starting transient',

24. See Carlos Palombini, 'Machine Songs V: Pierre Schaeffer—from Research into Noises to Experimental Music', *Computer Music Journal*, xvii/3 (1993), 14–19.

could transform its character, so that a bell stroke, for instance, would be changed into something more like an organ tone. Armed with techniques of this kind, he hoped to employ an array of gramophone turntables as 'the most general musical instrument possible', providing facilities for altering any sound derived from the real world (hence the term 'musique concrète' to denote this music created from 'concrete' sound sources, though behind the choice of word there may also have been the hope that new materials would revolutionize the art in the way that reinforced concrete had revolutionized architecture—an optimistic analogy cherished by many composers in the decade or so after the war).

Schaeffer's early studies, which include not only the railway piece but also others created from piano chords (played by Boulez) and saucepans, were broadcast by French radio on October 5, 1948 in what was billed as a 'concert of noises'. The result was immediate interest from the public and from fellow composers. Several young musicians visited Schaeffer's studio, and one of them, the Messiaen pupil Pierre Henry, remained to collaborate with him on what was the first extended electronic composition, the *Symphonie pour un homme seul* (1949–50), which uses a wide variety of sounds—vocal, instrumental, and orchestral, as well as many from everyday objects—in eleven short movements of diverse character, by turns sensual, whimsical, and menacing. The work received its première at the first public concert of electronic music, given at the Ecole Normale de Musique in Paris on March 18, 1950. With the arrival of the tape recorder later that year to ease production, and with the formal establishment by French radio of a Groupe de Musique Concrète in 1951, the way was open for a wider dissemination of the means of electronic music. For Boulez and Messiaen, the possibility of a precise control over sound and duration came at the opportune moment when music itself seemed to be demanding pristine process.

Variations: Nono

1948 begins to appear a key year: the year of the first musique concrète, the year when Messiaen completed *Turangalîla* and Boulez his Second Sonata, and the year when another avenue of modernism opened with the arrival of Hermann Scherchen (1891–1966) to teach a course at the conservatory in Venice, where his class included Bruno Maderna (1920–73) and Nono, both Venetians and both ex-pupils of Gian Francesco Malipiero.[25] Scherchen was a great instigator. He had conducted *Pierrot lunaire* on its 1912 tour, and given the first performance

25. I am grateful to Nicolas Hodges for giving me the benefit of his unpublished essay 'Luigi Nono: Compositional Development from *Variazioni canoniche* (1950) to *Composizione n.2 per orchestra—Diario polacco* (1958–59)'. The

Example 3   Luigi Nono, *Variazioni canoniche*

of Berg's *Wozzeck* fragments, among many premières; since 1933 he
had been living in Switzerland. He was active in the International Society for Contemporary Music, which, during the decade or so after
the war was still an important forum. And he had founded, in 1919,
the most influential new-music review: *Melos*. Rather unusually for
someone who had emerged from Schoenberg's circle, he had catholic
tastes, and seems to have encouraged young composers—first Nono
and Maderna, later Iannis Xenakis (1922–2001)—to stay independent
of all orthodoxies. On Nono his influence was decisive, though also
important at that 1948 course was the presence of Eunice Catunda, a
Brazilian composer and communist, who introduced both Nono and
Maderna to Spanish and Brazilian dance rhythms, and to the poetry
of Lorca. The Latin rhythms and the Lorca were to have a driving importance in Nono's music of the early 1950s; the communist allegiance
he already shared. Though it was not until 1952 that he joined the
party, his first public work was a homage to Schoenberg's most explic-

best published introduction to Nono in English remains: G. W. Hopkins, 'Luigi
Nono', *Music and Musicians,* 14/8 (1965–66), 32ff.

itly anti-fascist piece, *Variazioni canoniche sulla serie dell'op.41 di Arnold Schoenberg* (i.e., the *Ode to Napoleon*).

The title could be misleading. Nono's interpretation of both variation and canon is unconventional, and the work is not serial: rather the series is the music's gradual discovery, taking control of harmony in the third variation and of melodic counterpoint in the fourth, at the end of which—in the closing bars of the piece—the harp at last presents the twelve-note succession complete. Like Boulez at a similar point of close approach to Schoenberg (in the Sonatina), Nono immediately proves his separation and his individuality; but he does this not so much by contradicting Schoenberg as by hailing him from a distance, a distance expressed in features that were to remain characteristic. Among these are the treatment of the orchestra in choirs of like instruments (an old Venetian habit), the elemental simplicity, the Varèsian favouring of unpitched percussion for rhythmic messages, and the powerful thrust. Hopkins mentions also 'that sense of mystery whereby Nono seems to be a conjuror drawing sounds from the air as from a hat'. Example 3, from the lead-up to the second variation, may indicate many of these aspects. The insistence and the elementalness are there in the way a short-long-short rhythmic figure is stamped by the timpani in the fifth bar from out of the whispering percussion, and then becomes, in a second wave, the subject of a timbral crescendo from timpani to brass to strings, harp and piano in octaves. The magic unpredictability is present in the repeated surprise of a sudden boldness.

The work was composed in 1950, and Nono took it with him that summer when he went, as did Scherchen and Maderna, to the summer course that would provide the gathering European avant-garde with an annual meeting-place: Darmstadt.

2

Silencing Music

Cage, 1946–52

Rhythmic Structuring

The principal work of his own that Cage took with him on a visit to Paris in 1949 was his book of *Sonatas and Interludes* for prepared piano (1946–48), one of the largest of several compositions from that decade in which he adjusted the timbres of the piano by inserting foreign objects between the strings: the printed music includes a 'table of preparations' that gives instructions for the placing of screws, nuts, bolts and pieces of plastic and rubber to alter the sounds of forty-five notes, so that the piano comes to make largely unpitched noises like those of drums, gongs, and rattles. Preparation of the piano offered the composer the opportunity to explore and transform his sound material in a very direct manner, by inviting an empirical mode of working similar to that being made possible by the electronic medium. Indeed, the prepared piano was perhaps consciously developed as a homemade substitute for electronic synthesis. In 1937, Cage had expressed his optimistic view of the potential electronic evolution of music,[1] and in 1942—after he had made his first electronic experiments, beginning with the 1939 *Imaginary Landscape No. 1*, for instruments including two variable-speed turntables with frequency recordings—he had been more specific: 'Many musicians,' he had written, 'the writer included, have dreamed

---

1. John Cage, 'The Future of Music: Credo', *Silence: Lectures and Writings* (Middletown, Conn., 1961; London, 1968), 3–7.

of compact technological boxes, inside which all audible sounds, including noise, would be ready to come forth at the command of the composer'.[2] In this article he had gone on to describe the work he had recently done at a Chicago radio station, using electrical gadgets (buzzers, amplified coils of wire, a radio, and a gramophone) in various pieces made onto disc for broadcast.

If in their experimental approach to sound the *Sonatas and Interludes* relate to Cage's electronic essays, they also connect with his earlier works for his own percussion orchestra, such as the *First Construction (in Metal)* for six players (1939), since the prepared piano is effectively a one-man percussion group. This concentration on percussive sonorities was a central item of musical principle, for it dramatized the need, as Cage saw it, for music to be structured on the basis of duration (possessed by all kinds of sound, and by silence) rather than harmony (possessed only by pitched tones in combination). In his 'Defense of Satie'[3]—a lecture he delivered soon after the completion of the *Sonatas and Interludes*, and in which his productive naivety is apparent—he charges Beethoven with the 'error' of defining structure by means of harmony, and applauds Satie and Webern for correctly using duration as the measure: 'There can be no right making of music that does not structure itself from the very roots of sound and silence—lengths of time'. Later in the same talk he insists that the purpose of a musical composition is 'to bring into co-being elements paradoxical by nature, to bring into one situation elements that can be and ought to be agreed upon—that is, Law elements—together with elements that cannot and ought not to be agreed upon—that is, Freedom elements—these two ornamented by other elements, which may lend support to one or the other of the two fundamental and opposed elements, the whole forming thereby an organic entity'.

In the *Sonatas and Interludes,* he provided the most comprehensive demonstration of this combining of 'Law' and 'Freedom' in rhythmic structure. Each of the sixteen sonatas and four interludes is based on a number sequence that defines the durational proportions of the subsections and often appears also in smaller rhythmic units. In the case of Sonata I, for instance, the sequence is 4-1-3-4-1-3-4-2-4-2, and the movement, as always, falls into two repeated sections (Scarlatti, then, might be placed among Cage's ancestors, along with Satie and Webern) that correspond in their lengths to this sequence, the first being of four, one, and three double-dotted semibreves, the second of four and two double-dotted semibreves. Nor is this choice of the double-dotted semibreve as unit arbitrary, for the number sequence sums to twenty-eight, and the double-dotted semibreve is made up of twenty-eight

2. John Cage, 'For More New Sounds', in Richard Kostelanetz, ed., *John Cage* (London, 1971), 65.

3. Ibid., 77–84.

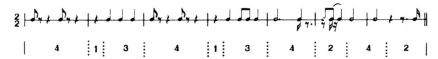

Example 4   John Cage, *Sonatas and Interludes*

semiquavers (sixteen plus eight plus four). So the entire sequence can be represented within any subsection. For example, the first subsection, with a length of four double-dotted semibreves, can equally be considered as containing twenty-eight crotchets, and so can express the sequence in terms of crotchets, as indicated in example 4, which shows only the rhythm of this subsection. Here, it is clear, the proportions are to some degree masked by what one must take to be 'Freedom elements', though these often state fragments of the 'Law' in miniature: the ratio 1:3, for instance, features several times, from the first bar onwards, as well as in its rightful places at bars 2 and 4. The sonata therefore displays the same proportioning on three levels: in the subsectioning of the whole, in the rhythmic divisions of subsections, and in the fine detail of the rhythmic divisions.

Cage had introduced this kind of self-repeating form in the *First Construction*, and continued with it in the works that came immediately after the *Sonatas and Interludes*, including the composition he began in Paris—the String Quartet in Four Parts (1949–50)—and the ensuing Concerto for prepared piano and orchestra (1950–51). In the former, the guiding number sequence governs the relative lengths of the four movements, which form a seasonal cycle from summer to spring. It is to these movements that the title alludes and not to the medium's polyphonic nature, for the quartet is not really polyphonic at all but essentially in one part: Cage described it as 'a melodic line without accompaniment, which employs single tones, intervals, triads and aggregates requiring one or more of the instruments for their production'[4] (by 'aggregates' he meant chords more complex than simple intervals and triads). The harmonies, reintroduced after a spate of works for largely percussive resources, are not to be interpreted as functional—indeed, the slow progress of unrelated chords defies an understanding in terms of harmonic consequence—but are rather single and independent events, each chosen for its colour and caused to occupy the space allotted to it by the numerical pattern. The string quartet thus becomes a kind of enlarged prepared piano, able to offer a very different range of sonorities, but similarly to be used as a reservoir of unconnected sounds. Cage pursued this mode of composition in writing for an orchestra of twenty-two soloists in the concerto, the players again contributing to a monorhythmic line of detached sound events.

4. Preface to the score.

As Cage recognized, his use of fixed-proportion rhythmic structures allowed him to place not only sound, noise, and silence on an equal footing but also East and West. Rhythm, not harmony, was what was fundamental to all musical cultures. And his own rhythmic practice related to the Indian concept of tala, or to the tiered speeds of Balinese gamelan music, which the work of Colin McPhee would have drawn to his attention.[5] The sounds of his works for percussion ensemble and for prepared piano also suggested those of Balinese music, and the *Sonatas and Interludes* had deeper links with Asia, coming from the time when Cage said he 'first became seriously aware of Oriental philosophy'.[6] It was after reading the works of Ananda K. Coomaraswamy that he determined in the *Sonatas and Interludes* 'to attempt the expression in music of the "permanent emotions" of Indian tradition: the heroic, the erotic, the wondrous, the mirthful, sorrow, fear, anger, the odious, and their common tendency toward tranquillity'.[7] Then in the String Quartet he was stimulated by Eastern associations of summer with preservation, autumn with destruction, winter with peace, and spring with creation.

Given Cage's interests in rhythm and in Eastern music, his relationship with Boulez in 1949 begins to make sense. For Boulez, here was a man whose use of rhythmic cells—albeit in strictly monophonic music—showed similar techniques of variation to his own, a man who was similarly iconoclastic (though, as it turned out, in his calm way far more ruthlessly so than the intemperate Boulez), and a man whose understanding of music was similarly global. Besides, Cage was an American in Paris, representative of a nation partly responsible for liberating France from its political and intellectual bondage, and representative, too, of a culture that might have appeared—to a young man seemingly immune to the siren call of the Soviet Union—to hold the key to the future. Falling between Boulez and Messiaen in age, Cage could have impressed Boulez as an older brother, and a proof that he was on the right path. Boulez was particularly struck by Cage's use of square charts setting out the durational relationships to be employed in a work, by his escape from temperament in writing for noise instruments, and by his handling of complex sounds not as agents of harmonic meaning but as events in themselves, and as events that suggested a pitch analogue for the rhythmic cell. 'The tendency of these experiments by John Cage', he was to write in 1952, 'is too close to my own for me to fail to mention them.'[8] But by that time, when Boulez

---

5. McPhee had an article, 'The "Absolute" Music of Bali', in the June 1935 issue of the influential journal *Modern Music*, to which Cage himself contributed.

6. Kostelanetz, ed., *John Cage*, 129.

7. Ibid.

8. Pierre Boulez, *Stocktakings from an Apprenticeship* (Oxford, 1991), 135.

had made the breakthrough into total serialism, Cage's retreat from Western rhetoric—to be observed progressively in the *Sonatas and Interludes*, the String Quartet and the Concerto for prepared piano—had set him on a very different course.

Towards Silence

The deceptive—perhaps even self-deceptive—nature of the link between Cage and Boulez is manifest from a comparison of the former's Concerto for prepared piano (summer 1950—February 1951) with the latter's first book of *Structures* (1951–52). Both composers made extensive use of number charts, but where Boulez's goal with these was total serial organization, Cage's was nonintention. For Boulez, objective rule was a guardian against traditional values, a guarantor of independence: he as composer was master of the rule. For Cage, always more radical, mastery of the rule was an idle conceit: he was delighted by the possibility of removing his own creative wishes. 'I let the pianist express the opinion that music should be improvised or felt,' he said of the Concerto's first movement, 'while the orchestra expressed only the chart, with no personal taste involved. In the second movement I made large concentric moves on the chart for both pianist and orchestra, with the idea of the pianist beginning to give up personal taste. The third movement had only one set of moves [dictated by coin tossing[9]] on the chart for both, and a lot of silences. . . . Until that time, my music had been based on the traditional idea that you had to say something. The charts gave me my first indication of the possibility of saying nothing'.[10]

The virtue of saying nothing was being borne in on him by his studies of zen under Daisetz T. Suzuki at Columbia University in 1951. Opening his work to chance decisions gave him some inkling of how to reach the goal. Through a mechanical procedure—at first coin tosses to pick places on number charts—sounds would arrive in a composition without the composer's will or decision, and so without any deliberate connection to other sounds. Nobody would be intending them; no musical language would be giving them a meaning. One could 'make a composition the continuity of which is free of individual taste and memory (psychology) and also of the literature and "traditions" of the art. The sounds enter the time-space centered within themselves, unimpeded by service to any abstraction, their 360 degrees of circumference free for an infinite play of interpenetration. Value judgments are not in the nature of this work as regards either composition, performance, or listening. The idea of relation (the idea: 2) being absent,

9. See Jean-Jacques Nattiez, ed., *The Boulez-Cage Correspondence* (Cambridge and New York, 1993), 94.
10. Note with Nonesuch H 71202.

anything (the idea: 1) may happen. A "mistake" is beside the point, for once anything happens it authentically is'.[11]

For the rest of his life—a period of forty years after this statement was published in 1952—Cage never wavered from this view. In a sense, therefore, the Concerto for prepared piano is his last composition, the last composition in which he exerted his will, though dyingly. Yet there is a paradox here. Nonintention was itself an intention, and what allows us to go on speaking of Cage as a composer after the Concerto is the unparalleled determination with which he pursued that intention through an extraordinary variety of ways and means. This is where 'individual taste and memory (psychology)' make their remarkable return, for a determined absence of determination had already been the central characteristic of his music, an absence revealed in his treatment of time as unmotivated extension, his choice of simplicity and repetition (found at an early extreme in the 1947 prepared-piano piece *Music for Marcel Duchamp*), his avoidance of rhetoric. And the future was to prove, despite his immense and worldwide influence in the 1950s and 1960s, that nobody could make unmeant music as he could.

One of his earliest and boldest ventures in that direction was his *Imaginary Landscape No. 4* for twelve radio receivers, first performed in New York on May 10, 1951. In order to remove his own preferences from the composition he entrusted it to 'chance operations', using, as in the last movement of the Concerto, coin tosses to derive positions on his charts: the particular stimulus was the *I Ching*, of which Richard Wilhelm's German version had been published in English in New York the previous year. Where the *I Ching* invites the user to cast lots and so be directed to one of sixty-four oracular pronouncements, Cage substituted for the latter his charts, of eight-by-eight arrays of numbers that he could use to dictate musical parameters—in this case, the wavelengths, durations, and dynamic levels to be set on the twelve radios. All these parameters are notated, but of course there is no way of knowing what will be broadcast on any given wavelength at the time of performance. It might therefore seem that the scrupulousness is ironic, even comic; but Cage was neither clown nor satirist. His folly was a kind of devotion. To accept the data of chance was to welcome anything. And to present those data in the form of a score was to demand a similar selflessness, trust, and tenacity from performers, so that his chance-composed works, so far from licensing irresponsibility, require and favour a rare degree of artistry.

He was lucky in some of his colleagues. Alongside *Imaginary Landscape No. 4* he was at work on a big solo piano work for David Tudor (1926–96), whom he had persuaded to give the first New York performance of Boulez's Second Sonata on December 17, 1950. Tudor was to

11. Cage, 'To Describe the Process of Composition used in *Music of Changes and Imaginary Landscape No. 4*', *Silence*, 59.

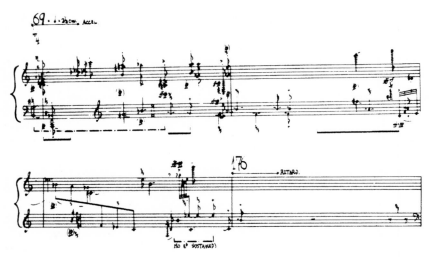

Example 5   John Cage, *Music of Changes*

remain one of his regular collaborators and friends; both men were associated with Merce Cunningham's dance company, and Tudor was the
destined performer or co-performer of much of Cage's music for piano
or electronics (towards which he moved in 1960). The work that
started this musical alliance was the *Music of Changes* (the New York
edition of the Wilhelm *I Ching* had been given the subtitle 'Book of
Changes'), which maintains the fixed-proportion rhythmic structure
of the earlier works, though time is here indicated principally by measured length rather than by traditional bars. Such notation, often called
'space-time notation', was widely adopted during the 1950s, 1960s and
1970s; for Cage it provided a way to symbolize time as a smooth extent,
into which conventionally notated durations fall. The proportional
rhythmic structure is now unregarded by the music: it simply provides
passages of time to be filled, and the filling is dictated again by coin
tosses that determine tempos, the number of simultaneous layers,
dynamic levels, pitches, and sound categories (whether single notes,
groups, aggregates, other complex events, such as clusters, silently
depressed keys, trills and glissandos on the strings, noises such as lid
slams, or rests); durations were derived from the Tarot pack. Often the
unwilled result is irrational: for instance, in example 5, which shows
the opening of the first of the four books into which the work is divided, the left-hand cluster gets in the way of other incidents. In such
cases 'the performer is to apply his own discretion'.

Perhaps the only thing that was intended of the *Music of Changes*
was that it should be a response to the Boulez sonata, with which it
was paired at its first complete performance, in New York on January 1,
1952. Everything else was ruthlessly nonintentional—except, crucially,

the ruthlessness. For one thing, few other musicians would have carried through the project of chance-composing every detail in a packed three-quarter-hour work, and of then going on in that direction: apologizing to Boulez in the summer of 1952 for the sketchiness of a letter, Cage remarked that 'I spend a great deal of time tossing coins and the emptiness of head that that induces begins to penetrate the rest of my time as well'.[12] The laborious mechanism of chance composition was not only a bulwark against creative intention; it withered creative intention. And yet by denying himself choice, Cage paradoxically intensified those features that had been most characteristic of his deliberate music: its openness to new and various sounds, and its cool unfolding, not troubled by passages of extreme activity or complexity, 'throwing sound into silence'.[13] Slowed beat in the String Quartet and the Concerto for prepared piano had already reduced the sense of music driving the machine of time. In the *Music of Changes*, by definition, there can be no moment-to-moment purpose. Time is a neutral expanse into which sounds come, and by offering it as such, Cage completed the revolution that Debussy had begun against musical progression.

He went on to apply coin-tossing methods to the electronic medium in *Imaginary Landscape No. 5* (1951–52) and *Williams Mix* (1952). Tape music was then in its infancy. The Russian-born Vladimir Ussachevsky (1911–90), who taught at Columbia University, gave a demonstration of the new medium's potential in 1952, and he was soon joined in his endeavours by Otto Luening (1900–96), who had studied with Busoni. They presented the first concert of electronic music in the Western Hemisphere, at the Museum of Modern Art in New York on October 28, 1952: representative of the pieces then heard are Ussachevsky's *Sonic Contours* and Luening's *Fantasy in Space*, based on the sounds of piano and flute respectively. Out of their efforts grew the Columbia-Princeton Electronic Music Center, which was formally founded in 1960.

Cage's interest in electronic music went back long before the Ussachevsky-Luening initiative to his 1937 essay and the works that had followed it; he had also had his enthusiasm reawakened by Boulez's news of working with Schaeffer.[14] But by now he was concerned not so much with new sounds as with tape as a holding medium. The notation of the *Music of Changes* already suggests a stretch of magnetic tape bearing sound imprints; *Imaginary Landscape No. 5*, devised for a dance, was to actualize that image, with the imprints taken from any forty-two source recordings. To make his own version he went to the studio of Louis and Bebe Barron (who in 1956 were to be responsible for the first electronic music made for a commercial film, *Forbidden Planet*), and

12. Nattiez, ed., *The Boulez-Cage Correspondence*, 133.
13. Ibid., 78.
14. See ibid., 119ff.

stayed on to create the vastly more complex *Williams Mix*, named in honour of the patron, Paul Williams, who had funded the work. *Williams Mix*, of which only a four-minute fragment was ever completed, required a host of coin tosses to determine the kinds and lengths of sounds to be spliced together onto eight simultaneous tracks, each sound belonging to one of six categories—'city sounds', 'country sounds', 'electronic sounds', 'manually produced sounds, including the literature of music', 'wind-produced sounds, including songs' and 'small sounds requiring amplification to be heard with the others'[15]—and subjected or not to control of frequency, overtone structure, and amplitude. For Cage, the work took him still closer to nonintentionality, since the choices of sounds and controls could be made by other people, following the chance-ordered plan. 'So that it is not "my" work'.[16]

But in another sense it is, for the usual reasons of discipline and openness, and also for the characteristic generosity to the small. Other works from the remarkable year of 1952 included *Water Music* (for a pianist also using a radio and other sound sources), the first of the *Music for Piano* series (in which Cage discovered a quicker way of creating chance music, by marking imperfections on a sheet of paper and placing notes there) and the opening piece in another series, of time-title works: *4' 33"*. But the celebrated silence of this last also stands at the end of a road, as one logical conclusion to Cage's quest for self-withdrawal from his work, and as a natural development from the yawning gulfs of the Concerto for prepared piano and the *Music of Changes*. It also presents the paradox of nonintentionality with peculiar intensity. Stray intentions persist. Cage sometimes seemed to accept the view that the piece is not silent at all, but rather a revelation of the sounds an audience would normally disregard or treat as disturbance. It is also mute theatre, in that the performer or performers (the première, at Woodstock, New York, on August 29, 1952, was given by Tudor, but the work was later made available to any forces) must make it clear that a musical performance is taking place. But these things are by the way. *4' 33"* is music reduced to nothing, and nothing raised to music. It cannot be heard, and is heard anywhere by anyone at any time. It is the extinction of thought, and has provoked more thought than any other music of the second half of the twentieth century.

Around Cage

Cage's rapid evolution in 1951–52—from the Concerto for prepared piano to *4' 33"* in eighteen months—may have been encouraged not only by zen studies but also by support from fellow artists with whom he was associated. In Tudor he had a dedicated performer (hence so

15. From Cage's note on the work in Kostelanetz, ed., *John Cage*, 109.
16. Nattiez, ed., *The Boulez-Cage Correspondence*, 132.

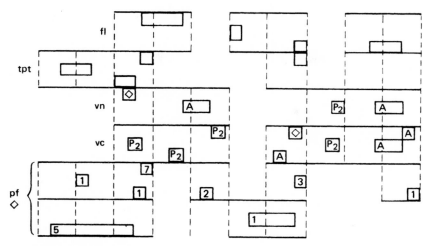

Example 6   Morton Feldman, *Projection II*

much piano music) and an assistant in the electronic studio. In Robert Rauschenberg, whom he met in 1948,[17] he found a painter with similar concerns for the small currency of experience. And in Morton Feldman (1926–87), Earle Brown (1926–2002), and Christian Wolff (b. 1934) he discovered younger composers willing to join his pursuit of non-intention: Feldman and Wolff came into his orbit in 1950; Brown joined the group two years later.

Some of Wolff's first pieces use radically limited materials: just three notes within the minimal chromatic range of a major second in his Duo for violins (1950). Meanwhile, Feldman was taking an almost opposite tack in prescribing pitch as little as possible. His *Projections* and *Intersections* are series of 'graph' compositions in which, as in the *Music of Changes*, time is represented by space, and in which the spaced boxes specify only instrument, register, number of simultaneous sounds, mode of production, and duration. The two series differ in that the *Projections* are to be consistently quiet, while in the *Intersections* 'the player is free to choose any dynamic at any entrance but must maintain sameness of volume'—though 'what is desired in both . . . is a pure (non-vibrating) tone'.[18] Example 6 shows the opening of *Projection II*, where the dashed lines mark off units of a second; the first sound heard is a five-note chord in the extreme bass of the piano, followed by a middle-range trumpet note, a note in the mid-treble of the piano, and so on. In other works of the same period, such as the *Extensions* series or *Structures* for

17. See David Revill, *The Roaring Silence: John Cage: A Life* (London, 1992), 96.

18. Statement by Feldman republished in *The Boulez-Cage Correspondence*, 104.

Example 7   Earle Brown, *December 1952*

string quartet, Feldman used conventional notation in order to achieve noncompulsion differently, by having delicate figures repeated over and over again. But the ideal is essentially the same: as Cage pointed out, 'Feldman's conventionally notated music is himself playing his graph music'.[19] The exceptions to his world of low-density, low-speed, low-volume music were few and extreme: the hectically eventful *Intersection III* for piano, or the unrealized and probably unrealizable *Intersection* for tape.[20]

The fact that Feldman had such a thing as a personal sound-world is emblematic of his distance from Cage; Brown's objectives were different again, and perhaps formed most by what he learned from the visual arts. By his own account, he was stimulated by 'the integral but unpredictable "floating" variations of a Calder mobile and the contextual rightness of Pollock's spontaneity and directness in relation to the

19. Michael Nyman, *Experimental Music: Cage and Beyond* (London, 1974), 45.

20. See note 23 to Heinz-Klaus Metzger, 'Essay on Prerevolutionary Music', published with EMI C 165 28954-7.

material and his particular image of his work'.[21] His aim was not the empty space of Cage, nor the quiet space of Feldman, but the decisive object—not the extinction of the composer, nor the liberation of the performer, but the creation of a well-made piece, one that would have a sure identity for all the variability of form and detail introduced by means of indeterminate notation. The more indeterminate the notation, the more the identity of the piece would have to be visual, until, very rapidly, he arrived at *December 1952* (example 7), which is at once the earliest, the most enigmatic (there being no instructions about how these shapes are to be realized as sound) and the most elegant of graphic scores. *4′ 33″* had elided the gap between music and life; *December 1952*, less ambitiously, elided that between music and design.

21. Quoted in Nyman, *Experimental Music*, 48.

3

Total Organization

Western Europe, 1949–54

The Moment of Total Serialism 1:
Darmstadt 1949 and Darmstadt 1951

It was around 1950 that Messiaen, through becoming a pupil of his pupils, became again their teacher. Speaking generally of his students, he once observed that 'their questions compelled me to undertake studies I might not have dreamt of, had it not been for them':[1] uppermost in his mind, surely, must have been his relationship with Boulez. However, his leap from the *Cinq Rechants* (1949) to the *Mode de valeurs et d'intensités* for piano (1949–50) might indicate some other catalyst, given that Boulez's most recent work at the time was the *Livre pour quatuor*. Conceivably the prompt came from Cage, who stayed in Paris for several months and played his *Sonatas and Interludes* both for Messiaen's class on June 7, 1949[2] and at a soirée when Boulez delivered a slightly circumspect introduction.[3] Boulez's reference here to 'duration, amplitude, frequency, and timbre—in other words, the four characteristics of a sound' echoes a statement of sound's quaternary nature in

1. Claude Samuel, *Olivier Messiaen: Music and Color* (Portland, Oreg.: Amadeus, 1994), 176.
2. See Jean-Jacques Nattiez, ed., *The Boulez-Cage Correspondence* (Cambridge and New York, 1993), 5.
3. Reproduced in ibid., 27–32.

Example 8   Olivier Messiaen, *Mode de valeurs et d'intensités*

Cage's recent essay 'Forerunners of Modern Music',[4] and suggests that the definition of these four parameters, which provided the organizational basis for total serialism, came from Cage. The setting-up of compositional algorithms, another essential feature of total serialism, also has clearer origins in Cage's principle of rhythmic proportioning than in Boulez's turmoil of motivic extrapolations. All that was needed was to add the twelve-note principle to these Cageian elements—the four parameters, automatic operation—and the *Mode de valeurs* (see example 8) would be the almost inevitable result.

The piece's dateline, 'Darmstadt 1949', points to other momentous encounters, though those were mostly in the future. The Darmstadt summer courses had been instituted in 1946 to bring young Germans— including Henze that first year—up to date with music unheard under the Nazis. Increasingly international, the courses had Leibowitz on board in 1948, Messiaen in 1949, and Edgard Varèse (1883–1965) in 1950, when Nono and Maderna were among the students.

Messiaen's preface to the *Mode de valeurs* describes how the piece is composed as a three-part counterpoint, each part using a different set

4. John Cage, *Silence: Lectures and Writings* (Middletown, Conn., 1961; London, 1968), 62–66; also republished in Nattiez, ed., *The Boulez-Cage Correspondence*, 38–42.

of twelve chromatic pitches and twelve 'chromatic durations'. These, following the principle of rhythmic arithmetic in the *Turangalîla* symphony, are on scales from a demisemiquaver to a dotted crotchet in the top part, from a semiquaver to a dotted minim in the middle part, and from a quaver to a dotted semibreve in the bottom part. Each of the thirty-six pitches is permanently associated with one of the thirty-six durations, and each also keeps the same values in the other two parameters, of which 'amplitude' is represented by seven dynamic levels and 'timbre' by seven different attack markings. The example shows the opening of the piece, which continues in the same manner. As Richard Toop demonstrated in an important article on the origins of total serialism, there is a tendency to maintain contiguous fragments of the duration scales (the two upper lines in the example, for instance, both begin one-two-three-four, and the one-two-three pattern is soon repeated in the middle part), but in no sense is the construction serial: decisions about the ordering of fragments appear to be based on the wish to avoid octaves and other overt suggestions of tonality.[5]

For Messiaen, the *Mode de valeurs* was at an extreme point of precompositional systematization. In the larger piano piece *Cantéyodjayâ* (1949) he had placed a fraction of similar music along with other elements in a dance of the possibilities open to him after the *Turangalîla* symphony; in later works he used sets of chromatic durations again—notably in the piano piece *Ile de feu II* (1950), the *Livre d'orgue* (1951), 'La Chouette hulotte' and 'Le Merle de roche' from the piano cycle *Catalogue d'oiseaux* (1956–58), the orchestral *Chronochromie* (1960), and the stigmata scene from *Saint François d'Assise* (1975–83)—but always with 'interversion' to make the haphazardness of the *Mode de valeurs* into decisive process. This technique he introduced in *Ile de feu II*, where a sequence of twelve chromatic durations is permuted by taking values successively from the centre; that generates the first 'interversion', from which the second can be obtained by repeating the process:

Original	12	11	10	9	8	7	6	5	4	3	2	1
Interversion 1	6	7	5	8	4	9	3	10	2	11	1	12
Interversion 2	3	9	10	4	2	8	11	5	1	7	12	6

The operation can be repeated further until the original sequence is reproduced—in this case as the tenth interversion. *Ile de feu II* unfolds the entire cycle, with less strictly organized episodes, but Messiaen later preferred sequences of thirty-two or sixty-four chromatic durations (the last piece in the *Livre d'orgue* has the title 'Soixante-quatre durées'), sequences whose interversions could intimate cosmic stretches of time.

5. Richard Toop, 'Messiaen/Goeyvaerts, Fano/Stockhausen, Boulez', *Perspectives of New Music*, 13/1 (1974), 141–69.

Ile de feu II and the *Mode de valeurs* were published with two other pieces as *Quatre Etudes de rythme*, of which Messiaen made a commercial recording, and it was in this audible form that the *Mode de valeurs* returned to Darmstadt in 1951. Among the students there was Karlheinz Stockhausen (1928–2007), who was immediately attracted by what he called a 'fantastic music of the stars':[6] what excited him, as this image suggests, was the music's presentation of itself as constituted of single notes, 'existing for themselves in complete freedom,' as he went on to put it, 'and formulated individually in considerable isolation from each other'. Hitherto he had written twelve-note pieces in traditional thematic style, pursuing a Schoenberg-Hindemith synthesis that had rapidly become the common language of postwar Germany. Now the experience of the *Mode de valeurs*—and of discussions with two other young men at Darmstadt, Karel Goeyvaerts (1923–93) and Nono—set him in a new direction.

It is worth noting that Stockhausen was awestruck first by the sound of the Messiaen piece, not by its mechanism, for the physical substance and the sensuous impact of sound were to remain essential to his work. But he consistently needed system too, and here Goeyvaerts could help. Goeyvaerts, after studies in his native Antwerp, had gone to the Paris Conservatoire, attended Messiaen's class in 1947–48, and been set on the serial road by his friend Jean Barraqué (1928–73), though apparently he had no knowledge of the *Mode de valeurs* before arriving in Darmstadt, bringing with him his opus 1, a Sonata for two pianos (1950–51).[7] The detached notes ('points' in Stockhausen's terminology) of this piece must therefore be an independent evolution from earlier Messiaen works via discussions with Barraqué, and surely even more so from the study of Webern's Piano Variations that Goeyvaerts had made in 1949–50, when he was still in Paris. (The possibility therefore arises that Goeyvaerts—as much as Boulez and Cage, and maybe more than either—was responsible for jolting Messiaen towards the *Mode de valeurs*.)

The Webern piece, though not itself definable as an example of total serialism,[8] proved to contain valuable pointers. Its second movement, for example, uses only three dynamic markings and five varieties of rhythmic cell; from this it was not too large a step to Goeyvaerts's use in the middle two movements of his sonata of seven duration values, seven modes of attack (as in the *Mode de valeurs*), and four dynamic levels. (The outer two movements, planned to contrast with the rationality within, are counterpoints of irrational cells derived more directly

---

6. K. H. Wörner, *Stockhausen: Life and Work* (London, 1973), 61.

7. See Toop, 'Messiaen/Goeyvaerts', 162.

8. See Peter Westergaard, 'Webern and "Total Organization": an Analysis of the Second Movement of the Piano Variations, Op. 27', *Perspectives of New Music*, ½ i/2 (1963), 107–20.

from Messiaen.) But the striking innovation of the sonata—certainly as far as Stockhausen was concerned—was its structural use of register, and this too had its roots in the Webern Variations, where pitch palindromes may be slightly upset by registral displacements of motifs, and in Messiaen ('Regard de l'onction terrible' from the *Vingt Regards sur l'Enfant Jésus*).

In the central movements of Goeyvaerts's sonata, cues from Webern and Messiaen are considerably developed. Initially a range of nearly five and a half octaves is available, gradually reducing to two and a half at the end of the second movement, and then widening again in the third. Two notes, A and D♯, remain fixed in register, but each time any other note recurs it is transposed up an octave, or if that would take it over the registral ceiling of the moment, it is reintroduced in the bass. Thus where Boulez had used fixity and mobility of register as an alternative to harmonic dialectic in his Second Sonata (no doubt also under the influence of Webern—perhaps specifically of the first movement of the Symphony Op. 21), Goeyvaerts's registral process created a form that depended neither on conventional models nor, as in the *Mode de valeurs*, on the composer's taste and judgment. Given a few simple rules, the music did not need to be 'composed' at all: the notes would be at play of themselves. Goeyvaerts had gone a step further even than Cage at this point towards music by algorithm, towards automatic composition.

Shortly after his Darmstadt visit Goeyvaerts wrote to Barraqué of what was on his mind: 'You know I want to arrive at a music where everything—absolutely everything—is contained in one fundamental generating idea. The pitch, the duration, the intensity, the density, the timbre and the attack are subjected to a general synthetic number with its subdivisions. . . . The whole thing appears as something immobile, static, which is, so to say, the analysis of the structure of "Being", its adaptation to time'.[9]

Stockhausen's susceptibility to this could not have been predicted from the pieces he had written before going to Darmstadt in the summer of 1951: the shock of the encounter with Messiaen and Goeyvaerts is all there in the leap from the Sonatina for violin and piano, completed soon before, to *Kreuzspiel* for piano with percussion trio and two woodwind instruments (see example 9), written in the immediate aftermath. One might even speak, again, of a conversion, especially when what exhilarated Stockhausen as much as Goeyvaerts was the spiritual dimension of their work: the possibility of liberating, more than creating, sound structures that would have nothing human in their composition, that would be images of divine unity.[10] Since at this point

9. Quoted in Paul Griffiths, *The Sea on Fire: Jean Barraqué* (Rochester, N.Y., 2003), 32.
10. See Richard Toop's review in *Contact*, 12 (1975), 45–46.

Example 9   Karlheinz Stockhausen, *Kreuzspiel*

Stockhausen was a devout Catholic, the form and title of his first piece
after the Darmstadt experience cannot have been accidental, though
the 'crossplay' is also a direct extension from Goeyvaerts's method of
shunting single notes, an extension complicated and enlivened by parallel processes applied to Messiaen-style chromatic durations (hence the
percussion), to dynamic levels, and to instrumental colours (hence the
woodwind). The necessary link between formal process and instrumentation may well have been, for Stockhausen, a further sign of deep
wholeness.

The example shows the opening of the first of the three main sections, up to the end of the opening statements of the pitch series and
two different duration series in triplet semiquavers: one pattered out by
the tumbas in even values, the other presented by the piano (11-5-6 . . .)
and by the tom-toms in 'transposed inversion' (2-8-7 . . .). Each of
these serial forms, whether of pitches or of durations, goes through a
crossover process that completes the section. In succeeding twelve-
note sequences, notes progressively move towards the edges of the
row, and then reappear at the middle. At the same time, they move in
register. To begin with, as shown in the example, they are evenly divided between the lowest possible placement and the highest; then,
starting at different times, they move, according to the pattern 0-1-5-
2-3-4-1-6 or its retrograde. As they reach the middle register, they are
taken over by one of the two woodwind instruments, oboe and bass
clarinet. So around the centre of the section most notes are played by
the woodwind, while at each end the piano predominates.

In the second section the processes of registral and instrumental
transfer are turned inside-out, so that the music starts at the woodwind
centre, moves out to the extremes of the keyboard, and then returns,
though there is the complication of an additional process playing itself
out in trichords on the piano. The third section then combines the
other two: piano and woodwind project a retrograde of the convergent-
divergent crossplay of the first section, while the piano also retrogrades
the divergent-convergent mechanics of the second. In the pure symmetry of this scheme, as well as in its development of the crossover
idea, the piece reveals its debt to the Goeyvaerts exemplar, while the
influence of the 'star music' of the *Mode de valeurs* is there in the piano
points (the very first pitch might be construed as a homage to Messiaen)
and in the attachment, within any section, of each note to a particular
duration (though there are structural exceptions to this rule, such as
the progressively increasing duration of C in the second section).

However, this is, already, a characteristic Stockhausen piece, not
only in its perfect digestion of its models but also in its intriguing introduction of discrepancies, its delighted newness, and its brio. Apart from
the durational changes just mentioned, the discrepancies include dis-
turbances to the pitch pattern when a pitched attack coincides with
one in the percussion: Stockhausen may have been concerned to make

some connection between the two streams; certainly the melding of pitched and unpitched sound was to become a priority in many subsequent works, notably *Kontakte*. As for the newness, out of the new system comes a new way of listening, though perhaps not directly. To follow the crossplay gambits cannot be considered; their effect, rather, is of a ruthlessly channelled disorder, of unseen hands moving notes according to unknown rules, as if one were observing a complex game with no prior knowledge of its etiquette. Where order is glimpsed—for instance in repetitions of intervalic motif—it will likely be fortuitous. *Kreuzspiel* flies free from the thematic-harmonic continuity that Schoenberg had wanted to preserve, and does so not by punishing that continuity, as Boulez had done, but by ignoring it.

In this lies one of the work's connections with non-European musical traditions: another would be its instrumentation, suggestive more of African or Asian ensembles than of German chamber music. Where such connections were deliberate in Boulez, in Stockhausen at this point they may still have been accidental; if the instrumentation, for instance, was not wholly a concomitant of the musical processes, its feel could have come from the modern jazz of the time. Jazz, too, is evoked—again, perhaps inadvertently—by the rhythm, the irregular accents within uniform pulsation (though the boogie-woogie slow movement of the Violin Sonatina is a long few months in the past). This uniform pulsation, which arises inevitably from the superimposing of lines in chromatic durations (and is, of course, emphasized by the tumbas of the first section), was something that Stockhausen soon became anxious to avoid, but in *Kreuzspiel* it makes a decisive contribution to the streamlined glide of process, and gives the game a tension of direction.

During the last two months of 1951, immediately after the composition of *Kreuzspiel*, Stockhausen went on to apply similar structural principles not to isolated points but to whole melodic and harmonic units, resulting in the movement later published as *Formel*, for twelve each of wind and strings with pitched percussion. This brought him a commission to complete an orchestral piece for the 1952 Donaueschingen Festival, and with the promise of a fee he set off for Paris in January 1952, there to study with Messiaen.

Interlude: The Patrons of Modernism

The names of Darmstadt and Donaueschingen have already suggested the importance those places had in propagating new music between the late 1940s and the early 1960s, and to a lesser extent thereafter. Each owed that importance to the determination of a music critic, to the fresh-start mood in the western sectors of Germany immediately after the war, and to the willingness of public authorities (local government agencies and radio stations) to sponsor new music—a willingness that some competitiveness among localities might have helped foster. Wolfgang Steinecke (1910–61) founded the Darmstadt summer courses, and vigorously supported the turn of events that took them, from 1956 onwards, out of the hands of men of his own generation (Hindemith, Leibowitz, Messiaen) into those of Boulez, Maderna, Nono, and Stockhausen. Heinrich Strobel (1898–1970), who had spent the war years in France, returned to his post in 1946 as editor of *Melos*, and the same year became head of music for the Südwestfunk (SWF), stationed in Baden-Baden. In 1950 the Donaueschingen Festival became part of his responsibilities, and he soon made its annual October weekend of concerts the most important public event in the new-music calendar: works first performed there under his jurisdiction included not only Boulez's *Polyphonie X* for eighteen instrumentalists in 1951 and Stockhausen's *Spiel* in 1952 but also the former's *Livre pour quatuor* in 1955 (first two movements), *Poésie pour pouvoir* in 1958, *Tombeau* in 1959, second book of *Structures* in 1961 and *Pli selon pli* in 1962, and the latter's *Punkte* in 1963, as well as Messiaen's *Réveil des oiseaux* in 1953, Xenakis's first acknowledged work, *Metastaseis*, in 1955 and Ligeti's *Atmosphères* in 1960.[11] It was through his influence that Boulez was encouraged to conduct the SWF orchestra regularly from 1958 onwards, and to make his home in Baden-Baden from the beginning of 1959. Meanwhile Stockhausen found his principal benefactor in the Westdeutscher Rundfunk (WDR) of Cologne, the city near which he was born, and in whose vicinity he stayed: not only was he engaged at the electronic music studio from 1953 onwards, but the WDR presented the premières of his *Kontra-Punkte* in 1953, *Gruppen* in 1958, and *Momente* in 1962.

The munificence of the SWF and the WDR provided an example to other radio stations, in Germany and elsewhere, to the extent that the leading composers of the Boulez-Stockhausen generation in Western Europe were all supported by broadcasting organizations—either directly as employees (usually in electronic music studios) or indirectly through the provision of the means for performance and recording. Their sole responsibility, therefore, was to create. (Only in the 1970s did Europe begin to bend towards the U.S. pattern of maintaining composers as university teachers.) Had that not been the case, it is hard to imagine that Stockhausen, in particular, could have achieved such a volume and intensity of compositional work, or felt free to pursue his instincts through the remarkable transformations his music was to undergo during the next two decades.

11. Recordings of many of these performances are presented on Col Legno AU 031 800, together with premières from the 1970s and 1980s of works by Holliger, Lachenmann, Rihm, and others.

The Moment of Total Serialism 2: Paris 1952

In Paris Stockhausen decided that *Formel* was too thematic, a cul-de-sac; it became relevant again only when he returned to thematic composition in the 1970s. (If this was indeed his process of thought, it indicates how his strategy was to draw up a scheme, follow it through, and then look at the results. Such an approach to composition would justify the use of such terms—much vaunted at the time—as 'experiment' and 'research', and would partly explain the pattern of Stockhausen's output, which to some extent he continued: a pattern of one-offs.) So to Donaueschingen he sent only the two subsequent movements as *Spiel*. Here he returned to points, and added to the *Formel* orchestra a large array of unpitched percussion instruments, used in the first movement to provide a vast repertory of attacks to coincide with the notes, which gradually come together in melodies (in this process, as in *Formel*, the vibraphone has a guiding role), and in the second to generate clouds of resonance out of which sustained points arrive as droplets of pitch condensation. This second movement, consistently slow, relates to his contemporary statement that the new 'through-organized' music demanded a kind of 'meditative' listening: 'One stays in the music . . . one needs nothing before or after in order to perceive the individual now (the individual sound)'.[12] Here is confirmation of what was said above about *Kreuzspiel*, that the process enacted in the music is a way of making it, not a way of hearing it. For the listener, the process lies hidden, and what is heard is a succession of instants, just as, for the observer of the world, elementary laws of physics and genetics—laws Stockhausen might have preferred to interpret as the purposes of God—are concealed behind and within a seeming chaos of phenomena.

The same paradox of rational, purposeful process and irrational, haphazard effect remains throughout the large body of work Stockhausen achieved during his year in Paris: *Spiel*, a quartet for pianist and timpanists (later revised as a trio), *Punkte* for orchestra (also later revised, and re-revised), the first four of a continuing sequence of piano pieces, a study in musique concrète, and the beginnings of *Kontra-Punkte* for ten players. Paris provided him with new opportunities, and new encounters—not only with Messiaen, but also with Boulez, who by this time was at work on total-serial projects of his own: two musique concrète studies and the first book of *Structures* for two pianos.

Like Stockhausen, Boulez was struck by Messiaen's *Mode de valeurs*, but perhaps more as a display of discipline than as a sound ideal. In the summer of 1951, he had quickly written the initial chapter of *Structures*, using the 'first division' of Messiaen's three-part mode as a twelve-note

12. Karlheinz Stockhausen, *Texte*, i (Cologne, 1963), 21.

series (E♭–D–A–A♭–G–F♯–E–C♯–C–B♭–F–B), combined with a twelve-duration series in demisemiquavers, again as in the Messiaen model. By its nature, the piece lies completely open to analysis—or at least to the analysis of how it was put together; the untangling that Ligeti published,[13] shortly after leaving Hungary and before he was well known as a composer in the West, is as much a classic document as the piece itself, and an almost inevitable companion to it. As Ligeti demonstrates, Boulez obtained his duration series by applying numbers to the pitch series, and then translating all the other serial forms into number sequences by using the same pitch-number equivalences: thus the retrograde inversion B–F–C–B♭–A– . . . translates as 12–11–9–10–3– . . . . Boulez also arranged the number sequences—twelve for the prime forms, twelve for the inverted forms (retrogrades can be simply read off backwards)—in two twelve-by-twelve squares, and obtained series of dynamic markings by reading the squares diagonally and interpreting the numbers on a scale from 1 = *pppp* to 12 = *ffff*.

Structures Ia is quite simply a presentation of the forty-eight forms of the pitch series, each with a different form of the duration series (so that pitches do not always have the same durations, as happens in the *Mode de valeurs* and generally within each major section of *Kreuzspiel*), and each with a particular dynamic level and attack marking. The serial forms are laid out in fourteen sections, these defined by the number of simultaneous forms (from one to six), the registral space, and the tempo. The sectional form owes something to the exposition from the Sonata for two pianos (1951) by Michel Fano (b. 1929), who had become a pupil of Messiaen the previous year, and whose piece is in some measure the missing link between the *Mode de valeurs* and *Structures Ia*[14] (though Fano was soon to turn from abstract composition to working in cinema as a musician and filmmaker). The rest of the Fano sonata, however, is a polyphony of rhythmic cells rather in the manner of Boulez's Second Sonata or *Livre pour quatuor*, if at a lower temperature of change. *Structures Ia*, on the other hand, retains its purity as a total serial construction, though one made not as an image of the pristine divine, it would seem, but rather as a way of approaching automatic composition. To quote Boulez himself on this: 'I wanted to give the first *Structure* . . . the title of a painting by Klee, "At the limit of fertile land". This painting is mainly constructed on horizontal lines with a few oblique ones, so that it is very restricted in its invention. The first *Structure* was quite consciously composed in an analogous way. . . . I wanted to use the potential of a given material to find out how far automatism in musical relationships would go, with individual invention appearing only in some very simple forms of disposition—in the

13. 'Pierre Boulez', *Die Reihe*, 4 (1958, English ed. 1960), 36–62.
14. See Toop, 'Messiaen/Goeyvaerts'.

matter of densities, for example'.[15]What Boulez here terms 'individual invention'—putting together a kit of serial forms that have almost invented themselves—is responsible for the shape of the piece, established by a palindromic arrangement of tempos, an increasing and increasingly stable density, and a variation in the fixing of notes within particular registers.[16] This last technique produces a markedly different effect here from the sense of desperate insistence or worrying it created in the Second Sonata: the impression is of something more abstract, of what Ligeti aptly calls 'knots' in the serial web. But what is most revealing in Boulez's statement is his dualism of the automatic (seen as generated by an impersonal process) and the individual (seen as resulting from the composer's free act of will). The virtue of automatism, for him, was that it provided an escape from tastes and learned techniques: there was no danger, for instance, of imitating past ways of shaping melodic ideas, because the shaping was done by the scheme. To that degree, it was an experiment that did not have to be repeated. Having been obliged to consider each note as an element in a schematic design, the composer could now consider each note for his own purposes.

But for Stockhausen, and even more so for John Cage, objective process and automatic mechanism were by no means so momentary or so negative in their implications. For example, where Boulez in *Structures Ia* grasped at what liberties remained in order to create an arbitrary form, a defiant display of his own hand, Stockhausen in *Kreuzspiel* took pleasure in making forms that were themselves automatic, and that sprang from how the material was constituted and deployed. It is a difference that he neatly stated in a remark on his contemporary: 'His objective is the work, mine rather the working.'[17] Both composers saw a need to generalize the serial principle, but for Stockhausen this entailed deriving single, through-composed forms from the basic ideas (*Spiel* was to be his last work in distinct movements until the mid-1970s), whereas Boulez was concerned to establish the foundations of a musical language, rules of musical grammar and vocabulary that composers could use to write scripts that would be their own.

Boulez's anxieties about total serialism may be reflected not only in his suspicion of his own achievement in *Structures Ia* but also in his rapid withdrawal of his *Polyphonie X*. This piece was the only one he completed of a projected volume of instrumental polyphonies—a volume that would seem to be an early example of an open work, allowing a free choice of pieces to be conjoined in any performance.[18] Its particular title indicates that it was an essay in 'cross polyphony', in the

15. Pierre Boulez, *Conversations with Célestin Deliège* (London, 1977), 55.
16. See Ligeti's analysis and Paul Griffiths, *Boulez* (London, 1978), 22–23.
17. K. H. Wörner, *Stockhausen: Life and Work* (London, 1973), 229.
18. See Nattiez, ed., *The Boulez-Cage Correspondence*, 80.

'diagonal' thinking that had captured Boulez's imagination from the first. As in Stockhausen's independently conceived works, the crossing involved exchanges of musical characteristics between two ideas from one point in time to another, as well as a reciprocity between melodic and harmonic composition, a kind of continuous arpeggiation on the grandest scale (this Boulez derived from Webern, and in particular from the Second Cantata). Beyond that, *Polyphonie X* was again an exercise in total serial control, though of a different kind from that shown in *Structures Ia*. The rhythmic organization, following the Second Sonata and the *Livre pour quatuor*, is based on quasi-serial transformations of cells rather than on chromatic durations: there are seven basic cells, and seven ways of altering them. Instrumentation, too, is numerically organized, their being, again, seven groups at any time.[19]

What Boulez later criticized in *Polyphonie X* was its 'theoretical exaggeration' and in particular its instrumentation by numbers,[20] but though it certainly contains moments of abrupt delivery, which caused some merriment at the first performance,[21] the composer may well have been just as unhappy at the time with the generally slow tempo of the piece and with its quantities of motivic imitation and recall— the same features that disappointed Stockhausen in *Formel*. Instead of advance there was regression, to patterns that seemed defunct (but that might subsequently become relevant again). So one moved on, as Boulez now moved on from *Polyphonie X* and from the endgame of *Structures Ia* to another piece for the latter book, *Ic*. *Ia* may have seemed a setback most of all for its mechanical rhythms, and especially for the tendency towards even pulsation that has been noted also in *Kreuzspiel* as a result of working with chromatic durations (and that Stockhausen typically turned into a plus), since *Ic* has a much livelier feel, even though it is still a bald presentation of serial forms.[22]

Structures Ib, the last piece of the set to be composed, is much the longest and most complex (becoming, in a little symptom of Boulez's concern for arranged form, the centrepiece of a symmetry rather than the finale of an explosion). It is also a piece of much greater weight, if not of greater historical moment, than the exceptional but crucial *Ia* (whose existence may have started Boulez wondering whether his purpose was to create archetypes or art). Boulez returns to his earlier

19. See Boulez's essay 'Possibly . . .', *Stocktakings from an Apprenticeship* (Oxford: Clarendon and New York, 1991), 111–40. The work is also discussed, with brief examples, in Jean Barraqué, 'Rythme et développement', *Polyphonie*, 9–10 (1954), 47–74 and in Antoine Goléa, *Rencontres avec Pierre Boulez* (Paris, 1958), 141 and 143.
20. See Boulez, *Conversations with Célestin Deliège*, 58–59.
21. Recorded on Col Legno AU 031 800.
22. See Philip Bracanin, 'The Abstract System as Compositional Matrix', *Studies in Music*, 5 (1971), 90–114.

Example 10 Pierre Boulez, *Structures Ib*

breadth and secrecy of serial usage, not laying out twelve-note sequences but using the series to generate 'a certain texture of intervals',
one in which the minor second and its octave transpositions inevitably
have pride of place, since there are five such intervals in the series. He
returns also to the flexibility of motion he had reached in the late 1940s,
reintroducing grace notes, irrational values, and, as in the slow movement of the Second Sonata, pauses to isolate what may be regarded
as interpolated commentaries. All these features are shown in example
10, a not untypical passage that may suggest how much Boulez had
honed his former self on the rigours of total serialism, which are still
evident in the detailed markings and perhaps too in moments of idealism (such as the coincidence of *fff* and *pp*).

The example shows how the two-piano medium is now used for its
antiphonal qualities, and not merely as a way of sounding six serial
forms at the same time. Formally, too, the piece takes up what had
earlier been a characteristic way of balancing different kinds of musical
motion. Short sections of two-part counterpoint in a strict fast tempo
are alternated with longer and more convoluted passages allowing mobility within a slow tempo range (example 10 illustrates, of course, the
latter type). The contrasts of tempo are extreme, but there is a disparity
between written and experienced tempo because the predominant
note values also change wildly. The opening 'Très rapide', for example,
sounds slower than the 'Lent' that follows it. In this way Boulez brings
about, as in later works, a double sensation of tempo: the possibility of
very fast slow music or of slow fast music.

Those various ways of generalizing serialism that Boulez had discovered in *Structures*, in *Polyphonie X*, and in his two studies in musique
concrète were set out—though curiously without acknowledged reference to those works—in his article 'Possibly . . .',[23] first published in a
special issue of the *Revue musicale* that marked a grand festival of contemporary art in Paris, 'L'Oeuvre du XXe siècle'. (Messiaen and Boulez
played *Structures Ia* at the festival, whose more prestigious events included an *Oedipus Rex* conducted by Stravinsky and staged by Cocteau.)
In this article Boulez insisted that 'any musician who has not experienced—I do not say understood, but truly experienced—the necessity
of dodecaphonic language is USELESS'. One might pause over the pa-
renthesis: Boulez was perhaps implying that commitment to serialism
was a matter of intuition, even passion, not logic, and thereby siding
with *Structures Ib* rather than its predecessor. About the message, though,
or about the path forward, there was no doubt.

The Human Voice 1: Nono

In the summer of 1952, when the Darmstadt summer courses recon-
vened, they were intellectually dominated not by Leibowitz and Messiaen but by Stockhausen, Nono, and Boulez, with the premières of
Kreuzspiel and *España en el corazon* (the first part of Nono's triptych *Epitaffio per Federico García Lorca*), and with performances of Boulez's Second
Sonata and tape *Etudes*. Among other works from the new generation
were what seems to have been the first piece combining live and electronic sounds, Maderna's *Musica su due dimensioni* for flute, cymbals, and
tape. But while the young composers at Darmstadt were united in their
zest for the new and their opposition to compromise—especially the
compromise of neoclassicism—they were no monolithic group. Nono,
in particular, could not go along with his fellows in their pursuit of total
serialism and their resulting fragmentation of texture. 'Pointillism', as
he later put it, 'is contrary to my technique of sound *relations*.'[24] His emphasis was accordingly not on separate organizations of the parameters
but on new, vigorous connections among them, and his *Polifonica—
monodia—ritmica* for five wind players, piano, and percussion (1951)
partitions the components only in order to propound continuity. In the
first section, polyphonic lines edge out from repeated notes and fragments of the chromatic scale; in the second, a long melody works towards a fierce climax; and in the third, with the wind instruments silent,
xylophone, piano, and percussion play against a persistent 3/4 metre.

It is not clear whether Nono's two works of 1951—this triptych and
the orchestral *Composizione*—were written before or after his meeting

23. Boulez, *Stocktakings*, 111–40.
24. Quoted in Michael Gorodecki, 'Luigi Nono: a History of Belief', *Musical Times*, 133 (1992), 10–17.

with Stockhausen and Goeyvaerts at Darmstadt, but the evidence of his next pieces is that these colleagues' ideas, projects, and achievements had astonishingly little effect on him. In most elements of style and technique, his music of 1951–53 proceeds directly out of his *Variazioni canoniche*. There is the same handling of instruments in 'cori spezzati' (the *Composizione* introduces the orchestral groups one by one: tuned percussion, strings, noise percussion, wind), the same use of nonserial chromatic segments and big formal gestures (the *Composizione* is composed entirely of nine notes until the percussion finale, where the timpani revel in the three notes that remain), the same unabashed display of figures rather than points: motifs, reiterated notes, vivid chords, powerfully urged metres (the finale of the *Composizione* is again in 3/4).

Nono now applied these principles on a larger plan in his first two published vocal works: *Epitaffio* for soloists, chorus, and orchestra (1952–53) and the ballet *Der rote Mantel* (1953), both fruits of his sense of a fraternal alliance with Lorca (the ballet is based on Lorca's play *Don Perlimplin*; *Epitaffio* sets Lorca's poetry along with a Neruda lyric that also treats of the Spanish Civil War). Just as Nono's orchestral writing had thrust unpitched percussion into prominence, so *Epitaffio* highlights speaking singers, employing a simplified form of the sprechgesang notation Schoenberg used in *A Survivor from Warsaw*, a work whose actuality and commitment may have provided a model. The epitaph—a memorial to Lorca and implicitly to all Republican victims of the war—is a set of three works, of which the first, *España en el corazon*, is itself a triptych. Its first section is a gentle piece for the soprano and baritone soloists entwining with clarinet over percussion; its third is similarly quiet and reflective, setting the soprano in sprechgesang against a larger ensemble. But the centrepiece vocalizes the violent, protesting manner of the *Variazioni canoniche*, and looks forward to the intensive third part of *Epitaffio*, *Memento*. In between these vocal panels comes a chamber concerto for flute, a wordless setting of Lorca's lament *Y su sangre ya viene cantando*, in which the three stanzas of the poem are represented by three musical sections in a fast-slow-fast pattern. Example 11, from

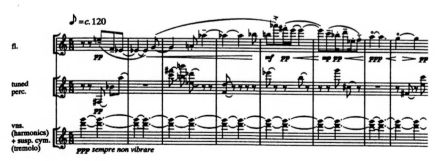

Example 11   Luigi Nono, *Y su sangre ya viene cantando*

the middle section, may illustrate Nono's tense hold on melody at a time when his contemporaries were finding melody impossible, and also his adoption of Schoenbergian complementarity, the tuned percussion supporting the flute by playing the notes it omits. Also characteristic is the use of a defective chromatic mode (omitting B and C#) in the flute part, and the high tremor of suspended cymbal tone, which continues with the held string harmonics almost throughout this section.

Nono's insistence on melodic line (*Y su sangre* was exactly contemporary with Stockhausen's *Kontra-Punkte*: see example 19) is one measure of the primacy of expressive force in his thinking. For him, melody could survive the absence of tonality and the loss of its function as theme; it could even gain thereby, and become, though passionate, objective. Free and unrepeating, it could speak of a hope for freedom, in a personless voice. And Nono made his music speak for the generality, too, in his use of the chorus, not only in *Der rote Mantel* and the flanking parts of *Epitaffio* but also in *La Victoire de Guernica* and—a rare removal from combat music—the *Liebeslied* he wrote for his wife. Just as he would use percussion instruments to give his orchestra power and actuality, so he would have his chorus (though not in the *Liebeslied*) speak. And when their music was less eruptive it would be—again as in the orchestral works—fundamentally melodic, not contrapuntal: a line in unison, or (so characteristic of Nono) a line threading itself from one vocal part into another. Atonality, being central to his antitraditional, antibourgeois activism, required a vigilance in the handling of pitch—a vigilance neatly displayed in the *Liebeslied*, where each half of the piece uses just five notes until the arrival of another to complete the hexachord. But there was still, remarkably, no question of serialism.

Electronic Music

One major problem with applying serialism to all the parameters had been the lack in other domains of anything corresponding to the equal-tempered scale or to the principle of octave equivalence: Messiaen's system of chromatic durations was an obvious cobbling—though undeniably useful to the composers of the *Mode de valeurs*, *Kreuzspiel*, *Structures I*, and *Polifonica—monodia—ritmica*. Boulez in 'Possibly . . .' had suggested that tempo might help. One could define twelve durations reproducing the frequency ratios of the chromatic scale (to a rough approximation the major triad would thereby have its durational equivalent in the threesome of, say, crotchet, crotchet plus quaver, and dotted crotchet), and then these basic durations could be 'transposed' by changing the tempo, a doubling of speed being equivalent to octave transposition.[25] But clearly this is still an arbitrary setup, since there is no true equivalence, in either psychoacoustical or formal mathemat-

25. Boulez, *Stocktakings*, 126–28.

ical terms, between change of tempo and pitch transposition. Most importantly, there is no durational counterpart here to the interval: a major third is always a major third, but Boulez's duration intervals (if such things may be conceived) would vary from one 'transpositional level' to another. Babbitt at this point was working on more sophisticated approaches to serial rhythm, but as yet his work was little known in Europe.

If rhythmic serialism was fraught with difficulties, then the serialization of timbre presented still more intractable problems. It was reasonable enough to establish a scale of attacks in piano music—from intense to gentle, as Boulez had done in the first book of his *Structures* —but there was no obvious way in which one might place in order, for example, the sound qualities of harp, cello, flute, and horn. Twelve-piece ensembles, such as Babbitt had used, could not provide anything more than artificial one-off solutions, nor was the basic problem of ordering addressed by the grouping schemes of Boulez's *Polyphonie X* and Stockhausen's *Formel*. One had to be able to 'tune' timbre, to control it. Stockhausen made an effort in that direction in *Spiel*, but seems to have realized that the solution would only come when composers could create timbres on tape. At the same time, the tape medium would make it considerably easier to realize durations with precision, and so to create a serial rhythm, whatever that might be, uncompromised by the needs, wishes, and habits of performers. The same impetus that led to total serialism therefore rapidly took composers into electronic music.

Schaeffer's studio provided the first stop, since it was virtually the only place where tape music was being made professionally in Europe in the early 1950s. Messiaen, Boulez, Barraqué, and Stockhausen all composed tape pieces, though Messiaen's *Timbres-durées*—a title expressive of what concerned all these composers—was put together by Henry. Something of the excitement of the adventure springs from the pages of Schaeffer's essay 'L'Objet musical', published in the same special issue of the *Revue musicale*[26] that contained Boulez's 'Possibly . . . '. Following up earlier suggestions of his own, but almost certainly influenced also by the group of young collaborators he had acquired, Schaeffer proposes serial manipulations of sound objects, objects that could be transformed in precise ways; he even theorizes about procedures that were to engage Stockhausen's attention throughout the next decade, such as the conversion of a complex event into a single sound, or the treatment of duration as a variable with the same capacity for complex relationships as pitch.

For the moment, though, the overriding concern was serial organization in all the parameters. In his *Etude sur un son* (1951), Boulez drew scales of timbre out of a recording of a stroke on a sansa (his

26. Pierre Schaeffer, 'Le'Objet musical', *Revue Musicale*, no. 212 (1952), 65–76.

choice of an African instrument indicative of his thinking still), and in the ensuing *Etude sur sept sons* went on in the same direction. However, the equipment was insufficient for Boulez's purposes, and both studies have an uncharacteristically inert sound. Boulez emerged from the studio totally disenchanted with its facilities and personnel,[27] and his continuing espousal of the need for electronic means seems to have been tempered—even during the decade and more when, much later, he was running his own studio—by misgivings.

Stockhausen, by contrast, learned from his experience with musique concrète that he would need other means: not transformation but electronic sound synthesis.[28] A new musical architecture demanded new material, not refashionings of the old. The work of Helmholtz and Fourier had suggested that any sound could be analysed as a collection of pure frequencies, of sine tones, and this was something that Stockhausen thought he had confirmed, in analysing instrumental sounds in Paris. So it seemed reasonable to suppose that the process could be reversed, that timbres could be synthesized by playing together a chosen group of sine tones at chosen relative dynamic levels. One could thereby form a repertory of artificial timbres that were related in defined ways, and therefore suited to serial composition. This Stockhausen tried, working with a sine-wave generator at the postal headquarters in Paris, but the practical problems were insuperable. Instead, in December 1952, he turned to using initial moments from prepared piano sounds in his first electronic composition, the *Etüde*.[29]

The following spring he returned to Cologne. Herbert Eimert (1897–1972) and Robert Beyer (1901–89) had begun experiments at the radio station, with which Stockhausen had already had contacts before going to Paris (he had been a student in Cologne), and there he found the equipment that enabled him to make the first sine-tone composition, his *Studie I* (1953), in which each sound is constructed from up to six pure frequencies taken from a table based on the proportions 48:20:25:15⅝:37½:30, that sequence being derived from the frequency ratios in the succession of falling minor tenth (12:5), rising major third (4:5), falling minor sixth (8:5), rising minor tenth (5:12), falling major third (5:4). The same sequence governs the rhythmic construction, and other six-unit series, made up of the first six whole numbers, determine

27. See his 'Concrète (Musique)', *Stocktakings*, 226–27.
28. See his 'The Origins of Electronic Music', *Musical Times*, 112 (1971), 649–50—though this needs to be read as what it is: self-vindication rather than history.
29. See Richard Toop, 'Stockhausen's *Konkrete Etüde*', *Music Review*, 38 (1976), 295–300, and 'Stockhausen and the Sine Wave: the Story of an Ambiguous Relationship', *Musical Quarterly*, 65 (1979), 379–91, of which the latter throws doubt on the above chronology, where Stockhausen's account has been followed.

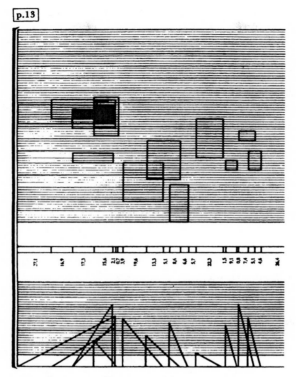

Example 12   Karlheinz Stockhausen, *Studie II*

other aspects: the number of sine tones packaged into each sound, their intensities, the dynamic curve applied, and the durations of pauses.[30] Nothing could better illustrate Stockhausen's will to achieve an image of perfect unity.

However, the sine tones obstinately failed to gel into the hoped-for new timbres, and so in his next electronic composition, *Studie II* (1954, see example 12), he tried another tack.[31] Again there is an artificial frequency gamut, this time a simpler one of eighty-one frequencies each related to the next by the ratio of one to the twenty-fifth root of five (approximately 1:1.07), chosen to produce an octaveless scale with uniform intervals of slightly more than a semitone. But now, instead of simply superimposing the sine tones, as he had in *Studie I*, Stockhausen spliced them together, always in groups of five, played the spliced tape in a resonant space, and then rerecorded the reverberation of the mixture. This brought a greater degree of fusion, though still the work's success in synthesizing unified timbres is modest.

30. See Karlheintz Stockhausen, *Texte*, ii (Cologne, 1964), 23–36.
31. See preface to the score, repr. in ibid., 37–42.

Failures of aim and technique, however, do not disqualify these pieces as objects not only of historical curiosity but of musical fascination. *Studie I* offers a surface of ringing chimes and deeper thuds: a slow percussion piece etherealized by the absence of sharp attacks. *Studie II*, by contrast, is brief and dynamic, its scintillating bundles of frequencies leaping about the novel pitch framework. Example 12, taken from the published score (this was the first electronic composition to appear in print), may give some impression of the piece at its most excited. The blocks in the upper part show the frequencies used in each note mixture; the numbers indicate durations in centimetres of tape (the speed being 76.2 centimetres per second); and the jagged lower part shows the dynamic envelopes imposed on the mixtures.

The Cologne studio's emphasis on synthesis from sine tones led to the coining of the term 'Elektronische Musik', partly to distinguish their work from the musique concrète of Paris, and for some years there was a mutual antipathy between the two institutions and their different ways of proceeding. There was no doubt, however, about which camp claimed the loyalty of the young composers who were starting to hear about the work of Stockhausen and Boulez, and to find something compelling in their vision of music reborn—composers like Henri Pousseur (1929–2009), who came to Cologne to work and learn. On October 19, 1954, the Cologne radio station broadcast a selection of compositions produced in their studio, including pieces by Stockhausen, Eimert, Goeyvaerts and Pousseur. Eimert's vision of a 'real musical control of Nature'[32] may have overstated the case, but a commitment had been made to building music from its most basic components, and that commitment had repercussions far beyond the half-hour programme.

The Human Voice 2: Barraqué

But among the young European composers of the early 1950s there was one who viewed the current necessity of music as something other than the building of a bold new future—who may have shared some of Boulez's premises, but who worked with an unfashionable concern (even an imperative) to make musical statements in the grand manner, guaranteed not by total organization but by total purposefulness. (It followed that those statements would be few.) Barraqué was also a pupil of Messiaen, and it was while under Messiaen's tutelage that he began his first acknowledged works, the Piano Sonata (1950–52) and *Séquence* for soprano and nine players (1950–54).

The latter, begun before the sonata but thoroughly revised afterwards, shows at once the scale of Barraqué's thinking. Not only is it an unbroken movement lasting for almost twenty minutes, but the writing

32. 'What is Electronic Music?', *Die Reihe*, 1 (1955; English ed. 1958), 1–10.

for both voice and ensemble has an ampleness quite without parallel in the contemporary works of Boulez or Stockhausen. And it is entirely characteristic of Barraqué that this ampleness should be so often and so unpredictably cut off, as if the music were striving for a Romantic rhetoric that the composer knows to be at once essential and unattainable, or indefensible. The instrumental ensemble—a traditional grouping (piano trio) vastly expanded or exploded by the addition of pitched and unpitched percussion—both permits this vision and gives the work a distinctive sound world, while the choice of poetic texts from Nietzsche, arranged by the composer for his purpose, makes it clear that the work's extraordinary blend of magnificence and impotence, eloquence and muteness, comes from a conviction that creative effort is at once irresistible and vain. Barraqué's vocal writing is fiercely demanding, with its wide intervals, different kinds of articulation and moments of violence, but lyricism persists. From a melancholic hyperaesthesia, the singer moves in the latter half of the work to identify herself with a stock figure of musical history, the abandoned Ariadne, and the ending comes, somewhat as in *Erwartung*, with an evaporation. The music becomes bone dry; flooding melodies turn to isolated points.

The Piano Sonata takes a similar course, and carries itself with a similar continuity and desperation, though it is twice the length. It is clear that Barraqué was impressed by Boulez's Second Sonata, and by its cellular conception. But where Boulez's rhythmic style tends to either obscure cells in polyrhythm or throw them against a steady pulse, Barraqué maintains an irregular momentum through great lines of dissimilar cells, and thereby gains a compelling thrust. Tempo is not imposed on the music, as in Boulez, but executed by it, and the antagonism of powerfully urged tempos becomes the work's sonata-style dialectic. Example 13 shows a typical passage in which the cells do not deny but rather establish, however uncertainly, a feeling of progression, to which imitations of rhythmic or intervalic contour lend weight. Also noteworthy in this example is the registral locking of pitches, which, though derived from the Boulez sonata, fixes on a median range to give rise to a more intense, more vocal frustration.

The first part of the work is a quasi-sonata development of two kinds of music: a 'free' type, marked by a more virtuoso use of the keyboard, by the presence of quintuplet figures and by the absence of registral locking; and a 'strict' type, in which register fixing goes along with a more sober musical growth (example 13 comes, plainly, from music of this second sort). The separate development and the interpenetration of the two reaches a climax when the musical continuity is devastatingly interrupted by a sequence of progressively lengthening pauses. In the second part the role of silence becomes ever larger as sections from the first part are brought back, reversed, and greatly decelerated (the slow movement of the Boulez sonata may have had an influence here, though the comparison shows how far Barraqué is from

Example 13   Jean Barraqué, *Piano Sonata*

Boulez's poise). In the poetic but apt language of André Hodeir, whose book did much to communicate Barraqué's importance: 'Whole slabs of sound crumble and vanish in the silence which engulfs all. Only the twelve notes of the series remain, and these are plucked off, one by one.'[33] The sonata, while being a huge creative accomplishment, turns at the end into self-extinction, as if it had all been for nothing. But this was not what the young soldiers of total serialism wanted to hear.

33. *La Musique depuis Debussy* (Paris, 1961), 173.

4

Classic Modernism and Other Kinds

The United States, 1945–55

The three great forefathers of modern music still alive at the end of 1945 were all United States citizens: Ives, Schoenberg, and Stravinsky. Ives as yet was little known, but the presence and the example of the other two may have encouraged a more moderate attitude to innovation on the part of many U.S. composers—Cage, who had studied with Schoenberg, always excepted. A late prose fragment by Schoenberg, dating from 1950, begins by restating a thought constant in his writings: 'I am at least as conservative as Edison and Ford have been. But I am, unfortunately, not quite as progressive as they were in their own fields.'[1] His works of his last years, while retasting the freedom and edge of the *Erwartung* period, by no means betray his lifelong commitment to orderly development and integrity of voice.

The orderliness, at least, communicated itself to many of his U.S. pupils and followers, among whom Babbitt—a follower, never a pupil —soon became one of the leading exponents of twelve-note music, both as a composer and as a professor at Princeton University. His contemporary, George Perle (1915–2009), promoted the same cause of rational twelve-note composition through his work as a teacher, theorist, and composer, developing a system out of Berg and Bartók whereby a traditional kind of harmonic coherence could be maintained in totally chromatic music. From the same generation, Leon Kirchner (1919–

1. Arnold Schoenberg, 'My Attitude Towards Politics', in H. H. Stuckenschmidt: *Schoenberg: His Life, Work and World* (London, 1977), 551–52.

2009), who, like Cage, studied with Schoenberg in Los Angeles, developed into a twelve-note composer able, like his teacher, to command the rhetoric of tonal symphonic music. One might also see the later music of Stravinsky, a U.S. citizen since 1945, within the context of this American serial school, though in his case the impulses came more from Europe.

The others' dependence on Schoenberg was not entirely unequivocal. Babbitt, in particular, was defiantly un-Schoenbergian in his belief in the importance of method, and almost as adamant as Boulez and Stockhausen in his new approach to form. What separates his work most distinctly from theirs is his insistence also on logic, within a work and within his extension of the twelve-note system on the basis of principles in Schoenberg and Webern. It is this logic that gives his work the classic dimension that marked the music of such elder contemporaries as Carter and Stefan Wolpe (1902–72) by virtue of their having started their creative lives before the war.

Schoenberg

As the Second World War came to an end Schoenberg was seventy. He had not left Los Angeles since arriving there in 1933, nor was he to travel during the remaining six years of his life. But friends, pupils, and colleagues made sure he was informed of his music's revival in Europe, where ideology or apathy had kept it from being heard since his emigration. Correspondents told him, for example, about performances of the Six Little Piano Pieces for Salzburg radio in September 1945, of the Second Quartet for Berlin radio in 1946, and of the First Chamber Symphony in Munich in 1947.[2] There were other marks of esteem. In 1946 he was named honorary president of the International Society for Contemporary Music and invited by the Bürgermeister to return to Vienna.[3] He also had news of the Darmstadt courses, to which Leibowitz asked him in 1949. Whether he was aware, too, of how his ideas were being adapted, extended, and rebutted by a new generation of composers is unsure: had he gone to Darmstadt in 1949 he would have met Messiaen and some of Leibowitz's young pupils (though not Boulez).

His music of these last years is sparse. In August–September 1946 he was seriously ill, and saved by injections into the heart: the illness, and the injections, were reflected in the String Trio he wrote during these months. Thereafter he was effectively an invalid, and his last works, all quite short, were achieved in brief bursts: in August 1947 came *A Survivor from Warsaw*, in June the next year a set of three folk song arrangements for unaccompanied chorus, in the spring of 1949

---

2. For these and other details, see ibid, 474ff.
3. See Erwin Stein, ed., *Arnold Schoenberg Letters* (London, 1964), 239.

the Phantasy for violin and piano, the choral piece *Dreimal tausend Jahre*, sketches for another choral work (*Israel Exists Again*) and the beginnings of a string quartet, and in June–July 1950 a setting of Psalm 130 in Hebrew. His final year was devoted to the words and music of a set of 'modern psalms', of which only one was partly composed.

For whatever reason—illness, age, recollection, the resuscitation of his music in Europe—he recaptured in these concluding works something of the brevity and fierceness of his first atonal pieces, though still with the insistent motivic echoing that the twelve-note method had encouraged. The shadows of returning tonality in the *Ode to Napoleon* and the Piano Concerto (both 1942) fall away, and there are no more large-scale tonal compositions, such as had played a large part in his output during the previous dozen years (the last tonal relics are just the folk song triptych and an ultimate canon). At the same time the links with standard forms and genres attenuate. The final chamber work is not a quartet but a trio, belonging to a much rarer repertory, and though the music is often patently developmental, parts of it are dislocated and the whole adheres to no traditional scheme: the single movement returns finally to its point of origin, having been interrupted by two self-contained episodes and several shorter divagations. A similar wheeling course, but over a reduced and smoother circuit, is taken by the only other instrumental work of this period, the Phantasy for violin and piano.

In terms of rawness, though, the String Trio's only companion is its more immediate successor, *A Survivor from Warsaw*. A narrator, delivering Schoenberg's own English text in sprechgesang, recalls a brutal experience from the Warsaw ghetto: semiconscious, in darkness, he hears trumpets, and a German officer demanding the inmates come out and number off. The orchestral accompaniment is a patchwork of ostinatos and sudden gestures, closely keyed into the text in the way of *Erwartung*, until the final surge that brings the men's chorus on to carry the work home. The narrator referred near the start to 'the grandiose moment when they all started to sing': it is to this that the work looks forward and builds. The message, unequivocally, is one of triumphant defiance; it is also, for the music, one of purposeful achievement, with the majestic Hebrew hymn rising up as a twelve-note chant from the earlier disintegration.

Schoenberg's next choral works were all concerned with another new creation, that of the state of Israel, to which he dedicated his setting of Psalm 130 for six-part speaking and singing chorus. The unfinished 'modern psalm' that followed was, characteristically, a prayer about the possibility of prayer—a prayer that could have been voiced by the Moses of the opera, and is similarly projected by a man through sprechgesang, the words being taken up and illuminated by a choir with orchestra. Schoenberg kept hoping he would be able to complete both *Moses und Aron* and *Die Jakobsleiter*, but nothing was added to those scores, and the *Modern Psalm* lapses at a corresponding point, where the words ask for the music of union with God.

Carter

Carter's self-reinvention was as striking an expression of the postwar climate as any, the swerve of a neoclassicist who now made change his prime subject. From his First Quartet (1950–51) onwards he was to work with materials in constant evolution: materials in which stability in one or more domains is necessary only to support and show the urgent movement in others. What the First Quartet also introduced was a polyphony of these dynamic streams, and in particular a polyphony of tempos, so that the music moves at several different rates simultaneously. Change does not happen simply because time is moving on; change is deliberately engineered and motivated.

There is a connection here—a connection of objectivity and rationalism—with the nevertheless very different music Carter had written before the late 1940s. Like other U.S. composers of his generation, he had studied in France with Nadia Boulanger, and learned from her a reverence for the neoclassical Stravinsky. But what was ironic and suppositional in Stravinsky became candid in the music of Boulanger's pupils, who seemed confident of a restabilization, and a renewal of contact with an audience predisposed by taste and education to music of the eighteenth and nineteenth centuries (U.S. neoclassicism often carried this subtext of democratic utopianism). Carter swam with that stream as far as his ballet *The Minotaur* (1947), where the allegiance is to Stravinsky's then recent Symphony in Three Movements, but his chamber pieces of 1948–49 began to introduce the new polyphony in characteristic terms of a polyphony of musical personality: the Cello Sonata, in particular, has this dialogue nature. Then he left New York to spend a year on a Guggenheim fellowship in the Arizona desert. 'I decided for once to write a work very interesting to myself, and so say to hell with the public and with the performers too.'[4] That work was his First Quartet (see example 14).

Thus where his almost exact contemporary Messiaen, just a day older, would seem to have gained encouragement from the young pupils who surrounded him in the late 1940s and 1950s, Carter moved forward most rapidly when he was artistically alone. U.S. popularism gave way to U.S. independence, and did so in the music too, where a sense of self-propelled movement asserted itself—a sense in this quartet of up to four separate lines of activity. Ives may have provided a spur here. Carter, born into a wealthy New York family, had been introduced

4. Allen Edwards, *Flawed Words and Stubborn Sounds: A Conversation with Elliott Carter* (New York, 1971), 35.

Example 14   Elliott Carter, String Quartet No. 1

to Ives by his school music teacher, and would surely have been familiar with Ives's Second Quartet, a work 'for 4 men—who converse, discuss, argue (in re 'politick'), fight, shake hands, shut up—then walk up the mountain-side to view the firmament.'[5] The essential difference in his own First Quartet is that the characters are not psychological, and certainly not identifiable consistently with the players, in the way that Ives's second violin enacts the role of his despised Rollo, the imaginary

5. Note on the manuscript.

guardian of musical propriety. Instead the flows at play in Carter's First Quartet are characters existing only in and as music—characters that may be introduced by particular instruments, but that can carry uninterruptedly from one voice into another. They are abstract characters, defined by their musical constituents—intervals, tempo, pulse unit— rather than by anything describable as mood. This may be another inheritance from neoclassicism; it is certainly a primary marker of Carter's music. For more than a quarter of a century after 1947 he wrote no vocal music, preferring to work with currents of musical movement that can be steered through instruments in small groupings (especially the string quartet) or through combinations of soloists and ensembles in works for orchestra (where Ives may again have provided an example: Carter's orchestral style is an abstraction of Ives's, with all the quotations and the local references taken out, to leave only the conflicting textures and energies).

Almost any dozen bars from his First Quartet would show its coursing, ranging polyphony; Example 14 comes from near the midpoint of the work, and suggests how different kinds of musical motion can be cross-related both vertically and horizontally. At the beginning of the example, cascading 9/16 semiquavers pass from the first violin into the cello, where they come to a halt on the one note, C♯, untouched during the four-bar, five-octave descent in major and minor seconds. Simultaneously, another train of thought, in pizzicato 3/8 quavers, transfers in the opposite direction, while the pulse units in the viola are drawn out, under the influence of the syncopated second violin, from three semiquavers to five, which the change of metre to 2/4 then reinterprets as four. This change of metre is an example of Carter's 'metric modulation', whereby a new metre is introduced as a translation of an old one, opening up the possibilities of pulses that would not have been easily available before, just as harmonic modulation changes the temporary tonic and thereby the pitch repertory. In this particular case, pulse ratios at the start of 2:3:9 per dotted crotchet in 3/8 (viola:cello:violin I) give way in the final momentary stalling to ratios of 8:15:20 per five semibreves in 2/4 (violin I:violin II:viola), where the 8 under the new dispensation is equivalent to 1.2 under the old. The music is performable because of regularities that bridge across: the quaver pulse that carries over from 3/8 to 5/8 in the first violin, or the pulse that stays the same across the change of tempo and metre at the double barline. These are classic means, extended from the two-against-three cross-rhythms of music from Brahms onwards. To that extent—as in the measure of his harmony, and his attachment to standard genres and weights of work—Carter is still a neoclassicist. But the colliding, jostling rushes of the First Quartet are new and distinctive, and were to be exuberantly taken further in the music of the next sixty years and more.

Revolutions usually require some kind of radical simplification, and so it is here, in that Carter found it necessary to identify each of his pulse layers by keeping it regular: always quavers in the first violin in the six bars before the double barline, always triplet minims in the second violin from that point onwards. In later works he would be able to make the movement inside each layer more flexible, without losing the identity of the layer, and also without damaging the sense that each layer is itself concerned with change, with executing a process. The vestiges of theme that remain in the First Quartet and the Variations for orchestra (1953–55) would then dissolve away, to leave pure mobility and development within musical layers identified by speed, instrumentation, and interval content. And the relatively simple processes of the First Quartet—represented by the elements of ostinato and scalewise movement in example 14—would give place to more complex sways and surges.

Carter's polyphony, in the First Quartet as in his later music, is one proof against subjectivity: because the music is happening in several speeds simultaneously, it has no speed of its own, and therefore allows no presumption that it speaks or sings (or, given the abundant pulsed rhythms, dances) the thinking of one person at one time. In form, the First Quartet celebrates this liberation from psychological time. It begins with several bars for the cello alone, and ends as a balancing, answering solo for the leader. At these points it has indeed a single voice— though the status of that voice is less certain at the conclusion, after so much polyphony of contradicting voices. Nobody is thinking this music. It is thinking itself.

The work's polyphony of tempos also has an effect on the notion of what constitutes a musical movement. Tempo in Carter is not something applied to music; tempo is enacted by the music as it becomes sound. A slow movement or a scherzo is a mode of behaviour, and can only take hold by means of a clearing away or suppression of other modes of behaviour. So it is here. There are four movements—a fantasia, a scherzo, an adagio, and a set of variations—but the music flows from one into the next, and the two interruptions dramatize the fact by cutting almost arbitrarily into the scherzo and into the variations (example 14 comes from the portion of the variations before this second break). Within the movements, too, the continuity of change removes the music from any normal pattern of recurrence: the themes of the variations, for instance, are not only several but tumbled into a process of swirling acceleration.

In its objectivity, and in its dancing rhythms, the First Quartet may still be Stravinskian, but it was also the first work in which Carter placed himself within the context of a wider divergence of modern masters: Ives, Debussy (whose *Jeux* and orchestral *Images* provided nearer examples of multiple tempos under supreme control), Schoenberg (for formal continuity and a disciplined atonality, though Carter had no use for the stabilization of motif implicit in classical serialism). Unlike Boulez, however, Carter never associated his music with a programme of modernist advance, and unlike Babbitt he taught only occasionally. In an age of polemic and controversy, there was no suggestion from him that his works instanced preferred aesthetic or theoretical criteria. Instead, for the two decades or so after the First Quartet he just went on producing a new big instrumental piece every few years.

Babbitt

Babbitt was a Schoenbergian from an early age. According to his own account,[6] it was for the sake of Schoenberg that he went to New York to study with Marion Bauer in the early 1930s; that gave him the opportunity to meet Schoenberg when the latter was staying in New York, in 1933–34. But during the next dozen years, he composed rather little and published nothing: the release came only after the Second World War, when he began a regular pattern of composing and teaching. His first published works were, he has remarked, 'concerned with embodying the extensions, generalizations, and fusions of certain techniques contained in the music of Schoenberg, Webern and Berg, and above all with applying the pitch operations of the twelve-tone system to non-pitch elements: durational rhythm, dynamics, phrase rhythm, timbre, and register, in such a manner as to preserve the most significant properties associated with these operations in the pitch domain when they are applied in these other domains'.[7] That final clause, implying a search for congruence among the organizational means used for the different parameters rather than for separation and conflict, draws attention to the fundamental division between Babbitt and Boulez.

Something of how Babbitt went about fulfilling his self-imposed programme may be illustrated with reference to *Three Compositions for Piano* (1947), his earliest acknowledged work, and one in which the principles of rhythmic serialism differ essentially from Boulez's techniques of unrestrained cellular variation and manipulating chromatic durations. Example 15 shows the start of the first *Composition*, which Perle analysed.[8] The serial forms have been marked here in accordance with the convention that 'P' represents a prime form, 'R' a retrograde, 'I' an inversion and 'RI' a retrograde inversion, the superscript numbers showing how many steps above C are needed to reach the first note.

No analysis is needed to notice how the music, in its even progress and its wit, is totally at odds with Boulez's contemporary Second Piano Sonata: despite the debt to Schoenberg, there is more connection with the oriental serenity of Cage's *Sonatas and Interludes* or his String Quar-

---

6. See Milton Babbitt, *Words about Music,* ed. Stephen Dembski and Joseph N. Straus (Madison, 1987), 5ff.

7. Note with CRI 138.

8. See George Perle, *Serial Composition and Atonality* (Berkeley, Calif., 1978), 99–101, 135–36, 139–41.

Example 15   Milton Babbitt, *Three Compositions for Piano*

tet. Babbitt and Cage were alike, too, in needing a precise reason for every creative decision. Cage found reason in his number sequences and charts, then later—the reason of no reason—in his dice-throws and other chance procedures. For Babbitt, reason came from the nature of twelve-note composition and the techniques to be derived therefrom. And those do need some analysis to untangle.

Babbitt characteristically bases his pitch organization on bringing together fractions of serial forms to produce 'aggregates', a term he uses to mean collections that contain all twelve pitch classes, but that are not instances of a work's series. (A pitch class—the term is again Babbitt's—is a virtual pitch, not yet ascribed to any register. A twelve-note series is a series of pitch classes, because a C in a series can be any C. Babbitt's nomenclature, more systematic than that of earlier serial composers, is required by music that is similarly more systematic.) In this case the fractions are simply hexachords, and it is easy to see how in each bar a pair of hexachords from different serial forms is combined to create an aggregate. The principle in operation here, developed from Schoenberg's use of hexachords in complementary relationships, is that of 'combinatoriality' (another key term in Babbitt's theory), specifically that of hexachordal combinatoriality. A twelve-note series exhibits this property if one of its hexachords can be combined with a hexachord from another form of the same series to produce an aggregate. Clearly, any prime form of any series will be combinatorial with the retrograde form that comes back to the same pitch class, and similarly any inversion with the retrograde inversion that takes the same path backwards. The possibilities are extended when a prime form is combinatorial with an inversion, a retrograde inversion, or a transposition, as will happen when there is some symmetry between the hexachords.

In the case of the *Three Compositions*, each of the two hexachords contains a chromatic group plus a note at each end a whole tone away (E, F♯, G, A♭, A, and B are, for example, the constituents of the first hexachord of P^4). This series is particularly rich in combinatorial relationships, since a given serial form is hexachordally combinatorial with a transposition (the association of bars 1–2), an inversion (bars 3–4), a retrograde (bars 5–6), and a retrograde inversion (bars 7–8). A set of this kind is said to be 'all-combinatorial', and it provides a whole network of connections the composer can use in ordering serial forms so as to ensure a perpetual circulation of the chromatic total and to achieve, as here, a density of correspondence that does not depend on thematic allusions.

Not only does the combinatorial property suggest which serial forms are to be superimposed, it also provides a clue for linear thinking. In example 15, for instance, each hand proceeds from one serial form to another in accordance with a combinatorial relationship: the second hexachord of P^4 forms an aggregate with the first of R^{10} (right hand, bars 2–3) and so on. There thus emerge what Babbitt refers to as 'secondary sets',[9] formed when one hexachord from a particular serial form is joined to a complementary hexachord from another. In this case the secondary sets are not emphasized, but in many later works they take on more importance. The combinatorial counterpoint and the secondary-set liaisons exemplify how Babbitt's world is a world of musical punning, in which particular elements (hexachords in this case) can be interpreted in more than one way. This may be one source—together with the rhythmic nimbleness—of his music's humour.

Example 15 also displays the use of nonpitch parameters to elucidate and mesh with the pitch organization according to Babbitt's stated principles. Four dynamic levels are associated with the four varieties of serial form—*mp* with the prime, *mf* with the retrograde, *f* with the inversion, and *p* with the retrograde inversion—and these associations are retained throughout the development that follows (they are 'transposed down' by two degrees, to *pp, p, mp,* and *ppp* respectively, in the eight bars that symmetrically close the piece). The organization of rhythm also proceeds in step with that of pitch. Babbitt chooses a basic set of 5-1-4-2, which may be interpreted in terms of duration (crotchet

    9. Milton Babbitt, 'Some Aspects of Twelve-Tone Composition', *The Score,* 12 (1955), 53–61.

tied to semiquaver, semiquaver, crotchet, quaver) or may alternatively, since it sums to twelve, be projected in the number of serial notes gathered together in bundles: 'durational rhythm' and 'phrase rhythm', to repeat Babbitt's terms, can both be organized serially, with reference to the same set.

It is phrase rhythm that is so organized in example 15, where the prime form of the rhythmic set occurs with the prime form of the pitch set (bars 1–2) and the rhythmic retrograde (2-4-1-5) with the pitch retrograde (right hand, bars 3–4, and left hand, bars 7–8). Rhythmic inversion may be more difficult to imagine, but the process of intervalic inversion does provide a model for a rhythmic counterpart. If the notes of a series are numbered according to their distance above C in semitones (e.g. C–D–A♭ . . . becomes 0-2-8 . . .) then the inversion can be derived by complementing these numbers to twelve (12 [i.e. 0]-10-4 . . . being C–B♭–E . . .). Thus, by a similar process of complementation to six, the set 5-1-4-2 can be inverted to yield 1-5-2-4, with a corresponding retrograde inversion of 4-2-5-1. As may be seen in example 15, these are indeed the rhythmic sets given to the inversion and retrograde inversion forms of the pitch set.

That eight bars of music may demonstrate so much evidence of order is some measure of Babbitt's ability to make everything in his compositions serve a constructive function, and to have a reason for everything. This no doubt reflects his cast of mind, but it may be symptomatic, too, of a postwar distrust of irrational genius (whose effects had been witnessed), and it was a position that gained support from the success of Schenkerian analysis in the United States. If tonal masterpieces could be shown to be full of structure unsuspected by the naive listener, it might well be possible that consciously evolved serial structure, though not identifiable by the unaided ear, would nevertheless contribute to music being perceived as homogenous and purposeful. This seems clearly to be so in the relatively simple case of example 15. The combinatorial relationships and the rhythmic serialism may not be noticed as such when the music is played and heard, but they surely contribute to the impression of lucidity, elegance, and pleasure the piece conveys. There is something watertight about the music: every detail has an immediate answer, suggesting that every eventuality has been prepared by the composer. What must also have contributed to the way Babbitt's music has been received is how his arguments on behalf of his music and methods have the same intellectual energy and integrity.

Those same writings, however, appear to assume that the comprehension of his music depends neither on some passive recognition of order nor on faith but rather on an active, conscious awareness of the rules of the game. That might explain why he took so long to establish the rules before he started to play, why he was so concerned to keep to the same basic rules, and why he felt able to apply the rules in gradually more complex and covert ways. Moreover, his demands for rigorous composition and rigorous listening need not be construed as idealist: they may rather be a composer's reasoned response to finding himself in a musical world where the general concert public has little use for Schoenberg or Schoenbergians, and where the listeners to advanced serial music are most likely to be found among fellow composers, musicologists, and committed lay adherents. In what is again an anti-Romantic gesture, Babbitt fulfils the desires of his audience.[10]

The second of the *Three Compositions for Piano* shows a further central element in Babbitt's technical repertory: the use of 'derived sets'. Following the example of such works of Webern as the Concerto Op. 24, he makes use of sets containing internal symmetries, these sets being derived from a parent by proliferation from a single fragment of two, three, or four notes. For instance, the first three notes of the form RI[11] from example 15 (F–D♭–C) can be used to generate a derived set if they are combined with their own inversion (B♭–D–E♭), retrograde inversion (A–G♯–E), and retrograde (F♯–G–B). This is the set presented in the right hand at the opening of *Composition II*, a set full of identities: by definition, each of its four trichords contains only one each of two different intervals. With derived sets the composer is thus able to explore, systematically, different harmonic areas contained within the original set: as *Composition II* proceeds, it unfolds and develops derived sets obtained from each trichord of the parent series in turn.

Babbitt pursued the techniques of *Three Compositions for Piano*—those of rhythmic serialism, combinatoriality, secondary sets, derived sets, and so on—in his *Composition for Four Instruments* (1948), *Composition for Twelve Instruments* (1948), and *Composition for Viola and Piano* (1950), each again with a title whose implications of 'abstractness and "formalism"' he declared himself happy to accept.[11] Where Boulez and Messiaen, in such works as the former's Second Piano Sonata and the latter's *Turangalîla* symphony, were producing music of great expressive force and dynamism, Babbitt and Cage were making their music as objective as possible. This difference at least balances the similarity between Boulez and Babbitt as serial composers, or that between Cage and Messiaen as anti-polyphonic musicians.

Homemade Music

If U.S. composers were beginning to feel some uncertainty about the general musical audience, that was not reflected in Carter's works, which

---

10. For a fascinating analysis of Babbitt's logic as a response to left-wing intellectual life in 1930s New York, see Martin Brody, '" Music for the Masses": Milton Babbitt's Cold War Music Theory', *Musical Quarterly*, 77 (1993), 161–92.

11. Note with CRI 138.

for some time were fully conventional in genre, comprising string quartets and orchestral scores. Cage, on the other hand, was finding and making his creative opportunities outside the norms of musical life, writing pieces for himself to perform, for close friends (notably Tudor), for dancers; his 1949 String Quartet was a rare venture into the traditional concert world.

In circumventing the usual routes and the usual public he was not alone in the U.S. Ives had done that, and the huge, multifarious output of Henry Cowell (1897–1965), an acquaintance of Ives and teacher of Cage, forestalls official culture's passions to delimit and define. Where West Coast composers closer to Cage in age are concerned, unorthodox musical behaviour becomes almost an orthodoxy. Harry Partch (1901–74), largely self-taught, devoted his life to designing, building, and writing for his own instruments made to a scale of forty-three justly tuned degrees per octave. Conlon Nancarrow similarly concentrated, throughout a long period of his life, on an unconventional medium: the pianola, or player piano. The music of Lou Harrison (1917–2003) suggests more a continuation from Cowell (who was his teacher, too) in its abundance, its generous simplicity, and its complete lack of European hauteur with regard to the instruments, forms, and tunings of other cultures.

Partch had come upon the gate to his independent road in Hermann Helmholtz's book on acoustics, translated into English by A. J. Ellis as *On the Sensations of Tone*. In the early 1930s he had written a few pieces for voice with 'adapted viola' (an instrument with a lengthened neck, and with its fingerboard marked to facilitate performance in just intonation), but it was only during the late 1930s and 1940s that he began to assemble a collection of instruments, and most of his works date from the period between 1949 and 1966. They consist principally of musical dramas, since for him just intonation and instrument construction were imbricated in an aesthetic of 'corporeal' music—of music as founded in natural vibration, and of music as a narrative art, rooted in speech. The history of Western music was, with rare exceptions (Musorgsky, for example), a contrary history of 'abstraction': closer to his ideals, he thought, were the musical cultures of ancient China and Greece, in which sound, display, word, and gesture were welded and magically potent. There is a striking kinship here with Artaud's ideas, which appealed so much to Boulez at just the time Partch was beginning to realize his first major projects.

The instruments Partch made or adapted include reed organs, plucked strings (kitharas, zithers, koto), marimbas with wooden or bamboo keys, and other struck percussion instruments made with found objects of glass or metal. To these might be added regular instruments, but the sound world would usually be dominated by the special percussion— as would the stage, for Partch clearly designed his instruments with an eye for spectacle.[12] He also gave them wonderful names: Mazda Marimba (made from light bulbs of different sizes), Spoils of War (including brass shell casings), Cloud-Chamber Bowls (of glass). In writing music for them, he tended to prefer simple textures, regular pulsation, and ostinato, for which his reasons might have included the need to work with student performers (his major performances were at universities in Chicago and Los Angeles), a wish to show off sonority, a way of working with stretches of music that—being equal in length and similar in rhythm—could be superposed, and a desire for elemental expression.

Two of his full-length dramas—all of which seem to call for dance and stylized action within the arena of the instrumentarium—are based on Greek plays: *Oedipus* and *The Bacchae* (transplanted into the contemporary U.S. in *Revelation in the Courthouse Park*). Of the others, *The Bewitched* is a sequence of scenes intended to reveal human conditioning ('We are all bewitched, and mostly by accident: the accident of form, color, and sex; of prejudices conditioned from the cradle up'[13]), and *Delusion of the Fury* is based on a Noh play in which vengeance gives way to enlightenment, with the appendage of a farce after an African tale.

Partch's combination of subtle intonation with primitive rhythm is neatly balanced by Nancarrow's pursuit of rhythmic intricacy using a medium that rules out any sophistication of tuning. But there are also parallels, and not only in the way both men existed outside musical convention—Partch scratching a hand-to-mouth existence in southern California for much of his life, Nancarrow living from 1940 onwards in isolation in a suburb of Mexico City. Both started to make serious progress in the 1940s; both began to achieve wider recognition late in life—Partch in the later 1960s, when his independent spirit and his magic dance dramas with resonant percussion instruments began to seem central and sympathetic, Nancarrow in the 1980s, when his patent complexity (as opposed to the concealed complexity of Boulezian serialism) could be recognized as in tune with a computer-oriented understanding of art and the mind.

Nancarrow began to compose for the player piano in order to realize tempo overlappings that proved beyond the performers he had to deal with at the time. But the player piano was more than a functional interim. It allowed him to create rhythmic canons (and most of his player-piano studies are canonic) in which the voices move at complex relative speeds: in Study No. 37, to take an extreme case, there are twelve voices, at tempos in the ratios 1:15/14:9/8:6/5:5/4:4/3:7/5:3/2: 8/5:5/3:7/4:15/8 (a rhythmic encoding of a chromatic scale in just intonation). Also, the studies exult in possibilities of keyboard sound be-

12. There are colour and monochrome photographs in his book *Genesis of a Music* (New York, 1974).
13. Ibid., 335.

Example 16   Conlon Nancarrow, Study No. 5

yond any keyboard player or combination of keyboard players: not only twelve-part canons, but colossal, precisely simultaneous chords and immense glissandos, all moving at speed with perfect accuracy. Example 16, showing a moment from Study No. 5, may give some indication of the kind of keyboard activity possible; note the tempo.

The prodigious rapidity and precisely executed extravagance of the music are among its joys and comedies: the joys and comedies of heavy loads lightly carried. For Nancarrow is one of the few great musical humorists. His techniques can be compared with those of animation, in that the preparation is an exercise of handicraft requiring concentration on items extracted from the continuity into which they will be absorbed (still pictures, single notes punched into the paper rolls that are the player piano's software) and that the laboriousness of this procedure results in an inherent disproportion between cause and effect (more than a year could be taken up in creating a five-minute piece[14]). Such disproportion is itself comic: so is the existence of worlds in which anything can happen, but everything must be preordained in detail. It may be for these reasons that animation lends itself most readily to comedy, and that Nancarrow's studies have the humour, as well as the

14. See Charles Amirkhanian's note with Wergo 6168.

dimensions, of the cartoon short (the longest of them play for around ten minutes; most last for between one minute and five).

They also resemble animated comedies in bringing brisk, simplified designs into movement, since Nancarrow's canons are not only abstract formal processes (often determinedly audible, at least up to the point—frequently reached and surpassed—at which the mind can no longer juggle with the number of lines in play) but also rules of behaviour for the small musical figures he commonly uses. Taking the relatively straightforward example of Study No. 5[15], this piece sets in play a variety of elements: an idle sort of vamp that lurches lopsidedly up to a cadence (it is characteristic of Nancarrow that humour should be present, as here, at the level of motif), twirls that are part way between scale and glissando, a fanfare of chords. Each of these ideas is on its own temporal plane: the vamp, for instance, repeats regularly throughout the piece, whereas other figures recur at increasingly shorter intervals. Example 16 shows a passage from about two-thirds of the way into the piece, and illustrates the polymetric density and the full keyboard texture Nancarrow can attain: at the beginning of the example, bars that have already begun have their time signatures placed in brackets; the repeating vamp is in 35/16, in the middle of the keyboard. The impression is of musical entities playing some game, dodging each other, while all the time more and more entities enter the game, to the point where, growing in frequency and in number, they meld: the whole process takes just over two and a half minutes. What also contributes to the comedy of the studies is the fact that an ignoble and outmoded machine is being used to create amazement.

Indeed, the studies are doubly mechanical: delivered by a mechanical instrument, and delivered too by machineries of rhythm in the form of mensuration canons. But, again like cartoon films, they thoroughly flout the notion that what is mechanical is ipso facto dead. Nancarrow's taste for complex cross-rhythms can be traced not only to his admiration for Stravinsky but also to his experience as a jazz trumpeter, and his ideas often have the syncopated spring of blues, ragtime, or boogie woogie. Letters written in vernacular style are posted along elaborate and sophisticated networks; material that high culture would deem debased is fantastically rescued and celebrated. And this rescue effort is in itself humorous.

Wolpe

Like Stravinsky—but a year before, in 1938—Wolpe moved to the United States after previous travels, which in his case had taken him

---

15. Kyle Gann, *The Music of Conlon Nancarrow* (Cambridge, 1995), 69, indicates that the studies up to No. 30 were composed between 1948 and 1960, which suggests a date in the early 1950s for No. 5.

from his native Berlin to Palestine. Like Varèse, he settled in New York. Like Messiaen, he became an important teacher—of Feldman among others. And like all those colleagues, he changed his music, or found his music changing, during the immediate postwar years. From Berlin and Vienna (where he had studied with Webern) he brought with him a mind set on counterpoint and chromaticism, but he was determined too on constant freedom to give motifs the stamp of character and to let them develop with vigour but without force. These are aspects of his music that he best expressed himself, for his prose accords with his music not only in its content but in its manner: even his problems with the language become solutions to the greater problem of creating a personal voice, rather as eccentricities in his music become essential, even natural. 'I very much like', he wrote, 'to maintain the flexibility of sound structures (as one would try to draw on water). That leads me to the promotion of a very mobile polyphony in which the partials of the sound behave like river currents and a greater orbit spread-out is guaranteed to the sound, a greater circulatory agility (a greater momentum too). The sound gets the plasticity of figures of waves and the magneticism and the fluid elasticity of river currents, or the fire of gestures and the generative liveliness of all what is life (and Apollo and Dionysus, and the seasons of the heart, and the articulate fevers).'[16]

The onwardness and the energy of his music have something to do with his appreciation of jazz, which he had known since his Berlin days, but which came closer up behind the surface of his music in the United States, most explicitly in his Quartet for the modern-jazz ensemble of tenor saxophone, trumpet, percussion, and piano (1950). In other works of this period, such as the sonata-weight *Battle Piece* for solo piano (1947) and the Violin Sonata (1949), the resemblance is not so much to the colour of jazz as to the unpredictability within a strongly forward movement. Wolpe typically sets up a regular, physical pulse, often at a brisk walking pace, even while lines of motivic development are going along in seeming independence of each other. As was soon to happen in Carter's music, a musical section (the Violin Sonata has four; *Battle Piece* is continuous) may not be identifiable as a 'movement': the music keeps the freedom to alter and contrast speed and character, almost from moment to moment. A collection of 'interval studies' (1944–49)—short contrapuntal essays 'for any instruments'—appears to have been the exercise book in which the composer devoted himself to the postwar demand for logical reconstruction.

But the moves in Wolpe's creative life were as bold (and as fully engaged, as wholehearted) as those in his music. During the summers of 1952–56 he taught at Black Mountain College in North Carolina, where fellow members of the faculty in his first year included Cage, Cunningham, Tudor, and Harrison. The works he wrote there, including

16. Note on the Violin Sonata, quoted in note with Koch 3 7112 2H1.

Example 17   Stefan Wolpe, Oboe Quartet

Enactments for three pianos (1953) and the Quartet for oboe, cello, percussion and piano (1955), bring an intermingling of the experimental into his recently developed style, as may be glimpsed in example 17, from near the end of the quartet. The pianist, in the last bar of this extract, is directed to get up from the keyboard, turn to the audience, and stamp 'in a dance-like movement' with left foot, then right; the percussionist repeats the stamps. Yet the effect, like the elementary ostinatos and the singing, is forged into the music's rhythm: something is flowing through this extraordinary passage on into more usual sorts of instrumental interplay. At the same time, the oboe part (and the oboist is effectively the work's soloist) shows a characteristic achievement of individual rhetoric—summons, playfulness—from elements of pitch and rhythm shared with the group: in that respect, jazz is still the ideal.

After Silence

4′ 33″ appears to have been followed soon by a much longer silence in Cage's output, one of several months.[17] Perhaps it seemed that no

17. See Jean-Jacques Nattiez, ed., *The Boulez-Cage Correspondence* (Cambridge and New York, 1993), 143.

more music was needed, that everything had been said in the saying of nothing. But there were endless ways of saying nothing, as Cage might have observed in the mute abundance of nature, from the mushrooms to the stars. There was, too, still a notional infinity of sounds waiting to 'become themselves', and it was perhaps on their behalf that he returned to composition—to the highly purposed business of creating music without purpose. He did so, between 1953 and 1956, exclusively on two fronts: in the *Music for Piano* series (still using the method of marking paper imperfections[18]) and in a collection of pieces measured to precise, chance-determined durations, a collection he referred to privately as 'The Ten Thousand Things'.[19]

The first of these were tiny, around a minute long, but those of 1954–56 became huge virtuoso exercises: *34′46.776″* and *31′ 57.9864″* for Tudor, *26′ 1.1499″* for any four-stringed instrument, and *27′ 10.554″* for percussionist. As in the *Music of Changes*, what is on display here is the complexity of chance phenomena: like the shapes of a broken glass, beyond what anyone could foreordain, are the similarly wild and irregular occurrences that enter these compositions. It necessarily followed that, though Cage was utterly simple in his bearing and in his behaviour as an artist, the demands he placed on performers were stringent, in works from the *Music of Changes* to such late pieces as the *Freeman Etudes*, and not least in 'The Ten Thousand Things', whose titles betoken a utopian accuracy of performance. The use of ancillary instruments, as in *Water Music*, adds further to the impression these pieces create of performance as action—of rhythm defined by rapidity of bodily movement, and of music becoming abstract theatre. Tudor gave the first performances of *34′46.776″* and *31′ 57.9864″* while on a European tour with Cage in October–November 1954: among the many European composers who were fascinated, Stockhausen was one of the first to apply what he had heard, not only in his piano writing but in his whole approach to performance.

This was another case, though, of Europeans mistaking the effect of Cage's music for its intention. If the exacting notation of 'The Ten Thousand Things' had any purpose, it was perhaps to screen off the habits and hopes of performers, just as chance operations screened off the habits and hopes of the composer. Having to offer so much attention to instructions, the players of these pieces could not at the same time offer any intention, and unaccustomed requirements—to play on the piano's strings or woodwork, use accessory instruments, deal with unusual notations—increased the defamiliarization.

18. See John Cage, 'To Describe the Process of Composition Used in *Music for Piano 21-52*', *Silence: Lectures and Writings* (Middletown, Conn., 1961; London, 1968), 60–61.

19. See David Revill, *The Roaring Silence: John Cage: A Life* (London, 1992), 178.

5

The Cold War

Eastern Europe seemed another world. And yet, as if aware of a postwar impulse for change, Andrey Zhdanov, holding high rank in the Soviet government, instituted in February 1948 a reinforcement of the cultural policy of socialist realism. Composers were called to account, and reminded of their duty to write music that put a socialist (i.e. optimistic) spin on a 'realism' that was now almost a century old, and that belonged to the bourgeois culture of late Tsarism: the diatonic-symphonic language of Tchaikovsky and Borodin. 'Formalism'—which in a Russian context embraced any projection of matters of technique, notably including innovations—was the enemy. What was stirring in the United States and Western Europe could have no parallel in the Soviet Union, nor in those neighbouring countries that had been liberated by Russian forces in 1945 and were coming under closer Soviet control in 1948. In Hungary, for example, a musicians' union was established in 1949 on the Soviet model, one of its functions being to have new compositions vetted by a panel of colleagues.

Noble ideals—of placing control in the hands of composers and of checking individual imagination against informed and sympathetic collective judgment—were compromised by the falsity of having to steer by an official aesthetic that was incoherent. A young composer recognizing that the musical world was changing fast but not so sure about the political one, as Ligeti was, would have to write one kind of music for the committee and another for the bottom drawer. Ligeti's works of 1949–53, Hungary's most viciously Stalinist period, include several that were passed for publication, performance, and broadcast, at least one (his Romanian Concerto) whose shortcomings he acknowledged and even emphasized when it came up for debate,[1] and several more he did not put forward. Among these last, *Musica ricercata* for piano (1951–53), though in no way serial, exposes just the kind of algorithmic thinking he was to analyse a few years later in Boulez's *Structures*. The first piece uses just one note (or, in Babbittian terms, pitch class), A, until another, D, is added just before the end. Succeeding movements are based on two, three, four notes, and so on, until all twelve are in play.

However, the distinction between imposed conformity and free thought—a distinction Ligeti underlined again and again after leaving Hungary for Western Europe in 1956—is not so clear. Many young people immediately after the war, Ligeti among them, welcomed socialism for its egalitarian aspirations, its state support of culture, and its antagonism to fascism. Even rule from Moscow would have to be an improvement on rule from Berlin. Ligeti's friend and colleague György Kurtág (b. 1926) wrote a choral 'Greeting Song to Stalin', and Ligeti himself produced a cantata for a youth festival in 1949. At the same time, *Musica ricercata* is nothing like as abstract as Boulez's music of similar date. It relishes connections with familiar ideas and folk music, as in the bristling dance of minor and major triads in the third piece of the set, shown in example 18, all very much in the spirit of Bartók, though with a playfulness that was Ligeti's own. In carrying forward the Bartókian heritage, connecting with folk music and connecting, too, with the needs of amateurs (who are welcomed here as they are not by *Structures*) and the expectations of audiences, *Musica ricercata* was just what members of the Hungarian musicians' union should have been looking for. Perversity and cynicism, intergenerational conflict and fear, may all have spoiled the chances for the real socialist music that socialist realism was not.

The situation throughout the Eastern bloc was difficult, even at times dangerous, and its complexity probably cannot be reduced to a story of oppression and resistance, such as has gained currency around the figure, in particular, of Dmitry Shostakovich (1906–75). There can be no doubt that Shostakovich took Zhdanov's criticism seriously. He put aside the violin concerto on which he had been working and turned instead to string quartets, bland cantatas, and a book of preludes and fugues for piano. (Fugues, having the mandate of history, were not 'formalist'.) It is also true that he delayed his next symphony, his Tenth, until after Stalin's death; the work had its first performance nine months later, in December 1953.

1. See Rachel Beckles Willson, *Ligeti, Kurtág, and Hungarian Music during the Cold War* (Cambridge, 2007), 41.

Example 18   György Ligeti, *Musica ricercata*

However, to read this symphony as a reaction to events—even as a portrait of the deceased leader—may be too much. The work is certainly a triumph of negativity, made with images of snarling, of forced movement, of empty bombast and worthless victory, but all these things can be found in the composer's sarcastic style from long before. He also inherited them from Mahler and from a deep vein of black humour in Russian culture. Moreover, one could interpret the symphony as marked by the same autodestructive urges as Boulez's Second Sonata, without the release of flinging out into new musical regions. It may have seemed to Shostakovich, as much as to Boulez, that the old tonal language was long worn out by the middle of the twentieth century. But, for whatever reasons of personal as well as official constraint, he had no alternative.

There is a whole knot of ironies around the fact that Shostakovich's music should have come to be prized as dissident by cultures, those of modern capitalism, whose aesthetic preferences are not so far from those of socialist realism. Of course, it may not be contradictory to admire Shostakovich because he shares our love-hate relationship with the musical language that remains dominant. The political affiliations, though, are confusing. Nono was by no means alone among younger composers in Western Europe and the United States in voting decisively on the Left, and yet the music these composers produced was banned from the Soviet Union and its satellites. The disfavour was certainly reciprocated: Shostakovich was anathema to Boulez, who seems only once, in 2002, to have conducted anything by the composer. Those who were beginning to assemble regularly at Darmstadt saw themselves as bringing in a revolution that would be more than musical, whether its aims were social-political (Nono), spiritual (Stockhausen), or undisclosed, perhaps unknown (Boulez). From the viewpoint of the Kremlin, however, they were bourgeois individualists.

The Central Intelligence Agency of the United States may have shared that opinion. The contemporary art festival lavishly presented in Paris in 1952, involving Stravinsky, Messiaen, and Boulez among many others, was clandestinely funded by the CIA through the Congress for Cultural Freedom, which had been set up in 1950 in the naive but not entirely dishonourable hope of demonstrating to left-wing intellectuals in Western Europe that capitalism was as hospitable to the arts as communism. But though Darmstadt in its infancy was also a U.S. intervention, sponsored by the military authorities in their sector of immediate postwar Germany,[2] officials appear rapidly to have washed their hands of these disputatious musicians.

This is not to say, of course, that the seeming permanence of the Cold War, and of the nuclear threat it entailed, did not hang over everything achieved during this period.

2. See Frances Stonor Saunders, *Who Paid the Piper?: the CIA and the Cultural Cold War* (London, 1999), 23.

6

Extension and Development

Western Europe, 1953–56

From Points to Groups

Punkte (1952), unperformed in its original version,[1] had apparently convinced Stockhausen that composing with points had its limitations: technical, in that there was no way to order timbre when working with standard instruments, and aesthetic, in that an orchestra of points became an undifferentiated mass, in the same way that, as both he and Boulez had found, layers of chromatic durations combined into regular pulsing. In the 1960s, in a sequence of revisions, he redrew the score for a larger orchestra, though one confined still to pitched instruments, and converted most of the original points into melodic lines, chords, and swarms of sound, so that the title became the relic of a history the piece had outgrown. More immediately he presented a creative criticism of the earlier score in *Kontra-Punkte* (1952–53), scored for an ensemble of ten players rather like that of Webern's Concerto, and carrying a title that may be understood as signifying 'Against Points', and even 'Against *Punkte*', as well as 'Counterpoints'. It was the first composition since *Kreuzspiel* in which Stockhausen found the musical means to keep pace with his intellectual élan, and he gave it the distinction 'Nr.1' in his catalogue of works. It was also one of the first pieces to become widely disseminated. The Viennese firm Universal Edition, the publishers of

1. For a note on this version, and a page from the score, see Robin Maconie, *The Works of Karlheinz Stockhausen* (London, 1976), 38–40.

most of Schoenberg, Berg, and Webern, printed the score in 1953 as part of a policy of promoting what their director, Alfred Kalmus, might well have seen as the twentieth century's second musical avant-garde (they also became the publishers of Boulez, and later Pousseur, Berio, Birtwistle, and others), and a recording was issued in 1956.

Kontra-Punkte—one of the few Stockhausen pieces for which Boulez was to profess unguarded admiration—expanded the range of thinking at this fiercely analytical time, and did so with a proud dramatic sweep that remained characteristic of the composer; that panache, as well as his personal charisma, was surely relevant to the commanding position he soon acquired among his colleagues, and held into the 1970s. In this case the drama comes about partly because the music's process is, at least in some measure, laid out to view. As it proceeds, so the instruments fall silent one by one, the six 'families' of the opening—flute plus bassoon, clarinet plus bass clarinet, trumpet plus trombone, piano, harp, and violin plus cello—giving place to the single timbre of the piano. At the same time, the ranges of dynamic level and rhythmic value are gradually curtailed, and a texture that began with isolated points ends with two-part counterpoint.

What chiefly distinguishes the piece, though, is the move from points to 'groups'. (It was a feature of the time that changes in technique were felt to need changes in terminology.) A group, for Stockhausen, was a collection of notes considered as an identity: if spread out through time, it was to be felt as an extended instant, and in order for that to happen, the texture of *Kontra-Punkte* consists largely of rapid arpeggiations, which give the piece an electric dynamism, realizing what Boulez had perhaps hoped to achieve in *Polyphonie X*. Example 19 shows a representative passage of counterpointed groups, and suggests how Stockhausen achieves the compelling small-scale continuity of the piece. The groups here set out more or less distinct harmonic fields, whose antagonisms are resolved in the large piano group at the end of the example—a group referring in bar 345 to the preceding harp group, in bar 346 to the clarinet group, and in bar 347 to the piano's own *sforzato* chord and group, while in the extreme bass there is a varied transposition of the flute group (an instance of the tritone-fifth/fourth motif, which Stockhausen, like Boulez, may have inherited from Messiaen). Four 'families' are thus conjoined, in a miniature image of what happens in the entire piece; the cello is perhaps to be considered as going its own way; the sixth 'family', the brass duo, has by this stage dropped out. The working with allusive harmonic connections relates to Boulez, who had of course been doing this at least since his Sonatina, but *Kontra-Punkte*, in a manner typical of Stockhausen, sets out as if from nothing but its own material, presenting a new world with joy and confidence.

As in *Kreuzspiel*, Stockhausen creates systems that result in vivacity. For example, the usual chromatic durations are combined with a division of the unchanging bar into up to twelve equal parts: hence the

Example 19   Karlheinz Stockhausen, *Kontra-Punkte*

abundant demisemiquavers of example 19—unless of course this effect preceded its supposed cause, and the system was chosen in order to justify a glittering rapidity. Another echo of total serialism lies in the zigzags of dynamic markings, which again may act to enliven performance. Less obvious in a brief example is the way in which a fixed system of proportions—of the sort described in the case of *Studie I* and present in all Stockhausen's works of this period as a guarantor of unity—governs the profusion of ideas. What we have, in the composer's words, is 'not the same shapes in a changing light [a description perhaps of his distant model, the Webern Concerto]. Rather this: different shapes in the same, all-pervading light.'[2]

2. Karlheinz Stockhausen, *Texte*, i (Cologne, 1963), 37.

Example 19 (continued)

Contemporary with *Kontra-Punkte* and *Studie I* are the first four of Stockhausen's *Klavierstücke*, opening a projected cycle of twenty-one. The scope of the cycle was presumably determined by some ordering of the first six whole numbers—an obsession in Stockhausen's early music (see the above discussion of *Studie I*)—but after sets of four, six, and one, all produced in the 1950s, any such pattern broke down, and the next pieces arrived much later as scenes in *Licht*, the operatic heptalogy he began in 1977. The first piece to be written, in Paris in 1952, was the one published as III, which is so brief that it can be quoted complete (example 20) and serve as a small model for exploring Stockhausen's formal procedures.

The organization of pitch has been interpreted in various ways: Robin Maconie[3] proposes a hearing in terms of three overlapping

3. Maconie, *Works*, 63–64.

Example 20   Karlheinz Stockhausen, *Klavierstück III*

chromatic segments (D–F, F–G♯, G♯–B), whereas Dieter Schnebel,[4] Jonathan Harvey,[5] and David Lewin[6] would all see the five-note set of the
first bar as the structural determinant, but neither approach is entirely
satisfactory, and perhaps what speaks most of the music is the doubt.
It is rather curious that young European composers of the early 1950s,
ostensibly erecting a theoretical framework that would be generally
valid, were cautious in describing their systems or procedures (unlike
Babbitt). Their works were to have been at once models of a new,
rationally based way of composing and inscrutable. Boulez's essay
'Possibly . . .' exemplifies the point. Insisting several times on technical
exploration as 'research' (a scientism to be repeated often in the theo-
rizings of composers at this time), and after indicating that his purpose
is to establish a musical 'grammar' that will last,[7] the author declines to

    4. Dieter Schnebel, 'Karlheinz Stockhausen', *Die Reihe*, No. 4 (1958, En-
glish ed. 1960), 121–35.
    5. Jonathan Harvey, *The Music of Stockhausen* (London, 1974), 24–26.
    6. David Lewin, *Musical Form and Transformation* (New Haven, 1993),
16–67.
    7. Pierre Boulez, *Stocktakings from an Apprenticeship* (Oxford: Clarendon
and New York, 1991), 115.

demonstrate how his general principles are applied. Probably the fear, which Boulez's colleagues shared, was that technical strategies would be taken as aesthetic meanings, in a way that was happening with Schoenberg, Berg, and Webern. Organization, on which these composers insisted, was distinct from effect, on which they remained largely silent. Subsequent analysts, working like detectives pursuing criminals who have done their best to leave the scene of the crime spotless, have often been concerned with how pieces were made, as Ligeti was in his analysis of *Structures Ia*. Lewin's analysis of Stockhausen's *Klavierstück III* is unusual in addressing perception.

Lewin asks us to hear the piece as a sequence of four passes through an elegant network of transformations of its five-note set—or rather through a network of networks. The smaller networks consist of sets related by inversion preserving the chromatic tetrachord (e.g., the opening A–B–D–A♭–B♭ and the partly overlapping B♭–A–G♯–B–F) and of those related to these by transposition through a tritone (e.g., F–E♭–D–E–A♭ in bars 2–3 and the largely simultaneous B–F–E♭–D–E); the larger network is a grouping of four such foursomes. Lewin provides a pitch-set abstract of the piece, a kind of chorale, as an exercise in teaching the ear to hear what he hears. By training ourselves in this way, we might think, we are being led to hear Lewin rather than Stockhausen: a particular photograph of a landscape that remains mute. So it may be, but we can never come directly to the landscape itself, to the piece unfiltered by the commentaries and interpretations of others, and by the prejudices we bring ourselves. (This dissolution of the musical work has been a key theme of the period.) As Lewin notes at the end of his analysis, after remarking—not without some dismay—divergences between his version and the more eclectic treatment of the piece by Nicholas Cook[8]: 'The differences in segmentation between Cook's analysis and mine should not be problematic, I think, except for those who believe that form is "a Form", something a piece has one and only one of in all of its aspects.'

What any analysis in terms of pitch-class sets must leave out of account is the twinkling of ambiguities between clear intervals (especially thirds and sixths, sevenths and ninths) and uncertain leaps, where the sensation of pitch is attenuated by isolation or extreme register. It may also be that the notes are sometimes to be understood more as programmes for action than as pitches, their placing on the keyboard in relation to one another being important for the effect on timing and attack. As Stockhausen put it, his concern in all four of these first piano pieces was with 'imparting a new way of feeling time in music, in which the infinitely subtle "irrational" shadings and impulses and fluctuations of a good performer often produce what one wants better than

8. Nicholas Cook, *A Guide to Musical Analysis* (New York, 1987), 354–62.

any centimetre gauge'[9]—though this may have been more a response
to how his music worked than a reason for its creation. In experimental art, the fortuitous need not be discounted, but rather welcomed and
celebrated.

If Stockhausen was indeed coming to recognize a fundamental difference between synthesized and performed music—a distinction that
was to be transcended in his next electronic works, *Gesang der Jünglinge*
and *Kontakte*—he was still, at least in the composing of *Klavierstück III*,
able to transfer into the instrumental world an electronic phenomenon, that of time reversal. In the fifth bar he progressively builds up a
three-note chord; in the seventh, more unusually, he progressively re-
linquishes notes. There are numerous more complex instances of this
effect in the second piece of the set, suggesting the composer might
have been trying out something discovered in Schaeffer's studio, rather
as *Klavierstück IV*, in Maconie's plausible view,[10] finds him leaning over
Boulez's shoulder at the worktable of *Structures* (though at this moment the two composers were so close that priorities are as hard to
establish as they are irrelevant).

'We are all', Stockhausen wrote, 'more or less treading on ice, and
as long as this is the case, the organizational systems being put forward
represent guidelines to prevent the composer from faltering. And one
has to face the fact that there are as many systems as there are grains
of sand, systems that can be dreamed up and set in motion as easily as
clockwork. Their number is probably infinite, but certainly only a very
few of them are acceptable systems, compatible with their means of
expression, and applicable without self-contradiction to all the dimensions of music. Of these, still fewer are so perfectly prefigured that they
yield beautiful and interesting music.'[11] This was another big difference
from Boulez. Where Boulez wanted one grammar to support a variety
of idiolects, Stockhausen went in search of a new system in each piece,
each time setting new conditions out of which a new musical universe
could evolve. Music's ability to elaborate itself of itself, which Boulez
wanted to control, Stockhausen would rather enable.

Systems of Organization

Mutual respect and rivalry, backed by the confidence they had gained
in achieving compositions as arresting and innovatory as *Structures*
and *Kontra-Punkte*, accelerated the next steps Boulez and Stockhausen

9. K. H. Wörner, *Stockhausen: Life and Work* (London, 1973), 32.

10. Maconie, *Works*, 67. In the 2nd edition, this view is tacitly withdrawn.

11. Stockhausen, *Texte*, i, 47. An unusually complete elucidation of a
Stockhausen system is provided by Richard Toop in his analysis 'Stockhausen's
"Klavierstück VIII"', *Contact*, 28 (1984), 4–19.

made. The workshop period was over; it was a time for works of great ambition and public intent, works such as Boulez's *Le Marteau sans maître* or Stockhausen's *Gesang der Jünglinge* and *Gruppen*. New journals— notably *Die Reihe*, whose first issue appeared in 1955—were founded to publish articles by and about the new music, and festivals and radio stations in West Germany continued to give it a forum. Boulez founded a platform in Paris, a concert series (the future Domaine Musical), whose first programme, in 1954, included works by Nono (*Polifonica— monodia—ritmica*) and Stockhausen (*Kontra-Punkte*) as well as Stravinsky, Webern, and J. S. Bach. Recordings of many of the new works introduced at the Domaine Musical were released on the Véga label and so more widely disseminated. Radio authorities and publishers (Schott as well as Universal Edition), too, continued to promote new music.

All this has helped to generate an impression in retrospect of something monolithic, though that may not have been how it appeared at the time. And total serialism, far from defining the music of these young composers, had been only a gateway through which they needed to pass. Boulez, in a 1954 essay,[12] chided his colleagues, and indeed his former self, for galloping too readily, too thoughtlessly, towards what he could only see as an illusory goal of total organization: 'One soon realizes', he wrote, perhaps with his own *Structures Ia* in mind, 'that composition and organization cannot be confused without falling into a maniacal inanity'. He went on to state his present wish for 'a dialectic operating at each moment of the composition between a strict global organization and a temporary structure controlled by free will' (which would explain the appeal to him of Stockhausen's *Kontra-Punkte*). Of course, it went without saying that the 'strict global organization' would in some way come out of total serialism. Organization would provide possibilities, among which the composer could direct himself by an alert marriage of intellect and instinct, with the late works of Debussy now admitted as potentially more useful models than Webern. Boulez's preference had always been for complexity and multiplicity—for Klee rather than Mondrian, as he had put it in a 1951 letter to Cage[13]—and it was to Debussian allusiveness rather than to Webernian strictness and symmetry that he appealed in *Le Marteau sans maître*.

In the same essay Boulez also points the way towards the aleatory principles that were to occupy him later in the decade. He speculates about the possibility of a composition existing as a set of 'formants', each linked to the organizational bases of the work as the formants of a timbre are linked to the fundamental, and yet each independent: the *Polyphonie* idea is reasserting itself, behind the guise of terms borrowed

12. Boulez, 'Current Investigations,' *Stocktakings*, 15–19.
13. Jean-Jacques Nattiez, ed., *The Boulez-Cage Correspondence* (Cambridge and New York, 1993), 116–17.

from acoustical analysis, and was to be partially realized in the Third Piano Sonata, a work predicted in the following passage, highly characteristic of Boulez's wish for fluidity, ambiguity, and freedom: 'Let us claim for music the right to parentheses and italics . . . a concept of discontinuous time made up of structures which interlock instead of remaining in airtight compartments; and finally a sort of development where the closed circuit is not the only possible answer.'

Such a labyrinthine conception, though manifested more obviously in the Third Piano Sonata, is already present in *Le Marteau sans maître*, as indeed it had been in the Second Piano Sonata or the Sonatina. After *Structures Ia*, Boulez had immediately returned to what had been his earlier practice: that of using principles borrowed and extended from Schoenberg and Webern in order to proliferate intervalic motifs and rhythmic cells in a whole variety of ways. The apparatus of total serialism persists in *Le Marteau*—the dynamic levels that change almost from note to note, the chromatic durations—and yet, in another sign of the small relevance of how a work is made to how it is received and appraised, the work's serial construction stayed a mystery for more than two decades, until elucidated by Lev Koblyakov.[14] Boulez's serial techniques, as described in what has been published of his Darmstadt lectures,[15] are so multifarious that almost anything could be derived from anything else, and his horror of the obvious may render a secure understanding of his compositional processes irretrievable.

Ligeti, who had abandoned the idea of analysing *Le Marteau* before tackling the transparent *Structures Ia*, pointed out in a later article for *Die Reihe*[16] that the original conventions of serialism—and even those of total serialism—had been so far adapted in the immediately subsequent works of Pousseur, Stockhausen, Boulez, and others that to describe those works as 'serial' would be almost meaningless. At best, only the essential principles—those of ordering a set of elements, and transforming that ordered set according to rules—remain. Babbitt felt this too, and recalled how, after his hopes had been aroused by news of endeavours seemingly similar to his own being carried out in Europe, his presumed comrades' 'music and technical writings eventually revealed so very different an attitude towards the means, and even so very different means, that the apparent agreement with regard to end lost its entire significance. . . . Mathematics—or, more correctly, arithmetic—is used, not as a means of characterizing or discovering general systematic, pre-compositional relationships, but as a compositional device. . . . The alleged "total organization" is achieved by applying

14. His doctoral thesis (1975–77) is published as *Pierre Boulez: a World of Harmony* (Chur, 1990).

15. Pierre Boulez, *Boulez on Music Today* (London, 1971).

16. Gyögy Ligeti, 'Metamorphoses of Musical Form', *Die Reihe*, 7 (1960, English ed. 1965), 5–19.

dissimilar, essentially unrelated criteria of organization to each of the components, criteria often derived from outside the system, so that— for example—rhythm is independent of and thus separable from the pitch structure; this is described and justified as a "polyphony" of components, though polyphony is customarily understood to involve, among other things, a principle of organized simultaneity.'[17]

Babbitt's distress, not unmixed with self-congratulation, is occasioned by little more than the fact that his European colleagues did not share his view of what constituted 'general systematic, pre-compositional relationships': one could as well criticize Berlioz for not being Bach. But at least his diatribe points up the great gulf at the time between composers in America and those in Europe with regard to the serial heritage. That gulf might be illustrated by comparing *Kontra-Punkte* or *Le Marteau sans maître* with his Second Quartet—a work of the same period, written soon before the essay just quoted. The Babbitt piece is lucid about itself: it is a demonstration of how it was composed. Its all-interval series is introduced interval by interval, as it were, with each new arrival initiating a development of the interval repertory thus far acquired, each development being argued in terms of derived sets. Important landmarks in the continuous progress are firmly underlined: Babbitt calls on harmonic octaves at the points where new intervals are brought into play, brings in a rare solo line when the first hexachord has been completed (bar 114), and has the first complete serial statement begun by all four instruments in unison (bars 266–68). It is all far away from Stockhausen's new systems as grains of sand— each, one must guess, unlike any other, and certainly unlike any systems familiar from the past. It is equally far away from Boulez's 'notion of a discontinuous time achieved thanks to structures which will become entangled'.

Le Marteau sans maître

Just as Boulez returned after *Structures Ia* to earlier musical ideals, so he returned to earlier poetic metaphors, but in both cases within a colder climate. In 1953, beginning his first new work after the book for two pianos, he went back again to René Char, but this time to an earlier collection, *Le Marteau sans maître*, where the verse is very much more concise, more abruptly obscure, more objective. In all these respects, the poems suited Boulez's purpose, which was not so much to set them to music, in the way that he had set the very much longer texts of *Le Visage nuptial*, but rather to make them the seed of an elaborate musical form—a form in which purely instrumental movements would be necessary, and not merely as interludes.

17. 'Some Aspects of Twelve Tone Composition', *The Score*, 12 (1955), 53–61.

As he had before, Boulez wrote an essay about his new work without naming it.[18] What mattered in music's contact with poetry, he declared, was structure: 'Structure: one of the key words of our time'. (This sentence alone conveys a thought, more poetic than analytical, to which every one of Boulez's compositions adds its commentary.) The poem must be more than 'a frame for the weaving of ornamental arabesques'; it must become '"centre and absence" of the whole body of sound': 'centre' because everything in the music is derived from the words, and 'absence' because the process of musical composition has completely consumed them. By applying himself thoroughly to the text, the composer would uncover 'a whole web of relationships . . ., including, among others, the affective relationships, but also the entire mechanism of the poem, from its pure sound to its intelligible organization.'

It was perhaps disingenuous of Boulez to assume that earlier composers of vocal music had not been excited by matters of 'pure sound' or 'intelligible organization' in the texts they chose to set: as so often, he conjures up a caricature of the Romantic artist in order to affirm his otherness. It was also disingenuous of him to imply that the 'expressive' qualities of the Char poems were somehow secondary, for the odd combination of violence and vagueness was essential to him—perhaps especially the vagueness, for *Le Marteau* as a setting of transparent, explicit texts is unthinkable. However, his emphasis on sound and structure was true to his practice, and true to the conscious concerns of many of his contemporaries. For example, Berio's responsiveness to verbal sound is evident right from his setting of three poems from Joyce's *Chamber Music* for female voice and trio, a work dating from 1953 (the year before he was drawn into the Darmstadt circle through meeting Maderna, Pousseur, and Stockhausen) and showing in its monotone second song a great number of patterns of timbre and rhythm suggested by patterns in the words. And as far as 'intelligible organization' is concerned, Babbitt's 'Spelt from Sybil's Leaves', one of a pair of settings of Hopkins sonnets for baritone and trio (1955), exhibits a neat parallel between the rhyme scheme and the serial forms used. Boulez himself was to derive musical reflections of sonnet form in later works based on Mallarmé, but the Char texts of *Le Marteau* are brusquely irregular, and the music seems not so much to echo them as to channel them into its own structural processes.

Partly that must be because of how the work cuts down the importance of its ostensible soloist, in contrast with the etiquettes of such widely differing examples of vocal chamber music as *Pierrot lunaire* and Ravel's Mallarmé poems: this is just one of its revolutionary features. Only four of the work's nine movements are vocal; two purely instrumental movements arrive before the singer enters; and the drama of the finale is the drama of the voice's being extinguished: first made

18. Boulez, 'Sound and Word', *Stocktakings*, 39–43.

wordless and a regular member of the ensemble, then replaced as principal part by the alto flute. There are no songs here, for the vocal movements are often dominated by instrumental qualities of rhythm, texture, and phrasing, and even the most songlike of them, 'L'Artisanat furieux', is a duet in which the alto flute has a comprimary role. The voice is a potential danger, which the music has to limit. Or, to put it another way, vocal expression has to force itself through a mill of musical purpose. It is not that the instrumental movements extend and elaborate the vocal settings, but rather that the voice and the Char texts offer commentary on what seems most essentially an instrumental action.

Boulez's wariness of the voice—at least in the period between the seductive 'Complainte du lézard amoureux' in *Le Soleil des eaux* and the fluid ornamented melismata of the *Improvisations sur Mallarmé*—was possibly a sign of a deeper and more widely shared wariness of music's ability to comport itself as if with a voice. His disdain of 'accompanied melody' in Messiaen,[19] his shattering of legato line in the Sonatina, and his insistence on polyphony—preferably on a polyphony of polyphonies, in which musical parameters are differently adjudicated—all point to this. In *Le Marteau* music tumbles forth, but from no source that we can project: it is too fast, too flickering in colour, too jagged in outline, too prone to sudden stops and changes of course. One virtue of these Char poems, besides their brevity, was that the voice they intimate (two of them include the first person singular pronoun) speaks intensely of things disconnected, and of things disconnected from itself.

There are three poems, each contributing, or contributed to, a cycle of movements. 'L'Artisanat furieux', sung in movement III, has a prelude (I) and a postlude (VII); 'Bourreaux de solitude' (VI) comes amid a chain of 'commentaries' that occupy the other even-numbered places; and 'Bel Édifice et les pressentiments' (V) has a 'double', or variation, at the end of the work. The interweaving of three separate cycles recalls Messiaen's practice in the *Turangalîla* symphony, except that in Boulez's case the interweaving goes further. Not only does the last movement explicitly recall moments from all three cycles, but the characteristics unique to each cycle—such as the pulsed rhythms and the suspended continuities of the 'Bourreaux de solitude' group—are compromised by distinctions that cut across the cycles (notably the distinction between vocal and purely instrumental movements) and by general features of the work.

Among these, most important is the instrumentation, which opened new possibilities for Western chamber music without there being subsequently any diminishment to the work's clang of novelty. The scoring is for contralto voice with alto flute, viola, guitar, vibraphone, xylorimba (a xylophone with an extended lower range), and unpitched

19. See Boulez, 'Proposals', in ibid., 47–54.

percussion (one player), a grouping of diversities into a new unity, enabled partly by a common middle-high register, partly by bonds of sound, and partly by an abrupt removal of the instruments into a special world of speed, dash, and harmonic restlessness. Also, heterogeneity is itself a unifying factor. Since none of the instruments is supported by any other, their gathered separations become a specific of the piece: this is music that is defined, and perhaps even made possible, by hazardous tanglings.

Its ancestries are also numerous. Derivation from *Pierrot lunaire* is acknowledged in the presence of a voice-flute duet (the setting of 'L'Artisanat furieux'), and Boulez has also suggested that the vibraphone relates to the Balinese gamelan, the xylorimba to the music of black Africa and the guitar to the Japanese koto,[20] to which one might add that the ensemble, like that of *Kreuzspiel*, is flavoured with the modern jazz of the period. *Le Marteau* is thus a pioneering essay in the 'music of the whole world' that Stockhausen was to take as an ideal[21]— though it draws away from embracing exotic qualities of modality, rhythm, or ritual presentation: refusal is still what partly gives Boulez's music its energy, and this particular piece its quick temper.

As for the liaisons between instruments, those too have been described by the composer, in noting that the voice connects with the flute as an instrument of breath (so that the flute can seamlessly but also awesomely assume the vocal role at the end), the flute with the viola as an instrument able to sustain sounds, the viola (pizzicato) with the guitar for its plucked strings, the guitar with the vibraphone as a resonator, and the vibraphone with the xylorimba as an instrument to be struck.[22] The unpitched percussion (used only in the 'Bourreaux de solitude' cycle and the omnium-gatherum finale) he leaves out of account as 'marginal', though the xylorimba's high noise-content establishes some rapport.

Boulez's commentaries on *Le Marteau* have concerned themselves only with these matters of apparatus and descent, and the very elusiveness of his published Darmstadt lectures is enough to suggest, again, a view of detailed compositional technique as something to be withheld. The cause for this need not be interpreted as artistic *pudeur*, still less as a wish to protect trade secrets. Boulez's privacy is, rather, a silent statement of principle—of the principle that the creative means are, and should be, engulfed in the final work, so that to retrieve the compositional process would be impossible or, if it could be done, futile. Koblyakov's painstaking retrieval is, correspondingly, an astonishing analytical achievement, and a resounding disproof of the impossibility, if not the futility, since the question remains as to how the process

20. Pierre Boulez, 'Speaking, Playing, Singing', *Orientations*, 330–43.
21. See, for example, his note on *Telemusik* in Wörner, *Stockhausen*, 57–58.
22. See Boulez, 'Speaking, Playing, Singing'.

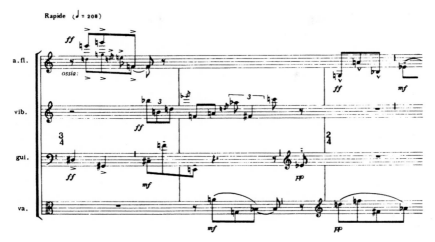

Example 21a   Pierre Boulez, *Le Marteau sans maître*

Example 21b

confers or determines the work's meaning and value. After all, *Le Marteau sans maître* had been installed as a modern masterpiece—and hailed by Stravinsky, who attended a performance Boulez conducted in Los Angeles in 1957[23]—long before anyone but its composer had any knowledge of its moment-to-moment compositional workings.

Example 21a shows the opening of the work, and Example 21b an indication, based on Koblyakov, of how the basic series can be 'multiplied' by any one of its five constituent groups to yield a new series in which every original note is replaced by a transposition of the multiplying group onto that note. (It is unclear whether this was Boulez's independent extension from Webernian serialism or his formalization of Stockhausen's group technique.) In this case the 'factor' is group *c*, the minor third, and the new series is transposed as a whole up a semitone so that the new *dc* is equivalent to the old *c*. The music is in two parts, one shared between the alto flute and the vibraphone, the other between the guitar and the viola, and this latter part begins with groups *a*, *b* (the D has to be borrowed from the vibraphone), *ac* (the C has to be borrowed, again from the vibraphone), *dc* (the same C must do duty

23. See Igor Stravinsky and Robert Craft, *Memories and Commentaries* (London, 1960), 123, and Robert Craft, ed., *Stravinsky: Selected Correspondence*, ii (London, 1984), 350.

here too) and *bc* (with the A and the E♭ borrowed from the flute), while the flute-vibraphone line also moves through *bc* (beginning of the second bar) and *e* (beginning of the third bar), among other groups.

Koblyakov's analysis, carrying across the entire length of the work, is far more convincing than may appear in reference to a short extract, and its formidable detail defies summary. However—and not only on the historical grounds of the work's prior valuation—one must doubt that the music is heard as a succession of multiplied serial units. Not only is the division into such units not always clear (the C–E♭, split between vibraphone and guitar, and involved in both parts, is a case in point), but even the nature of the music as two-part counterpoint is constantly being jeopardized by the crossings of parts and the splittings of lines between dissimilar instruments, especially when the speed is such that triplet quavers are gone in a tenth of a second (both the prelude and the postlude to 'L'Artisanat furieux' race at double the speed of the setting, as if they were harmonics of the vocal movement). Pace and fracturing, one might conclude, are more at issue here than polyphony—though with the polyphony vital for the pace and fracturing to be felt. Also, polyphonic order is expressed in the music most directly not by chains of serial multiplication products but by correspondences of shaped motif.

In example 21a one may note the prominence of rising thirds (usually minor), with or without falling ninths or sixteenths (usually major): it is almost as if the alto flute were announcing a three-note motif, one to be answered successively, in Webernian fashion, by the guitar (though with mild distortion) and the viola (in retrograde inversion) along a time line of consecutive quavers, a time line that then continues as far as the middle of the third bar. (Webern's Concerto would again be the work in the background here.) Regularities, of motif and of pulse, are played against irregularities, in ways that echo, though they do not precisely duplicate, the compositional process of taking units from a mechanical scheme (the successions of units in Koblyakov's analysis come from diagonal traverses of five-by-five squares of multiplied series) and then interpreting them with apparent freedom in matters of note order, registration, rhythm, and dynamics. In Boulez's terms, the basic elements were produced automatically; it was then necessary to author them by what musical means remained. There had to be this dialectic between process and freedom, between organization and composition, between the rational and the irrational.

Boulez has been consistent about such dichotomies, and about their irreplaceability. 'One used to find, especially in country towns, cafés where two walls with mirrors ran parallel. And when you entered these cafés you saw yourself into infinity; but if you took one mirror away, you saw only one reflection. I think that the imagination is situated between irrational and rational invention just as between two mirrors: if it deprives itself either of the irrational or the rational, then it can see itself only once.'[24] Even his unusually candid illustration of irrational invention, in this same article, finds excitement in an opposition: 'When you are out walking you can see the play of light on the leaves of the trees, and if you look at the leaves intensely enough you may suddenly be struck by the play of one structure in comparison with another. I have selected the example of leaves because I have seen for myself the relationship between one fixed arrangement of light and the flexible arrangement of leaves.' *Le Marteau sans maître*, on many levels of pitch, rhythm, and instrumentation, is Boulez's most complex and endlessly fascinating, endlessly frustrating play of such relationships between the fixed and the flexible.

A more violent description of such an encounter comes at the end of his 'Sound and Word', where he invokes Artaud again—'hearing him read his own texts, accompanying them with shouts, noises, or rhythmic effects, has shown us how to make the phoneme burst forth when the word can no longer do so' (a striking indication of what the effect of *Le Marteau* should be, but has been less and less in Boulez's five successive recordings[25])—and concludes: 'I increasingly believe that to create effective art, we have to take delirium and, yes, organize it.' No doubt this is what he would have wished: to compose with the daemon upon him, and to wrest from the struggle a form. However, his procedure in *Le Marteau sans maître* suggests much more someone taking organization and throwing it into delirium, and his awareness of this—his awareness that he belonged to a different class of artists, those needing a conscious structure to wield or fight against—may have been responsible for the decline in his output, and the virtual extinction of his ability to commit himself to a finished work, after the first performance, when he was thirty, of what was to remain his most signal achievement.[26]

Sound and Word

Le Marteau sans maître was one of three closely contemporary works that Stockhausen discusses, along with Nono's *Il canto sospeso* (1955–56) and his own *Gesang der Jünglinge* (also 1955–56), in what is a rare

24. 'Music and Invention', *The Listener* (22 January 1970), 101–2.

25. See Paul Griffiths, 'Le marteau de son maître, or Boulez selon Boulez', *Pierre Boulez: Eine Festschrift zum 60. Geburtstag am 26. März 1985* (Vienna, 1985), 154–58.

26. The work was scheduled for the 1954 Donaueschingen Festival but shelved, apparently because it stretched the guitarist. Boulez then revised it before the first performance several months later, on June 18, 1955 at the ISCM Festival in Baden-Baden, though the original version had already been published. For an anecdote from that première, see Elliott Carter, 'For Pierre on his Sixtieth', in ibid., 12–13.

document in showing a composer of this time (or indeed any time) observing his fellows.[27] As he intimates, his views of his colleagues are coloured by his own preoccupations: in particular his concern with treating the comprehensibility of words as a variable. It was characteristic of him that he could not be satisfied with Boulez's and Berio's derivation of music from verbal sound and structure: there must be some general principle that a single work would be enough to demonstrate completely—some system a work could bring into being. Such a system he found in the organization of degrees of comprehensibility, across a range from the candour of speech to the total incomprehensibility of wordless music. This would require electronic means. He needed 'to arrange everything separate into as smooth a continuum as possible, and then to extricate the diversities from this continuum and compose with them',[28] and he found the way to do that through attending, between 1954 and 1956, classes in phonetics and information theory given at Bonn University by Werner Meyer-Eppler. Since, as he there discovered, vowel sounds are distinguished, whoever is speaking, by characteristic formants (emphasized bands of frequencies), it seemed it ought to be possible to create synthetic vowels out of electronic sounds, so that synthesized music could begin to function as language.[29] Working from the other end, the whole repertory of tape transformations was available to alter spoken or sung material and so move it towards pure, meaningless sound.

Thanks to these techniques Stockhausen was able to create in *Gesang der Jünglinge* a model union between music and language. The synthesized electronic sounds are composed according to principles analogous to those operating in vocal sounds, and the recorded voice, that of a boy treble, is carried into the electronic stream by studio alteration and editing: superimpositions creating virtual choruses, reverberations to suggest great distance, scramblings of words and parts of words, changes of speed and direction. Nothing on either side, therefore, is quite foreign to the other, and Stockhausen invites his audience to attend to degrees of comprehensibility by using a text with which he could expect them (the work was intended for projection in Cologne cathedral) to be familiar: the German translation of the prayer sung in the Apocrypha by three young Jews in Nebuchadnezzar's furnace (hence the title, 'Song of the Youths'). Even so, the choice of this par-

27. Stockhausen, 'Music and Speech', *Die Reihe*, 6 (1960, English ed. 1964), 40–64.

28. Ibid.

29. See Stockhausen's 'Actualia', *Die Reihe*, 1 (1955, English ed. 1958), 45–51, in which he adopts Boulez's way—perhaps designed to convey the authority of objectivity—of discussing a work without naming it; see also his 'Music and Speech'.

ticular prayer—rather than, say, the 'Our Father', which would have been even more familiar—cannot have been uninfluenced by what Stockhausen could have envisioned would be the imagery of the piece, with the boy's singing surrounded by flames of electronic articulation.

In using natural alongside synthetic sound, Stockhausen mediated not only between speech and music but also between the musique concrète of Paris and the 'Elektronische Musik' of Cologne, opening the middle ground for exploration. His example—in this as in so many other things—was widely followed. Berio, for instance, transformed a passage of recorded recitation from Joyce's *Ulysses* to produce a stream of comprehended and half-comprehended utterance in his tape piece *Thema—omaggio a Joyce* (1958), though with a physical, sensuous handling of the female voice that connects more with the vocal writing of his concert works, such as *Chamber Music*, than with the ecstatic purity of the treble in *Gesang der Jünglinge*. Ligeti, too, was impressed by Stockhausen's achievement, and in his *Artikulation* (1958) made a more ambivalent, half-comic essay in electronic sound mimicking language.

Equally influential was Stockhausen's introduction of a spatial dimension into electronic music. *Gesang der Jünglinge* was originally prepared for five tape channels, later reduced to four, and its ebullience is greatly enhanced by antiphonal effects. Stockhausen himself was to apply in many later works the discoveries he had made here in the treatment of language and of space, of which the latter was already claiming his attention in *Gruppen* for three orchestras. But perhaps the deepest lesson of *Gesang der Jünglinge* was that music of all kinds, whether naturally or electronically produced, is made of sounds rather than notes, and that the first task of the composer is to listen. 'More than ever before', Stockhausen wrote, 'we have to listen, every day of our lives. We draw conclusions by making tests on ourselves. Whether they are valid for others only our music can show.'[30]

Il canto sospeso, the third work Stockhausen considered in his essay on music and speech, is a setting of fragments from the farewell letters of condemned political prisoners—characteristically highly charged material, which Nono projects in characteristically highly charged music for soloists, chorus, and orchestra. There is certainly no Boulezian suspicion of 'expressive relationships' here, though at the same time Nono contrasts movements whose words can be understood (such as the fifth, for tenor and orchestra) with others in which the sense is almost wholly confounded by his serial mechanics. He adopts this latter course, Stockhausen interestingly suggests, when the words are such as would shame musical interpretation.

Example 22 shows the start of the second movement, which is the usual example, since in this piece for unaccompanied chorus the

30. Ibid.

Example 22　Luigi Nono: *Il canto sospeso*

composer's procedures are manifest.[31] The movement is characteristic, however, in that the meaning of the text—'I die for a world that will shine with such a strong light and with such beauty that my sacrifice is nothing'—is obscured by having the four contrapuntal lines divided across the eight-part chorus. The contrapuntal lines move in units of quintuplet semiquavers, semiquavers, triplet quavers, and quavers, in each case in units from the Fibonacci series, 1-2-3-5-8-13, which in Stockhausen's music of this period, too, was often used to define proportions (Le Corbusier's 'modulor' system may have been the common source). All four lines are drawn into a single unfolding of pitches, simply repeating one of Nono's favoured all-interval series in which the

31. For a very much more far-reaching analysis, see Kathryn Bailey, '"Work in Progress": Analysing Nono's *Il canto sospeso*', *Music Analysis*, 11 (1992), 279–334.

intervals expand wedgewise: A–B♭–A♭–B–G–C–F♯–C♯–F–D–E–E♭. There is also a quite separate quasi-serial organization of dynamic levels. What Boulez saw as a problem—the struggle between organization and invention—becomes in Nono a dramatic emblem of his subject matter, as if we were hearing not so much prisoners as a prison itself singing.

. . . how time passes . . .

'Music consists of order-relationships in time.' So begins Stockhausen's essay '. . . how time passes . . . ' (1957), whose title perhaps punningly speaks of bemusement at what had happened within the space of six years, as well as of his recent and present concerns with tempo (on the large scale), with the momentary fluctuations and vibrations of sound (on the small scale), and with relationships across the divide. These were the concerns of the fruitful phase that had followed *Kontra-Punkte*, the concerns of *Gesang der Jünglinge*, of the second set of *Klavierstücke* (*V-X*, though *V* was revised, *VI* and *VII* were replaced,[32] and *IX* and *X* were not finished until 1961), of *Zeitmasze* for five woodwind, and of *Gruppen*.

Work on his electronic *Studien* had given Stockhausen a practical demonstration of how pitch and duration—the two parameters whose parallel ordering had been such a problem to total serialism—are aspects of a single phenomenon, that of vibration. A vibration of, say, 32 Hz will be perceived as a pitched note, whereas one of 4 Hz will be heard as a regular rhythm, and somewhere in between the one will merge into the other. So for different reasons—to do with acoustics rather than mathematics—Stockhausen came to the same conclusion that Babbitt had reached a little earlier, that some deep coherence had to be sought between the principles applied to pitch and to rhythm in forming a work. The scale of chromatic durations was inadequate, in Stockhausen's view, because it contradicted acoustical reality, being an additive series and not a logarithmic one, such as lay behind the chromatic scale of pitches; moreover, it led to absurdities and inconsistencies, such as the tendency towards regular pulsation when many lines are superimposed, or the undue weight of long durations.

To be troubled by these things was not, of course, new. Boulez in *Le Marteau sans maître* had developed his techniques of transformation to the point where he could range from strongly pulsed music to plastic counterpoint propelled by irregular beats or to completely ametrical

32. For remarks on the earlier versions of VI and VII, see Richard Toop's articles 'On Writing about Stockhausen', *Contact*, 20 (1979), 25–27, and 'Stockhausen's Other Piano Pieces', *Musical Times*, 124 (1983), 348–52. For a presentation of V and VII, see Karlheinz Stockhausen, 'Clavier Music 1992', *Perspectives of New Music*, 31/2 (1993), 136–49. This item is particularly valuable as a seemingly unedited transcript of the composer's speech.

movement: rhythmic variety, to which he had been led before by intuition and a sense of history, could now be justified within the system.
Nono in *Il canto sospeso* had broken up regularity simply by overlaying
streams in different units. Stockhausen himself, in *Kontra-Punkte* and
Klavierstücke I-IV, had added equal divisions of the bar to chromatic
durations. But now he wanted to base his organization on the nature
of sound. To create a true confluence with the phenomenon of pitch,
he introduced a logarithmic scale of twelve tempos—a scale that could
be 'transposed' by altering the rhythmic unit: for example, a change
from crotchets to semibreves, and therefore a deceleration by a factor
of four, would be the equivalent of a downward shift of two octaves.
Within this system, the obverse of the one proposed earlier by Boulez,[33]
a rise of a perfect twelfth would have its analogue in a change of tempo
in the ratio 3:2 (the frequency ratio of a perfect fifth, if one discounts
the small discrepancies of temperament) coupled with a halving of the
rhythmic unit. So any pitch line could be turned into a duration-tempo
succession, a melody of rhythm, and one could also change the timbre of the rhythm, as it were, by adding 'partials' in the form of other
duration-tempo successions going on at the same time, their number
limited only by the practicalities of performance. For instance, the first
group of *Gruppen* has a 'fundamental' represented by minims in the
violas, combined with 'overtones' of crotchets (cellos), triplet crotchets
(harp), quavers (wood drums), and so on up to the 'tenth harmonic'
(flutes). In this way each group in the work is composed as the image
of a particular pitch in a particular octave with a particular timbre: as
Jonathan Harvey has shown, the whole rhythmic structure is the vast
amplification of a serial melodic thread.[34]

This equivalence leads naturally to the work's novel layout, for if
different 'fundamentals' are to be heard at once—if the melody is to
branch or be harmonized or counterpointed—there must be some way
of maintaining different tempos simultaneously, and if each 'fundamental' is to have a rich spectrum of 'overtones', there must be a generous supply of instruments: hence *Gruppen* for three orchestras, each
separated from the others and having its own conductor. But having
derived the need for orchestral antiphony from his structural scheme,
Stockhausen was characteristically drawn to take advantage of the opportunities for spectacle, notably in the sonorous climax where a brass
chord is hurled from one orchestra to another across the auditorium.
Or perhaps one should regard structure and spectacle as simultaneous
imperatives: Stockhausen's artistic success, and his prowess among his
peers, depended partly on this knack of discovering systems that would
unfold into impressive and unprecedented results. *Gruppen* also be-

33. Boulez, *Stocktakings*, 126–28.
34. Harvey, *The Music of Stockhausen*, 59–61; see also Gottfried Michael
Koenig: 'Commentary', *Die Reihe*, 8 (1962, English ed. 1968), 80–98.

longed securely in his history as an exploration—despite its scale—of relatively small, highly variegated ensembles: this had been his preference in his *Drei Lieder* (at least to judge from the published revision), *Formel, Spiel,* and *Punkte,* and it seems to have been stimulated by a wish he shared with his colleagues, a wish to avoid the traditional string-based orchestra, to use different colours as freely as different notes, and to bring forward the percussion. Each orchestra of *Gruppen* is accordingly made up of three dozen players, about half of whom are strings, the rest being constituted equally of woodwind, brass, and percussion, both pitched and unpitched. The articulation of a new kind of rhythmic structure becomes—has to become, in obedience to that structure—a virtuoso exercise in orchestral sound.

As with *Kontra-Punkte,* the new work's innovatory exuberance powerfully impressed Stockhausen's contemporaries. Nono and Berio both wrote pieces for orchestras in groups: the former's *Composizione per orchestra No. 2: Diario polacco* of 1958 and the latter's *Allelujah II* of 1956–57. So, in his *Doubles* (1957–58), did Boulez, who was one of the conductors at the first performance of *Gruppen* (Cologne, March 24, 1958), when the piece brought together three leading composers of the new wave to lead the performance (Maderna was the third)—with another, Ligeti, in the audience—of what could be seen as not only a new assault on space and time but also a symbol of fraternal cooperation.

Statistics

Hardly less influential than *Gruppen* on the orchestral sound of the later 1950s was the music of Xenakis, whose promptings came not from acoustics but from architecture (of which he had practical experience at this time, working in Le Corbusier's studio) and mathematics. After arriving in Paris from Athens in 1947, he had some lessons in composition—in Messiaen's class, and as a protégé of Hermann Scherchen, who conducted several of his early performances—but he was always an independent, and not least in his rejection of his contemporaries' methods of working. His article 'La Crise de la musique sérielle',[35] is a remarkable document for its time in denouncing directions that, at the moment of *Le Marteau sans maître* and *Gruppen,* were commanding widespread enthusiasm. 'Linear polyphony', Xenakis wrote, with implicit reference to such works as Boulez's *Structures,* 'destroys itself by its very complexity; what one hears is in reality nothing but a mass of notes in various registers.'

Of course, this was precisely what had attracted Stockhausen to the 'star music' of the *Mode de valeurs*: Xenakis's criticism was only a statement of how the recent music of his contemporaries departed

---

35. Iannis Xenakis, 'La Crise de la musique sérielle', *Gravesaner Blätter,* 1 (1955), 2ff.

from traditional linear consequence, and its object was not so much the music itself as the justification of that music in terms of serial order and grammar. For him, though, the conclusion had to be that another theoretical base was needed. If the effect was to be 'nothing but a mass of notes', the means to produce that effect should be sought in the branch of mathematics that had been developed to deal with such statistical phenomena: in 'the notion of probability, which implies in this particular case, combinatory calculus'. He therefore turned to the laws of stochastics, which describe phenomena that can be defined only in the large (Xenakis gives as examples 'the collision of hail or rain on hard surfaces, or the song of cicadas in a summer field'[36]), and so derived 'stochastic music'. By interpreting curved planes—his architectural speciality—as massive overlays of glissandos, as if the strings of an orchestra were playing a blueprint, each instrument drawing its own line, he had introduced a new and widely imitated texture in his first published piece, *Metastaseis* (1953–54). His second, *Pithoprakta* (1955–56), initiated stochastic music with highly differentiated textures calculated according to laws of probability.

Stockhausen was interested in those laws too, and again the starting point was his work with Meyer-Eppler on the nature of sound. One could, he had learned, define the formant spectrum of a complex sound—such as an unpitched percussion stroke, of the kind he had been using keenly since *Spiel*—without being able to know just which frequencies would be present at any particular instant. *Gruppen* suggests how he may have wanted to express this by having some frequencies (in their rhythmic embodiments) present throughout, while others make only a fleeting contribution. In the case of this work the image is fixed, as indeed it is in *Pithoprakta*, so that the score is in the nature of a still picture of something potentially in motion: to realize the motion—to create a score open to macroscopic rhythmic uncertainty—would be hazardous in works for large forces. But it would be possible with soloists or small groupings, and it was this ideal of a constrained mobility that Stockhausen went after in his second set of piano pieces and in *Zeitmasze*.

Writing these compositions after a period of intensive work in the electronic studio on his *Studien*, he was determined also to take advantage of musical possibilities peculiar to live performance, among which rhythmic freedom coincided with the tendency in his theoretical thinking. It was perhaps only after the fact that he had been able, in the case of the first group of piano pieces, to delight in performers' rhythmic imprecision. In *Zeitmasze* and the new piano pieces such imprecision is made part of the structure, in that tempos (and in *Zeitmasze* the relative tempos of the five players) are here dependent less on notational pre-

36. Iannis Xenakis, *Formalized Music: Thought and Mathematics in Composition* (Bloomington, 1971; Stuyvesant, N.Y., 1992), 9.

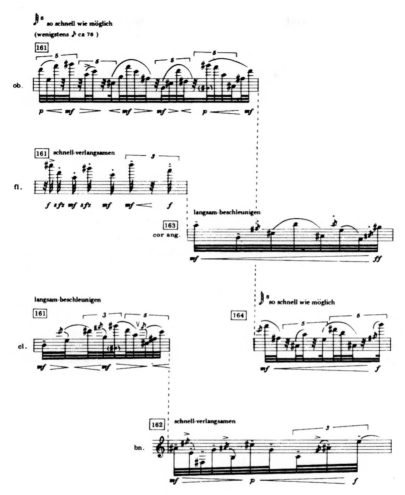

Example 23   Karlheinz Stockhausen, *Zeitmasze*

scription than on limitations of technique and feasibility. *Zeitmasze* becomes an elastic play of five time-strands, each of which mixes passages
in strict tempo with others whose speeds are determined by, for example, the musicians' capacities to play as fast as possible, or as slowly as
possible within one breath (hence the need for this to be a wind piece:
aim and medium mesh in a manner characteristic of Stockhausen).

Each of the piano pieces in the *V-X* set similarly combines fixed
rhythms with elements whose rhythmic characters will depend on
the player's dexterity; each also brings together determined pitch structures with others that contradict these, or that contribute only a generalized effect: Stockhausen had been impressed by David Tudor's extension of piano technique in performing Cage, during the European

tour the two U.S. musicians made in 1954, and he dedicated the set to Tudor. The massive clusters and cluster-glissandos of *Klavierstück X* are among the most striking of the statistical phenomena, or super-groups, where the character of the whole matters much more than the detailed contents. But this piece is unusual only in its flamboyance: its companions also uncover new techniques and sonorities, or formalize what had come out of Tudor's Cage. *Klavierstück VII*, for instance, beautifully exploits the resonance effects obtained when strings are freed by silent depression of the keys.

Notwithstanding the piano pieces' qualities of sound and shapeliness, *Zeitmasze* is Stockhausen's most ambitious work in integrating metronomic definition with free tempo, and fixed metre with scatterings of notes. At the same time, like some of the piano pieces, it mixes points and groups in what the composer—again wanting to present musical decisions as instituting new modes of practice—called 'collective form'.[37] Example 23 gives some indication of this, and also of the work's counterpointing of time layers, as well as its profusion of cross-references in matters of interval and contour (compare, for example, the cor anglais and clarinet lines). Clearly such music poses great problems of coordination; at the same time it liberates the bounding energy of the ideas. No work better displays the self-confidence felt by Stockhausen and his colleagues at this point, nor the exhilaration they experienced in pursuing and capturing new possibilities in sound.

37. Stockhausen, *Texte*, i, 235.

1956

Nikita Khrushchev's repudiation of Stalin's 'cult of personality', in February 1956, signalled a change of mood in the Soviet leadership. The previous month, RCA released the first record they had made with a new singing star: Elvis Presley (1935–77). Both events were to have long and significant repercussions in the world of composition.

The 'Khrushchev thaw' was sometimes misconstrued, as by the Hungarian government, with cruel effect in October–November 1956. Yet it could also sometimes permit an opening to new music from Western Europe and the United States. Just two weeks before Warsaw Pact tanks rolled into Budapest, the city of Warsaw had witnessed a contemporary music festival. There was no repetition the next year, but from 1958 this 'Warsaw Autumn' became a regular event, with guests that year including Nono and Stockhausen.

Russian musicians had a direct link to the source in Philipp Herschkowitz (1906–89), who had studied with Webern in the 1930s and was now sought out by many aspiring composers. Among them, Andrey Volkonsky (1933–2008) composed in 1956 what may have been the first twelve-note composition by a young Russian, his *Musica stricta* for piano—though the thaw was less noticeable in Moscow than in Warsaw, and such ventures had to remain underground until the 1960s.

Progressive composition was spreading not only more widely but also more deeply as the Presley generation came of age—a generation that also included Harrison Birtwistle, Peter Maxwell Davies, Alfred Schnittke, Arvo Pärt, and Helmut Lachenmann, all born within a few months of Elvis.

There were some ironies in this synchronicity. Young composers in the first decade after 1945 had believed themselves to be building a new music, as indeed they were. Now a new music of a different sort was arriving, and sweeping the world. It had, moreover, very little in common with the tradition Presley's aforementioned contemporaries found themselves in. Where modern jazz still had something to say to Babbitt, Barraqué, Boulez, and Stockhausen, there was no communication with rock 'n' roll. Many of its principal features, not least the heavy regular beat that most defined it, were anathema to these avant-garde masters, to their colleagues, and to the ever growing new generation of composers. That would change, of course, but not immediately.

7

Mobile Form

1956–61

Cage

Hitherto Cage's impact on European music had come in short, though perhaps decisive, shocks: in 1949, when he made his music and his thinking known to Boulez and Messiaen in Paris, and in 1954, when he and Tudor gave performances in several European cities, and when Stockhausen met them. By the mid-1950s, however, many of the most prospering musical developments in Europe—Stockhausen's concern with statistical events, Boulez's pursuit of open form, extensions of instrumental and vocal technique by Berio and Mauricio Kagel (1931–2008), almost everyone's effort at electronic music and so at ways of composing untempered sounds—were making Cage seem far more relevant than could have been the case earlier. In 1957 Maderna discussed Cage's work at Darmstadt, and an issue of *Die Reihe* included, between Stockhausen's ' . . . how time passes . . . ' and an elucidation by Pousseur of the current state of his technique, a short piece in which Cage described the compositional process required to create his *Music for Piano 21-52* (1955) by means of chance operations[1]—this in what had been the journal of total organization. Change was in the air, and the next year Cage and Tudor were themselves at Darmstadt.

---

1. John Cage, 'To Describe the Process of Composition used in "Music for Piano 21-52"', *Die Reihe*, 3 (1957, Eng. ed. 1959), 41–43.

Shortly before, on May 15, 1958, they had taken part in an all-Cage concert mounted at Town Hall, New York, to celebrate the silver jubilee of the composer's first published works. Written to provide the evening with a climax, *Concert for Piano and Orchestra* (1957–58) was exuberantly indeterminate, created by a composer who avowed, in his programme note, that his 'intention [sic] in this piece was to hold together extreme disparities, much as one finds them held together in the natural world, as, for instance, in a forest or on a city street'[2] Accordingly, the work is an encyclopedia of notational possibilities, laid out in parts for piano and thirteen other instruments, any or all of which may be used in performance, together with other material (pieces from the *Music for Piano* series could also be overlapped at will). 'I regard this work', his note concludes, 'as one "in progress," which I intend [again] never to consider as in a final state, although I find each performance definitive'. This Joyceian notion of the constantly continuing work had been part of 'The Ten Thousand Things',[3] and suggests that after *4′ 33″* Cage had to consider his compositions as endlessly mutable, though it was only at this point in his career, after the *Concert*, that the emphasis in his music shifted from the solo piece to the unsynchronized ensemble.

At the same time there was a shift from relatively conventional notation to new forms requiring a contribution from the performer. Example 24, from the solo part of the *Concert*, provides an instance. The player has to draw perpendiculars from either the upper or the lower horizontal line to the slanting lines. Measurements from the base line to the points of intersection with the wavy lines are then used to determine values for the four musical parameters (pitch, duration, dynamic, attack) according to scales the player also determines. The numbers show by their differences the time available for sounds derived from references to each of the slanting lines: 1.5 seconds in the case of the first, for example.

Stockhausen and Boulez

By now it was clear that the interests of Stockhausen and Boulez were differently based, even though the Darmstadt comradeship continued until 1965,[4] the last year Boulez was present. Stockhausen was driven on by what he could learn about the nature of sound, whereas Boulez's essays of the mid-1950s speak of aesthetic issues and models from literature. Both their closenesses and their differences are revealed in the

2. Richard Kostelanetz, ed., *John Cage* (New York, 1970, 1991; London, 1971), 130.

3. See Jean-Jacques Nattiez, ed., *The Boulez-Cage Correspondence* (Cambridge and New York, 1993), 143.

4. See Dominique Jameux, *Pierre Boulez* (London, 1991), 117.

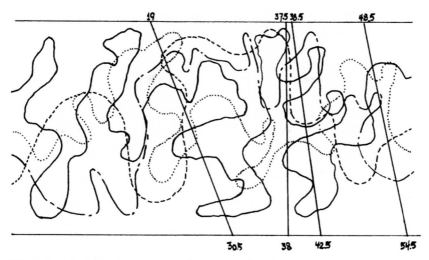

Example 24 John Cage, *Concert for Piano and Orchestra*

extraordinary conjunction of Stockhausen's *Klavierstück XI* (1956) with Boulez's Third Piano Sonata (1955–57), the two first classics of open form in European music.

Stockhausen's piece presents the player with nineteen groups disposed on a single large sheet of paper. According to the instructions, the performer 'begins with whichever group he sees first', 'casts another random glance to find another of the groups', and continues in the same manner until a group has been reached for the third time. There is thus no guarantee that all the groups will be played, and similarly their order is entirely free, though Stockhausen makes some effort at linkage into what he may have seen as a Markov chain, 'a sequence of mutually dependent symbols',[5] since at the end of each group he gives a 'registration' of what tempo, dynamic level, and mode of touch must be used for the next, whichever that may be. Whether or not this is a borrowing from information theory, Stockhausen characteristically identifies his work as something new in musical history, having nothing to do with earlier examples of mobile form in the music—say, of Cage, Brown (whose *Twenty-Five Pages* of 1953 may be combined successively or simultaneously in any way and played on any number of pianos up to twenty-five), or Henry Cowell (whose 'Mosaic' Quartet dates from 1934), everything to do with research into sound. '*Klavierstück XI*', he said, 'is nothing but a sound in which certain partials, components, are behaving statistically. . . . As soon as I compose a

5. For a different approach to Markovian music see Iannis Xenakis, *Formalized Music: Thought and Mathematics in Composition* (Bloomington, 1971; Stuyvesant, N.Y., 1992), 43–109.

noise . . . then the wave structure of this sound is aleatoric. If I make a whole piece similar to the ways in which this sound is organized, then naturally the individual components of this piece could also be exchanged, permutated, without changing its basic quality.'[6]

Perhaps for the first time in their relationship, Boulez was mistrustful of one of Stockhausen's new departures, finding in it 'a new sort of automatism, one which, for all its apparent opening the gates to freedom, has only really let in an element of risk that seems to me absolutely inimical to the integrity of the work'.[7] That word 'automatism', conjuring up the stalemate of *Structures Ia* and the disappointments of Cage, suggests how deeply Boulez was worried. Leaving any aspect to chance produced exactly the same effect as being forced by some scheme: the composer's presumed liberty of action was compromised. This Boulez would not countenance, and yet there seemed no way to justify the composer's freedom other than by recourse to the mystique of the individual imagination, which again was not very satisfactory. Boulez's technique was presenting him with multiple possibilities, but no grounds for choice. However, by a far-reaching development of the open forms of Cage and Stockhausen, it might be possible to defer choice to the point of performance: to present the work with its alternatives intact, and to ask the performer or performers to choose from among them.

In a crucial article on aleatory composition,[8] Boulez proposes that chance can be 'absorbed' in musical structures dependent on a degree of flexibility, perhaps in tempo: there were already examples of such structures in his own music (*Structures Ib, Le Marteau sans maître*) and in Stockhausen's (*Zeitmasze, Klavierstücke V-X*). Chance could also be accommodated, he ventures, in mobile forms, and that possibility he explored most deeply in his Third Piano Sonata, which could even have been intended as a creative criticism of Stockhausen's *Klavierstück XI*. The performer is now asked not to give a 'random glance' but rather to prepare a way through the options provided, and the work is—or rather was planned to be, since only two of its five 'formants' have been published[9]—a compendium of opportunities for alternative route, ossia, and ad libitum.

Boulez's return to the term 'formant' is a reminder that his thoughts on open form go back to before *Klavierstück XI*—to his 1954 report 'Current Investigations',[10] and perhaps even to the *Polyphonie* enterprise—

---

6. Jonathan Cott, *Stockhausen: Conversations with the Composer* (London, 1974), 70.

7. Antoine Goléa, *Rencontres avec Pierre Boulez* (Paris, 1958), 229.

8. Pierre Boulez, 'Alea', *Stocktakings from an Apprentice* (Oxford and New York, 1991), 26–38.

9. A fragment from another, *Antiphonie,* was published as Sigle in 1968 in a Universal Edition piano compendium.

10. Boulez, *Stocktakings*, 15–19; see above, p. XX.

and that he too, in this respect at least, was open to ideas presenting themselves in the nature of sound. He has also suggested that there might be 'développants'—other movements 'complete in themselves but structurally connected with the original formants'.[11] However, the essentially literary nature of his approach is revealed by the layouts of the two printed formants, *Trope* and *Constellation-Miroir*. The former is a ring-bound sheaf of four items to be played in various possible orders— a 'Texte' that is the subject of a 'Parenthèse', 'Commentaire' and 'Glose', while *Constellation-Miroir* ('mirror' because what we have is, for reasons undisclosed, the retrograde of a notional *Constellation*) sprinkles fragments over several large pages, and so recalls the appearance of Mallarmé's *Un Coup de dès*, which Boulez had planned to set in 1950.[12] At that time, instead of *Un Coup de dès*, he had written *Structures Ia*: now *Constellation-Miroir* would take up Mallarmé's invitation towards a music of immanent variability in a different way, and find a route, in its teeming variety of routes, to defy compulsion.

The structural link between the formants is at the level of the basic series, which in *Trope* is considered as a succession of four units suggesting cyclical concatenations of serial forms (see example 25a)[13] and also serving as the germ of the formant's circular mobility. Two of the serial units together, *b* and *d*, make up a transposition of *a* down a minor third; the foreign group *c*, a symmetrical pairing of minor thirds, is a 'trope' which both imitates and interrupts the larger symmetry. The formant is a vast magnification of this material, not only in its cyclical permutability but also in its inclusion of commentaries that are interpolated into the skeleton structure or else superimposed upon it. Not only are three of the large sections commentaries on the root 'Texte', but they contain within themselves parentheses and glosses that are sometimes obligatory, sometimes optional: example 25b, from the opening of 'Parenthèse', shows one of the latter inserted into a straightforward serial chain, which is that of example 25a.

The music's movement by allusion is a characteristic that goes back to the Sonatina of a decade before, and beyond that to the late Debussy that Boulez had invoked as a model in his 1954 essay ' . . . Near and Far'.[14] For example, one may notice the accelerando run of *c* units within the brackets referring to the preceding *c* group marked 'un peu précipité', or the parenthetic *d* groups similarly relating to the corresponding group in the main text, or the registral fixing of the A–G minor seventh. What is unusual here—though repeated later in *Domaines*

---

11. Pierre Boulez, '"Sonate, que me veux-tu?"', *Orientations* (London, 1986), 143–54.

12. Nattiez, ed., *The Boulez-Cage Correspondence*, 80.

13. See Pierre Boulez, *Boulez on Music Today* (London, 1971), 73–74, and Iwanka Stoïanowa, 'La *Troisième sonate* de Boulez et le projet mallarméen du Livre', *Musique en jeu*, 16 (1974), 9–28.

14. Boulez, *Stocktakings*, 141–57.

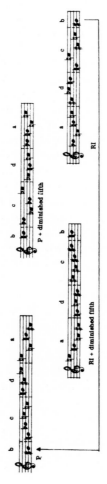

Example 25a

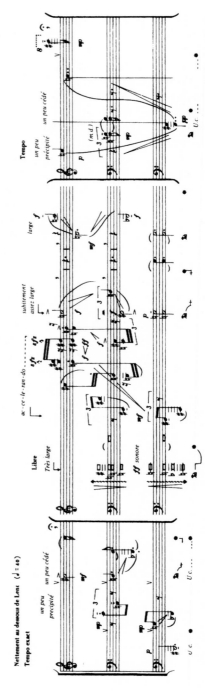

Example 25b   Pierre Boulez, Piano Sonata No. 3

for clarinet and ensembles (1961–68)—is the clear demarcation between a strict framework of serial unfolding and its vast possibilities of extension: that demarcation is even emphasized by the move out to another world of tempo, rhythmic variety, and density, and then by the return, through what may be sensed as a correction when the obligatory music repeats an E–F fall just heard in the free material. But if the formant is, in this regard, doctrinaire, that may have been in its purpose as a teaching instrument and example. It is the *Structures Ia* of aleatory form, and *Constellation-Miroir* the *Ib*.

This other piece, planned as the central sun around which the four smaller formants revolve (in that their placings were to have been variable), is considerably more ambiguous about the strategies by which simple material ('points': sequences made up essentially of single notes) is related to more complex ('blocs': massive chords and arpeggios). There is a brief mixture of the two types at the start, followed by three sections of 'points' alternated with two of 'blocs', and this large form is fixed. But within each section Boulez provides numerous possible ways of linking the fragments, so that the player 'must pick his way through a close network of paths' as he confronts what the composer has likened to a map of an unknown town.[15] More subtly and ambiguously than in *Trope*, unforeseen connections infiltrate the paths, and give any performance of the formant some sense that it is indeed the traverse of a maze, though hardly less important to the musical effect is the fluidity of movement (a controlled rubato is generally demanded) or the wide variety of sounds obtained by means of scrupulously marked pedallings and resonance effects. There were intimations of these in example 25b, where, for example, the depression of the sustaining pedal near the start of the bracketed material, just after the *fortissimo* arpeggio has been played, captures the echo from the strings. But *Constellation-Miroir* has many more, so that the visual distinction of the printed music, which uses red ink for 'blocs' and green for 'points', is matched by its sonorous appeal.

Boulez and Berio

Apparently it was only after completing the first version of his Third Sonata that Boulez came to know of Mallarmé's dream of a Book that would be endlessly mutable, a Book whose segments could be chosen and ordered at will for public readings. Learning of this could only have intensified his feelings of proximity to a poet who had overturned existing grammar and trodden a similar path to his own between chance and necessity, and almost inevitably a large-scale Mallarmé setting was his next major project—not a return to *Un Coup de dès* but an assembly of poems into a new book: *Pli selon pli* for soprano and orchestra, of

15. Boulez, '"Sonate, que me veux-tu?"', 151.

which he assembled a first version between 1957 and 1962. The Third Sonata is related to this work rather as the first book of *Structures* is related to *Le Marteau sans maître*, in that both later compositions give voice to poetic implications and discoveries that had already arrived in purely musical form. In principle, *Pli selon pli* is considerably less open in structure—partly for the practical reason that the sonata's multitude of options could not be imitated in a work for large forces without loss of the control Boulez was zealous to maintain. However, the work's revisions, continuing into the 1980s, kept it alive to change, even while gradually rescinding the original formal liberties.

The five movements, if all are to be played, must be given in a pre-scribed, symmetrical order, beginning and ending with pieces for large ensemble in which the voice is present only momentarily (*Don* and *Tombeau*), and reaching inwards to a song for soprano and nine-piece percussion ensemble (*Improvisation sur Mallarmé II*). Revisions of the other two movements, the first and third *Improvisations*, increased their scale to enhance this palindrome, and at the same time deprived *Impro-visation III* of its status as the work's one great area of unpredictability, withdrawing the performers' freedom to choose and order material. The work's elasticity thus became much more a matter of variable tem-pos, and of the superimposition of orchestral streams flowing at differ-ent rates, as in *Gruppen*, though requiring only one conductor. (And requiring, one might almost add, the composer himself to be that con-ductor, since most of his works since the late 1950s, when he began to give concerts regularly, have needed his own kinds of precisions and virtuosities: perfect ensemble playing, exact rhythm, and the ability to respond quickly to alternatives.)

For the outermost movements Boulez chose one of Mallarmé's earliest published poems ('Don du poème') and one of his last ('Tom-beau', his homage to Verlaine). These movements therefore represent the birth and death of a poet, and stand too for the birth and death inherent in art: the birth of the creative impulse, and its death to the artist once it has been expressed. 'Don du poème' is further the cele-bration of a literary birth, in that it looks forward in metre and imag-ery to the poet's 'Hérodïade', and Boulez's *Don* similarly looks forward to the remainder of *Pli selon pli*. There is a dedicatory setting of the opening line of the poem, and then the text disappears (becomes 'cen-tral and absent', to recall Boulez's terminology); the music goes into the state of nascence that the silent words are at once describing and illustrating—a state, as musically interpreted, of suspended chords, through which prefigurings of the four movements to come are drawn forward in reverse order and lost. In *Tombeau*, completing the symme-try, the singer emerges at the end with the final line of the text, and the piece is extinguished by a *sforzato* chord that recalls the opening crack of *Don*. The end is as the beginning; a window is opened and shut.

The *Improvisations sur Mallarmé*—improvisations only for himself as composer and, in their fluidity of tempo, as conductor—allow the poem to be present as well as central (though this was not entirely the case in the early versions of the third), and so there can be a little less doubt about how the music relates to the words.[16] As in *Le Marteau sans maître*, the relation takes place simultaneously on different levels of imagery and structure, the former represented by, for example, the ornate vocal melisma for the undulating lace curtain of 'Une Dentelle s'abolit' in *Improvisation II*, or the use of registral fixing now to give a stationary effect for reasons traceable to the text, or the choice of a scintillating, resonant instrumentation to correspond with metaphors of coldness, transparency, whiteness, and reflection. Meanwhile, perhaps a little naively, Boulez reacts to verbal structures with changes from melismatic to syllabic singing at formal junctures (all of the poems except 'Don du poème' are sonnets), or by deploying different compositional principles for masculine and feminine endings, or by musical eightnesses for the eight syllables of the lines.

Lessons from *Pli selon pli*—lessons concerned with the musical matching of verbal sound and sense, with the exploration of stationary harmonic fields, and with the notion of the work as a collection of fascicles—were absorbed and developed by Berio in an important group of pieces composed during the same period. Also crucial, to him and to others, was a lesson dramatized in *Le Marteau sans maître*: the rediscovery, following the fragmentation of the heyday of total serialism, that an instrument (specifically the flute) could command the rhetoric of a voice. (Nono alone had no need to learn this lesson, since instrumental vocality and drama had been manifest in his music all through—not least in his flute concerto *Y su sangre*.) The flautist Severino Gazzelloni, a regular performer in *Le Marteau*, was one of the first star soloists of the European new-music circuit, and responsible for the prominence of the flute in the music of that world; for him Berio wrote two chamber concertos, *Serenata I* (1957) and *Tempi concertati* (1958–59), as well as *Sequenza I* (1958), the first of a continuing series of virtuoso solos concerned with dramatizing performance.

Tempi concertati is a drama too. The 'concerted tempos', and the disposition of the orchestra into four groups, suggest another look at *Gruppen*, albeit on a smaller scale than in *Allelujah II* (where again the flute had a determining role), but *Tempi concertati* proceeds in quite a different fashion (and in quite a different fashion from *Serenata I*) as an interplay between solos and choruses, an interplay of declamation and revolt, suggestion and response, song and silence, in which the flute

---

16. For Boulez's own explanations, see his 'Constructing an Improvisation', *Orientations*, 155–73, and also *Conversations with Célestin Deliège* (London, 1977), 94–95.

has to hold its primacy against solo activities from members of the groups, especially the violin and the two pianos. Together with the contemporary works of Kagel (different anyway in their concerns with debasement and criticism rather than brilliance and play), the piece stands at the head of a modern tradition of instrumental theatre.

After these three flute-centred works, Berio returned to the voice of his wife Cathy Berberian (1925–83), who was another of the small group of performers devoted to new music in the 1950s (a short list would have to include also the names of David Tudor and Yvonne Loriod), and the singer on whose voice he had already created *Chamber Music* and *Thema*. In his next work for her, *Circles* with harpist and two percussionists (1960), he turned from Joyce to cummings, and set three poems, two of them twice, to make a palindrome *ABCB'A'*. Since the poems are, in the order *A-C*, of increasingly dislocated syntax, one circle of the work is from words as information to words as sound and back again, and that circle is repeated in different aspects of the musical design. For example, both settings of the first two poems use conventional rhythmic notation, whereas *C* is in the proportional notation that Cage had introduced (Berio had already used this in *Sequenza I* and *Tempi concertati*), and *A* and *A'* feature the harp (in the latter case with mostly pitched percussion), whereas *C* is altogether noisier. Example 26, a passage from this central section, shows its typical qualities as well as the work's more general response, in instrumental as much as vocal writing, to the phonemes and meaning of the text: particular instances include the white noise of hi-hat and suspended cymbal connecting with the sibilants in the voice, or the drumrolls that unashamedly answer the text, or, still more obviously, the outburst at the word 'collide'.

The percussion notation in this passage, and elsewhere, owes something to Stockhausen's recent solo piece *Zyklus* (1959), with which the work also shares a combination of circular with directed form, though where Stockhausen had taken up Boulez's idea of ring-binding to create his cyclical composition, *Circles* has a fixed starting point: the circling is left implicit in the palindrome, a palindrome being a circle opened and stretched out. As for the directedness, that comes in the treatment of the voice. The ornamented lyricism of the first setting is progressively stripped away as the work proceeds towards its centre, with a change to syllabic singing in *B* and the introduction of speech and rounded Italian kinds of sprechgesang in *C* (see example 26, where the rectangular note heads indicate approximate pitch and the open ones speech). But then, instead of recovering its embellishments, the voice is drawn more and more into the musical ambits of the instruments in *B'* and *A'*, and this integration is demonstrated on the concert platform by having the soloist move to positions nearer the ensemble. (The mobile performer was as much a phenomenon of the period as instrumental

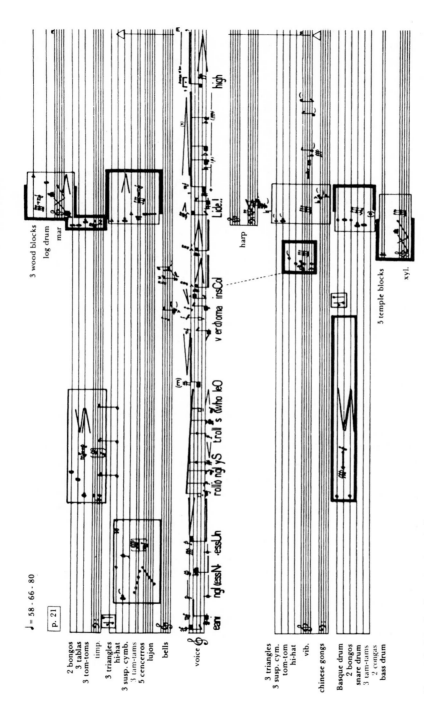

Example 26 Luciano Berio, *Circles*

theatre, and a phenomenon that was to reach its apogee in the actor-musicians on stage in Stockhausen's *Licht*.)

Berio's use of different vocal styles to articulate a form—a technique dependent on Berberian, whose mimic agility Cage had exploited in his *Aria* (1958)—is on show in three works completed soon after *Circles*: *Epifanie* for voice and orchestra (1959–61), the theatre piece *Passaggio* (1961–62) and *Folk Songs* for voice and septet (1964). These works also display Berio's range, from provocation to charm. *Folk Songs* is a garland of numbers from around the world, delightfully done (Berio's involvement with folk music was to go much deeper in such later works as *Coro* and *Voci*); *Passaggio* is ostensibly an attack on bourgeois society, an attack in the form of a mirror. The unnamed protagonist, She, moves among different stations, as in *Circles*, each station being associated with a different musical-dramatic aura: she is prisoner, prostitute, performer, and the audience discovers that their expectations of the theatre singer—expectations focussed during this period on such women as Judy Garland, Edith Piaf, and Maria Callas—are what the piece is about. Choruses of singers and speakers, the latter placed among the audience, identify and exaggerate modes of response (the work was evidently designed to instigate and to accommodate uproar), but though this might suggest an alignment with Nono's political art (recently brought to a larger public through the performance of his opera *Intolleranza*), Berio, as always, is more concerned with means of communication than with messages. *Passaggio* is a play of different soprano-esque ideals (heroine, victim), of different relationships between words and music, of different avenues of response from the audience.

In that respect it is, as David Osmond-Smith suggested, an 'open work' of the sort defined by the composer's longstanding friend and collaborator Umberto Eco, an example of works that 'although physically completed, are nevertheless "open" to a continuous germination of internal relations that the spectator must discover and select in the act of perceiving the totality of stimuli'.[17] This is the kind of indeterminacy—an indeterminacy of meaning, brought about by a use of languages (verbal and musical) of high ambiguity, by an avoidance of finality in any statement, and by rich networks of cross-reference operating both within the work and across to other works of the composer's own or by other composers (hence Berio's endless fascination with arrangement and recomposition)—that Berio preferred to a Cageian indeterminacy of sound or a Boulezian indeterminacy of form. His interest was not so much in a new language as in all languages, old and new, and he was therefore disinclined—disinclined too, perhaps, by temperament—to resist echoes of tonality. The thirteen-note series of his orchestral piece

17. Quoted in Osmond-Smith's notes in the programme book for the Berio festival held in London in January 1990.

Nones (1954), for example, had emphasized major and minor thirds, through which he achieved a suaver harmonic texture than most of his colleagues would have countenanced, though he avoided Henze's path towards a restoration of tonal kinds of form and behaviour. This is a sophisticated world in which tonal harmonies can be found among many others, and favoured not so much out of nostalgia as for their ease and sensuousness of sound. There seems to be a similar amenability in the material when Berio worked with electronic resources, as in *Perspectives* (1956) and *Momenti* (1957).

Another of his electronic pieces, *Visage* (1961), is again based on Berberian's voice. Following the example of *Gesang der Jünglinge* (but not of his own *Thema*, which had used only vocal sounds), Berio here presents a mélange of the vocal and the purely electronic, with the difference that the voice by no means resists interpretation as a character. She is heard in a natural recording almost throughout, but only at two points does she stumble towards verbal expression, towards verbal expression at an emblematically elementary level (of all words she retains only 'words' itself, in Italian 'parole'). For the rest she laughs, moans, sighs, cries, and gabbles in nonsense language, creating a fluid stream of musical-dramatic suggestions on a private and intimate level to contrast with the public agony of *Passaggio*. Both *Visage* and *Thema* were composed at the RAI electronic studio in Milan, where Berio and Maderna were directors, and where guest composers included Cage in the winter of 1958–59 and Nono in the 1960s. Another work Berio prepared there was *Différences* for quintet and tape (1959), concerned with borderlands not between vocal sense and senselessness but between live instrumental playing and the widened possibilities of the same ensemble subjected to electronic processing. Again the piece is an open work in Eco's sense, though Berio did also achieve one example of the Boulezian open form in *Epifanie*.

This was a collection of seven orchestral pieces, which could be played separately as *Quaderni* ('exercise books'), and five vocal items to texts by various European writers set in their original languages, all twelve sections to be performed in one of several possible sequences. But where for Boulez, in the Third Sonata, mobile form was an acceptance that order had ceased to matter, in *Epifanie* order mattered very much. 'The chosen order', Berio noted, 'will emphasize the apparent heterogeneity of the texts or their dialectical unity', and in his recording he preferred the latter, creating 'a gradual passage from a lyric transfiguration of reality (Proust, Machado, Joyce) to a disenchanted acknowledgement of things (Simon)'[18] and so to Brecht's warning that words should not be allowed to seduce us from deeds. However—and this is why the past tense has been necessary here—his definitive revision of the score, to create *Epiphanies* in 1991–92, set the music in a

18. Note with RCA SB 6850.

fixed succession. There is a striking parallel with Boulez's revision of *Improvisation sur Mallarmé III* to remove variability, and indeed with a general disenchantment with mobile form after the mid-1960s.

But in the late 1950s and early 1960s this was still a hot topic. Alongside the Third Sonata and *Pli selon pli*, two other works were occupying Boulez's attention then: the orchestral piece *Figures-Doubles-Prismes*, which was mobile only in the sense that most of its rare performances found it revised and extended, and the second book of *Structures* for two pianos, which is inherently an open form, begun in 1956, the year after the sonata. It may be that Boulez saw these two major keyboard projects, embarked upon as his period with Barrault's company was coming to an end, as material for recitals, and that their long (in the case of the sonata, indefinite) deferral came about because his performing medium changed during the late 1950s from the piano to the orchestra. He gave the first performance of the sonata at Darmstadt in 1957 (apparently all five formants were represented), and the same year played *Structures* (including some of the second book) with Yvonne Loriod in London and Germany. The new book of *Structures* was finished in 1961—or perhaps abandoned then, since several years passed before it was published, and its flexible plan could accommodate other 'chapters' besides the two provided. Since this book is based on the second division of Messiaen's pitch mode for the *Mode de valeurs*, there remains the possibility of a third book based on the last division.

Boulez's use of the term 'chapters' is another sign of the literary bent of his thinking in the later 1950s; he has also described the second book of *Structures* as 'a fantastic succession, in which the "stories" have no rigid relationship, no fixed order',[19] and Robert Piencikowski has suggested the influence of the *nouveau roman*, especially of the work of Michel Butor, himself influenced by new music and especially by Boulez.[20] In the first chapter mobility remains implicit—implicit in the 'fantastic succession' of fragments, some of which are in strict time and require the exact coordination of the players, others being solo breaks loosened by the flurries of grace notes that permanently entered Boulez's music in this work and the *Improvisations sur Mallarmé*. Usually these solo passages—ranging in length from a short bar to the substantial cadenzas that both pianists have soon after the middle of the chapter, are accompanied or supported by sustained resonance—and the two kinds of sound are linked by shared or overlapping harmonic fields, these fields being built up by the multiplication technique. So music that is newly played, present and visible to the audience, subject to momentary whim or error, falls into line with music that is reverberating,

19. Programme note for the definitive first performance, again by Boulez and Loriod, at the 1962 Donaueschingen Festival.
20. See Piencikowski's note with Sony MK 42619 and Butor's essay 'Mallarmé selon Boulez', *Melos*, 28 (1961), 356ff.

past and invisible, fixed. This is a source of great beauty, of flashing events reflected in still pools; but there is also a hopelessness in the music's inability to break free from the ice trap of what has been: the beauty and the hopelessness are those of the Mallarmé sonnet set in the first *Improvisation*, and they seem to combine in what is both an image and a demonstration of Boulez's predicament. The rushing evolution of the past decade had brought him the means for one masterpiece, *Le Marteau sans maître*, but beyond that he had come again to 'the end of fertile land', where he was condemned to magnificent repetition.

The work's second chapter, fully mobile, has one notional stream of continuity that begins as a glacial succession of chords in both pianos (both with bass strings freed by the sostenuto pedal to reverberate) and opens into arpeggios in the second piano, among and over which the first piano introduces self-contained items, which can be played at different points in accordance with a system of musical cuing, or which may in some cases be omitted. These items, like the fragments of the first chapter, are distinguished by harmony, rhythmic character, and register: the two longest of them, both to be performed as fast as possible, are confined respectively to the extreme treble and the extreme bass, tightening Boulez's toccata manner to a point where energy is turned by the harmonic fixing into whirling rotation, where fury is all manner. For the splendour of its piano writing (vacant though that splendour is becoming), for the reflections it sets up between the pianos, for its stimulating and influential projection of performers as sportsmen and signallers, and for its loneliness as the single work from the two decades between *Le Marteau* and *Rituel* that Boulez completed and left unaltered, the second book of *Structures* is a key work, and perhaps unsurpassed in all Boulez's career since 1955.

Barraqué

In 1956, the year after he had completed *Séquence*, Barraqué was introduced by Michel Foucault to Hermann Broch's novel *The Death of Virgil*, in which he discovered a sympathetic demand for a philosophically aware art, a sympathetic grand reach through whatever fragmentation, and sympathetic material, in the book's dense web of meditations on death, on the act and purposes of creation, and on the inevitability of failure and incompletion. 'All dies, all goes', the composer later wrote. 'Every trustee of creation must accept that, as he accepts his own death. Even on the technical level his art must evolve towards death; it must be completed within "incessant incompletion".'[21] The hungering for evolution, the self-motivated drive to complete what

21. Jean Barraqué, 'Propos impromptu', *Le Courrier musical de France*, 26 (1969), 75–80.

Example 27   Jean Barraqué: . . . *au del du hasard*

could not be completed, did not by any means lead Barraqué to join
any of the revolutionary musical movements of his time: to the contrary, one of the most remarkable features of his art is its consistency.

   La Mort de Virgile was planned as a universe of works in five books,
one for each part of the novel, and a fifth of commentary. Of course,
commentary is inherent all through, in that Barraqué created texts
around quotations from Broch, and in that his whole project was a
commentary on the novel. However, there is a deep difference between *La Mort de Virgile* and such contemporary works of musical commentary and mobility as Boulez's *Pli selon pli*: a difference of voice.
Barraqué's voice, whether in vocal or in instrumental lines, is desper-
ately engaged; this is the voice of a consciousness uttering the words
for itself, not commenting upon them, as may be suggested by example
27, from . . . *au delà du hasard* for four instrumental groups and one of
voices (1958–59). The moment is characteristic of Barraqué in its richly
figured and strongly dynamic polyphony, which is a real polyphony

Example 27 (continued)

of individual but interlaced lines, and not a Boulezian heterophony of
similar parts. Where Boulez's technique of chord multiplication ratio-
nalized static harmony, Barraqué kept to the principle of the twelve-
note sequence, which he made contribute to his music's linear force.
The perpetual circulation of pitch classes is the rule, the force that
drives the wind; reiterations, within and between lines, stand against
the rule, like trees in the wind. There are numerous instances in example 27: both linear repetitions, especially in the vocal part, and network repetitions, emphasized by registral locking (for example, of B and
F♯ in the second and third bars)—another technique that has a static effect in Boulez and a dynamic one in Barraqué.

Possibilities are widened in . . . *au delà du hasard* by the music's layout as a polyphony of polyphonies, an assembly of five groups that
tend to be contrapuntally—as they are timbrally—relatively homogeneous: the first is of brass, saxophones, and vibraphone, the second of
tuned percussion, the third of untuned percussion, the fourth a quartet
of clarinets, the fifth a female chorus with solo soprano. She is the chief

bearer of the music's voice here—as in *Séquence*, and as in the other two parts of *La Mort de Virgile* that were completed: *Le Temps restitué* with chorus and orchestra (1956–68) and *Chant après chant* with piano and percussion ensemble (1965–66)—though there is almost as much a sense of vocal utterance—linear, dynamic, phrased—in Barraqué's instrumental writing. Fluid, but intensely pressured, and maintaining a rhythmic drive despite—or because of—flickerings in the basic pulse, these instrumental voices may contain an echo of modern jazz, which is also suggested by the lineup of . . . *au delà du hasard* in particular, and came from Barraqué's friendship with his supporter André Hodeir.

The grand rhetoric of this work—evident on the small scale in example 27 in, for instance, the setting of 'volonté', the graphic clarinet image at 'chûte', and the emphatic rush throughout—comes to a head in the tenth of the thirteen sections, the one that sets a quotation from Broch: 'Blinded by the dream and made by the dream to see, I know your death, I know the limit which is fixed for you, the limit of the dream, which you deny. Do you know it yourself? Do you want it so?' A long orchestral passage is suddenly cut off, and the music stops for fifteen seconds; there is then an immense orchestral crescendo in two phases, followed by a further fifteen-second silence, before the untuned percussion loudly usher in the sibylline utterance of Broch's words. Such magniloquence, arising from a context of impatient and despairing rapidity, is characteristic of Barraqué, and unique in the period.

All three completed parts of *La Mort de Virgile* use a technique of 'proliferating series', which would seem to have been a pitch-class adaptation of Messiaen's method of rhythmic interversion. Two serial forms are taken, and one is regarded as a permutation of the other; a third form is then obtained by applying the same permutational process to the one. For instance, if the basic series of . . . *au delà du hasard* (C–A♭–G–D♭–E–D–B♭–E♭–B–F–F♯–A) is understood as a permutation of its retrograde inversion (A–C–C♯–G–D♯–G♯–E–D–F–B–A♯–F♯), then repeating the permutation and ignoring enharmonic differences (A goes to C, C goes to A♭/G♯, C♯/D♭ goes to G, etc) will produce a new series that is not related in any classical way to the other two: A♭–D–D♭–G–B♭–E♭–F♯–E–F–B–A–C. By constantly changing the interval sequence within twelve-note successions, the technique eradicated one remnant of stability in classic serialism, and contributed to the sense of perpetual and turbulent self-renewal in much of Barraqué's music. Serial proliferation also ensured that, as he wished, derivations could never be unambiguously unravelled, despite the fact that—as in example 27 and so often in his music—serial forms are clearly presented.[22] 'Analysis', he

22. For further details of Barraqué's serial practice see Bill Hopkins, 'Barraqué and the Serial Idea', *Proceedings of the Royal Musical Association*, 105 (1978–79), 13–24; François Nicolas, 'Le souci du développement chez Barraqué', *Entretemps*, 5 (1987), 7–24; André Riotte, 'Les séries proliférantes selon Barraqué:

wrote, 'must concern itself with the final result: that is, with the work as part of history. . . . The composer's thinking remains his marvellous secret.'[23] And though he was thinking here of Debussy, Debussy was his great model of renovation, just as Beethoven was his great model of development.

Barraqué's proliferating series matched the poetic proliferation inherent in the Broch project, which was to have embraced works on different scales (sketches exist for a piece for eighteen voices *a cappella*; there was also to have been an opera), and which the composer surely cannot have expected to complete. Incompletion was written into the artistic contract; *La Mort de Virgile* was his response not only to Beethoven's dynamism and Debussy's fluidity,[24] but also to the work that had set him on his course as a composer: Schubert's 'Unfinished' Symphony.[25] Each part that he did achieve is a protest against the dissolution and hopelessness inherent in the project: that is one source of the music's energy, to be always fighting itself into existence. It is music of becoming, which Barraqué registers in leaving off double bar lines (his works do not end, but rather fade into an acceptance of silence), in the complexity of his polyphony, in his constant interplay of sound with silence and with noise, and in his impatience with anything stable or achieved.

Exit from the Labyrinth

Mobile form was a neat solution to the problem of how to effect progress and closure in music that had outgrown the supports of tonality and metre. Serial procedures came up with multitudinous alternatives, not chains of succession; mobile form respected that, and also accorded with a new understanding of the work as manifold, a site of actions and reactions rather than an object. It might seem curious, then, that it has to be spoken of in the past tense, for it did fade rapidly from most composers' interests after the early 1960s. Three of its most lavish instances—not only *Pli selon pli* and *Epifanie* but also Stockhausen's *Momente*, which came from the same period—were all revised by their composers with all mobile elements removed. Earle Brown, whose concern with mobiles began earlier, coming through Calder, and who had contributed to the heyday of open form in Europe with such works

---

approche formelle', *Entretemps*, 5 (1987), 65–74; and Andrew Fathers, *Jean Barraqué and L'inachèvement sans cesse* (diss., Oxford, 1993).

23. 'Debussy ou la naissance d'une forme ouverte', quoted in François Nicolas, 'Le souci du développement chez Barraqué', *Entretemps*, 5 (1987), 13.

24. See, besides his book on Debussy, his analysis of *La Mer*, edited by Alain Poirier as 'La Mer de Debussy ou la naissance des formes ouvertes', *Analyse musicale*, 12 (1988), 15–62.

25. See Barraqué, 'Propos impromptu'.

as *Available Forms I* for sixteen-piece ensemble (first performed at Darmstadt in 1961), went on producing scores that may similarly be assembled in many different ways, but in this he went on virtually alone, so
that mobile form became his signature.

Perhaps two reasons may be given for its general demise, of which
the first would be the practical difficulty of rehearsing a large-scale
work with variable elements and the extra attention demanded of a
soloist who must not only navigate the territory but put it together.
Also, mobile form was rapidly understood not as a wide-ranging principle but as a passing fashion. The rhythm of Darmstadt, with composers getting together each summer to compare notes, imposed the expectation that change would come every year—a condition Stockhausen
came near fulfilling with his astonishing inventiveness in the 1950s
and 1960s, but one that Boulez recognized as unsustainable and dangerous. The abandonment of mobile form, circa 1962, was an early sign
of the regression towards the norm that was to overcome music during
the next decade.

8

Elder Responses

One striking measure of the avant-garde's success as a movement is the unprecedented impact composers still in their thirties and forties were having on thoroughly established figures—even the most thoroughly established. Perhaps Stravinsky was a special case: a composer with a constant inquisitiveness and intellectual rapacity. Messiaen, too, was maybe in an unusual position as the man who had had both Boulez and Stockhausen in his classroom, and whose prestige as a teacher brought him into daily contact with young composers. But there were many others whose music grew leaner, less diatonic, more contrapuntal, and often more systematic, including not only Carter and Wolpe but also Luigi Dallapiccola (1904–75), Michael Tippett (1905–98), Giacinto Scelsi (1905–98), Witold Lutosławski (1913–94), Benjamin Britten (1913–76), and Henri Dutilleux (b. 1916). In some cases—Carter's and Scelsi's, for example—the change would seem to have come about independently. Nevertheless, change there certainly was.

Stravinsky

Stravinsky's development was facilitated by Robert Craft, who joined the composer's household as assistant in 1949. Three years later, when Craft was recording the Op.29 Suite of the recently deceased Schoenberg, Stravinsky was there and became fascinated with the work's serial construction—a fascination that fed into his Cantata (1951–52) and Septet (1952–53), the latter an almost explicit response to the

Schoenberg. A few months after those Schoenberg recording sessions, in May-June 1952, Stravinsky was in Paris for the twentieth-century festival and heard Boulez and Messiaen give the first public performance of *Structures Ia*.[1] For the moment this may have provided the right kind of echo, but the more important impulses were coming from Craft—his performances of Webern as well as Schoenberg—and perhaps Carter. Stravinsky's next composition after the Septet was his first with ordered sets, the springtime triptych of Shakespeare songs for female voice with a slightly Webernian trio of flute, clarinet, and viola (1953), after which came his first to use the same set throughout: *In memoriam Dylan Thomas*, a song for tenor and string quartet between 'dirge-canons' for four trombones (1954).

The poet's death had come just as Stravinsky and he were about to embark on an opera, whose subject could not have been more suitable for Stravinsky's music at this point: the piece was to have been about the reinvention of language following a catastrophe, and these first serial songs are beautifully careful essays in the renaming of features that had long been characteristic of Stravinsky—features such as repeated notes (which alone place his serial music at a distance from Schoenberg and Webern, though not from Babbitt), verse-refrain forms, counterpoint in two or three parts, wide-gapped chords and sprung rhythm. Like the songs Stravinsky had written nearly four decades before, during the early years of his Swiss exile, the Shakespeare and Dylan Thomas settings are moving essays in self-education.

Another signal quality of *In memoriam Dylan Thomas* is quite straightforwardly that it is a memorial. Many of Stravinsky's ensuing serial compositions were also to be monuments (*Epitaphium, Introitus, Requiem Canticles*), others sacred commemorations (*Canticum sacrum, Threni*). One of the values of serialism was that it suggested fixity, order, and objectivity—that it offered exactly that canonical rule which 'neoclassicism' had been supposed to provide. So Stravinsky's evolution during the 1950s—though perceived as a defection by those for whom modern music was divided between Stravinsky as neoclassicist and Schoenberg as serialist—was more an arrival than a new departure. The fundamental Stravinsky-Schoenberg dichotomy was between block form and development, pulse and metre, objectivity and subjectivity, and here nothing changed.

Not all Stravinsky's serial compositions were funerary or religious: *Canticum sacrum* (1955), an exercise in twentieth-century Venetian music, was written during an interlude in the composition of the abstract ballet *Agon* (1954–57), whose long gestation helped make it a meeting ground of the explicitly tonal and the explicitly twelve-note,

---

1. See Robert Craft, ed., *Stravinsky: Selected Correspondence*, ii (London, 1984), 349, from the section in which Stravinsky's letters and Craft's notes elucidate the composer's relationship with Boulez.

of the French baroque and of the modern Viennese. And his next work, the solemn, ceremonial *Threni* (1957–58), was followed by a nervy piano concerto, *Movements* (1958–59). Whether by accident or intention, there were severe sacred pieces for Europe (*Threni* too was written for Venice, where Stravinsky spent the late summer each year from 1956 to 1960), and lively instrumental designs for the United States.

However, *Movements* is a European work in being the site of Stravinsky's closest contact with the Darmstadt-centred avant-garde. In November 1956 Boulez, Stockhausen, and Nono had visited him in hospital in Munich, and for a few years thereafter he and Boulez were in regular communication. He was present when Boulez conducted *Le Marteau sans maître* in Los Angeles in March 1957, and when Boulez, Stockhausen, and Rosbaud rehearsed *Gruppen* in Baden-Baden in October 1958; presumably he was also brought into contact with the music of these composers when Craft recorded *Le Marteau* and *Zeitmasze* in the early months of 1958, in which case these encounters might have provided the trigger, since *Movements*, which begins as if with a triggered release, seems to have been begun soon afterwards.

Two strikingly new features of the piece are its polyrhythms and its flickering instrumentation, both illustrated in the closing bars, shown in example 28, and both suggesting how Stravinsky's new-found admiration of Webern[2] was conditioned by his experience of Stockhausen and Boulez. The music ends, as it had begun, with a statement of the basic series, but much of the work is built up from elements derived by nonstandard means: rotating notes within hexachords, overlaying four serial forms to obtain a sequence of four-note sets.[3] These are Stravinsky's own techniques, but the effect of them is like the effect of Boulez's techniques in *Le Marteau* or Stockhausen's in *Kontra-Punkte*: to create a field of action so broad that almost any move (and *Movements* is a sequence of moves as in a game, as well as a chain of five miniature musical movements and a succession of different speeds, different ways of moving) can be justified in terms of the 'system'. What actually happens, then, is likely to be determined by the composer's aims and tastes—by those matters of intention and personality that Cage (and briefly Boulez) had wanted to eradicate. In the particular case of *Movements*, Stravinsky's authorship is evident in many features: the remaining weight of strong beats in barring that is much more than a notational convenience; in parallel with that, the remaining weight of intervals and chords from the vocabularies of his earlier works (the chord heavily affirmed in the 9/16 bar is surely not an arbitrary choice); the role of the piano as more obbligato than solo; the light counterpoint;

2. See the interview with him printed as an introduction to Hans Moldenhauer and Demar Irvine, eds., *Anton von Webern: Perspectives* (Seattle, 1966).

3. See Stephen Walsh, *The Music of Stravinsky* (London, 1988), 246–54, and Claudio Spies, 'Impressions after an Exhibition', *Tempo*, 102 (1972), 2–9.

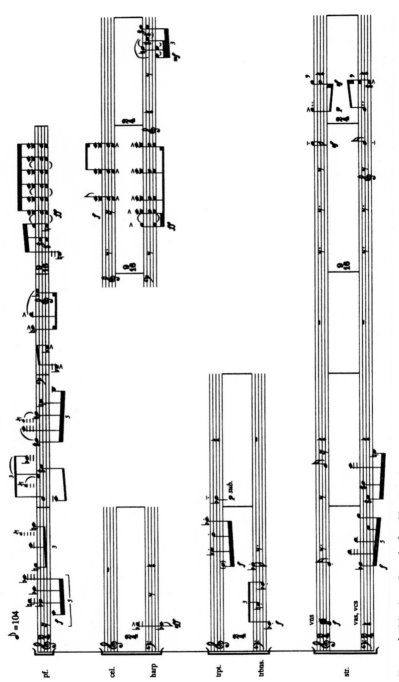

Example 28 Igor Stravinsky, *Movements*

130

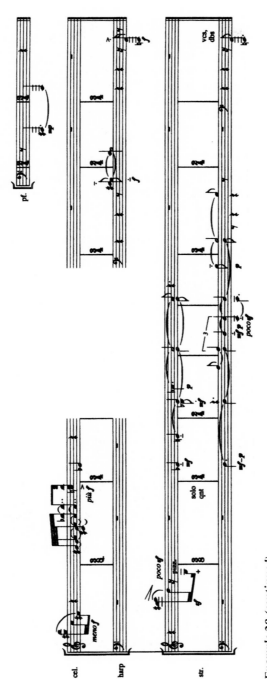

Example 28 (continued)

the deployment of the orchestra as a nesting set of ensembles; the projection of music as abstract drama (a drama whose most spectacular event in example 28 is how the piano disappears, only to reappear, like Petrushka, in ghost form, as the celesta, unheard since near the work's beginning). What is equally typical of Stravinsky is that new circumstances should have produced a new composer.

Messiaen

Messiaen's direct participation in his juniors' enterprises was brief—limited in the case of electronic music to *Timbres-durées* and of total organization to the archetype, *Mode de valeurs et d'intensités*, as well as to elements in some of the piano and organ pieces that immediately followed. By 1951 the phase was over, and in that year he made a first step into a new world, of music made from birdsong: this modest but crucial reinitiation was *Le Merle noir* for flute and piano, which was followed by *Réveil des oiseaux* for piano and orchestra (1953), *Oiseaux exotiques* for piano, wind and percussion (1955–56), and the *Catalogue d'oiseaux* (1956–58), consisting of thirteen piano pieces with a total duration of over two hours.

The departure was not entirely new: there are birdsong imitations in earlier works, including notably the *Quatuor pour la fin du temps* and *Turangalîla*. But making birdsong the sole substance of a work certainly was new. *Réveil* has no other material than that which Messiaen himself collected in the field, and though both *Oiseaux exotiques* and the *Catalogue* admit other kinds of music, birdsong is still the overwhelming source, and everything else has to be justified either as armature (the percussion engineering with Greek and Indian rhythmic patterns that underlies large sections of *Oiseaux exotiques*) or else as descriptive context (the occasional passages in the *Catalogue* where a sway of chords is introduced to convey, in Messiaen's usual synaesthetic manner, the colour of plumage or landscape). The reasons for this recourse to nature surely included those he gave himself: that he took great joy in the songs of birds, that he saw their music as a cornucopia of divine creation, that he understood them—being winged, aerial, and beautiful—as earthly harbingers of the angels. 'I do not believe one can find in any human music, however inspired, melodies and rhythms which have the sovereign liberty of birdsong.'[4] But none of this quite explains the sudden conversion of 1951, which may have been a reaction to the implication of the *Mode de valeurs*, the implication that composition required the separate ordaining of each note. Under such conditions, human melodists would have to fall mute, leaving only the birds singing.

4. Antoine Goléa, *Rencontres avec Olivier Messiaen* (Paris, 1960), 234.

In the case of *Réveil*, nature provides not only the material but also the form. According to the score's preface, the music replays birdsongs heard in springtime between midnight and noon, though it does so through time that is doubly bent: accelerated fortyfold in order to compress nature's half-day into twenty minutes in the concert hall, and simultaneously decelerated so that rapid songs can be brought down, in both tempo and tuning, to a human scale of hearing. Messiaen explained how his transcriptions of birdsongs—nearly always based on field observation—had to be slowed, reduced in pitch, and expanded uniformly in interval size for the necessities of human performers and listeners, and he likened his procedures to those of composers of musique concrète.[5] Calls that seem by nature already adapted to human time he tended to avoid: the cuckoo and the turtledove, for instance, never appeared again in his music after their débuts in *Réveil*. The songs he preferred were the florid roulades of warblers, thrushes, and larks, and the strident cries found more often among tropical than temperate species—preferences that may have been prompted by the greater challenge these songs presented to the composer as listener and reinterpreter, having to register long melodies in the one case and complex timbres in the other. After all, if he had wanted simply to make use of birdsongs as musical material, he could have done so in the musique concrète studio: the point was to exercise his own artistry, in company with the birds, to celebrate with them, and to do so, as they did, extrapersonally, to achieve a creaturely innocence in the rendering of nature. The art of composition became the art of imitation, of copying nature not from a consistent viewpoint, in the manner of a landscape painter or the composer of a symphonic poem, but item by item, piece by piece: not a Sibelian scene with cranes but a *Catalogue d'oiseaux*.

Réveil des oiseaux, the first of Messiaen's major birdsong pieces, is an extinction of creative personality as complete as its great contemporary *4' 33"*, and as incomplete. In principle, material and form are given; however, fingerprints mark the choice of found material and its handling. Silence was already Cage's signature, and performed silence still more so. Messiaen, in choosing birdsongs from among all the sounds of nature, chose in accordance with the history of his own music, which was in part a history of quasi-neumatic repetitions of rhythmic-melodic formulae in music of toccata-style speed and insistence; at the same time, he revealed his authorship in the way he treated birdsongs. Several of the songs in *Réveil des oiseaux* conform to the same setting of one of his most characteristic modes, the 'second mode of limited transpositions': C–D♭–E♭–E–G♭–G–A–B♭–C, this being one of the mode's three possible transpositions, underlying the melodies ascribed to quite different

5. See Claude Samuel, *Olivier Messiaen: Music and Color* (Portland, Oreg. 1994), 95.

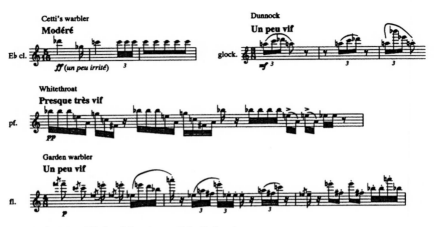

Example 29   Olivier Messiaen, *Réveil des oiseaux*

species, as shown in example 29. And though in later works his bird-song transcriptions became modally more complex and often more fastidiously defined and decorated, links to his particular harmonic world would remain; besides which, by the end of the 1950s he had effectively defined instrumental birdsong imitation (just as Cage had defined silence) as his realm. But this was by inadvertence. The essential was the effort, which he shared with Cage and in some respects with Boulez, to make art objectively, even if it would be impossible to make art objective. By endeavouring to reflect back, perfectly, the perfection of creation, Messiaen's birdsong pieces of 1951–60 (including the orchestral *Chronochromie*) participate in his spiritual project, even though this period was unique in his output for its lack of explicitly religious subject matter.

The birdsong pieces also belong with the rest of Messiaen by virtue of their objectivity of pattern and form: their adherence not to the experiential time of smooth onward flow but to a nonhuman time of cyclic repetition, abrupt change, and potentially endless continuity—not one arrow but many arrows. If repetition and alternation (of pitch, of rhythmic value, of motif) are important in the birdsong detail of *Réveil des oiseaux*, its larger plan is also one of oscillation, since Messiaen interprets the midnight-to-midday span as a sequence of solos for the piano (nightingales at midnight, a blackcap after sunrise, later a blackbird, and a medley at midday) interspersed with choruses for piano and orchestra. After the work's first performance—at the 1953 Donaueschingen Festival, signifying Messiaen's abiding status as a senior member of the avant-garde—there was a silence of very nearly two years before the beginning of *Oiseaux exotiques*, perhaps because *Réveil* appeared to its composer a solution that left no possibility of development. He found that possibility by releasing the solo-chorus antiphony from its descriptive intentions, providing it in part with underlays of rhythmic mosaic formed from the ancient Greek and Indian figures that had long featured in his music, removing the strings from his orchestra, and extending his ornithological frontiers to include, as the title intimates, birds from many different countries. *Réveil* had perhaps been too simpleminded an attempt to copy nature; *Oiseaux exotiques* exults in the possibility of attaining objective form by other means—by the reiteration and accumulation of musical objects—and of releasing the bounds of verisimilitude in the dynamic scale and the conjoining of species. Birds from India, the Far East, the Canaries, and North America sing together, and sing loudly. The work also makes more assertive use of signal cries, especially the jubilant E-major-ish calls of the Indian shama that clamour for the music to close.

The *Catalogue d'oiseaux* ostensibly returns to the naturalist intentions of portraying birds—all French birds—in their habitats, but there are the same structures of alternation and palindrome, along with further infiltrations of nonbirdsong material. Usually this material is justified as illustrative, but the mechanisms of illustration are codes peculiar to Messiaen, the most important being his equivalences of colour and harmony. For example, E major seems to represent the blazing gold of the oriole and of summer sunlight in 'Le Loriot', just as it worked similarly in *Oiseaux exotiques*, and A major conveys the blue of the sea and of the bird's plumage in 'Le Merle bleu'. Black, absence of light, has no chord to represent it, since chords in Messiaen's vocabulary are instances of resonance, and resonance is the sounding image of light. The dark of night in 'La Chouette hulotte' ('The tawny owl') is introduced rather as a three-part counterpoint in a mode of pitches, durations, and intensities, so that what had been, just a few years earlier, the whole thrust of Messiaen's endeavour—towards a music of abstract speculation—is now the antithesis, the contrary to his music of reimagined nature and of colour.

Abstraction—especially the abstraction of musical arithmetic effected by rhythmic cells or chromatic durations—can alternatively be a frame for birdsongs, as it was in *Oiseaux exotiques* and 'Soixante-quatre Durées' from the *Livre d'orgue*, and as it is in several of the *Catalogue d'oiseaux* pieces and in *Chronochromie* (1959–60). Though this last work is a final climax to the birdsong period, Messiaen's title, backed by his pronouncements,[6] insists on it as an exercise in colouring time, in marking out segments by percussion attacks and identifying them with the colours of string chords (the combination of resonance with continuous tone may reflect an awareness of Stockhausen's efforts at timbre synthesis). This is what happens in the two 'strophes' of the score, in each of which interversions of a sequence of thirty-two durations are laid out under birdsongs. More birdsongs—those of two Messiaen

6. See ibid., 135–36.

favourites, skylark and song thrush—alternate in the corresponding 'antistrophes', and the ensuing 'epode' is a tangle of eighteen birdsong lines for solo strings. The strophe-antistrophe-epode triad follows the form of Greek choral odes, a model Messiaen had previously used in 'Le Chocard des alpes' from the bird catalogue; in *Chronochromie* not only are the strophe and antistrophe doubled (repeated with variation) but the whole assembly is placed between an introduction and a coda, which again are doubles of each other. And these outer sections add more, nonavian elements to the composer's imitation of nature: *fortissimo* chromatic chords hurled in rapid interchange from different orchestral sectors to represent rocks, and a 'torrent' passage in which, according to a note in the score, 'the tumbling sound of the water is rendered principally by the violas and cellos' and the trills of violins and basses are 'vapour and confusion'. Following one of Messiaen's preferences among the works of nature, *Chronochromie* is a mountain walk of music, where birds from Japan, Sweden, and France can all be heard, and time is parcelled out in moments of harmony. 'For me', Messiaen said, 'the only real music has always existed in the sounds of nature. . . . The harmony of wind in trees, the rhythm of waves on the sea, the timbre of raindrops, of breaking branches, of stones struck together, the different cries of animals are the true music as far as I am concerned.' Cage might have said the same, except that his interpretation of 'nature' would have included the human and the industrial, and that his aim was to imitate not nature's sounds but nature's selflessness. These are differences on which one might ponder in comparing another pair of near-coincident scores, *Chronochromie* and *Atlas eclipticalis*.

The first performance of *Chronochromie*—again at the Donaueschingen Festival, in 1960—was again succeeded by a hiatus in Messiaen's composing. Then came another septenary, the *Sept Haïkaï* for piano and small orchestra (1962), stimulated by his first visit to Japan, and including, besides two birdsong movements in the alternating solo-chorus manner of *Oiseaux exotiques*, one of his rare attempts at a similar sketch of human music: 'Gagaku', in which a piece from the repertory of the imperial court ensemble is transcribed as if it were a birdsong or the rush of a mountain stream—alien sound whose imitation would divert the composer's art along the objective pathways of record (the melody for the shawmlike hichiriki is taken by a trumpet with oboes and cor anglais in unison, while eight violins reproduce the accompanying chords of the shō, a mouth organ). Large parts of the *Sept Haïkaï* are again hung on frames of rhythmic patterning measured out by percussion: an Indian scheme in the introduction and coda, interversions of thirty-two chromatic durations once more in 'Gagaku' and in 'The Park at Nara and the Stone Lanterns' (the first of two movements compacting elements from Japanese landscapes), Greek metres elsewhere. What is unusual for Messiaen in the arithmetic of this work is the pres-

Example 30   Olivier Messiaen, *Sept Haïkaï*

ence of so much irregular rhythm, suggesting that, like Stravinsky, he
was impressed by the recent work of Stockhausen. Example 30, from
'The Park at Nara', illustrates this, and illustrates too how the music is
often composed of several independent temporal layers. Such com-
pound textures recur in Messiaen's music from the 'Crystal Liturgy' of
the *Quatuor pour la fin du temps* onwards, and they help, as in so much
music of this period, to split the viewpoint—to provide, in this instance,
an impression of things heard and seen (the piano and the prominent
marimba, however much the latter recalls Messiaen's 'style oiseau',
might suggest the stone lanterns, the chromatic clarinets the envelop-
ing darkness) with no person in the picture hearing and seeing them.
What they create—overlapping flows differing in speed and direction—
is open form more completely than may be found in most of the period's
mobiles.

Contact with Japan might have reinforced—if that had been possible—Messiaen's taste for simultaneous alterities, for the eternities of
slow motion and repetition, for a long view of tradition. In his interviews with Claude Samuel, he speaks of Japan almost as if it were
paradise: 'It's a country where everything is noble: in the streets in

Japan, one sees no drunks, no beggars. . . . [What struck me] was also the beauty of the men and women—their marvellous black hair, which remains black as ebony to the ends of their lives. . . . Nara . . . has several temples and, in the parks surrounding them, immense thousand-year-old trees. . . . In these parks, does, stags, and fawns roam freely and approach visitors with no apprehension.'[7] In Europe, in the resolutely positivist Europe of the 1950s, he might easily have felt himself out of place and out of time: that would have been another reason for his recourse to given musical material, and for the unusual gaps in his output. Japan showed him that he was not, after all, alone (though that lesson was now coming from Europe and North America, too, with the increasing appreciation of his music from the early 1960s onwards). Japan was a new home, and an old one: a place that had experienced no Renaissance to uproot its art from sacredness, and yet a place that was fully attuned to new ways of thinking and working. Japan—it would have the same effect for Stockhausen a little later—restored him.

His next work after the *Sept Haïkaï* was based on a similar ensemble of piano, clarinets, and tuned percussion, but with orchestral brass instead of the eight violins: *Couleurs de la Cité Céleste* (1963). There are similarly constancies and changes in the musical material: still present are the birdsongs, the chords of colour, the chromatic durations, and the Indian and Greek rhythmic patterns; gone are the irregular rhythms; newly arrived (or restored) are the plainsong quotations and the breadth of form, the work playing continuously for over a quarter of an hour. Also new, or returning, is the exalted subject, which is that of several earlier and later works: the life of the resurrected, especially as revealed in the last book of the New Testament. The 'colours of the Heavenly City' are those of the precious stones that St. John describes as forming the foundations of the New Jerusalem, and that Messiaen interprets as harmonies similarly anchoring his work, whether they are presented resplendent as chords or used to enhance the chants and birdsongs: sardonyx, chrysoprase, emerald, sapphire, amethyst, and the rest. At the same time, the colours of the work are its fragments, studded together like the pieces of coloured glass in the windows of Chartres or the Sainte Chapelle—to suggest an analogy that his own admiration for those windows makes inescapable. In that respect, the illustrations of the subject—the harmonic gemstones, the alleluias of the heavenly host, the 'star that holds the key to the abyss' (a musical pictogram of piano appeal, lightning stroke and *fortissimo* strokes of low gongs and tam tams)—dissolve into the swirl of lit sound. Messiaen's participation in the avant-garde, as teacher and taught, had vastly widened his scope during the fifteen years since the *Turangalîla* symphony, and made it possible for him to move from that work's powerful harmonic surges

7. Ibid, 99–100.

and rhythmic pulsations into the fractured time of *Couleurs de la Cité Céleste*—a structure appealing at once to the verse-refrain forms and antiphonies of the Middle Ages and to modern predilections for sudden shift and ceaseless change.

Varèse

In several ways Varèse was Messiaen's dialectical opposite: American rather than European (though both were born in France), secular rather than sacred, urban rather than rural, spasmodic in creativity rather than continuous, solitary rather than being revered by hundreds of pupils and devoted performers. But the similarities outweigh. Both were impressed by ancient cultures. Both produced some of their best work for ensembles of wind and percussion. Both took from Stravinsky the principle of construction in disjunct blocks. Both were attracted by the ondes martenot, and both used ideas from electronic music (reversal through time, change of speed and register, sound synthesis) in works for instruments. Both—to pick up a tiny point of what seems to have been convergent evolution rather than borrowing—used an ensemble of violins to imitate the Japanese shō (the Varèse piece was his unfinished *Nocturnal*). Both, finally, enjoyed a creative renewal around 1950.

In Varèse's case it is hard to know how much this depended on the rising generation. As a member of the 1950 Darmstadt faculty he would have encountered Nono, but he seems to have had no meeting with Boulez until 1952, in New York,[8] or with Stockhausen until December 1954, in Paris, when *Déserts* was given its first performance with Boulez introducing the piece and Stockhausen controlling the tape relay[9]— a prime moment in the history of the avant-garde. Besides, he had started *Déserts*—the key work in his regeneration: his first new achievement since 1936[10]—before the summer of 1950. He may have known of Cage's work before this, but the overwhelming stimulus for *Déserts* came from the access to a tape recorder he gained in 1952.

The plan of *Déserts*, unprecedented, was that electronic and orchestral music be brought face to face: three sequences of 'organized sound' on tape are interpolated into a composition for an orchestra of wind, piano, and percussion. Babbitt has drawn attention to the subtlety with which Varèse assembles timbres from his ensemble,[11] and indeed much of the scoring suggests an almost Webernian care for timbre-melody—

8. See Fernand Ouellette, *Edgard Varèse* (London, 1973), 177–78.

9. See Michael Kurtz, *Stockhausen: A Biography* (London, 1992), 76.

10. Discounting the unpublished *Etude pour 'Espace'*, which had no performance after its 1947 première until 2009, and the tiny 1949 dance score for Burgess Meredith.

11. See 'Edgard Varèse: a Few Observations of his Music', *Perspectives of New Music*, 5/1 (1966), 93–111.

something quite new in Varèse's music, the instruments being used, for example, to vary the colours of the sustained pitches that are stations of polarity in the musical progress.[12] The correlative qualities of moderate speed and passivity provide a striking contrast with most of Varèse's earlier music, whose assertive gestures, repeated here, now fail to initiate movement. Their forcelessness may be understood in the light of his intention to refer to deserts of all kinds: 'All those that people traverse or may traverse: *physical* deserts, on the earth, in the sea, in the sky, of sand, of snow, of interstellar spaces or of great cities, but also those of the human *spirit*, of that distant *inner* space no telescope can reach, where one is alone.'[13] (And here is another contrast with Messiaen, the world of nature for Varèse being silent and alien, typified by the desert, whereas Messiaen at the same time was rehearing the forests in *Réveil des oiseaux*.)

Varèse's further intention for *Déserts* was that it should be experienced in company with a film, one that would have to be 'in opposition with the score. Only through opposition can one avoid paraphrase. . . . There will be no action. There will be no story. There will be images. Phenomena of light, purely. . . . Successions, oppositions of visual planes, as there are successions and oppositions of sound planes.'[14] Varèse's horror of 'paraphrase' between sight and sound was typical of the time: it was shared by Cage and Cunningham in their collaborations, and reflected in the seeming desuetude of opera. Post-1945 modernism was distinguished by separation—the separation of notes, the separation of rhythm from pitch contour, the separation of vision from sound—since only through separation, so it was thought, could phenomena be defined and structured.

However, Varèse's dream of a grand simultaneity had its realization in the superior *son et lumière* show that took place at the 1958 Brussels Exposition, in a futuristic pavilion designed for the Philips company by Le Corbusier (with the help of his assistant Xenakis). Varèse's contribution to this was his *Poème électronique* (1956–57), which stands with *Gesang der Jünglinge* among early electronic masterpieces. By contrast with the tape inserts for *Déserts*, the *Poème* is strongly defined, exuberant, and rich. It includes electronically generated melodies, wedges of distorted organ sound (a potent image that also occurs in the *Déserts* interpolations), industrial noises, and fragments from the recording of the composer's *Etude pour 'Espace'*. The drive that presses through material so diverse and so expressively resonant is irresistible; in its origi-

12. See Arnold Whittall, 'Varèse and Organic Athematicism', *Music Review*, 28 (1967), 311–15.

13. Quoted in Georges Charbonnier, *Entretiens avec Edgard Varèse* (Paris, 1970), 156.

14. Ibid., 66.

nal location, relayed through numerous loudspeakers and experienced with projections, it must have been astonishing.

For Varèse, who had been looking forward to electronic music since the First World War, it was the appropriate culmination. Between 1954 and 1958, he had spent a good deal of time in Europe, working on his two major electronic works in Paris and Bilthoven, and perhaps not resisting the role of father figure thrust on him by Boulez and Stockhausen. He then returned to New York, put away his tape machine, and spent his last years on various projects connected with themes of night and death, of which *Nocturnal* was completed by his pupil Chou Wen-chung.

Symphonists and Others

Where Varèse, like Stravinsky, stood in a paternal, even grandpaternal relationship to the post-1945 avant-garde, Dutilleux and Lutosławski were those composers' seniors by only a decade. Still, having begun as artists before the war, they represented an earlier generation; they were also more attached to older ways of doing things. This was not necessarily a matter of cause and effect, for Henze was showing a similar kind of temperament in preferring customary genres—opera (e.g., *Elegy for Young Lovers*, 1959–61), symphony (No. 5, 1962)—in which to unfold music that sought no severance from the prewar music of Berg and Stravinsky, and even from the lyric Romanticism of Schumann and Mahler. In Lutosławski's case, there was also the common lingering concern in Eastern Europe for matters of affect and continuity, a concern of which socialist realism may have been more symptom than motive. Attitudes could differ in other respects. Henze, after his departure from Germany for Italy in 1953, seems to have had little contact with or interest in his erstwhile Darmstadt coevals, whereas both Dutilleux and Lutosławski listened carefully to the fragmentation engineered by their younger colleagues and proceeded to symphonize it, Dutilleux in his *Métaboles* (1962–65), Lutosławski in his Second Symphony (1965–67).

Lutosławski's first engagement with the avant-garde had come earlier, in his *Jeux vénitiens* for chamber orchestra (1960–61), which must be one of the most discreet essays ever in adjusting to Cage. But then, the prompt was discreet, too: no more than 'a short fragment' of the *Concert for Piano and Orchestra* heard over the radio, according to the composer's own account.[15] This, however, was enough, suggesting the possibility of freeing the coordination of instrumental (or vocal) parts from time to time, a technique Lutosławski used in many subsequent

15. See Zbigniew Skowron, ed., *Lutosławski on Music* (Lanham, Md., 2007), 99.

works, including his Second Symphony. The effect he valued was rhythmic and textural: 'The rhythms that result from the introduction of the element of chance are very sophisticated and it is impossible to achieve them in any other way. . . . The most complex textures and rhythms are achieved by the performers with no effort.' Yet he retained what was most important to the symphonic character of his music: 'full control of the pitch organization, particularly over its harmony'.

Wolpe was another who took account of the avant-garde and certainly kept 'full control of the pitch organization', but within an environment much more hospitable to innovation. In the late 1950s and early 1960s he went regularly to Darmstadt, to learn as well as to teach, which again brought a change in his music: a greater abstraction (though he would accept, as he had in the Black Mountain works, his music's development towards the world of some other composer or style), sometimes a greater density, and an effort to organize aspects of tempo, rhythm, and instrumentation in parallel with his ways of using pitch cells. But what remained, as forcible as ever, was the push of musical implication in the motifs of which his music was made. Carter was similarly observant of his junior contemporaries, if from a greater distance, and may have felt emboldened thereby in pursuing greater complexity in his Second Quartet (1959) and spectacular Double Concerto (1961), scored for piano and harpsichord, each with its own ensemble.

The most radical members of this generation were as yet unsung. Nancarrow and Partch remained away by themselves, probably not aware of much music but their own, which was still all but unknown. Another isolated figure was Scelsi, who apparently travelled through India and Nepal, and suffered some kind of mental breakdown before re-establishing himself as a composer in Rome in the early 1950s. Concentration and singleness became his purposes. At first his music was essentially monodic and modal, often with an Indian flavour. This occasionally resurfaced in the melodic protraction and decoration of his later pieces, though from the late 1950s onwards his music became much more thoroughly itself, investigating sound as if from within. Whole movements would be based on a very slow drift through the pitch spectrum, or on an antagonism between two notes, or even on just a single note, as in the two works that opened this mature period: the String Trio (1958) and the *Quattro pezzi* for chamber orchestra (1959). With pitch held static, or almost so, there was the opportunity to work with microtonal fluctuations and with timbre, and Scelsi's writing in particular for string instruments—or that of his amanuensis, Vieri Tosatti, who transcribed his taped improvistions—became intensively exploratory.

Example 31 shows a passage from his Fourth Quartet (1964), a work which traces a single slow curve throughout its ten-minute dura-

Example 31   Giacinto Scelsi, String Quartet No. 4

tion. At this point, the glide up from the opening C is reaching A♭ (typically blurred by quarter-tone dissonances, with G half-sharp and A
half-flat) and then, briefly, A. Separate notation for the four strings of
each instrument helps create a fabric that is continuously in change
but also continuously the same. His own term, the 'sphericity' of
sound, aptly describes the effect, which is of an invisible object turning
to reveal new parts of itself—especially new harmonics, which may be
actually played or else sounded as a result of strained performing techniques (including the use of special mutes in such works as the Second
Quartet and *Khoom*, dating from 1961 and 1962 respectively), as if
from a fundamental that remains in place or slowly shifts. A true bass
in his music is rare: the cello's third string is seldom used in this quartet, its fourth never. The octaves and estranged octaves (estranged by
dissonant inflection, as in gagaku and other Asian traditions with
which the composer could have been familiar), here on three registral
levels, relate to an imaginary hum. Something close to motionlessness
is combined with fizzing activity in the trills and tremolandos that
Scelsi characteristically uses to make his glissandos as imperceptible as
may be.

String instruments, allowing fine tuning of pitch and adjustment of timbre, suited him well, and he wrote much for them. But he also favoured low brass for their weight of sound, and again for their adaptability, through the use of mutes, while the voice, generally wordless, could powerfully transmit the incantatory character of his music, whether in unaccompanied vocalises (*Wo-Ma* for bass, 1960, the *Canti del Capricorno* for soprano, 1962–72) or in abstract narratives of solitary tragedy (*Khoom* for soprano, string quartet, horn, and percussion) and corporate upheaval (*Uaxactum* for chorus and orchestra, 1966). Just as his music seems to be at once very slow and very fast, so its microtonal dissonances can be felt as simultaneously ferocious and calm, in dispute and (because found on the same sphere of sound) in accord.

9

Reappraisal and Disintegration: 1959–64

Questioning Voices: Ligeti, Bussotti, Kagel

There is something emblematic in Boulez's recourse to the personal in the works he began during the second half of the 1950s: to the solo voice, even to song (the cantabile of the *Improvisations sur Mallarmé* has no precedent in *Le Marteau sans maître*), to music for himself to perform (*Le Marteau* dates from before the beginning of his concert-hall career; *Pli selon pli* and *Figures-Doubles-Prismes* developed in parallel with that career, and became repositories for practical discoveries in terms both of the orchestra and of his own performing skills as the pianist of the Third Sonata and *Structures* grew into the international conductor), to a personal world of brilliantly figured, static sound. The idea of the work as a model embodiment of new musical thinking—the idea behind the first book of *Structures*, *Le Marteau*, and everything Stockhausen had written from *Kreuzspiel* onwards, an idea that belonged with the Darmstadt notion of the composer as his juniors' exemplar—was perhaps harder for him to sustain as it became clear that there was no such thing as 'the avant-garde', that the years of mutual interests were passing, and that composers were going their own ways. Ironically, Nono coined the term 'Darmstadt School'[1] just at the point, in 1958, when solidarity was breaking down.

1. In his lecture, 'Die Entwicklung der Reihentechnik', published in his *Texte* (Zurich, 1975), 30.

Xenakis's earlier criticism had come from outside the central group, and so perhaps could be brushed off, but in 1960 Ligeti made some of the same points within the pages of *Die Reihe*,[2] citing examples from Boulez, Stockhausen, and others to show how serial principles had either proved self-defeating or been replaced by 'higher order' principles, such as those governing the temporal structure of *Gruppen*. Out of this analysis he derived the notion of 'permeability' in music: a musical structure is said to be 'permeable' if it allows a free choice of intervals and 'impermeable' if not (he gives the example of Palestrina's music—a symptomatic choice for a contrapuntalist—as being strictly defined by harmonic rules and hence 'impermeable' to an unusual degree). But permeability and impermeability could also be features of texture, rather than harmony, as was the case in contemporary music. Using the example again of *Gruppen*, he noted how 'a dense, gelatinous, soft and sensitive material can be penetrated *ad libitum* by sharp, hacked splinters. . . . "Soft" materials are less permeable when combined with each other, and there are places of an opaque complexity beyond compare'—beyond compare, that is, in late 1958, when Ligeti wrote the article. By the next year, he had completed his orchestral piece *Apparitions*, whose first performance, at the 1960 festival of the International Society for Contemporary Music, caused so much stir among composers as to indicate that something significant was taking place: a challenge to the orthodoxy of complexity.

Until this point Ligeti had been known in the West as an associate of Stockhausen's at the Cologne electronic studio and as the painstaking analyst of *Structures Ia*: a composer, therefore, firmly at the centre of advanced music. Perhaps what bothered his colleagues about *Apparitions* was not so much the resort to orchestral clusters and the reduction of music to shifting or contrasted types of sound as the rationale provided by his essay: Stockhausen in *Carré* (1959–60) had arrived at a similar handling of the orchestra (if without the dramatized weirdness and comedy), and 'texture music' was in vogue—as witness the works that suddenly established Krzysztof Penderecki (b. 1933), such as his *Threnody—to the Victims of Hiroshima* for string orchestra (1960), in which Xenakisian cluster glissandos are given a searing affect. But for a composer of the Darmstadt-Cologne axis to wonder about the musical disciplines of the last several years was troubling.

Ligeti went on to develop his cluster technique more thoroughly and masterfully in his *Atmosphères* for orchestra (1961) and *Volumina* for organ (1961–62), in which there is no longer any attempt to deal with units of pitch, duration, loudness, and timbre in a serial manner, or indeed any other. Ligeti's conclusion was that musical atoms could

---

2. György Ligeti, 'Metamorphoses of Musical Form', *Die Reihe*, 7 (1960, English ed. 1965), 5–19.

not, or could not yet, be composed into meaningful structures, by which he presumably meant that the kind of compositional method he had revealed in *Structures Ia* was not intelligible in performance. What he left out of account was the possibility of meaning introduced subsidiarily, whether by the composer (as one would guess to be the case with the quasi-motifs at the start of *Le Marteau*), by the performer (who might—perhaps must—present a particular view even of such recalcitrant material as that of *Structures Ia*), or by the listener (whose ways are the most difficult to determine). The sound of these massive exemptions is there in the music, in the suppression of differentiations that *Atmosphères* solemnly accomplishes. Rhythmic movement is eliminated by staggering instrumental entries (a technique for which Ligeti introduced the term 'micropolyphony'), emphasizing sustained sounds (the work, unusually for this period, is for an orchestra without percussion) and avoiding all sense of pulse; harmony is held in suspension by the use of clusters. All these effects of continuity provoke an experience of sound as texture—the sort of experience that Ligeti had indicated in his 1960 essay (in the terms of that essay, the textures of *Atmosphères* are peculiarly permeable). Along a different route he had arrived at the position of Boulez in *Structures Ia* or Cage in the *Music of Changes*: he had reacted to the immediate past by effacing it, clearing the ground for his later works to make a progressive rediscovery of modes of particularization which might be, in his terms, comprehensible.

The beauty of *Atmosphères* must depend on the fastidiousness of its scoring, but when writing for a soloist, in *Volumina*, Ligeti could achieve similar effects by simply blocking in areas of the keyboard graphically. Here again he was marching with others. At Darmstadt in 1959, the year following Cage's visit, it had become clear that introducing chance into composition would have much more far-reaching consequences than those allowed in the mobile forms of Stockhausen and Boulez that had been heard for the first time there two years before. A course in 'music and graphics' included performances of Cage's *Concert*, and of European pieces that had been stimulated by Cage's innovations in notation and Tudor's style of playing, among them Kagel's *Transición II* for pianist, percussionist, and tapes (1958–59), *Five Piano Pieces for David Tudor* (1959) by Sylvano Bussotti (b. 1931), and Stockhausen's *Zyklus* for percussionist (1959). There was also a lecture by Stockhausen[3] in which he spoke of a 'music for reading' made conceivable by the 'emancipation of the graphic from the acoustic element', a feature he detected in the scores of Cage and Bussotti. As if to demonstrate that emancipation, Cage had already the previous year given an exhibition of his scores as pictures, when the art critic of the *New York Times* had

3. Karlheinz Stockhausen, 'Musik und Graphik', *Texte*, i (Cologne, 1963), 176–88.

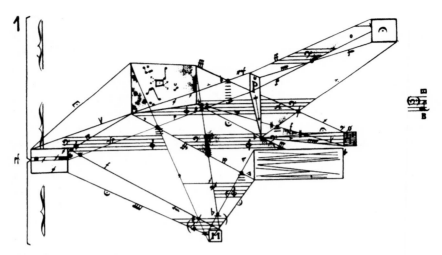

Example 32   Sylvano Bussotti, *Per tre sul piano*

found in them 'a delicate sense of design . . . that transcends the purely technical matter of setting down music'.[4]

But of course that was not Cage's intention. Nothing was Cage's intention. Whether the pages of his *Concert* look beautiful (as one may easily agree they do)—whether the work sounds beautiful—has to do with the observer: like a flower or a cloudscape, such a piece does not strive for beauty. And the new kinds of notation—far more various than one illustration (example 24) can indicate—arose directly from new kinds of compositional method. It was different with Bussotti. Example 32, from his *Per tre sul piano* (one of his *Sette fogli* of 1959), may work as 'music for reading', but the aim is surely much more to excite the performers' imaginations. Cage was concerned with action, Bussotti with feeling. In this particular case the piano becomes, in Richard Toop's words, 'a prone body, alternately caressed, cajoled and assaulted by its suitors'.[5] (The eroticism was to remain characteristic of Bussotti's work, representing a self-consciously excessive satisfaction of what bourgeois culture desires of artists, so that decadence turns into social criticism.) In a prefatory note to the published edition of *Sette fogli* (a collection surely prompted by Earle Brown's *Folio* of 1954, within which *December 1952* came to be included) the composer remarks that he had

4. Dore Ashton, 'Cage, Composer, Shows Calligraphy of Note' [the paper's headline style has not changed], *New York Times* (May 6, 1958), repr. in Richard Kostelanetz, ed., *John Cage* (New York, 1970, 1991; London, 1971), 126.
5. Note with EMI EMSP 551.

originally planned an explanatory apparatus, such as many scores carried during this period of rapid notational change, but that the works had established their own performing tradition during the decade that passed between composition and publication.

(To the extent that this performing tradition has been interrupted, Bussotti's music will go on surviving only in the form of recordings: it is, as much as Stockhausen's *Studien*, a set of fixed electronic objects. But it is not alone in this regard. Remarkably few works by young European composers of the 1950s and early 1960s continue in regular performance: outside the works of Boulez, Stockhausen, Ligeti, and Berio, almost none. As the governing culture in the Western world has become less tolerant of innovation, so the music of this acutely radical phase has fallen into neglect. On the other hand, works of this period were created in a spirit of revolt, and their nature may therefore be compromised when they are treated as modern classics. To the extent that their revolution has succeeded—as it may be judged to have done in the person of Boulez, who by the mid-1970s was conducting major orchestras on both sides of the Atlantic and planning a research institute in Paris—their original contrariety may have become an embarrassment, which might partly explain Boulez's repeated eagerness to revise and transform many of his older compositions. Then again, such reforming zeal may express an awareness that progressive music cannot outlast its historical moment, that the original recording, thrusting a work into the world it was made to alter, and not the score is the form in which a piece must live on. Perhaps the whole history of music since the introduction of the LP record, around 1950, has been swayed by the existence of a means whereby not only could listeners repeatedly hear the same piece—which would be an encouragement towards subtlety and complexity—but also the performing criteria of the time would be permanently emplaced in the music.)

Bussotti's casting of the musician as seducer or rapist was a theatrical extension of what Tudor had shown possible in performing the most recent Cage: exploring the whole body of the piano for the sounds it can produce, and so extending earlier work by Cowell and Cage himself. Kagel was also stimulated by this, as well as by Cage's calligraphy, but instead of pressing player and instrument into a sensual encounter, he preferred to view the behaviour of the investigatory performer with a certain ironic detachment, and to enjoy the other irony of highly detailed notation giving rise to impure results. In its outlandish sophistication, with rotatable discs and moveable slides, the score of his *Transición II* (1958) proceeds from that of Boulez's Third Sonata, while its promised intention to fuse 'in one single declension' the musical present (heard in performance) with the past (returning on tape) and the future ('pre-experienced' in the form of previously prepared recordings of music to come) suggests a Stockhausen-like will to compose with time itself.[6] And yet in performance the work could hardly fail to seem an absurd spectacle in which two musicians, operating on a piano, undertake meticulous actions in the service of musical aims that remain obscure, and in that respect the piece presents itself as a caricature of contemporary avant-garde endeavour.

Kagel had already started down that road, notably in his *Anagrama* for four singers, speaking chorus, and eleven-piece ensemble (1957–58), which was the first piece he completed after arriving in Cologne from Argentina in 1957, and which had its first performance in the city at an ISCM Festival concert that also saw the première of Ligeti's *Apparitions*. These two composers, both drawn to Cologne by Stockhausen's presence and coming as at least partly formed artists, enjoyed an outsider's prerogative to mix curiosity with scepticism. *Anagrama* is a response to *Gesang der Jünglinge* and a challenge, exploring possibilities of interaction between verbal and nonverbal sounds without electronic resources but with extraordinary sonic imagination and also with a sharp sense of comedy. Textually and musically the work is elaborated from the Latin palindrome in Dante's *Divine Comedy*, out of which the composer draws a rapid shuffle of scenes for voices using several languages to address each other, the audience, and no one in particular. As example 33 may intimate, Kagel wielded a heroic complexity of means in creating musical situations that are at once profuse, innovatory, and absurd. Comic in its nonsense dialogues, quick changes, and bizarre simultaneities, the work contributed decisively to an explosion of interest in the impurities and extremities of which both voices and instruments are capable.

Kagel's exposure of musicians as actors continued to convey a more comic and critical attitude than could be found at the same time in the instrumental theatre of Bussotti or Berio. Often he showed too, as he had in *Anagrama* and *Transición II*, an interest in neglected possibilities of sound. *Sonant* (1960), scored for the unusual ensemble of guitar, harp, double bass, and drums, comes near Feldman in its unsynchronized parts and its absorption with extremes of quiet, but the players' bashfulness also has a theatrical import quite alien to Feldman, and Kagel went still further in taking the then unusual step of requiring his musicians to speak. Also from this period is *Sur scène* for bass, mime, speaker, and three keyboard players (1958–60), whose fundamental idea was 'to create a spectacle out of elements borrowed from traditional musical life: instrumental playing, exercises that precede performance (scales, vocalises, etc), the commentaries of a musicologist. . . . Music becomes a character on stage, which represents the reversal

---

6. See the composer's note with Mainstream 5003, and also his articles 'Tone, Clusters, Attacks, Transitions', *Die Reihe*, 5 (1959; English ed. 1961), 40–55, and 'Translation-Rotation', *Die Reihe*, 7 (1960; English ed. 1965), 32–60.

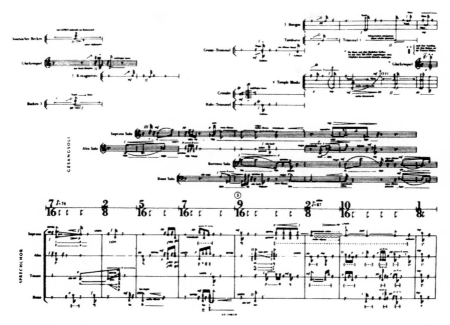

Example 33   Mauricio Kagel, *Anagrama*

of the situation in opera.'[7] Almost from the first then, Kagel's satires and explorations were directed into the wider musical culture and not only into the areas of his colleagues' immediate concerns.

Stumbling Steps: Kurtág

Ligeti's emigration, and Kagel's, involved not only a change of location but also a new visibility within the world of new music. It was different for György Kurtág, a classmate of Ligeti's in Budapest immediately after the war, who remained in Hungary, and whose work was little known outside until the 1980s. Ligeti and he form a neat pair of opposites: the one wild-white-haired (at least since his late forties), articulate, productive, international, the other almost shaven-headed, almost silent, almost nonproductive (at least until his late forties) and spending his life teaching chamber music at the academy where the two had met. At that first encounter, in 1945, Ligeti had been impressed by 'Kurtág's timidity, his introverted attitude and his total lack of vanity or presumption. He was intelligent, sincere, and simple in a highly complex

7. Jean-Yves Bosseur, 'Dossier Kagel', *Musique en jeu*, 7 (1972), 88–126.

way. Later he told me that he, for his part, had taken me for a student of protestant theology.'[8]

Both Ligeti and Kurtág had gone to Budapest in search of the spirit of Bartók; both of them later found also the spirit of Webern, though in Kurtág's case this seems not to have happened until 1957–58, when he was in Paris for a year, attending Milhaud's and Messiaen's classes, receiving psychological therapy from Marianne Stein (to whom he dedicated his Op. 1, a string quartet), and copying out by hand Webern's entire works.[9] During this year he was at rock bottom: 'I felt, to the point of desperation, that nothing in the world was true, that I had no grip on reality. I was living with another of Marianne Stein's pupils, an American actress, and in exchange for my room I would take her two children for walks in the park. That was the Parc Montsouris, a magnificent wilderness with fantastic trees. The experience of trees in winter was perhaps the first reality. That carried on almost until spring, when birds appeared as a second reality.'[10]

This anecdote—almost a Kurtág composition itself in how it opens a world of feeling with a few quick strokes—suggests what became the manner of his creativity: to start with nothing, to take nothing for certain, and then to make something utterly simple, utterly trustworthy. When he began to compose again, it was for some years exclusively in small instrumental forms: miniatures on a Webernesque scale—where a three-minute movement is Brucknerian and the average is the sixty-second spurt or flagging—but combining the imitative counterpoint of serial Webern with the rare timbres and ostinatos of atonal Webern, and introducing personal qualities: bleak humor, scrawniness, sometimes moments of intense light. 'The cockroach seeks a way to the light' was to have been the programme of the first movement of the quartet; 'The overtone chord symbolized the light, and in between the dirt'.[11]

By 1963, when he was thirty-seven, Kurtág had only five works ready for publication: about a minute of music for each year of his age, and with a wind quintet the largest ensemble.[12] During the next five years he produced about as much music again, all towards one piece, *The Sayings of Péter Bornemisza*, a 'concerto' for soprano and piano (per-

8. György Ligeti, 'Begegnung mit Kurtág im Nachkriegs-Budapest', in Friedrich Spangemacher, ed., *György Kurtág* (Bonn, 1989), 14–17.

9. See Peter Szendy, 'Musique et texte dans l'oeuvre de György Kurtág', *Contrechamps*, 12–13 (1990), 266–84.

10. Bálint András Varga, *György Kurtág: Three Interviews and Ligeti Homages* (Rochester, N.Y., 2009), 6.

11. Ibid., 7.

12. For an excellent introduction to Kurtág's music, see Stephen Walsh, 'György Kurtág: an Outline Study', *Tempo*, 140 (1982), 11–21, and 141 (1982), 10–19. A postscript is provided by his 'A Brief Office for György Kurtág', *Musical Times*, 130 (1989), 525–26.

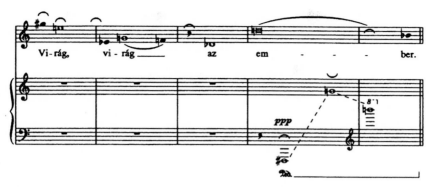

Example 34 György Kurtág, *The Sayings of Péter Bornemisza*

haps so called by analogy with the sacred concertos of Schütz), whose four sections are made up once more of fragments. Bornemisza was a writer and Protestant preacher of the sixteenth century, and his 'sayings', assembled by the composer, cut to the quick. A new doctrine of personal accountability makes its demands. The text also has the newness of being couched in what was then an emergent language, lusty and rugged, with some sniff of the plough still among the biblical phrases. Tone and style were right for a composer who was, similarly, cutting himself a new language, and for whom the liberty to do so imposed a need for unflinching self-observation and self-criticism in the act of composing. The words also encouraged him, in his first published vocal work, to push the voice to its limits of expression (the piano too: Barraqué's Sonata provides the work's lonely company in points of strength, freedom from precedent, and certainty—and it is a tantalizing coincidence that both composers should have been set on their paths by hearing Schubert's 'Unfinished' when they were children[13]), those limits including not only violent declamation and almost deranged, jubilatory savagery, as if the voice were intoxicated with the horrors of which it sings, but also a breathtaking lyrical nakedness—more breathtaking and more naked because it requires the singer to be absolutely on target. Example 34 shows such a passage.

There could hardly be less here and still be something. On the other hand, there could be more and nothing at all.

One might venture that Kurtág's achievement—well established by this point—was so to particularize the momentary gesture that it released itself from musical syntax. This is what we mean by realism, whether in Monteverdi or in Musorgsky, but Kurtág is able go further (as each realist must go further than the last), in that his miniature

---

13. See Varga, *Három kérdés?*, and Jean Barraqué's 'Propos impromptu', *Le Courrier musical de France*, 26 (1969).

forms can virtually preclude syntax, and in that the disintegrated state of musical language extends the freedom of the gesture. No less crucial, to a realist, is the ability to invent gestures that are almost onomatopoeic, caught up in what they connote: the slow, soft, wide span of the voice in example 34, or the piano glissando rising like a wisp of smoke.

Listening Ears: Cage, Young, Babbitt

After the celebration embodied in his *Concert for Piano and Orchestra* Cage began to concern himself again with electronic media, for which he found opportunities in Europe during a six-month tour in 1958–59. He produced a tape version of *Fontana Mix* (a kit composition rather in the manner of example 24) at the RAI electronic music studio in Milan, and created two more realizations of the score for himself to perform on Italian television: *Water Walk* and *Sounds of Venice*. By now theatre was not just a by-product of his music but a prompting force: back in the United States he created *Theatre Piece* (1960), for eight performers in multifarious activities, as well as *Cartridge Music* (also 1960), in which he invented live electronic music.

Cartridge Music has several players generating sounds by inserting objects into gramophone cartridges or by acting on pieces of furniture to which contact microphones have been attached. The aim, so Cage said, was not only to create the possibility of electronic performance (indeed, one might add, of electronic theatre, since the sounds are out of proportion to the actions one sees), but also 'to bring about a situation in which any determination made by a performer would not necessarily be realizable. When, for instance, one of the performers changes a volume control, lowering it nearly to zero, the other performer's action, if it is affected by that particular amplification system, is inaudible. I had been concerned with composition which was indeterminate of its performance [because of the overlay possibilities of the *Music for Piano* series and the *Concert*, for instance]; but, in this instance, performance is made, so to say, indeterminate of itself.'[14]

He could go no further—unless to allow the total indeterminacy of improvisation, which he had always resisted as an immediate return to personal taste. Here were more paradoxes. In 1961 Cage's scores began to appear from the C. F. Peters Corporation in New York, greatly improving the dissemination of his music to cope with the increasing worldwide demand at a time when he was producing almost nothing new. The same year his first collection of lectures and essays, *Silence*, was published, and installed him as the guru of a new libertarian avant-garde, who heard his message that everything could be music—but ignored the disciplines he had adopted to keep self at bay.

14. Kostelanetz, ed., *John Cage*, 145.

In New York this avant-garde was represented by the Fluxus group. La Monte Young (b. 1935), an early member, had come into contact with Cage at Darmstadt in 1959, though he had already begun writing strangely simple pieces, opening out from the fascination with sounds of long duration that went back, so he has said, to listening to the wind from inside the log house in which he grew up. His Trio for Strings of 1958, which has gained the aura of a classic and of the great progenitor of what became known as 'minimalism', is a serial composition, but with notes and rests extremely distended, so that sound or silence becomes the focus of attention, encouraging a listening into the extended present. The new pieces of 1960 went beyond notation, being set down as verbal instructions, and quietly indicating that the 'composer' was now first listener:

> Turn a butterfly (or any number of butterflies) loose in the performance area.
> When the composition is over, be sure to allow the butterfly to fly away outside.
> The composition may be any length but if an unlimited amount of time is available, the doors and windows may be opened before the butterfly is turned loose and the composition may be considered finished when the butterfly flies away.[15]

Elsewhere in New York, Babbitt was using electronic means in a different way from Cage's in *Cartridge Music*, though similarly to explore the further reaches of what could be heard. In 1957, still seeking a rhythmic analogue for pitch class, he had introduced the notion of 'time points' in *Partitions* for piano and *All Set* for jazz ensemble (a typical title from a verbal as well as musical punster). The time point of a musical event is a measure of its position within the bar. Thus, if the time signature is 3/4 and the unit of measurement is the semiquaver, a note attacked on the first beat is said to occur at time point zero, a note attacked a semiquaver later is at time point one, and so on. Where the 'interval between two durations' is a concept of obscure meaning, the interval between two time points is quite simply a duration. And where there is no justification for regarding twelve durations as completing a durational octave, the time-point equivalent to the octave is very present in the bar. For example, the interval between time points zero and six, in the case just outlined, is six semiquavers; if the second time point is delayed until the next bar, then this interval becomes a bar plus six semiquavers.

However formally neat, though, the time-point system placed extreme demands on articulation in performance, which was one reason (along with the general lack of performers and performances) for Babbitt's exclusive and belated concentration on electronic composition

15. Composition 1960 No. 5.

between 1961 and 1964. He made all his pieces on the RCA Synthesizer at the Columbia-Princeton Electronic Music Center in New York,[16] a machine that, having little in common with the voltage-controlled synthesizers developed later in the 1960s, could generate a wide variety of sounds or else alter sounds in quite precise ways. Oscillators and noise generators provided the raw materials which the composer, giving the synthesizer its instructions on a punched paper roll, could obtain at will with a high degree of control over pitch, timbre, and volume. The apparatus was a kind of super-organ, with an enormous range of stops, and it appeared most happily employed when used to form, as in Babbitt's compositions, quasi-orchestral polyphonies within the equal-tempered twelve-note scale.

Babbitt's first two works wholly on tape were the *Composition for Synthesizer* (1960–61) and *Ensembles for Synthesizer* (1962–64), of which the former moves to a climax that shakes at a single chord, while the latter, in keeping with the development in his music at the time, is a composite of many tiny and ingeniously worked fragments, one that begins as an alternation between short counterpoints and chords from which notes are successively removed, then continues as a closely integrated mosaic of more diverse 'ensembles'. The composer acknowledged the instrumental character of his electronic music, and voiced reservations about works that, like Stockhausen's *Gesang der Jünglinge* or *Kontakte*, are based on postulates particular to electronic means. 'Perhaps', he wrote, 'a system founded on the unique resources of the electronic medium, and on premises hitherto unknown and not as yet even foreseeable, will be discovered and vindicated. Meanwhile, if it is only meanwhile, there is still an unforeseeably extensive domain in which the electronic medium uniquely can enrich and extend the musical systems whose premises have been tested, and whose resources barely have been tapped.'[17] What speaks here is his wariness not only of Stockhausen but of that whole generation of European composers, whose serial extrapolations he could not but find unsystematic and therefore, in his terms, illegitimate.

Yet his caution did not keep him from taking advantage of the dramatic possibilities of electronic music in his *Philomel* for soprano and tape (1963). This work—a scena for the soloist to an invisible accompaniment of recorded soprano and synthesized sounds—is set at the instant when the tongueless Philomel of the Ovid story undergoes metamorphosis into a nightingale. That transformation can be accomplished in the mirror of the loudspeakers, the voice coming now from the human soloist, present in the flesh, now from a disembodied entity

16. See his 'An Introduction to the R.C.A. Synthesizer', *Journal of Music Theory*, 8 (1964), 251–65.

17. Milton Babbitt, 'Twelve-Tone Rhythmic Structure and the Electronic Medium', *Perspectives of New Music*, 1/1 (1962), 49–79: 79.

cousin to her; there is an echo song for the two. At the same time the dense interweaving of electronically synthesized polyphony gives the work an imposing musical continuity while making a poetic contribution in evoking the night forest through which Philomel flees and flies. There is, also, a sympathy between the intensive punning of John Hollander's text—'Feel a million filaments; fear the tearing, the feeling trees, that are full of felony'—and the perpetual reinterpretation of basic elements that is central to Babbitt's music.

Exploiting the Moment: Stockhausen

Stockhausen's tendency to describe himself as an originator, influencing many but influenced by none, is understandable in view of the way his works from *Kreuzspiel* to *Gesang der Jünglinge* were received, by composers from the very youngest to the most distinguished of the time, Stravinsky. But it seems possible that the arrival of Kagel, Ligeti, and the young Cornelius Cardew (1936–81), all of whom came to live in Cologne in 1957, had an effect on him: at least it extended his circle, which also included the critic Heinz-Klaus Metzger, the poet Hans G. Helms, various people in the art world, and colleagues from the early days of the WDR electronic music studio, notably the composer Gottfried Michael Koenig. In such an intellectual environment, questions of priority are undecidable: things that appear first in scores by Ligeti or Kagel might have been provoked by suggestions from Stockhausen, and vice versa. Indeed, Stockhausen's whole career, since *Kreuzspiel*, had shown how he could seize opportunities provided by encounters with others, and his success in the electronic studio (the high place of *Gesang* in the electronic repertory seems unassailable) was probably helped by his skill in teamwork. The important difference now was that Cologne, where Stockhausen was living until he moved out in 1964 to the house he had designed at Kürten, began to provide what Darmstadt had before: a forum of debate and artistic stimulation.

Inevitably there was a change in what he was producing. The completion of *Gruppen*, also in 1957, brought an end to a phase of highly detailed and rapidly changing music; the next group of works—*Zyklus* for percussionist (1959), *Refrain* for a chiming trio of piano, celesta, and vibraphone (1959), *Carré* for four choral-orchestral groups (1959–60), *Kontakte* (1958–60), an electronic piece to be played either alone or with pianist and percussionist, and *Klavierstücke IX* and *X* (1961)—shift the centre towards slowness, more complex sounds, and greater latitude in the execution of detail. Also noteworthy is the move from works that would have to be played on mixed programmes to works that chosen performers (Tudor and other pianists, especially Aloys Kontarsky and Frederic Rzewski, and the percussionist Christoph Caskel) could perform at all-Stockhausen concerts. There were the beginnings here of the ensemble that regularly presented his music between 1964 and the early 1970s, and for which most of his works from that period were written. For him, as for Boulez, contributing to a movement was becoming less important than pursuing individual explorations.

Zyklus was Stockhausen's masterpiece of graphic invention, using indeterminate signs for indeterminate sounds—sounds that cannot be completely defined by conventional notation (marimba and vibraphone, the two instruments of precise pitch, are used only in glissandos), and that may be prescribed merely as a scatter of attacks on a particular instrument within a given time. Characteristically, Stockhausen establishes a scale of nine degrees of uncertainty that may exist within an event, and uses that scale to mediate between what is prescribed and what is loose. Equally characteristically, he creates the piece as the image of a sound, a complex vibration in which nine constituents follow staggered cycles of growth and decay: in the musical metaphor there are nine chief instruments, and the player turns to them in turn in moving through a circle within the battery. Spiral binding, as in Boulez's *Trope*, makes it possible to start the circuit at any point. The need to complete the cycle gives *Zyklus* an onwardness that Stockhausen had wanted to avoid in *Klavierstück XI*, but at the same time the freedom in the notation, including a freedom to introduce optional elements, means that the implicit dynamism can be either endorsed or countered by the performer, whose wheeling, clocklike movement makes this Stockhausen's first contribution to manifest instrumental theatre. However, the greater visual achievement is the score's, and Stravinsky's reservation ('very attractive to look at, too—one almost wishes it didn't have to be *translated* into sound'[18]) was perhaps shared by Stockhausen himself, with his talk of music for reading.

Refrain is also an elegant package, but a simpler and sharper design in letting chance into a determined framework. Taking up the technique of timbre composition he had developed not only in electronic works but also in orchestral pieces from *Spiel* to *Gruppen*, Stockhausen assembles sounds from the three principal instruments, using additional percussion instruments and vocal enunciations to colour attacks and resonances. The vocal interventions, in particular, give to the piece the aura of a ritual enactment, while the resonant sound world and the long suspensions additionally make the piece a striking prefiguration of the direction in which Stockhausen would travel after his first visit to Japan, in 1965–66. This is the framework. The chance element concerns the placing of the 'refrain' material, with its clusters, its glissandos, and its far more dynamic feel. On the single-page score, this music is notated on a transparent strip that can be revolved to different positions against the six 'verses', which are therefore printed partly (where the 'refrain' can fall) in concentric circles. Thus the score itself—a typi-

18. Igor Stravinsky and Robert Craft, *Memories and Commentaries* (London, 1960), 118.

cal European reinjection of intention into a Cage prototype (the kit score of *Fontana Mix*)—displays that 'curvi-linear' form[19] that Stockhausen was hoping to achieve by combining the stasis of randomness with the dynamism of goal-orientation.

The intimacy of *Refrain* is unusual for Stockhausen; so is the brevity. Its technique of composing timbres from vocal and instrumental sounds he transferred to a more typical scale in *Carré*, whose similarity to *Gruppen*, in being a work for spaced groups, is deceptive. *Gruppen*, like *Klavierstück XI* and *Zyklus*, was a magnified image of sound's behaviour; *Carré* and *Refrain* return to more direct concerns with making sounds. They mark a change from the speculative to the empirical, and from variety to a concentration on static events. Stockhausen recalled how the idea of *Carré* came to him during his first tour of the United States, when he spent a lot of time in aeroplanes, and 'I was always leaning my ear . . . against the window, like listening with earphones directly to the inner vibrations. And though a physicist would have said that the engine sound doesn't change, it changed all the time because I was listening to all the partials within the spectrum'.[20] Here was another, and important, discovery about musical time: that listening— the movement of aural attention within the sound—could be a dynamic activity.

Carré accordingly became Stockhausen's purest and most comprehensive essay in timbre composition with conventional resources: music which, like the second movement of *Spiel*, calls for active contemplation of sounds that succeed one another without any strong sense of logical connection. But the work does not rely entirely on the dynamism of listening, for its sounds generally have built-in gradual change in the form, for example, of a slow glissando or the layering of more precisely figured detail onto a smooth surface, and the work's tranquil unfolding is several times interrupted by the insertion of episodes that vigorously exploit the possibility, as at the climax of *Gruppen*, of having sounds spin in the centrifuge of the separated ensembles.

One other innovation in *Carré* is significant. Having planned the work, Stockhausen handed over much of the task of realization to Cardew,[21] which suggests a mode of working more characteristic of the architectural practice than of the composer's desk. No doubt Stockhausen had got used to working with associates in the electronic studio; there was also the point that he was pressed for time, since while *Carré* was in progress he was simultaneously at work in the studio on

19. Note by the composer in K. H. Wörner, *Stockhausen: Life and Work* (London, 1973), 42.

20. Jonathan Cott, *Stockhausen: Conversations with the Composer* (London, 1974), 31.

21. See Cornelius Cardew, 'Report on Stockhausen's "Carré"', *Musical Times*, 102 (1961), 619–22, 698–700.

Kontakte. But the practical circumstances are less important than the assumptions that made them possible—the assumption, in particular, that one could separate the plan (Stockhausen's term, which he used when speaking of many of his works, is 'form scheme') from the detail, with the implication that the plan is paramount. Serialism had supposed a method of working from the small to the large; Stockhausen had substituted a reverse process, and at the same time indicated that the essence of composition is in the setting-up of musical situations, whose particular conduct is relatively unimportant: whole sections of *Carré* can be omitted.

Kontakte belongs with *Carré* in being for four sound sources at compass points (but now loudspeakers), in its slowly changing sonorities, and in its swirling of sounds through space. But at the same time it capitalizes on properties unique to the electronic medium, as Stockhausen firmly asserted in a radio talk on the piece.[22] He draws attention to four 'criteria' that distinguish electronic from instrumental music—or that, one might rather say (since all four had been interests of his instrumental compositions), presuppose an electronic, analytic experience of sound and correspondingly lend themselves to electronic creativity. For example, two of them are old concerns of his—the composition and 'de-composition' of timbres, the making of scales between pitched tone and noise—that can be more easily and thoroughly pursued in a medium where smooth transitions between dissimilar states can be engineered. A third criterion is the possibility of scales of loudness, which had been a rather unconvincing postulate of total serialism, and which Stockhausen now uses, in a characteristic move from theoretical integrity to display, for illusions of depth. By carefully regulating volume and reverberation, he creates in *Kontakte* the effect of distinct screens of sound receding from the listener, screens that may be transparent to the ear, or that may be drawn back to reveal others 'behind' them. In this artificial space, as important to the work as the real space separating the loudspeakers, sounds may appear to come out of the distance and then, dropping in pitch to imitate the Döppler effect, fly past the listener, irresistibly suggesting the aeroplane engines that stimulated *Carré*.

But the most significant special feature of electronic music, and the one Stockhausen places first, is the opportunity it provides to show and to use the coherent unity of the three parameters of timbre, pitch, and duration, or—as Stockhausen preferred to call them, his emphasis shifting from the atomic, written note to the substantial, heard sound—'coloristic composition, harmonic-melodic composition and metrical-rhythmic composition'. The continuity of the parameters, their common basis in the phenomenon of vibration, had of course been a

22. Karlheinz Stockhausen, 'Die Einheit der musikalischen Zeite', *Texte*, i (Cologne, 1963), 211–21.

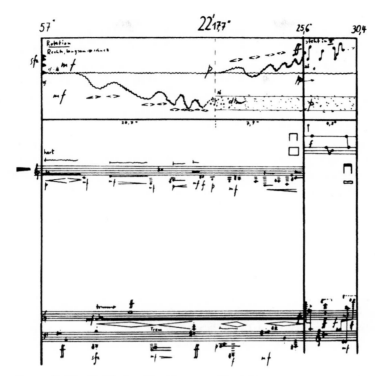

Example 35   Karlheinz Stockhausen, *Kontakte*

primary subject of the preceding group of works associated with the essay ' . . . how time passes . . . '. But *Kontakte*, typically for this period, makes the whole business more concrete. Example 35 shows a clear instance—clear even in the graphic representation of the electronic music—where a complex sound is progressively stripped of its components, each of which appears to float away and degenerate into the basic material from which the work was made: single impulses. Progressive deceleration of the constituents takes them smoothly from the realm of timbre to that of pitched sound and so to that of rhythm.

The 'contacts' of the title may thus be understood as happening among the parameters, and also between the domains of pitched sound and noise, since the slowing components slip not just from pitch to rhythm but from pitch to rhythmic noise. But there are also metaphorical contacts between sounds that appear familiar, because they resemble sounds we meet in life (including music, especially the music of percussion instruments—though everything here is artificially synthesized), and sounds that are unknown, that we cannot immediately categorize. In the alternative version, with pianist and percussionist contributing a new level of 'contacts' with the tape, the electronic images of instrumental sounds create the opportunity for a dramatic interplay:

the performers may seem to capture sounds from out of the ether, or the tape may appear to hijack instrumental material and develop it way beyond instrumental possibility. Or to quote the composer's description: 'The known sounds give orientation, perspective to the listening experience; they function as traffic signs in the unbounded space of the newly discovered electronic world.'[23] There is a case of instrumental-electronic contact in the final segment of example 35, where both players join the tape in blobs of sound in the upper register.

Example 35 may also suggest how *Kontakte* is a bundle of processes, a matter more of forming than of form, going further in the composer's characteristic direction. The processes come to a suitable conclusion, in a spinning swish of sound that disappears into the far distance and so makes an effective withdrawal, but Stockhausen said that this ending is arbitrary.[24] In both *Kontakte* and *Carré* he sought alternatives to directional music, but left behind the mobile-form option of *Klavierstück XI*, *Zyklus,* and *Refrain*. His new means were long duration (*Kontakte* lasts for more than thirty minutes, and *Carré* can take almost an hour, both works playing continuously: now unremarkable, such expanses of sound were quite exceptional at the time) and a diminishment of causal connection between segments. As he said of *Kontakte*: 'The musical events do not take a fixed course between a determined beginning and an inevitable ending, and the moments are not merely consequents of what precedes them and antecedents of what follows; rather the concentration on the Now—on every Now—as if it were a vertical slice dominating over any horizontal conception of time and reaching into timelessness, which I call eternity: an eternity that does not begin at the end of time, but is attainable at every *moment'.*[25]

This is the first and basic statement of Stockhausen's concept of 'moment form',[26] a kind of musical structure in which the 'moments', each with its distinctive character and way, are to be heard as individual, as implicit eternities, rather than as stations on a journey. Where Schoenberg in his serial works had attempted to find forces to compensate for the loss of the directed thrust of diatonic harmony, Stockhausen and his colleagues were moving along without. Barraqué found in Hermann Broch's novel *The Death of Virgil* an embedding of his own conclusion that now there could be no conclusion, that music's dynamic must be one of striving for unreachable attainment. Boulez explicitly contrasted the old universe of tonal gravitation with the new universe 'in constant expansion'. And Stockhausen arrived at moment form, soon grandly celebrated in *Momente* for soprano, four choral groups, brass octet, two electronic organs, and three percussion players.

23. Note with Vox STGBY 638.
24. See Wörner, *Stockhausen*, 110.
25. Ibid., 46–47.
26. See also his 'Momentform', in *Texte*, i, 189–210.

(The highly irregular formation is a testament to the optimism and the funding that still buoyed up the key players in the European musical vanguard. From Stockhausen's point of view, the choice of resources was an essential creative idea, and ought to be unrepeatable.)

Momente may well have been meant, like *Punkte* and *Gruppen*, as the apotheosis and the exemplary instance of its declared technique (Stockhausen cannot have been unaware of the function each new piece would have as a teaching instrument at the next Darmstadt session), and the individuality of the moments is made manifest in an unusual return to mobile form.[27] However, the score's variability is greatly circumscribed by the composer's care for mediation, and also, in the final version of 1972, by the sense of occasion that infuses a long, exhilarating section that could never be anything but an opening.[28] In neither version are the moments freely interchangeable; rather they must be organized like planets around the three suns that each concentrate on one of the fundamental parameters, which are again those that Stockhausen's acoustic studies had taught him were fundamentally unified: duration, melody, and timbre. The planetary moments mix these categories in different combinations, or else ignore them, and the permissible forms are governed by associations of similarity and contrast. Moreover, Stockhausen sprinkles the work with foretastes of moments to come or reminiscences of moments past, so that, characteristically, ideology is not immune to the claims of drama.

As a result, *Momente* is impressive not as a haphazard succession of isolated events but as a spectacle and a grand synthesis.[29] It follows on from *Gesang der Jünglinge* in ignoring any boundary between speech and music, the solo soprano and the choirs enjoying a vast Kagelian repertory of modes of vocal and nonvocal behaviour. With *Kontakte* it shares a refusal to acknowledge any division between the pitched and the unpitched, and it also ranks with that work as a crowning achievement in timbre composition, using its superficially limited but in effect very versatile ensemble (an ensemble that of course holds the speech-music and pitched-unpitched mediations implicit) to create a wealth of complex sonorities, often dark and enclosed in the music of 1961–64, more extravert and brighter in the sections written later. (The early 1960s found Stockhausen unusually recoiled both personally and professionally. His invention of moment form was symbolic at a time when the unified thrust of the 1950s seemed to have gone from music, and

27. Sketches for the work have been published as *Ein Schlüssel für 'Momente'* (Kassel, 1971).

28. On the two versions, see Robin Maconie, *The Works of Karlheinz Stockhausen* (London, 1976, 1990), 137.

29. See Stockhausen's note on the work in Wörner, *Stockhausen*, 48–53, for insights into the philosophical thinking on which the synthesis was partly based.

his affair with the U.S. visual artist Mary Bauermeister forced him to rethink himself.)

The Last Concert: Nono

Momente became a momentous public statement only in the later stages of its development, but even while Stockhausen was working on the earlier version several of his colleagues were starting to concern themselves with music directed beyond the circuit of specialist festivals that was by now giving them perhaps too comfortable a time. For Nono, the existence of a new-music culture was artistic and political death: he was interested in disrupting bourgeois conventions, not in creating a new one. For Boulez too, the lapse from engaged attack into ordinary life seems to have been dispiriting. Since 1945 he had been able to see himself as the leader of a group in determined opposition; now there was no group, and nothing to oppose. The works he had begun in 1956–57—the Third Piano Sonata, the second book of *Structures*, *Figures-Doubles-Prismes* and *Pli selon pli*—remained the last new pieces he brought to performance for almost a decade. As his conducting career took off (at first mostly in programmes of twentieth-century music with German radio orchestras and his own Domaine Musical ensemble), he entered that long period during which most of his creative work has been refashioning.

Nono found an alternative to that in continuing the attack on other fronts. His *Intolleranza* (1960–61) was the first opera by one who had not fled the ranks of the avant-garde (as Henze, for example, had), and in it he projected onto the stage that spirit of contra-bourgeois feeling and thinking he had seen as inherent in postwar musical practice. The work is a protest against capitalist society's heartless treatment of an immigrant, a protest made as a sequence of short scenes that encapsulate incidents of inhumanity and, through the almost constant presence of the chorus, both universalize them and teach from them. All the most broad and vigorous features of Nono's previous output are brought to a culmination: the strident handling of orchestral sonorities out of *Diario polacco* and *Incontri*, the range of choral disposition from keenly divided, extenuated textures to powerful massings, the solo melodic lines of fierce expressive insistence. But for the first time these are combined with electronic sounds of a penetrating force. Nono had made a belated acquisition of studio techniques in Milan, producing his *Omaggio a Emilio Vedova* in 1960 (Vedova was the painter whose stark images were projected during the first performances of *Intolleranza*), and he began to realize that electronic music could provide him with both the musical material and the forum for continuing his offensive against bourgeois society. After two more sets of songs for voices and instruments, the *Canti di vita e d'amore* (1962) and the *Canciones a Guiomar* (1962–63), he turned his back on the resources of normal concert life.

1965

The phenomenon known as 'the sixties' effectively began in 1965, the year President Lyndon Johnson initiated both his 'Great Society' and U.S. engagement in Vietnam, when the abolition of the death penalty in Britain opened a short era of liberalizing reforms, and when the Beatles performed at Shea Stadium in New York.

As far as new music of other kinds was concerned, the success of the various avant-gardes—those who had their spiritual homes in Darmstadt, in Princeton, or in the nowhere and everywhere of Cage—was bringing about their dissolution, as composers of a new generation, reacting to their elders (whether positively or negatively), went off in different directions. But still there were directions to go off in. Progress remained as much an ideal as it had been for Boulez twenty years before, except that it was much harder in this increasingly various world to find a uniform historical imperative, and progress without need provided the recipe for fashion. Even in the mid-1950s, the newest works of Boulez and Stockhausen, in particular, had been rapidly imitated by younger composers, as if those works provided the key to the future: *Gruppen* was followed by numerous scores for spaced orchestral groups, *Le Marteau* by a host of adamantine ensembles. By the middle of the next decade, the pursuit of fashion and the splintering of factions had together created a turmoil of simultaneous developments, requiring some loosening of the already loose chronology being followed here: the next chapters follow streams that ran concurrently.

Something else that mattered was the increasing seriousness, range and appeal of popular music. The Beatles' album *Revolver* (1966) was just one symptom of rock musicians' urge to develop their language, and to do so, in part, by looking over the wall: the Beatles' next release, *Sgt. Pepper's Lonely Hearts Club Band* (1967) enshrines Stockhausen among the gurus on its cover. And classically trained composers were reciprocating the interest.

10

Of Elsewhen
and Elsewhere

Though the passage of time irrevocably obscures novelty of any kind, one of the most striking features of the avant-garde music of the 1950s and early 1960s remains its isolation, in so many respects of aim and technique, from any immediate precedent. Separation from the past became an item of belief: every feature cherished in the great Western tradition was now to be abandoned, whether by destruction, in Boulez, by blithe disregard, in Cage, or by intensive searching elsewhere, in Stockhausen. Of course, the extreme apartness of 1951–52—the period of Cage's *4′ 33″*, Stockhausen's *Kreuzspiel*, and Boulez's first book of *Structures*—was soon compromised in all kinds of ways, and rapprochements were made: Cage returned to writing music, and Boulez and Stockhausen found themselves caught up in more continuous ways of moving through time. But making things new was still the ideal.

Boulez has consistently been the most vociferous spokesman for this position, despite his vigorous conducting activity, especially during the 1970s, within the museum of musical tradition. Writing in the middle of that decade, fanfaring the foundation of his Institut de Recherche et de Coordination Acoustique/Musique (IRCAM) in Paris, he insisted that: 'Our age is one of persistent, relentless, almost unbearable inquiry. In its exaltation it cuts off all retreats and bans all sanctuaries; its passion is contagious, its thirst for the unknown projects us forcefully, violently into the future. . . . Despite the skillful ruses we have cultivated in our desperate effort to make the world of the past serve our present-day needs, we can no longer elude the essential trial: that of becoming an absolute part of the present, of forsaking all memory to forge a perception without precedent, of renouncing the legacies of the past, to discover yet undreamed-of territories.'[1]

But this is perhaps too lyrical to be true, even allowing for the fact that Boulez was hoping to justify the considerable state expenditure involved in establishing and maintaining his institution. The position is—given the replacement of a thirty-year-old's abruptness by a fifty-year-old's more mannered discourse—little changed since the days of *Le Marteau sans maître*, except that where Boulez in the mid-1950s could plausibly feel himself to be spearheading a great musical movement, by the mid-1970s this was no longer the case, and the adherence to an old revolutionary rhetoric was to stymie both IRCAM and Boulez's own creative endeavours. For by 1974 it had become very clear that 're-nouncing the legacies of the past' was no simple matter. What about the revolutionary asceticism that was itself a legacy of the past? Amnesia is the privilege of the young, and even by the later 1960s the new wave was growing up. As that wave broke up, as the arrow of determined progress splintered, so the possibilities multiplied of touching back to what had been.

The Distant Past

The achievement of the eighteenth and nineteenth centuries remains the great sun of the Western musical solar system: the repertory that dominates performance and recording. Composers who approach it must either maintain their ironic distance, as Stravinsky did, and later Ligeti, or be content to turn into its orbit, adopt its premises and its modes of thought. The further past offers less gravitational pull—partly just because it is further off, but also partly because its forces seem to be complemented by, rather than at war with, those of our own age. Pertinent here is Stravinsky's progress during the 1950s: forward to Webern and Boulez, but at the same time backward to Gesualdo and to pre-Renaissance music. The more general growth of interest in 'early music', following behind Stravinsky by a decade or so, may be evidence of a community of thought and feeling; it has also made it possible for composers to write for instruments that had been extinct for centuries, as Kagel did in his quite un-Renaissance-sounding *Musik für Renaissance-Instrumente* (1965). As for matters of compositional technique rather than instrumental means, the medieval view of rhythm as number suggests comparison with the attitudes of Messiaen and of those composers who, influenced by him, developed rhythmic serialization in Europe: Barraqué drew attention to that in an article on rhythm, where, with no sense of incongruity, he moves directly from Machaut's *Messe*

1. IRCAM press brochure (Paris, 1974), 6–7.

Example 36a   *Victimae paschali laudes*

Example 36b   Peter Maxwell Davies, *Taverner*

de Notre Dame to *The Rite of Spring*.[2] Also, as Charles Wuorinen (b. 1938) pointed out, the rhythmic complexities cultivated by composers of the post-Machaut generation are such as to make *Le Marteau sans maître* appear quite normal.[3]

But these are instances of correspondence rather than influence. For examples of the latter, British music of the 1950s and 1960s provides the richest field, perhaps for various reasons: the fact that British musicians and musicologists were taking a leading part in the rediscovery of early music, the fact that composers of an older generation, such as Britten and Tippett, had interested themselves in Tudor music and Purcell, the fact that musical culture in Britain had last been actively progressive in the age of Dunstable. Three composers who were fellow students in Manchester during the early 1950s—Alexander Goehr (b. 1932), Harrison Birtwistle (b. 1934), and Peter Maxwell Davies (b. 1934)—were quite aware that what they were learning from the recent music of Boulez and Nono had its parallels in the pages of *Musica Britannica*.

Davies's concern with the further past stayed intense, and the role of pre-Baroque music in his work has been various and profound. A great many of his works are founded—as the music of the medieval and Renaissance polyphonists was founded—on fragments of plainsong; example 36 shows an instance of this in a comparison of the opening of the Easter sequence *Victimae paschali laudes*, transposed up a semitone, with the cello solo from the final scene of the composer's opera *Taverner* of 1962–70. Clearly, his processes of transformation leave little kinship between the music and its seed: even in his transcriptions—and he has made many, of works by Machaut, Dunstable, Purcell, Buxtehude, and others—the original is often twisted into alien, and sometimes perversely alien, harmonic or instrumental territory. At the simplest level, a plainsong theme may be subjected to octave displacement of its pitches,

2. Jean Barraqué, 'Rythme et développement', *Polyphonie*, 9–10 (1954), 47–73.

3. Charles Wuorinen, 'Notes on the Performance of Contemporary Music', *Perspectives of New Music*, 3/1 (1964), 10–21.

melodic alteration, and a very un-chantlike rhythmic presentation, combining sixteenth-century techniques of parody with nineteenth-century variation and twentieth-century serialism. In the particular case from *Taverner,* as Stephen Arnold has pointed out,[4] the plainsong serves not only as a musical source but as a symbol of resurrection by virtue of its text. (For Taverner, the Catholic composer who turns himself into a zealous despoiler of his heritage, it is a deceptive resurrection he attains in having the White Abbot put to death.) The use of plainsong themes at once for their musical qualities and for their associated meanings is common in Davies's music, though normally the relationship between chant and variant is more complex.

A counter-example is provided in Messiaen's music. Like Davies, Messiaen was alive to the textual connotations of the melodies he used, and when he returned to explicitly religious subject matter, in *Couleurs de la Cité Céleste* for piano, wind, and percussion (1963), he began bringing appropriate chant melodies into his music. One instance is the alleluia for the eighth Sunday after Pentecost, *Magnus Dominus,* which Messiaen accepts without melodic change and integrates into his musical world by means of harmonization (in this case using his fourth mode of limited transpositions) and orchestration (for wind and bells). Because his music is essentially modal, rather than, like Davies's, essentially chromatic, this acceptance is musically possible. But it is also spiritually essential in the music of a man whose first creative effort, as he said, was 'to express . . . the existence of the truths of the Catholic faith'.[5]

Davies has another standpoint. His is a music not of exposition but of questioning, even to the extent of negation—negation that can be musically effected by the gradual melodic transformation of a melody into its precise inversion,[6] and that stands behind his abiding concern with themes of betrayal. In his dramatic works, betrayal is staged: Taverner betrays himself in extinguishing what was good and creative in his personality; the protagonist in *Vesalii icones* for dancer, cellist, and quintet (1969) betrays the image of Christ he has presented by turning, finally, into a vision of Antichrist, cavorting to a foxtrot. Outside the theatrical context, music itself can be betrayed by means of this sort of parody—the parody of distortion and mockery, rather than the expressively neutral parody of elaboration conducted in Renaissance masses.

Many of Davies's earlier works are parodies of parodies, in that they are based on polyphonic pieces themselves based on plainsongs: examples include the wind sextet *Alma redemptoris mater* (1957) after a Dunstable motet, the String Quartet (1961) and other works linked in

4. Stephen Arnold, 'The Music of Taverner', *Tempo,* 101 (1972), 20–39.
5. Claude Samuel, *Olivier Messiean: Music and Color* (Portland, Oreg., 1964), 20.
6. See Arnold, 'Music of *Taverner*'.

some way to the Monteverdi Vespers, and a larger family of compositions derived from the Benedictus of Taverner's *Gloria Tibi Trinitas* mass—a family including not only the opera *Taverner* but also two orchestral fantasias (1962 and 1964) and the *Seven In Nomine* for chamber ensemble (1963–65). In these works, Davies's parody is to a large degree secret and, for that reason, not expressed, though the music in other respects may be fiercely expressive, in ways that strike back to Mahler and Schoenberg. In pieces from the late 1960s, however, parody becomes overt and takes on its modern sense, dramatized in the theatre works (such as *Taverner* and *Vesalii icones*), but no less disturbing in orchestral and chamber works, where it may be felt to infect the whole substance of the music.

Davies has described his 'foxtrot for orchestra' *St Thomas Wake* (1969) as being based on 'three levels of musical experience—that of the original sixteenth century "St Thomas Wake" pavan, played on the harp, the level of the foxtrots derived from this, played by a foxtrot band, and the level of my "real" music, also derived from the pavan, played by the symphony orchestra.'[7] But there remain the questions—as evidently Davies's scare quotes show he recognizes—as to how 'real' his 'real' music can be, and why we should accept one level of music as being more 'real' than the foxtrots that crop up in so many of his works of this period (see also, besides *Vesalii icones*, the *Fantasia on a Ground and Two Pavans* after Purcell), and that may even be felt to identify those works. There is no obvious reason why his post-Schoenberg style of endless development should be presumed to have a 'reality' not shared with the other guises his music was capable of taking—or why, to look at it the other way, that style should not also be interpreted as a manner of pastiche. These uncertainties Davies seemed to be acknowledging in concluding his Second Taverner Fantasia—which powerfully enshrines the Schoenbergian weight and drift of argumentation—with a woodwind dispatch that swiftly and grotesquely parodies half an hour of searching, string-led music. The pathos and musical tension accumulated through a long and troubled development are simply cast aside, and at the same time redoubled by being cast aside, because now the foundations are under attack: the music is questioning its own assumptions, even its own honesty.

His bigger orchestral work of this period, *Worldes Blis* (1966–69), Davies has presented as a recuperation, 'a conscious attempt to reintegrate the shattered and scattered fragments of my creative persona'.[8] This is again an immense musical edifice founded on given material—a medieval English song—but now there is no separation of levels and

7. Programme note for the first performance of *Vesalii icones*, at the Queen Elizabeth Hall, London, on December 9, 1969; the note is reprinted in Paul Griffiths, *Peter Maxwell Davies* (London, 1981), 152–54.

8. Ibid., 150.

no blatant autodestruction: the quest for reintegration imposes rather a steady progress in which constant self-interrogation answers itself. As Stephen Pruslin has observed: 'The main allegro pays only lip-service to closure and after the transition the music careens through a whole series of sections, all of them unclosed. The effect is that of amassing a series of left-hand parentheses without bothering about the corresponding right-hand ones, so that one builds up a large "structural overdraft".'[9] Where the Second Taverner Fantasia had presented a process of growth whose premises were alarmingly shaken at the end, *Worldes Blis* advances in momentous instability, and only in conclusion comes overwhelmingly to affirmation. Its thirteenth-century source, speaking of bitter resignation to the vanity of the world, seems to have offered not only musical stimulus but also a poetic metaphor for this harsh vision.

(The Imaginary Past)

In avoiding the close, familiar past of the central tradition, avant-garde techniques lent themselves to summoning not only the future but also prehistory, as foreshadowed in Varèse's incantatory *Ecuatorial*. There are many examples of such hypothetical musical archaeology in the works of Xenakis, such as his score for the *Oresteia*, first performed in 1966, and Scelsi, whose *Uaxactum* for chorus and orchestra, redolent of ancient Mexico, dates from the same year. Another composer fascinated by lost musical cultures was Maurice Ohana (1913–92), who spent his adult life in Paris but had been brought up in Morocco and Spain. Between 1966 and 1976 he devoted himself almost exclusively to a sequence of magical works whose titles all start with 'S'. Among them, *Sacral d'Ilx* (1976) is for the trio Debussy planned for his fourth sonata, comprising oboe, horn, and harpsichord, a grouping Barraqué included in his Concerto and to which Boulez alluded in *Domaines*, where the harpsichord is updated into an electric guitar. Ohana characteristically uses estranged sonorities—third-tones and 'multiphonics', or chords produced by means of particular fingerings—as evocative of strangeness, while chantlike melodic lines and a percussive use of the harpsichord suggest mysterious ceremonial. ('Ilx' is the ancient name for the Spanish town of Elche, an important site of Phoenician settlement.)

The Distant or Not So Distant East

Davies's engagement with medieval and Renaissance music, and with techniques of parody, may perhaps be a legitimation (a legitimation according to Boulezian criteria that structure be articulable but not ar-

---

9. Stephen Pruslin, 'Returns and Departures: Recent Maxwell Davies', *Tempo*, 113 (1975), 22–28.

ticulate) for a composer whose musical business is essentially modern and Romantic: the violence with which he has treated his source material (most dramatically in the arrangements of his 'expressionist' period, such as the *Seven In Nomine* and the *Fantasia on a Ground and Two Pavans*) may almost suggest as much, since the effect is not so much to cherish as to dismember. It is from a modern, even modernist, viewpoint that retroversion becomes a cause for anxiety; those who are determined to move forward have most to lose by looking back.

Composers disinclined to progress, though, risk nothing: found materials for them are objects requiring placement, not subjects demanding consideration. Hence the very different tone of Messiaen's appropriation of medieval material, and his ability to make use of materials from other places, as well as other times, with the same combination of care and detachment: the Indian rhythmic figures he found in an encyclopedia, or the gamelanlike metallophone section he incorporated in the orchestra of *Turangalîla* and many later scores, or the complete tradition copied into the 'Gagaku' movement of *Sept Haïkaï*. Messiaen's imitations regard Asian music (and also avian music) as closer to the timelessness of paradise, and it is perhaps the lack in such music of post-Renaissance Europe's manifold dynamisms (harmonic, metric, formal) that is responsible for its claim on so many composers since the abandonment or destruction of those dynamic principles became an aim around 1945. It was no accident that Messiaen, open to non-European music, should have been the most prestigious European composition teacher from the 1950s to the 1980s, or that non-Western composers should then have begun to contribute significantly to what had hitherto been a predominantly Western tradition.

In Japan, Tōru Takemitsu (b. 1930) showed quite explicitly how close European and U.S. composers had come, in the late 1950s and early 1960s, to oriental ways of considering time as unthrusted blank space, of accommodating the unpredictable, and of attuning art to nature. His solo piece *Piano Distance* (1961), for example, has connections with Boulez's Third Sonata and second book of *Structures* in its feeling for resonance, and with Cage in its inscription of sound calligrams on silence. Other works of this radical period include *Ring* for flute, guitar, and lute (also 1961), whose four movements can be played in any order, with a graphically scored improvisation interpolated, several electronic pieces, and—following a meeting with Cage in 1964—happenings. *November Steps* (1967) combined a Western orchestra with Eastern soloists (on shakuhachi and biwa), but marked a withdrawal from experiment back to developing the francophone style of Takemitsu's earliest works. Much of his later music is close to Messiaen, though with a gentler, more yielding character.

Takemitsu's acceptance in the West—where his music has been performed far more than that of any other Asian musician—may have to do not only with his music's quality but also with Western expectations

of Asian art as serene, passive, decorative, and subsidiary, since it remains difficult for even the most sympathetic Western observers to
separate a real appreciation of Asian art from an idolization of stereo-
type, or for even the most sympathetic Western composers to accept
Asian music on its own terms rather than draw it into Western contexts. Equally, there must be problems for Asian musicians who seek,
as Takemitsu sought, a particularly Asian understanding of what remain
fundamentally Western media, such as the orchestra or twelve-note
equal temperament.

Some intriguing if innocent, perhaps insolent, responses to these
questions came from Lou Harrison, who, like his teacher Cowell before, was excited by the variety of musical cultures he found around
him in San Francisco and kept himself open to learning non-Western
instruments and traditions, which he would not so much incorporate
as advance towards with whatever Western means he chose to keep
(notably the notions of composer and score), and on which he would
also draw in gently undermining Western privileges. From reading
Partch's *Genesis of a Music* he came to prefer just intonation, and in the
early 1970s he and William Colvig, his life partner, constructed an
'American gamelan' of justly tuned metallophones, which he used in,
for example, *La Koro Sutro* ('The Heart Sutra', translated into Esperanto)
with chorus and his Suite with solo violin, works written in 1972 and
1974 respectively.

Harrison's music exhibits a rare humility in the face of non-Western
traditions. More generally the ideas, ever prone to wishful interpretation, have flown faster than any deep acquaintance with traditions and
instruments, and fusions, whether made by Western or non-Western
composers, have had to take place on Western territory, using Western
media. The point was made satirically in reverse by Kagel in his *Exotica*
(1971), which depends precisely on the lack of familiarity and expertise that six European musicians will bring to a collection of at least
sixty non-European instruments. When Boulez and Stockhausen took
up ideals of instrumentation from Asian or African music, they did so,
like Messiaen, with European ensembles, as in the former's *Le Marteau
sans maître* and *Improvisations sur Mallarmé* or the latter's *Kreuzspiel* and
Refrain.

The possibility that non-Western artistic practices and philosophies
will unsettle Western music more profoundly remains for the future,
however much noise there has been. Even Cage, in his pursuit of a zen
music of nonintention, could not escape Western conditions of musical
communication (the score, the rehearsal, the concert, the recording),
let alone Western notions of artist and oeuvre. With other composers,
even the attempt is doubtful. Boulez, for example, has recorded that,
when he first heard examples of Asian and African music on records,
he was struck not only by their beauty but also 'by the concepts behind
these elaborate works of art. Nothing, I found, was based on the "mas-

terpiece", on the closed cycle, on passive contemplation or narrowly aesthetic pleasure. In these civilizations music is a way of existence in the world of which it forms an integral part and with which it is indissolubly linked—an ethical rather than simply an aesthetic category.'[10] This insistence on music as an active mode of being in the world is arguably a legacy more from Artaud than from Messiaen, but by this point in Boulez's career (the article was first published in 1960) there was a contradiction, or at least a tension, between such inflammatory pronouncements and the man's musical routines. (That contradiction or tension was most famously exposed in 1967, when in an interview with *Der Spiegel*[11] he called for opera houses to be blown up, while at the same time he must have been preparing to conduct *Parsifal* at Bayreuth the next summer and *Pelléas* at Covent Garden the following year.) The Third Piano Sonata, which provided the occasion for this article, surely was intended as a 'masterpiece', and a masterpiece indeed by virtue of—not despite—its innovation in respecting 'the "finite" quality of western art, with its closed circle, . . . while introducing the element of "chance" from the open circle of oriental art'.[12] Besides, this talk of chance and openness suggests that Boulez was really talking about Cage rather than about anything directly from the east, which might explain the bleak decisiveness of his last statements on Eastern music, in another interview of 1967: 'The music of Asia and India is to be admired because it has reached a stage of perfection, and it is this perfection that interests me. But otherwise the music is dead.'[13]

Quite apart from the problem that Cage appeared to have taken out rights in music east of the Indus, Boulez seems to have been caught between a fascination with oriental art and a horror of imitation or even conspicuous reference. The things that captivated him in music from outside the cultivated European tradition were sounds and the sense of time: suppleness and fluidity of pulse, hospitality to improvisation, slowness and length, a comparative unimportance of the end. In publicly introducing his second *Improvisation sur Mallarmé* in 1960, for instance, he remarked how he had 'heard Andean peasants in Peru playing harps with a most extraordinary sonority and learned from them the use of the instrument's highest notes and a variety of "dampings"',[14] while the third *Improvisation*—at least in the version that was current between 1959 and the mid-1980s—clearly shows both kinds of indebtedness: to exotic sounds in its clattering heterophonies for homogeneous percussion ensembles (of two xylophones, three harps, etc) and

10. Pierre Boulez, '"Sonate, que me veux-tu?"', *Orientations*, 145.

11. In No. 40 of that year.

12. Pierre Boulez, 'Alea', *Stocktakings from an Apprenticeship* (Oxford and New York, 1991), 35.

13. Boulez, *Orientations*, 421.

14. Ibid., 158.

its immense opening soprano melisma delicately inflected with quarter tones, and to new temporalities in its long suspensions, its offering of alternatives, and its loose coordination of overlapping blocks. But that was as far as Boulez was prepared to go. He praised Messiaen for providing the lesson 'that *all* can become music',[15] but in his own work he could never have accepted the extraneous allusions of Indian rhythms, plainsong melodies, or imitation gagaku: the need—as in learning from Debussy or Webern—was to analyse, and then to construct from basic particles whose origins would be as deeply buried as the worldwide music in *Le Marteau*.

So it was with Stockhausen until, in the early months of 1966, he made an extended visit to Japan in order to compose an electronic work in the Tokyo radio studios. Michael Kurtz has suggested that dislocation —an experience confined before the present age to refugees and immigrants, who have other problems—elicited a new outlook. 'Could he compose exactly the same kind of piece in Tokyo as in Cologne? If so, why travel to Tokyo?'[16] Stockhausen's own accounts confirm that it was being in Japan that made it possible for him 'to take a step further in the direction of composing not "my" music, but a music of the whole world'.[17] This was *Telemusik*. Here exotic music is not analysed but accepted, in the form of recordings, and only afterwards submitted to electronic techniques of modulation and integration. As Stockhausen explained, the work contains '"electronic" passages, which are of today, together with tape recordings of music, for example from the south Sahara, from the Shipibo of the Amazon, from a Spanish village festival, Hungarian, Balinese music, recordings from temple ceremonies in Japan, . . . music of the highland dwellers of Vietnam, etc.'[18] He also insisted that the piece is not a collage but rather 'an untrammelled spiritual encounter',[19] because the different kinds of music are both carefully assembled and made to affect one another. The stage is provided by purely electronic sounds—often piercing high frequencies, which introduce what was to be for several years in Stockhausen's music a common image of listening to shortwave broadcasts: in such works as *Kurzwellen* (1968) shortwave receivers are used in performance, so that the 'music of the whole world' becomes part of the live piece. The meetings of musics in *Telemusik* are engineered by studio procedures that the composer also elucidated: 'I modulate the rhythm of one event with the dynamic curve of another. Or I modulate electronic chords, regulated by myself, with the dynamic curve of a priestly chant, then

---

15. Programme note for a concert at Severance Hall, Cleveland, on December 5, 1970.

16. Michael Kurtz, *Stockhausen: A Biography* (London, 1992), 142.

17. Karlheinz Stockhausen, *Texte*, iii (Cologne, 1971), 75.

18. Ibid., 79.

19. Ibid., 76.

this with the monotonous song (therefore the pitch line) of a Shipibo song, and so on.'[20] This technique of 'intermodulation', to use Stock-hausen's own term, generates complex textures and dense events in which the original recordings, when they can be distinguished at all, sound as if they are being jammed by interference—the interference of other recordings that collide with and obscure them.

The use of Japanese percussion instruments to signal each new section is a nice gesture of deference to the composer's hosts, but in dedicating *Telemusik* to the Japanese people Stockhausen was concerned with deeper issues. 'I have learnt', he wrote, '—especially in Japan— that tradition does not simply exist, but that it must be created anew every day. . . . Let us not forget that everything we do and say must be considered as a moment in a continuing tradition.'[21] Hitherto Stock-hausen had written about his music as if each work were a pure thought experiment, dependent only on methods and ideals chosen for that work. From now on, as Robin Maconie has observed, he 'is eager to discover parallels between his own and other music (especially tradi-tional music of oral cultures) as proof that his personal intuitions are in tune with universal forms of musical expression'.[22] And in beginning to search out roots and linkages he was, not for the first time, thinking and acting for his generation.

Quotation

Telemusik also belongs with the best of early Stockhausen—with *Kontra-Punkte*, *Gesang der Jünglinge*, *Kontakte*, and the piano pieces—in making a composition out of a solution to a problem, and so in achieving a compelling unity of material and design. Only this material—ethnic music that would provide abundant variety without triggering imme-diate recognitions and responses in any likely listener—was suitable for intermodulation; only intermodulation could unify this material. But around the same time other composers were starting to use found ideas that would, on the contrary, be recognized, and that would by inten-tion create a disparity between material and design—that would appear as quotations in alien contexts.

The rediscovery of Ives may have played some part in this, though more probably Ives arrived as confirmation rather than influence. The reasons for the tide of quotations in music of the mid-1960s are likely to be deeper, and to include a wish to engage with aspects of the domi-nant culture from which postwar composers had held themselves apart (a wish growing as musicians born in the 1920s now entered middle

20. Ibid., 80.
21. Ibid., 76.
22. Robin Maconie, *The Works of Karlheinz Stockhausen* (London, 1976; 1990), 210.

age), a desire to make contact with audiences for that culture, and a hope that music might adjust to the multiple and simultaneous sensory stimulation easily available in a world where, during the 1950s and 1960s, most Western homes had acquired television sets and record players.

Cage, in particular, was struck by this change, and by Marshall McLuhan's analysis of its meaning in *The Gutenberg Galaxy* (1962) and later books and articles. McLuhan, he wrote, 'has given a dramatic cause (the effect of electronics as opposed to the effect of print on sense perceptions) for the present social change. . . . New art and music do not communicate an individual's conceptions in ordered structures, but they implement processes which are, as are our daily lives, opportunities for perception (observation and listening). McLuhan emphasizes this shift from life done for us to life that we do for ourselves.'[23] But though these words come from a short article entitled 'McLuhan's Influence', again the case was more one of confirmation. Cage's production of unordered, multifarious music went back a decade before *The Gutenberg Galaxy* to *Williams Mix*, and a further decade before that he had composed a collage of a simpler sort in *Credo in Us* (1942), where a gramophone record provides one voice in a counterpoint otherwise for piano and percussion (Cage suggests the use of something by Beethoven, Dvořák, Sibelius, or Shostakovich—music, therefore, from a wholly alien world of harmonic-symphonic form).

Nevertheless, the contact with McLuhan—and with another prophet of optimistic millenarianism, Buckminster Fuller—came at a time of change in Cage's work, the time when he had almost abandoned composition in favour of writing and lecturing. The texts of 1961–67 collected in his second volume, *A Year from Monday*, resonate with the joy he felt in his new status as a cultural phenomenon—joy that did not imply diminished responsibility; joy that was responsibility. In *0′ 0″* (1962) he overstepped his usual proscription of improvisation, and at the same time inscribed himself in his new status into the piece. What is presented here is not Cage's music but Cage himself, since he was the first and designated performer of the score's single instruction: 'In a situation provided with maximum amplification (no feedback) perform a disciplined action'. Like *Telemusik*, the work was a product of its composer's first visit to Japan: at the première, in Tokyo, Cage's disciplined action was the writing-out of the score. Like *Telemusik*, too, it marked its composer's awareness of himself as a global figure. On the world stage, and at a time of rapid, widespread social transformation, composing perhaps began to seem inconsequential—even evasive, too much a matter of 'an individual's conceptions'—and both Cage and Stockhausen returned from Tokyo to devote themselves more com-

23. Richard Kostelanetz, ed., *John Cage* (New York, 1970, 1991; London, 1971), 170.

pletely to group endeavours (especially in live electronic music) and to regroupings of music other than their own.

For example, most of Cage's rather few published compositions of 1963–68 belong to the *Variations* series and propose a multiplicity of activities: the sanctioned recordings of *Variations V* (1963), performed by Cage and Tudor, present vast sweeps of musical excerpts and other sound detritus. *HPSCHD* (1967–69), on which Cage collaborated with Lejaren Hiller as computer programmer, became in its public stagings a carnival of live musicians (up to seven harpsichordists playing music from Mozart to the present), tapes (up to fifty-one of them, each in its own temperament), slides, and films. Other 'works', never published, were perhaps only intended to happen once, like the *Musicircus* (1967) to which Cage invited various composers and performers, and the music went on along with films and slides in a large space with floating balloons and refreshment stalls.

These things were temporary—as temporary as the balloons and the hamburgers—and Cage's failure to publish *Musicircus* or the next year's *Reunion* may be taken as an acknowledgment of that. To revive those works could only be an exercise in 1960s nostalgia; anarchy—as Cage's subsequent output so magnificently demonstrated—constantly has to be reinvented, for otherwise it is form and custom.

Other composers were introducing quotations in a quite precise way for their affective and often nostalgic resonances, an outstanding example being George Crumb (b. 1929). Crumb described himself as having 'an urge to fuse unrelated elements and juxtapose the seemingly incongruous',[24] as in his *Night of the Four Moons* for contralto and four players (1969), of which Richard Steinitz has remarked that: 'The direct quotations from Bach, Schubert or Chopin, heard through Crumb's strange and unworldly soundscape, acquire an amazing aura of distance both cultural and temporal. Surrealist museum exhibits, their mummified beauty seems utterly remote, like a childhood memory of warm, homely security.'[25] It worked. But it worked only as long as tonal and atonal were strictly separate categories, implying a similarly strict separation between ancient and modern. Once composers began re-establishing tonality, and working again in traditional genres (and Davies was doing both from the mid-1970s), such quotations as Crumb's lost the shock, the inadmissibility, on which their effect depended.

The problem of integrating quotations into a foreign musical substance—a problem that barely arises in the otherwise very different works from this period by Cage and Crumb—becomes, in the remarkable Cello Concerto of 1969 by Hugh Wood (b. 1932), the problem of

24. Note with Nonesuch H 71255.

25. Richard Steinitz, 'The Music of George Crumb', *Contact*, 11 (1975), 14–22.

forcing back or accepting what a chosen genre most wants to convey. Right from the start of this work, the cello has been coming up with echoes of the Elgar concerto—falling semitones approached through a larger lift—while endeavouring to track its own route of intimate melancholy. Repeatedly its efforts have been greeted by the orchestra with derision (vehement passages close in tone to contemporary works by Maxwell Davies), menace, or coercion. Forced on again, but with a quietness that is chilling, the cello is eventually left with nothing to say but what it has said before, said in that other great concerto it has been circling around, striving to avoid.

This ominous weight of the past marks most of what Bernd Alois Zimmermann (1918–70) wrote during his last decade. A few years older than most of his Darmstadt colleagues, Zimmermann had always been less adamant about the need, or the feasibility, of a completely fresh start, and alongside post-Webernian essays, such as his *Perspektiven* for two pianos (1955–56), he had written works with deeper roots in common practice, like his trumpet concerto *Nobody knows the trouble I see* (1954). (Two generations of Austro-German composers, from Hindemith and Krenek to Zimmermann and Henze, saw in jazz and blues at once a challenge and a solace, an instance of music being vigorously new and popular.) His resolution of this divergence was a doctrine of 'pluralism', first put into practice in his opera *Die Soldaten* (1958–64), which not only uses the full panoply of musical means—speech, song, and sprechgesang, a vivid score for large orchestra, and electronic sounds on tape—but also introduces quotations from Bach and other composers. Zimmermann's technique here derives from the Violin Concerto of Berg, whose *Wozzeck* is a major influence on the opera as a whole, in the measure that Jakob Michael Reinhold Lenz, on whose play of 1776 the work is based, was an influence on Büchner. A work from the same period, *Monologe* for two pianos (1960–64), overlays and comments on quotations from Bach and Messiaen, as shown in example 37. The found materials are presented each in its own harmonic-rhythmic realm, and yet they exist together in a larger world that also has room for the original music that starts to arise around them, partly as commentary.

Zimmerman's 'pluralism' was stimulated by his view of the musical world in which he found himself: the claims of the future and of the past—the claims of *Perspektiven* and of *Nobody knows the trouble I see*— could be reconciled only by accepting both, at the cost of stylistic unity. 'We should have the courage to admit that, in the light of musical reality, style is simply an anachronism.'[26] Hence the deliberate oppositions of his *Antiphonen* (1962)—not only between the viola soloist and the orchestra, as in any concerto (and he returned again and again to this most combative of forms), but also between recalled and original

26. From *Intervall und Zeit*, quoted in note with Teldec 9031 72775.

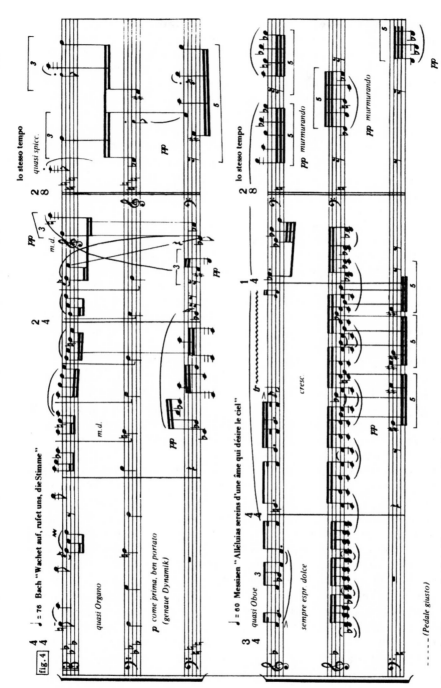

Example 37 Bernd Alois Zimmermann, *Monologe*

181

materials, and between instrumental sound and speech from the players. Work on *Die Soldaten* appears to have released several other pieces in which confrontations between new and old are worked out, including *Présence* for piano trio (1961), in which the three players are cast as literary characters—Don Quixote (violin), Molly Bloom (cello), and Ubu (piano)—whom the music leads through diverse encounters sharpened by quotations from Bach, Prokofiev, and others.

Unlike Davies, Zimmermann did not take the view that the music he composed was more real than the music he quoted: both were necessary to his works, and therefore equally integral and authentic. Bach in Zimmermann, or Bach in Berg, is not the same as Bach in Bach: something has happened, and it is the later composer who, responding to his musical situation, has made it happen. At least, this seems to be the position from which Zimmermann set out. 'One cannot avoid observing that we live in harmony with a huge diversity of culture from the most varied periods; that we exist simultaneously on many different levels of time and experience, most of which are neither connected with one another, nor do they appear to derive from one another. And yet, let's be quite honest—we feel at home in this network of countless tangled threads.'[27] Quite soon, though, the quotations in his music began to take on a more ominous resonance. In his orchestral *Photoptosis* (1968), there is no longer the attempt to conjure citations out of original music; instead, Beethoven, Wagner, and the rest gather to observe the passing of a tradition, framed and supported by brilliant but empty rhetoric. Zimmermann's last works, before he committed suicide, are bleak essays on the death of art and the extinction of hope: the *Requiem für einen jungen Dichter* (1967–69) and the 'ecclesiastical action' *Ich wandte mich und sah an alles Unrecht, das geschah unter der Sonne* (1970).

The curve of Zimmermann's career suggests a gradual collapse of the ability, or perhaps even the wish, to control the material and affective power of the music of the past: his output seems to tell a story of ghosts who return. Kagel never lets them come so close. As an ironic observer of the musical world, he took the opportunity of the vogue for quotation—which usefully coincided with the Beethoven bicentenary —to ask questions about the phenomenon of the great composer. His chamber orchestral version of his multipurpose *Ludwig van* (1969) reduces Beethoven themes to banality by empty repetition and distortion, and so provides an image of how music in Western culture has its meaning changed in similar ways, through the endless repetition of the standard repertory and the distortions of performers. As with several other works of this period, Kagel also made a film version, in which the same points are made more explicit by the use, again ironic, of modes characteristic of 'serious' television, such as the historical documentary and the panel discussion.

27. Ibid.

Other composers besides Kagel were prompted by the Beethoven anniversary to subject 'Ludwig van' to some scrutiny. Stockhausen, for example, created in *Opus 1970* a realization of his *Kurzwellen* in which Beethoven material on tape (fragments from the works and readings from the Heiligenstadt Testament) replaced the original shortwave radios as sources of ideas for intuitive elaboration by live electronic ensemble. According to the composer, the performers should be able 'to hear familiar, old, pre-formed musical material with new ears, to penetrate and transform it with a musical consciousness of today',[28] so that the music is explicitly removed from the musical and social contexts with which Kagel was concerned, and by which Zimmermann found himself oppressed. At least, that was perhaps the intention. Because of the tightness with which contexts are bound into Beethoven's music—the fact that just a bar, maybe even a chord, is enough to summon all kinds of images way beyond the structural effects and implications of the notes—irony is far more difficult to escape than had been the case in *Telemusik*. Stockhausen, lacking a sense of irony, may nevertheless have noticed something amiss, for *Opus 1970* had no life and no progeny after the occasion for which it had been made.

Meta-Music

The chatter of quotations in new music became noisiest at some time close to the Beethoven year, and then subsided. It indicated what was perhaps the sharpest crisis in music since the eruption immediately before the First World War, a crisis that was again a crisis of confidence, productive in some cases of creative collapse or hysteria. Few composers were untouched. Apart from those already mentioned—musicians as diverse as Cage and Davies, Stockhausen and Zimmermann—composers who introduced quotations into their works included such established figures as Shostakovich, who cited excerpts from Wagner and Rossini's *William Tell* overture in his Fifteenth Symphony (1971), and Tippett, who arrived at the *Schreckensfanfare* from Beethoven's Ninth Symphony in his own Third (1972). Both were probably aware of younger colleagues close at hand: Davies, Robin Holloway (b. 1943), who startlingly came forward with an orchestral exploration of material from cherished lieder, *Scenes from Schumann* (1970), and Alfred Schnittke (1934–98).

The moderated freedom of the late Khrushchev years, and the resultant visit of Nono to the Soviet Union in 1962, brought for many Russian composers a feeling of fresh opportunity, and Schnittke travelled the serial road awhile. By the end of the 1960s, however, he had come to the conclusion that serialism did not offer the means to command big, continuous forms, and so he began to work with combinations of tonal and atonal elements. Also, Nono's visit had perhaps opened

28. Note with DG 139 461.

a Pandora's box. If style was not vouchsafed by a tradition, if one could define one's own terms, then the possibility of creative integrity—of music arising and presented without artifice or manipulation—was over. This might be a cause for joy (creativity no longer being encumbered with Romantic ideology) or gloom (the guidelines of artistic morality having disappeared). In Schnittke's case, a wild hilarity in much of his music of the 1970s seems to hold despondency implicit.

Schnittke's first major expression of what he called 'poly-stylistics' was his First Symphony (1969–72), which includes quotations from Haydn, Beethoven, Chopin, Johann Strauss, Tchaikovsky, and Grieg, as well as jazz episodes in its hour-long continuous stream. The breakdown of unity is demonstrated, too, theatrically, in that the work starts out with just three musicians on the platform; the rest then enter, in a chaos of improvisation to which the conductor has to call a halt. In mirror fashion, most of the players go off before the end, leaving just a violinist, whose reminiscences of Haydn's 'Farewell' Symphony bring them back.

Resistance to music about music was generally restricted to those who fell silent (such as Boulez, silence being another response to crisis) and those who quoted not the substance of past music but its basic vocabulary in repetitive minimalism. The ending of the avant-garde thrusts had left a musical world with no great project, no direction ahead. A music of quotations could celebrate that freedom from history, react savagely or sombrely to deracination, or create new forms in which quotation is a necessity.

All these points of view fuse in the examinations Dieter Schnebel (b. 1930) made of revered masterpieces and called *Re-Visionen*, this being one of several cycles on which he worked at the time, along with *Maulwerke*, exploring nonstandard vocal resources, and *Für Stimmen (. . . missa est)*, whose subject is church music, a topic of special interest to a composer who is also a theologian. His project in *Re-Visionen* was 'to tap into the potential of the past, to carve out its perhaps undiscovered possibilities' and so bring about 'encounters with the past as a new country—and even as the future'.[29] In the first of these pieces, for example, *Bach—Contrapunctus I* (1972), the source material is simply transcribed for voices, five to a part, and yet this is enough to awaken echoes with much more recent music, by Schnebel himself and by Kagel, to whom he was always close. The singers are distributed in space, as Schnebel liked to do, and their humming, so unlikely for the 1740s, fits precisely with the composer's other choral music, besides giving the unnerving impression of a music stifled.

The disquieting presence of the same composer is enabled in *Leonce und und . . .* (1966), a scene Rolf Riehm (b. 1937) planned for an opera after Büchner's *Leonce und Lena* that got no further. Here the source is

29. Note with Wergo WER 6616-2.

the B flat minor fugue from *The Well Tempered Clavier* (first book) and the processing wavers between frank arrangement and shadowy allusion. One might have the impression that the characters are being pulled by strings from the past—and, beyond the characters, the supposedly new score in which they are contained. Violence in both music and characters is provoked, and wild fantasy, while all the possibilities of pathos seem prearranged by the original fugue. One of this composer's earliest published works, *Leonce und und . . .* announced a career that would be centrally concerned with asking questions about the received musical culture.

More celebratory, the middle movement of Berio's *Sinfonia* for vocal octet and orchestra (1968–69) achieves a complex irony, since not only is it a wash of quotations, but that wash is contained within what is itself a quotation: the scherzo from Mahler's 'Resurrection' Symphony, a movement whose meandering river-like progress is found now to be carrying an abundant flotsam of memories. What was form in Mahler (music made of notes) becomes meta-form in Berio (music made of other music)—though this is not a complete change, since there is evidence of deliberate allusion in the original (the form was already meta-form),[30] and since, too, Berio's treatment may be just the virtuoso actualization of associations any listener might bring to an experience of the Mahler (form becomes meta-form in the way that it is received). Berio's task was not to compose so much as to de-compose (to block out more or less of the Mahler movement as it went along), to assemble (to select at each moment the elements that could take their places on the Mahler stream) and to comment, largely in the vocal parts, which keep up their own current of cross-references impinging on a recitation from Beckett's *The Unnamable*.

Example 38 shows the opening of the movement, where the first discernible quotations come from the start of the 'Jeux de vagues' from Debussy's *La Mer* (bars 4–5: reeds and strings, plus figure in glockenspiel and harp) and from the beginning of Mahler's Fourth Symphony (bars 2–7: flutes and snare drum, with men humorously adding directions from the score). These citations are duly recognized by the two sopranos, but the second contralto has noticed also the arrival of the wholesale borrowing of the Mahler scherzo in something close to its original scoring (bars 7ff: woodwind and timpani). The connections, already, are of various kinds: connections of oeuvre (Mahler's), of rhythmic character (elements of ostinato in both the Mahler samplings, and of scherzo in both the Debussy and the gathering Mahler matrix), of harmony (the G major of the Fourth Symphony lighting the approach of C minor with the Second), of verbal association (the Mahler scherzo started out as a song, 'Des Antonius von Padua Fischpredigt',

30. See David Osmond-Smith, *Playing on Words: A Guide to Luciano Berio's Sinfonia* (London, 1985), 41–43.

Example 38   Luciano Berio, *Sinfonia*

and so has a watery link to the Debussy). In its gentle reminder of the many varieties of musical understanding, the movement stands out against the 1950s-Boulezian insistence on material structure alone. It also has a superbness of public effect that the status of the erstwhile avant-garde was beginning to make possible: the ultimate version of Stockhausen's *Momente* is another witness to this brief time when modern music was starting to reach large audiences—the large audiences who had recently participated in the rediscovery of Mahler.

However it may have been planned, the rest of the work seems to lead towards and then depart from the centrepiece, whose strong presence created problems of containment not settled until Berio added a fifth movement to the original four. The other movements could hardly be simulacra of the Mahler reworking, but nor could they ignore it. Continuity of sound was provided by the webbing of amplified voices and instrumental drifts (the work was conceived for the Swingle Singers, whose speciality was scat singing Bach); continuity of manner came from the absorption throughout in processes of generation and reworking. For example, the finale is, Berio said, at once the first movement's completion and a further commentary on everything that has gone before: 'The first four parts of *Sinfonia* are to the fifth as Mahler's scherzo is to the third.'[31] The work ends, then, in self-quotation, in meta-meta-music.

Crossing great swathes of time, seeming to evoke the origins of music in the burgeoning cries and calls of the first movement, the *Sinfonia* is yet very much a work of its age, packed with its age's hope that the analysis of underlying structures would reveal similarities between the apparently dissimilar, and carrying the fresh-found voices of its world: Mahler, Lévi-Strauss on the beginnings of myth (quoted in the first movement), Martin Luther King (for whom the second movement is an elegy). As a work of reportage, it takes its imagery, as *Telemusik* did, from radio, from tuning in. Radio had given composers of Berio's generation their main opportunities, both in presenting concerts and in providing facilities for electronic music (such as Berio and Maderna had enjoyed as directors of the Italian radio electronic studio in Milan in the late 1950s and early 1960s); radio also, by placing the knob-turning listener in seemingly immediate control, provided a positive experience of contemporary confusion. Hence the importance of radio as a metaphor for composers as they moved away from the search for a new language to the discovery of the many languages already existing.

For Berio, the many languages included not only those from the history of Western music he placed in the middle movement of the *Sinfonia* but also the languages of folk music from around the world. In *Folk Songs* (1964), written for Berberian, he fashioned a cycle of

31. Rosanna Dalmonte and Bálint András Varga, *Luciano Berio: Two Interviews* (London, 1985), 108.

sophisticated arrangements not so distant from those of Stravinsky, Ravel, and Falla, but later works place ethnic materials in much larger and more complex structures of cherishing and analysis. *Coro* for forty singers and forty instrumentalists (1975–77), for example, takes up not particular tunes but models of musical language and behaviour from different traditions—the art song of Western Europe, the heterophony of central Africa, the shape of Yugoslav melody—in 'an anthology of different modes of "setting to music"'.[32] But where the *Sinfonia*, even in its lament over King, had held out the prospect of a new dawn of jostling multiplicity, *Coro* is more commemorative than celebratory, repeatedly gathering its many performers and many cultures into clustered monoliths on a line of Neruda: 'Come and see the blood in the streets'. The mood of 1968 had changed.

That change can be heard, too, in Stockhausen's music, in the shift from the optimistic universality of his electronic *Hymnen* (1966–67) to the autobiographical dreams of *Sirius* (1975–77) and the works beyond. *Hymnen* repeats the intermodulatory techniques of *Telemusik*, though on a much larger scale (*Telemusik*, at seventeen and a half minutes, is an item, whereas *Hymnen* has the two-hour span of an entire concert) and to quite different effect, since now the raw materials are chosen to be recognizable and to elicit associations: they are the national anthems of numerous countries, sampled from recordings. Another difference is in the variety that spaciousness makes possible, for where *Telemusik* was quick and electric, *Hymnen* is grandly loose. It voyages from what sounds like poor reception (again the radio experience) into the clear exposure of an anthem, or from passages that take up the methods of *Kontakte* (operating, before the listener's ears, processes of transformation and decomposition on the recordings) to purely verbal sequences, like the multilingual litany on the word 'red' or the ominous calls of a croupier. And the scale and the range of the material are matched by the versatility of the work, which is, Stockhausen said, 'composed in such a way that various screenplays or librettos for films, operas and ballets can be written to the music'[33]. Not only that, but 'the order of the characteristic sections and the total duration are variable. Depending on the dramatic requirements, regions may be extended, added or omitted.' The work can therefore, by design, preserve its character through deformation; it has that amplitude and that resilience. Stockhausen had moved from the kind of locking process at work in *Kreuzspiel* through moment form to a libertarianism that *Hymnen* exemplifies in both structure and content. His own radical alterations to the original tape include a version with a live electronic ensemble to imitate what they hear and forge connections between anthems, and one in which, additionally, an orchestra plays along in the third of the

32. Berio's note with DG 423 902.
33. Preface to the score.

four 'regions'. This last version was, like Berio's *Sinfonia*, written for the New York Philharmonic. Both composers had spent long periods in the region of San Francisco—Berio, based in the U.S. between 1963 and 1972, taught at Mills College in Oakland, besides the Juilliard School in New York, and Stockhausen was at the University of California at Davis in 1966–67—and so both were close to the source of the new spirit of revolt that embraced resistance to the Vietnam War along with demands for the emancipation of blacks, women, and homosexuals. At least for a while, around the time of the *Sinfonia* and *Hymnen*, their work seemed to be part of a global upsurge and to embody the new pluralism as it was coming into being.

11

Music Theatre

In the 1950s, when attention generally was fixed on musical fundamentals, few young composers wanted to work in the theatre. Indeed,
to express that want was almost enough, as in the case of Henze, to
separate oneself from the avant-garde. Boulez, while earning his living
as a theatre musician, kept his creative work almost entirely separate
until near the end of his time with Jean-Louis Barrault, when he wrote
a score for a production of the *Oresteia* (1955), and even that work he
never published or otherwise accepted into his official oeuvre. Things
began to change on both sides of the Atlantic around 1960, the year
when Cage produced his *Theatre Piece* and Nono began *Intolleranza*, the
first opera from inside the Darmstadt circle. However, opportunities
to present new operas remained rare: even in Germany, where there
were dozens of theatres producing opera, and where the new operas of
the 1920s had found support, the Hamburg State Opera, under the
direction of Rolf Liebermann from 1959 to 1973, was unusual in commissioning works from Penderecki, Kagel, and others. Also, most composers who had lived through the analytical 1950s were suspicious of
standard genres, and when they turned to dramatic composition it was
in the interests of new musical-theatrical forms that sprang from new
material rather than from what appeared a long-moribund tradition.
(It was already a truism that no opera since *Turandot* had joined the
regular international repertory. What was not realized until the late
1970s was that there could be a living operatic culture based on rapid
obsolescence.) Meanwhile, Cage's work—especially the piano pieces he

had written for Tudor in the 1950s—had shown that no new kind of music theatre was necessary, that all music is by nature theatre, that all performance is drama.

Opera and 'Opera'

Ligeti no doubt spoke for most of his colleagues in the late 1960s and early 1970s when he declared that 'I cannot, will not compose a traditional "opera"; for me the operatic genre is irrelevant today—it belongs to a historical period utterly different from the present compositional situation.' No doubt he spoke for many, too, in going on to say that, nevertheless, 'I do not mean at all that I cannot compose a work for the facilities an opera house offers.'[1] (At this point he had written *Aventures* and its sequel *Nouvelles Aventures*, two pieces for three singers and ensemble that can be staged, though their flux of minuscule wordless dramas, careering from comedy to pathos, is freer and more immediate without theatrical trappings. They show how he was able to profit from his position as a mature student of the Western European avant-garde: by following his models—in this case, Kagel's *Anagrama*—while at the same time exaggerating them, and bringing to them his own charm and perfectionism.) But by the time he came to write his 'Opernhaus-Stück', *Le Grand Macabre* (1975–76), there had been a change in his view, and a change too in the musical climate. The age of anti-opera had passed; the new work would have to be, as he said, an 'anti-anti-opera'.

During the decade or so before *Le Grand Macabre* opera had been the preserve of composers willing and able to deal in some way with the genre's traditions, whether by following them (Henze and Zimmermann), by analysing them (Berio), by countering them (Kagel), or by seizing on the single truth that opera gives music a tongue with which to speak (Nono). Nono's was a rare escape. Why the power of tradition should have been felt so much more strongly in opera than in, say, orchestral or piano music (there are no operatic equivalents to *Gruppen* or the sonatas of Boulez and Barraqué) is a complex matter, having to do, perhaps, with the rigidity and smallness of the standard opera repertory, and therefore with the costs of experiment (financial and aesthetic costs) and the pressure to conform. The great lesson of the standard repertory is that the story is paramount, that the music should be in synchrony with the story's narrative flow. Diatonic music, with its progressive narratives of harmonic movement and thematic transformation, is very good at that, which is why opera flourished during the era of diatonic music's supremacy, from Monteverdi to Puccini and Strauss. Atonal opera is opera in crisis: *Erwartung*, *Wozzeck*. And crisis is

1. Ursula Stürzbecher, *Werkstattgespräche mit Komponisten* (Cologne, 1971), 43.

hard to perpetuate. Hence the need for later composers either to acknowledge tradition in writing operas, or else to find new forms and new kinds of narrative, whether in oriental theatre, in folklore, in contemporary Western drama, or in unstructured 'happenings' of the kind enabled by Cage and the Fluxus composers.

Henze, the most prolific and most performed opera composer since Britten, remained so by virtue of his warm, thorough-going acceptance of opera's history and conditions. Where Berg in *Wozzeck* wrote a symphony at some ironic remove from the action, as if to suggest how the normal world of diatonic-thematic narrative was now broken and suspended, Henze's symphony in *The Bassarids* (1965)—a reworking of the *Bacchae* of Euripides, for which W. H. Auden and Chester Kallman wrote the libretto—is plushly in the foreground. As he has explained, the first movement is a sonata which establishes the conflict between the principals, Dionysus and Pentheus, as a musical conflict between fluid, unmeasured, ululating voice (the call of Dionysus, a tenor) and staccato trumpet fanfare.[2] The second movement is a scherzo in the form of a suite of Dionysian dances; the third, incorporating Dionysus's hypnotizing of Pentheus, is an adagio succeeded by a fugue; and the finale is a passacaglia.

The Bassarids was the culmination of the sensuous, unashamedly nostalgic style Henze had pursued since moving to Italy a decade before. The symphonic structure, recalling not so much Berg as Mahler, is ample enough to include gestures made in diverse directions, from the knowing, deliberately vulgarized pastiche of Baroque French cantata style in the intermezzo interrupting the slow movement to quotations from Bach, both as an earlier master of the siciliana rhythm on which the opera floats (Henze belongs squarely, even self-consciously, in the line of German artists rhapsodizing the Mediterranean) and as a source of references to support a parallel between the Crucifixion and the sacrifice of Adonis. (Here is an example of how what are being treated here as separate waves—historicism, theatre, politics—were flowing together and interpenetrating.) The integration of varied materials and opposed themes, as displayed in the opera, is in Henze's view a characteristic of the 'segregated' artist, the 'outlaw'. Undoubtedly he saw himself in this role, at odds with conventional society by virtue of his homosexuality, and artistically contrary both to tradition (though ever less so) and (ever more so) to the avant-garde, since he turned aside from the tentative approach to total serialism he had essayed in his Second Quartet (1952). His inclusion in 1958 in the issue of *Die Reihe* devoted to 'young composers'—along with Stockhausen, Boulez, Nono, and the rest—had already been an anachronism; by the time of *The Bassarids* the divide was absolute: *Momente* had already been

2. See 'The Bassarids: Hans Werner Henze talks to Paul Griffiths', *Musical Times*, 115 (1974), 831–32.

written. 'Never would he aim at an accord with the basic tendencies of his time', Henze writes of his chosen type; instead he must devote himself to a minority 'which merits his sympathy and which excites his sensual and spiritual substance'.[3]

Henze's concern with the individual as a feeling being—even with himself as a feeling being—was part of his grand Romantic inheritance, and it inclined him, as it did the Romantics, to another genre in which these relationships with sympathetic minorities and uncomprehending masses could be played out: the concerto. *The Bassarids* was followed by a rush of such works: chamber concertos for double bass and for oboe and harp (several such works were written by various composers for the marital duo of Heinz and Ursula Holliger), and the determinedly autobiographical Second Piano Concerto. But then this absorption in his own personal and artistic situation was joined by a commitment to the interests of all those ignored or oppressed by bourgeois society. The darling of the Salzburg Festival, for which *The Bassarids* had been written, became a revolutionary; the poet of the soul began to shout about social iniquities. It was 1968.

In the quasi-operatic oratorio *Das Floss der 'Medusa'* of that year, dedicated to Che Guevara, Henze dealt with the historical episode in which a group of shipwrecked men were abandoned to a raft by their officers, and left to face the perils of drowning and starvation. After the experience of its abortive Berlin première, lost amid struggles between police and left-wing students, Henze spent a year in Cuba, writing his Sixth Symphony, and expressing in that score his delight in the sonorities and rhythms of Cuban music, as well as reaffirming his alignment with socialism by including in the elaborate polyphony quotations from Vietnamese and Greek protest songs.

But apart from the appearance of a new edge and anger in the music, and a partial, momentary relinquishment of continuity, not so much had changed. The Caribbean was a new Mediterranean: a new south, a new sensuality, a new escape. And the revolutionary activist— whether appearing as a character in the works or writing them—was a new guise for the Romantic hero. Henze's awareness of this is perhaps signalled by his preoccupation not so much with revolution as with the problems of being a revolutionary artist—problems he addressed in his first post-1968 piece designed for stage presentation, the 'show' *Der langwierige Weg in die Wohnung der Natascha Ungeheuer* (1971), scored for baritone and several ensembles. How, this work asks, can the left-wing intellectual justify the part-way commitment of pushing for revolution in his work but taking no active part in the class struggle? The music, like much that Henze wrote during this period, abounds in quotations and opportunities for more or less directed improvisation, as well as in broader references to cultural types, bringing out the nature and force

3. Hans Werner Henze, *Essays* (Mainz, 1964), 32.

of the alternative siren songs by which the artist hero is beset. A *Pierrot* quintet, dressed in hospital overalls, represents the sick bourgeoisie (as so often for composers of this generation—not least Boulez—Schoenberg is a Freudian-Oedipal father). A brass quintet, with police helmets, are the agents of the oppressive state machine, a role the brass in *The Bassarids* perform for Pentheus. A rock group provides the voice of the underground. And there are two instrumental soloists: a percussionist, whose violent, physical activity is a metaphor for the complete engagement from which the hero withholds himself, and a Hammond organist as plutocrat.

Henze took up the contradictions exposed in this perhaps necessarily confused score in another concerto—his Second Violin Concerto of the same year—and dealt with them on a more abstract level, though still theatrically. The soloist is here cast, in a dramatization of what had been the case in this composer's earlier concertos, as the self-willed Romantic virtuoso, trying at once to relate to the system (the orchestra) and to prove his independence: his quixotic condition (and a male soloist does seem to be necessarily implied) is displayed in his being costumed as the Baron von Münchhausen of German story. He plays; he speaks. And the music unwinds around a poetic commentary by Hans Magnus Enzensberger on Gödel's theorem, that any complex system contains propositions which, within that system, can be neither proved nor refuted. From this the work conjures the extrapolation that any system—especially any musical or social system, one is led to infer— must destroy itself.

Undoubtedly Henze's own system of political expression was doing so. The allurements he felt were, perhaps beyond those of *Natascha Ungeheuer*, the dreams and fantasies and pleasures of his earlier music— things he had carried with him, as he had carried his southern attachments to the New World. His Cuba, as sung in his Sixth Symphony, in his dramatic 'recital' *El Cimarrón* (1969–70) and in his 'vaudeville' *La Cubana* (1973), is not that of Castro and the struggle to build a socialist society but that of the tropical forest, of plantations lying under the beating sun, of seedy urban night life and exotic dance rhythms. His sympathies, as expressed in *Das Floss der 'Medusa'*, *El Cimarrón*, *Natascha Ungeheuer*, *La Cubana*, and the Second Violin Concerto, are with the individual rather than the mass, which is customarily presented, Romantically, as wanting to have a restraining influence on the flood of life and love in the individual's breast (*Der Prinz von Homburg*) or else as following blindly in the charismatic leader's wake (*The Bassarids*). Henze's personal and artistic apartnesses remain, of course, relevant.

The single striking difference in his explicitly revolutionary output was the absence of opera, as if that most bourgeois of musical institutions had to be spurned, and replaced by the alternative concert-hall theatrical forms of such works as *El Cimarrón*, *Natascha Ungeheuer*, and the Second Violin Concerto. Not until a decade after *The Bassarids* did

Henze return to opera with *We Come to the River* (1974–76), and by then his political alignment was becoming moderated. His decisive, if still uneasy, rapprochement with German tradition was marked by a new batch of string quartets at the same time.

For Henze, opera became a problematic medium at the time of his political engagement; for Nono and Berio, it was the proper arena for controversy and provocation. Nono's commitment seems to have led him to opera even at a time when the genre seemed most outmoded: *Intolleranza* was a spurt of energy against the nature of the medium, doing away with story and display, insisting on the powerful presence of the chorus, and introducing into the theatre the brutally new sound world of electronic music. In the case of Berio, his theatre works of the 1960s are more overtly political than anything else in his output, even if the message gets more complexly overlaid along the line from *Passaggio* to *Laborintus II* (1965) to *Opera* (1970).

Laborintus II is a double labyrinth of words and music, one in which the Ariadne's thread is a spoken narration written by Edoardo Sanguineti around phrases and images from Dante's *Inferno*. As this line of text unwinds, so it triggers music from an ensemble of voices and instruments covering a broad spectrum of styles from madrigalian euphony to contemporary jazz: we hear the voice of a lover, of a mob, of a flute, a trumpet or a harp, of the electronic constructs on tape. The ranging is typical of the time, but where Henze in *Natascha Ungeheuer*, for instance, used different styles as distinct social tokens, Berio's purpose is to tease out musical connections: what most distinguishes the score is the fluid movement from one situation to another, the hazy in-between rather than the specific reference. The work lies also in between music and language, in an area Berio had already explored in such works as *Thema*, *Circles*, and *Epifanie*. As in his *Chemins* series, where a previously composed instrumental solo is surrounded by music for ensemble, the voices and instruments of *Laborintus II* provide an oblique commentary on the spoken text, while at the same time the text is an oblique commentary on the music—a kind of running poetic programme note. Yet another in-betweenness of this opalescent score is its midway status between concert hall and theatre. It has no explicit action, but in concert it tends to sound like an unstaged opera. Perhaps its home is in the medium for which it was written, and to which so much of this period's music appeals, in grateful thanks: radio.

The maze structure of *Laborintus II*—another constant of the time, as witness Boulez's Third Sonata or Stockhausen's *Momente*—is also a feature of Berio's first opera, whose title is a signal that its concern is with the genre itself. Berio probably would have echoed Ligeti's statement about the impossibility of writing just another opera, a contribution to a history. His answer was to take that history as his subject, both by self-consciously creating operatic forms, as Berg had done in *Lulu*, and by searching back to the origins of opera, beginning each act with an 'Air' to a text from Striggio's libretto for Monteverdi's *Orfeo*. *Opera* is a celebration of opera, and also—because it refuses to abide by the rules it entertains—an implicit criticism. The history of opera is to be seen as a history of dissolution and decline, going on in parallel with other sliding catastrophes the work presents: the history of Western capitalism and the sinking of the *Titanic*.

Music Theatre

If opera seemed to progressive spirits in the mid-1960s to be in its dot-age, there appeared to be new possibilities in smaller, more flexible combinations of music and drama, often denoted as 'music theatre'. A sporadic history of such works was claimed: *Pierrot lunaire* and *Histoire du soldat* were the classic twentieth-century examples ubiquitously cited; Monteverdi's *Combattimento* was a distant ancestor. But there was no precedent for the sudden and brief flowering that happened now, and that could be seen in the work of composers as removed from the avant-garde as Britten (in his church parables).

The explosion of music theatre out of opera was more than a meta-phor in the case of the new genre's most active proponent, Davies, whose work on his opera *Taverner* sparked off an interrupting suc-cession of dramatic pieces for smaller forces, beginning with *Revelation and Fall* for soprano and sixteen players (1965–66). His model was de-cisively Schoenberg rather than Stravinsky or Monteverdi, and he was instrumental in founding a performing ensemble—originally called the Pierrot Players, later the Fires of London—based on the *Pierrot* lineup, for which most of his later music-theatre pieces were composed. *Revelation and Fall*, though scored for a larger group, makes musical refer-ence to Schoenberg, and also enters that Viennese period by way of its Trakl text and its allusion additionally to Lehár, in a characteristic love-hate embrace of light music. It is also typical of Davies in taking the expression of extreme emotion as by itself dramatic. He is a dramatist of the individual (and especially of the individual under stress), not of relationships, and all his best theatre pieces are for soloists: the scarlet-habited nun of *Revelation and Fall*, screaming into a megaphone at the moment of crisis, the even more unhinged male vocalist of *Eight Songs for a Mad King* (1969), the nude male dancer of *Vesalii icones* (also 1969).

Based on a story that King George III in his madness tried to teach birds to sing, *Eight Songs* places its instrumentalists in giant cages to wit-ness and suffer the manic ravings of the soloist, whose part calls for a huge range, both in pitch and in vocal colour. If this is the most spec-tacular of Davies's dramatic inventions, *Vesalii icones* is the most intense. The dancer, whose gestures mirror both the engravings in the sixteenth-century anatomy text by Vesalius and the Stations of the Cross, lays bare the agonies of Christ, while the instruments—among which the cello has the principal role as the dancer's shadow, partner, or ideal—

add further layers of analysis and distortion, in which Davies's character-istic use of hidden and overt parody keeps the music on the disquieting border between commitment and mockery.[4] At the eighth station, for instance, there is a complex masquerade of musical images stimulated by the episode in which St Veronica wipes Christ's face and receives the imprint of his features on her cloth. The opening of this section has the cello declaiming a theme from Davies's *Ecce manus tradentis* for soloists, chorus, and instruments (1965), a work itself based on the plainsong setting of those words: the chant of betrayal is thus doubly betrayed by the time it reaches *Vesalii icones*. At the same time the piano decorates a second plainsong theme in the style of a nineteenth-century salon piece. Subsequently the material is bent to allude to the scherzos of two Beethoven symphonies, to Pierre de la Rue's *L'Homme armé* mass, and to Davies's own *Missa super L'Homme armé*. There are also more flagrant, even exhibitionist parodies, as at the sixth Station, where the mocking of Christ is the occasion for twisting the *L'Homme armé* tune into a comfortable Victorian-style hymn (that style itself a sort of blas-phemy, the music insists) and later into a foxtrot, which the dancer is to play on a honky-tonk piano. Parody and drama in this work spring from the same source: the violence shown on stage is a violence the music is doing to itself.

Davies's dependence on Schoenberg is parallelled by the relation to Stravinsky in the work of his colleague Birtwistle—to the clear-cut forms of such works as the Symphonies of Wind Instruments and *Agon*, and to the rustic theatre of *Renard* and *Histoire du soldat*. (The com-posers continued their association after Manchester: the Pierrot Players were founded under their joint direction.) Birtwistle's first major the-atre work was the chamber opera *Punch and Judy* (1966), which is based on the old puppet shows, and which presents a gallery of characters who are part clown, part monster, all of them still puppetlike in their abrupt and grotesque behaviour, their appalling passions and their mur-derous savagery. Parody was part of Birtwistle's arsenal too, but more important was a pure fury of gesture: for example, the high woodwind chords of screeching alarm that entered his music in *Tragoedia* for en-semble (1965).

Punch and Judy is, like Stravinsky's *Renard*, closed and cyclic: a rite of death and resurrection, night and day, winter and summer. Its highly symmetrical structure includes, for example, four 'Melodrama' sec-tions in which Punch traps his victims in wordplay, each followed by a 'Murder Ensemble' which is the celebration of a ritual execution; and these larger sections are filled with tiny, compact forms, often strung together in patterns of verse and refrain. Though the work is nominally an opera, it relates to the music-theater tradition not only in its links

4. See Michael Taylor, 'Maxwell Davies's *Vesalii icones*', *Tempo*, 92 (1970), 22–27.

with *Renard* but also in its reduced scale and its dramatic style. The action is to be presented as if from a puppet booth, in which the characters go through their motions and in which also a wind quintet is seated, the pit orchestra consisting of just ten further players. As for dramatic style, the cyclic ceremonial necessarily discards narrative continuity, and the characters are sharp-featured, bright-coloured figures in formal patterns of ferocious hate and consuming lust.

Instrumental Theatre

The antiphony in *Punch and Judy* between the stage quintet and the pit band is just one example of how Birtwistle's drama is as much instrumental as sung, projecting ideas of display, signal, independence, combat, and repetition to be found in such concert works of his as *Tragoedia* and *Verses for Ensembles* (1969), the latter a ritual play for instrumentalists on different platforms. Three percussionists have one level for their noise instruments and another for their xylophones and glockenspiels; five woodwind players are seated at the left when playing high instruments and at the right when using their lower equivalents; a brass quintet has its own station; and there are also antiphonally separated desks for trumpet duets and for woodwind solos accompanied by the horn. Example 39 shows the opening of the first of two climactic sections of echoing and answer placed within the sequence of 'verses' for different groupings—sections which in their severe pulsation look forward to the time-measuring that underlies many of Birtwistle's works of the next decade. The arresting quality of the music in performance can be imagined.

Musicians in movement had already appeared in, for example, works by Berio (*Circles*) and Boulez (*Domaines*), but the more fundamental idea here is that musical performance is by nature dramatic, and that a soloist in concert dress, playing on a platform, is an actor. The drama of performance is a current in all of Birtwistle and in all of Berio, even where it is not emphasized by movement or by unusual orchestral layouts. It is a current, too, in all of Kagel, though often spilling over into a drama of situation. His *Match* (1964), for example, is a musical contest between rival cellists, refereed by a percussionist: the extreme difficulty of the cello parts may be judged from example 40, and if the calculated absurdity of the enterprise is not evident from the score, it is abundantly clear in the composer's film version. (*Match* is one of several Kagel pieces that seem to demand the close-up, deadpan inspection of the camera, and that belong to a cinematic tradition of wordless comic shorts.)

Another Kagel piece, *Der Atem* (1970), is one of many works in which he addressed the pathology of performance and performance as pathology. According to his description: 'A retired wind player devotes himself to the continual repetition of the same thing: maintaining his

Example 39   Harrison Birtwistle, *Verses for Ensembles*

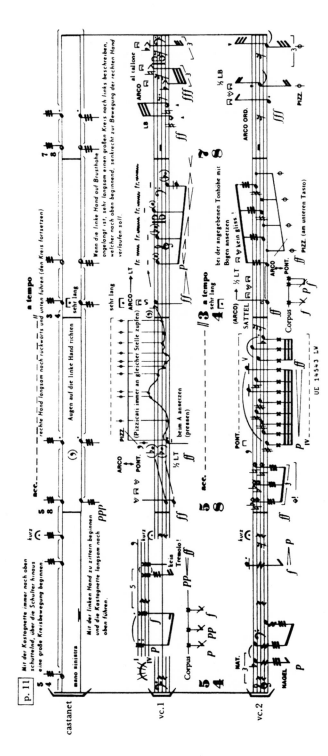

Example 40 Mauricio Kagel, *Match*

200

instruments. At each moment he goes to the cupboard, takes out the instruments and puts them back, oils them, blows into them, wipes the saliva traps, warms the reeds and the mouthpieces, silently does some exercises; often he talks to himself while polishing away all the time. Occasionally he happens to play, properly speaking.'

It was Kagel, almost inevitably, who created the anti-opera that Ligeti had anticipated and been obliged to go beyond, for Kagel's amused, ironic eye could hardly fail to turn the opera house inside out. His *Staatstheater* (1967–70) uses all the resources of such an institution —principals, chorus, orchestra, corps de ballet, scenery, costumes—in activities that satirize, ignore, or contravene customary purpose, the soloists being brought together in a crazy sixteen-part ensemble, the dancers put through their paces in gymnastic exercises. But not all Kagel's theatre works of the period were so absurd or so loosely structured. In *Tremens* (1963–65) he considered the effect of hallucinogenic drugs on aural experience: the subject was presented in a hospital cubicle, forcibly encouraged by a doctor to listen to tapes of music which a live ensemble distorted, as if projecting the subject's imagined versions. And in *Mare nostrum* (1973–75) he played with the idea of a party of Amazonians trying to make sense of Mediterranean culture, so that the work displays the relativity of norms, musical and social, and the danger of condescension in anthropology.

Stockhausen, his sense of spectacle already apparent in *Gruppen* and *Kontakte*, exemplifies the post-1945 history of neglect followed by abundance in the sphere of dramatic music, since until 1968 he had composed almost nothing with a theatrical component (the single exception was *Originale*, a 1961 version of *Kontakte* that took the form of a regulated happening, with contributions from Cologne artists and other 'originals'), whereas after 1971 almost all his works were representational dramas. The first was *Trans*, which presents its audience with the awesome spectacle of a string orchestra seated in close rows behind a magenta-lit gauze, solemnly unfolding a sequence of still, dense harmonies. From further back come the amplified but indistinct sounds of wind and percussion groups in marching chords or swirling melodies, this music impervious to the implacable crashes of a weaving shuttle (heard at irregular intervals from loudspeakers), to which the strings respond each time with a change of chord. All this, like Kagel's *Match*, came to its composer in a dream, and there is a further connection with Kagel in the four moments of surreal comedy that are superimposed on the rest: the first of these has a viola player performing a virtuoso cadenza, 'like a little wound-up toy instrument'[5] switched on by a marching drummer. What is indelibly Stockhausen's is how the piece is at once bold and tacky, magnificent and failing.

5. Jonathan Cott, *Stockhausen: Conversations with the Composer* (London, 1974), 63.

The larger *Inori* (1973–74) is comparable in this respect, and in its massive orchestral sonorities, which map out the development of a melody through a two-hour span in phases concentrating on rhythm, dynamics, melody, harmony, and polyphony, as if in a résumé of musical history. But where *Trans* made theatre out of orchestral performance, *Inori* adds the actions of a mime, or pair of mimes, in attitudes of worship taken from many different cultures, these actions of prayer seeming to be amplified by the orchestra: the Japanese title has the meaning of 'Adorations'. Soon after, in *Harlekin* for dancing clarinetist (1975), the composer introduced the concept of the instrumentalist-actor, performing in costume, and so prepared the way for his *Licht*, in which the main characters are more likely to be represented by instrumentalists than by singers. Opera and instrumental theatre are one.

12

Politics

Cardew

'The ideology of a ruling class is present in its art implicitly; the ideology of a revolutionary class must be expressed in its art explicitly. Progressive ideas must shine like a bright light into the dusty cobwebs of bourgeois ideology in the avant-garde, so that any genuinely progressive spirits working in the avant-garde find their way out, take a stand on the side of the people and set about making a positive contribution to the revolutionary movement.'[1]

The words of Cornelius Cardew express a hope shared by several composers of his generation in the early 1970s, as it became clear both that political establishments in the West were retreating from the idealism and reform, and that, on a more local level, the musical avant-garde had compromised its opposition to the dominant culture. Boulez, who had been a firebrand as a young man in Paris, was now conducting Brahms in London and New York. The most iconoclastic music of Cage had been embraced by the publishing, recording, and broadcasting industries. The early works of Stockhausen were being taught in colleges and conservatories. If any kind of music could become acceptable, then emphatic political expression seemed to many younger composers to provide the only way of being unacceptable.

---

1. Cornelius Cardew, *Stockhausen Serves Imperialism* (London, 1974), 86.

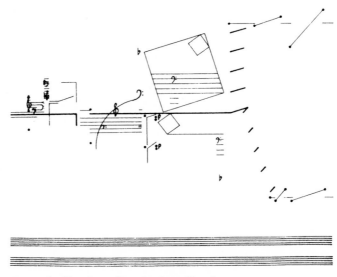

Example 41 Cornelius Cardew, *Treatise*

Cardew had gone on from his work with Stockhausen to align himself more with Cage, and to produce in his *Treatise* (1963–67) a magnum opus of music as graphic design, as game without instructions, map without key: example 41 shows a representative extract. The work was, by intention, both triumph and disaster. 'Psychologically', Cardew wrote, 'the existence of *Treatise* is fully explained by the situation of the composer who is not in a position to make music.'[2] The only music he could make at this time was improvised music, as a member of the London performing group AMM, who worked with conventional instruments and electronics, and who sought, through communal concentration and discipline, to exceed their individual boundaries as musicians trained in jazz or classical traditions. For Cardew, and for other musicians, the experience of improvisation was a politically radicalizing influence, for its lessons of fruitful cooperation and productive freedom seemed ready for application to the wider world.

First they might be applied to the wider musical world. Cardew went on from *Treatise* to make settings in *The Great Learning* (1968–70) of the first seven paragraphs from a classic Confucian text—settings to bring professional musicians and amateurs together. *Paragraph 2*, for instance, simply offers twenty-six drum rhythms and twenty-five rudimentary melodies of five or six notes. The performers are divided into several groups, each consisting of a drummer and singers. The drummer chooses one of the rhythms and repeats it continuously, while the singers, following a leader, proceed slowly through one of the melodies. Then all move on.

2. Cornelius Cardew, *Treatise Handbook*.

Work on this piece led to the formation in 1969 of the Scratch Orchestra, a group of composers, musicians, and nonmusicians who joined together idealistically to continue to break down barriers between professional and amateur. A musical training provided no special privileges and might even be a handicap; the atmosphere was one of benign anarchy. Scratch Orchestra programmes included compositions from the new generation of U.S. experimental musicians, including La Monte Young, Terry Riley (b. 1935), and Frederic Rzewski (b. 1938), and by members of the group, as well as scratch performances of popular classics and 'improvisation rites', which were designed so that they did not 'attempt to influence the music that will be played' but rather tried to 'establish a community of feeling, or a communal starting-point, through ritual'.[3]

Producing a new classic was not on the agenda, but it happened in the case of Wolff's *Burdocks* (1970–71). Like Cage in his *Concert for Piano and Orchestra*, Wolff drew here on a variety of compositional practices he had developed in recent years, sometimes using staff notation of a simple kind allowing multiple possibilities, sometimes conveying an idea or approach in words—or even just a single word in the case of one of the ten pieces: 'flying'. As usual with him, the score conveys not so much prescriptions as suggestions, just enough to allow and encourage the performers to work on shaping and reshaping a certain melodic motif, on responding to one another, on learning as they go. Because the musicians are invited to make decisions on the spot about how to treat the material and each other, realizations of *Burdocks*, or of Wolff's later collection of fourteen *Exercises* (1973–74), will tend to pause unexpectedly, go back, turn off in a new direction (which may be a cul-de-sac), and invest time in rather modest activities—though Wolff's small tunes are remarkably unlike anything else, prompting Cage, after an *Exercises* performance, to speak of 'the classical music of an unknown civilization'.[4] Lack of conventional success, though, is evidence of fundamentally new ideas at work—or very old ideas, of music as a cooperative activity in which anyone may take part.

Like a revolutionary cadre, the Scratch Orchestra was from the first to be alert to its own evolution, and almost inevitably that evolution led it from the modelling of egalitarian relationships in music to active political engagement. News of the Cultural Revolution in China was welcomed as showing the way forward—a way that led through subjection to public criticism (or at least to criticism within the group) and a horrifying willingness to abandon anything but the slogan of the moment. For a performance of the first two paragraphs of *The Great Learning* in 1972, Cardew made a new translation of the characters, so that the call for keen introspection in the Ezra Pound version—'*The*

3. Cornelius Cardew, 'A Scratch Orchestra: Draft Constitution', *Musical Times*, 110 (1969), 617.

4. Quoted by Frederic Rzewski in his note with New World 80658-2.

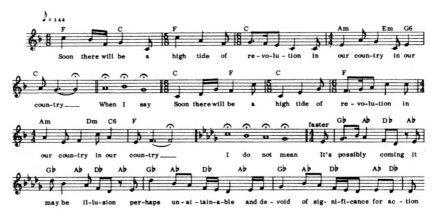

Example 42   Cornelius Cardew, 'Soon'

Great Learning takes root in clarifying the way wherein intelligence increases through the process of looking straight into one's own heart and acting on the result; it is rooted in watching with affection the way people grow'—took on a doctrinaire political cast: '*The Great Learning* means raising your level of consciousness by getting right to the heart of the matter and acting on your conclusions. *The Great Learning* is rooted in love for the broad masses of the people.' It was also at this point that he began to attack his erstwhile mentors Cage and Stockhausen, and to repudiate his own earlier works, as politically irrelevant if not downright pernicious. He began to write simple didactic songs, to make arrangements of impoverished material from Beijing, and to produce piano transcriptions of Chinese and Irish revolutionary ballads in the manner of nineteenth-century salon music. The opening of one of the songs, 'Soon' (1971), shown in example 42, may indicate how far Cardew had travelled in the few years since *Treatise*.

Rhythmic irregularity alone lives on as an avant-garde heritage, and yet the musical quality of 'Soon' is not the point, any more than the musical quality of *Treatise*, being inaudible, could possibly be the point—or any more than the musical quality of *Structures Ia* is the point. Each is a victory of ideology, but with the difference that in 'Soon' that ideology is political. Thereby it marks the moment—as surely as such other phenomena of the period as minimalism and historicism—when the idea of musical progress was abandoned, or perhaps had to be abandoned. Progress now, for Cardew and composers who thought like him, could only be political progress, and music must relinquish all its own hopes and histories in order to serve that cause.[5]

5. For a conspectus of Cardew's musical and political development, see Richard Barrett, 'Cornelius Cardew', Michael Finnissy and Roger Wright, eds., *New Music* 87 (Oxford, 1987), 20–33.

Rzewski

Among those who shared Cardew's view were composers from the United States, including Rzewski and Wolff, both of whom, like Cardew, had roots in the classic avant-garde: Wolff as a pupil of Cage, Rzewski sharing Cardew's own background as an associate of Stockhausen's. In 1966 Rzewski, with other U.S. musicians in Rome, founded one of the first live electronic ensembles, Musica Elettronica Viva, whose broad interests are suggested by one of their publicity statements: 'Tapes, complex electronics—Moog synthesizer, brainwave amplifiers, photo-cell mixers for movement of sound in space—are combined with traditional instruments, everyday objects and the environment itself, amplified by means of contact mikes, or not. Sounds may originate both inside and outside the performing-listening space and may move freely within and around it. Jazz, rock, primitive and Oriental musics, Western classical tradition, verbal and organic sound both individual and collective may all be present.'[6]

MEV began by playing determined compositions by members, but soon turned more to improvisatory pieces, following the example of jazz and rock groups, and following too the nature of the medium. This was not music for standard instrumental lineups that could be reproduced around the world and for decades to come; it was music made for what was to hand, music for the moment. That temporariness was an invitation to deal with issues of the moment, be they musical or political; there was also the evidence from improvisation, as with AMM at the same time, that musical issues were political issues in microcosm. *Spacecraft*, performed by MEV on numerous occasions in 1967–68, had the programme of leading each player from an 'occupied space' of personal inclination to 'a new space which was neither his nor another's but everybody's'.[7] Then in *Free Soup* (1968) Rzewski asked that the audience should play with the ensemble, who were 'to relate to each other and to people and act as naturally and free as possible, without the odious role-playing ceremony of traditional concerts.'[8]

Rzewski's first outspokenly political works, *Coming Together* and *Attica* (both 1972), both call for an unspecified instrumental ensemble to give cumulative force to a repeating melody, rather as in his earlier improvisation piece *Les Moutons de Panurge* (1969), and along the lines of the early music of Philip Glass (b. 1937), in whose ensemble he briefly played. But the 1972 pieces also include spoken texts, taken from moving and noble statements made by prisoners involved in the Attica revolt of September 1971, and now it seems that the driving music is

6. Quoted in Michael Nyman, *Experimental Music: Cage and Beyond* (London, 1974; Cambridge and New York, 1999), 110.

7. Frederic Rzewski, quoted in ibid., 110.

8. Ibid., 111.

driving home the words. Rzewski went on to produce a set of thirty-six piano variations on the Chilean protest song '¡El pueblo unido jamás será vencido!' ('The People United Will Never Be Defeated!', 1973), placing occasional avant-garde elements within a virtuosity inherited from Liszt and Busoni. The adaptation of past styles to present political needs becomes, perhaps, a way of rescuing those styles from their bourgeois origins. It also demonstrates that the composer has refused the role of artistic pacemaker, the role that bourgeois culture had assigned the avant-garde in order to defuse it.

The Composer in the Factory

Like Cardew and Rzewski, Nono was very aware of the power of the dominant culture to appropriate musical innovation; like them he was struggling—and for much longer had been struggling—with that power. But he could never accept that the answer was to forsake all hope of musical advance, since for him political and musical revolutions went hand in hand. 'I see no reason', he wrote, 'why music today should not take part in the discovery, the formation of new dimensions—human, technical, virtual and real—which exhibit and express the fundamental historical movement of our time: the fight by the international working class for socialist liberty.'[9] Revolutionary thought demanded revolutionary means, and the way to avoid assimilation was to move entirely out of the official arena, by rejecting the network of institutions— concert halls, festivals, modern music ensembles, recording companies —through which capitalist culture had domesticated the avant-garde. Accordingly Nono began to present his music in factories—especially *La fabbrica illuminata* for soprano and tape (1964), which uses the words of factory workers and the noises of factory machinery—and to write for new media. Most of his works from this point on use electronics, for reasons both musical and, on several levels, ideological. Studio composition made the composer himself into a worker: using his hands, having responsibilities to colleagues, dealing with actual material rather than with mental figments. Also, the use of recorded factory noises—not only in *La fabbrica illuminata* but in several succeeding works—was designed to place the music within the experience of workers, and estrange it from the experience of bourgeois concert-goers. Finally, through tape it was possible to bring into the music direct signals of political involvement: the sounds of street demonstrations in *Contrappunto dialettico alla mente* (1967–68) or of Castro reading a letter from Che Guevara in *Y entonces comprendió* (1969–70).

The sounds of actuality give Nono's works of this period vividness, but they also contribute to a broadening of detail. Though the music

9. Luigi Nono, 'Der Musiker in der Fabrik', *Mitteilungen der Deutschen Akademie der Künste*, 5 (1967), 6–8.

still makes use of abstract constructive techniques the composer had developed in works leading up to *Il canto sospeso*, especially in the handling of rhythm, the pitch realm is less differentiated—partly because of the recorded material, partly for artistic reasons in which Nono's electronic experience may have played a part. Strident, anguished sounds are very much to the fore in his first tape piece, *Omaggio a Emilio Vedova* (1960), and in another, *Ricorda cosa ti hanno fatto in Auschwitz* (1966). But then of course such sounds are proper both to his voicing of protest and to the urban, mechanized world he wanted his music to echo, and they are instrumentally embodied in the clusters and sustained, searing sonorities of his orchestral writing from *Incontri* onwards. The essential difference in the later music is that the expressive urgency of such sounds makes it impossible to hear them as merely a by-product of compositional research. In *Per Bastiana–Tai-yang cheng* for orchestra and tape (1967)—a work dedicated to the composer's second daughter, and taking its subtitle from the Chinese revolutionary song 'The East is Red', which is immersed in the music—the fury swerves into the foreground. Nothing could more forcibly demonstrate Nono's distance from the China-watching songs of Cardew and Wolff.

Per Bastiana is unusual among his works of this period in returning to the concert hall, but such a return was inevitable in order to work with large forces, and the compromise was reduced when he could work with musicians who, like Claudio Abbado and Maurizio Pollini, sympathized with his musical and political ideals. For them he wrote *Como una ola de fuerza y luz* (1971–72), a memorial to South American freedom fighters; it was also Abbado who facilitated his return to opera. Like Berio, he had been fascinated by the new techniques introduced by U.S. theatre companies: he had used part of the Living Theatre's Vietnam war protest play *Escalation* in *A floresta è jovem e cheja de vida* for voices, clarinet, bell plates, and tape (1966), and the experience left an impression on the open structure of his second opera, *Al gran sole carico d'amore* (1972–74), which is not so much a narrative as it is a documentary anthology focussed on the plight of the lone principal character, an unnamed Mother. Like *Intolleranza*, the work is boldly and blockily scored for soloists, chorus, orchestra, and tape, but it also takes advantage of the more direct methods Nono had discovered in the intervening compositions—not least in its projection of the solo female voice against orchestral or electronic backcloths as a 'symbol of life, of love, and of freedom from all new forms of oppression'.[10]

10. Nono's note with Wergo 60067.

13

Virtuosity and Improvisation

The Virtuoso

The history of music is a history of performers continuously transcending what were thought to be limits, but rarely as rapidly as in the 1960s and early 1970s. Wind players learned to produce not only multiphonics but also percussive noises (by tapping on parts of the instrument) and microtones, as well as unusual sounds created by means of more or less severe alterations to the embouchure and mouthpiece. Many of these devices were also possible on brass instruments. On strings, new sounds could be obtained by unconventional bowing pressures, by bowing on unconventional parts of the instrument, by striking the instrument in various ways, and so on. Changes in piano technique tended to be more straightforward tightenings of traditional demands in terms of dexterity except for occasional ventures, post-Cage, into the interior of the instrument (plucking or tapping strings) and onto its frame, but percussionists found vastly wider scope, in terms of their instrumentaria, their techniques, and their musical importance. It is enough to note that a virtuoso percussionist could hardly have existed in Western music before the 1950s—Stockhausen had to write *Zyklus* because no percussion test pieces existed—whereas percussion ensembles and soloists are now a normal part of musical life.

One could simply use the new resources for their poetic effects, as Henze did, for example, in his *Heliogabalus Imperator* (1971–72), where woodwind multiphonics create effects of festering decadence within what is a conventional symphonic poem. Or, like Berio, one could take them as deepening and ramifying the relationships connecting an instrument's physical nature with its history and with its performer. Each of Berio's many works for soloists, whether unaccompanied or concertante, seems to arise in a very direct manner from the instrument or voice concerned: from the physical exercise of playing it, and from the history and repertory it has. What follows is that technical effects—and new technical effects all the more so—are engrained in how the music is: they are not embellishments, nor are they curlicues of adventitious difficulty. The works of his *Sequenza* series are showpieces, certainly, but the showiness is not an extra. In *Sequenza VI* for viola (1967), frenetic tremolo chords are the substance of the piece. *Sequenza V* for trombone (1966) could not exist without the new effects of the period, especially singing into the instrument. *Sequenza III* for female voice (1965–66) is not a song with new vocal techniques, but new vocal techniques that make a song. If later members of the series tend to withdraw from these new sounds, that is partly because music as a whole has done so, and partly because Berio grew more concerned with the histories of instruments than with their practicalities. Another difference is that the earlier members of the series were written for a rather narrow band of new-music practitioners, including Severino Gazzelloni (*Sequenza I* for flute, 1958), Cathy Berberian (*Sequenza III*), Vinko Globokar (*Sequenza V*), and Heinz Holliger (*Sequenza VII* for oboe, 1969), whereas the later pieces have entered a world far more densely populated with ready performers.

All the *Sequenza* pieces are composed performances; what also distinguishes the earlier pieces, especially those for voice and for trombone, is that the performances are theatre as much as music—that they belong with the music theatre of the time. *Sequenza III* is a setting of a short poem by Markus Kutter, but the main concern, as in the earlier electronic pieces *Thema* and *Visage*, is with vocal behaviour rather than verbal meaning: the words, deliberately elementary, are there to be confused. Example 43, from near the opening of the piece, shows something of the variety of vocal styles required, and shows too Berio's characteristic use of psychological cues ('tense', 'giddy' and so on). The music does not express a dramatic situation; it is that situation. So the work belongs with others in Berio's output, such as *Circles* and *Epifanie*,

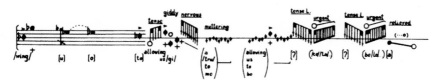

Example 43   Luciano Berio, *Sequenza III*

which, written with Berberian's many voices in mind, make music the generative force of theatre. This was a lesson studied by many other composers—perhaps most profitably by Georges Aperghis (b. 1945), whose *Récitations* (1977–78), written for the singer-actress Martine Viard, again use diverse kinds of articulation, but now to create characters expressing themselves in monologue or dialogue within compact, strip-cartoon frames. As for the operas Berio himself went on to write, these can be seen as successive attempts to create much larger musical forms that would have the same autonomy, the same supremacy over words and action.

If *Sequenza III* is typical of Berio in its dramatic nature and in its dwelling at the frontiers between music and language, it also displays, like all its companions in the series, his command of hectic activity within closely defined harmonic limits, his obsession with repeated return, redefinition, and re-elaboration. *Sequenza VII*, for example, is a flurry of escapes from, decorations of, and rejoinings to a note sustained throughout the piece as a drone. (An abiding characteristic of the composer was his fascination with the musical world in which he found himself—even with the popular musical world, as witness his arrangements of Beatles numbers—and his response to the advent of minimalism was typically alert.) Often the urge to re-elaborate cannot be confined within the piece, and produces richer versions, as in the case of *Sequenza II* for harp, which, in *Chemins I* (1965), was embedded in an orchestral tissue developing its ideas in diverging directions. Writing of this work Berio remarked that: 'A thing done is never finished. The "completed" work is the ritual and the commentary of another work which preceded it, of another work which will follow it. The question does not provoke a response but rather a commentary and new questions.'[1]

Sequenza VI was a particularly fruitful source of proliferating avenues. Berio first wrapped the viola solo in music for an instrumental nonet to create *Chemins II* (1967), and then surrounded this work with orchestral divagations to make *Chemins III* (1968). A further, oblique route from *Chemins II* is taken in *Chemins IIb* (1970), an orchestral commentary from which the solo part has been removed, and this in turn gave rise to *Chemins IIc* (1972), which adds back the solo thread but now allots it to a bass clarinet. The three directly linked works— *Sequenza VI, Chemins II,* and *Chemins III*—are related to each other, Berio said, 'like the layers of an onion: distinct, separate, yet intimately contoured on each other: each new layer creates a new, though related surface, and each older layer assumes a new function as soon as it is covered.'[2] There is thus a two-way flow of musical thought, outwards

---

1. Programme note for a concert at the Palais des Beaux-Arts, Brussels, on December 18, 1966.
2. Note with RCA LSC 3168.

from the original solo to the orchestra, and inwards to the centre. The process may be one of unfolding, as when latent harmonies in the solo are explicitly stated by the nonet or the orchestra, but it is more likely to be one of development and change.

The principle of commentary, enshrined in these three works in exemplary fashion, belonged to the age. Composers of Berio's generation had learned that the ideal of the immediate postwar years, that of starting music again from scratch, could not so easily be accomplished, or at least that it could not be repeatedly accomplished. Stockhausen had spoken of the limitless availability of new systems, waiting to be discovered, but the experience of the 1960s was that history stayed around, even if it was only the history of each composer's own works. Composition was not pure invention; it was adaptation. And the consciousness of that seems to have led composers to make adaptation the point. Berio, whose *Sinfonia* is the great classic of music as commentary, produced not only expanding versions of his own scores but also orchestral treatments of works by Brahms, Mahler, and Verdi.

His leaning towards commentary led him naturally to two genres in which the text-commentary duality is inherent: settings of words, and concertos, the latter including not only the *Chemins* series but also other recompositions and new works created immediately in concertante format, such as *Points on the Curve to Find . . .* (1973–74), in which a small orchestra fills out the harmonic potential in an almost exclusively monodic solo piano part consisting mostly of rapid trills and tremolos, and in which the brass, by providing sustained pitches and chords in what is otherwise an excited polyphony, underpin a nervous movement towards the resolution of the final unison D. Another example is the Concerto for two pianos and orchestra (1972–73), which has a more complex but equally sure harmonic ground plan, beginning over an E pedal, and coming in its second half to an increasingly firm definition of G as tonal centre, this finally affirmed by G major chords. Here again, Berio was sensitive to the time—and to his own inclination to deal with history, not write it off—in seeking a greater harmonic continuity than had been characteristic of music in the 1950s and early 1960s. However, the harmonic statements and processes in his music are unambiguous only on the largest scale: at any moment they may be surrounded by alternatives that nudge at the music's basic principles, and keep it in the world of questions rather than answers. Berio's Concerto—the only one of his many concertante works to have that title until Concerto II (1988–89), subtitled *Echoing Curves*, the echoed curves being those of *Points . . .*—is by implication and by deed a commentary on the whole concerto form, as much as his *Sinfonia* is a commentary on the symphony. And just as the *Sinfonia* tries at moments to escape from being a symphony, so the Concerto at times evades concertoness, as when the nominal soloists begin to become accompanists to members of the orchestra.

The notion of music as commentary, so fecund for Berio, seems to have been for Boulez—previously so insistent on innovation—a cause at once of excitement and despair. 'When I have in front of me', he has said, in terms which call to mind his *Trope*, 'a musical idea or a kind of musical expression to be given to a particular text of my own invention, I discover in the text, when submitting it to my own kind of analysis and looking at it from every possible angle, more and more possible ways of varying it, transforming it, augmenting it and making it proliferate.'[3] Much of his output since 1960 has consisted of reworkings, and his biggest project of this period, *Pli selon pli*, exists in so many versions that perhaps one should consider it less a work than a nexus of possibilities, which, 'fold by fold', have multiplied. Other examples include the orchestral *Notations*, begun in 1977 as vast amplifications of piano miniatures from 1945, and *Eclat/Multiples*, in which the proliferation of musical ideas and ensembles is the modus operandi.

So it is too on a more compact scale in *Domaines*, which, like so many of Berio's works, finds the commentary idea at home in concertante form, for the work is a sequence of dialogues between the clarinet soloist and the six ensembles in turn, these elaborating ideas in the solo part. This is Boulez's sole contribution to the virtuosity of display, for his piano sonatas, though certainly hugely demanding, do not make a point of virtuosity, and though his orchestral scores, developed through his performing experience, require a virtuoso conductor, their virtuosity virtually eliminates showmanship. Even in *Domaines* he shows the lack of interest in new instrumental techniques, offering his clarinetist the option of including multiphonics but specifying only the principal note, which seems less an advancing of aleatory freedom than an admission that marginal sounds are only decorative. It was not so for Berio, at least in his works of the mid-1960s, and it was not so for composers who were themselves instrumentalists, such as two for whom Berio wrote *Sequenza* solos: Vinko Globokar (b. 1934) and Heinz Holliger (b. 1939).

The latter studied with Boulez, whose influence is evident in the orchestration of his oboe concerto *Siebengesang* (1966–67), and also in the work's transposition into instrumental music of the form and feeling of a Trakl poem, 'Siebengesang des Todes'. But in writing for the oboe, Holliger was writing for his own voice, and he seems to have put into the work everything he then knew about playing. The work is a 'seven song' in being divided into seven sections, in having orchestral groupings in sevens (to a total of seven-squared players), in using sevenfold divisions of time, and in concluding with a seven-part female chorus to vocalize on syllables from the poem's last line. But the response is to the imagery as well as the numerology of the poem—to the image of death as a beautiful voyage, with the oboist riding 'shimmer-

3. Pierre Boulez, *Conversations with Célestin Deliège* (London, 1977), 15.

Example 44 Heinz Holliger, *Siebengesang*

ing torrents, full of purple stars' in calling on different orchestral ensembles to serve either as foils (glockenspiel, celesta, and two harps, in the second section) or as assemblies of colleagues (alto flute, cor anglais, horn, and viola, in the fourth). The solo part requires multiphonics—as shown in example 44, from the virtuoso utterance with which the work opens (not shown is the complex, delicate arpeggio of cymbals, celesta, and violin harmonics at the first bar)—as well as, at the end, the ability to sustain a soft high A for about fifty seconds (Holliger's own method of 'circular breathing' made this feasible), while in the sixth section, to great dramatic effect, the player has to take up an instrument with a microphone inserted into it, and use techniques that make this amplified oboe able to imitate almost anything the orchestra can come up with, from disruptive staccatos in the brass to woodwind chords or the highest jitterings of the violins. Holliger's immediately subsequent works tended to push the exploration of virtuosity—rather as in Kagel's music—into denatured terrain, and thereby to provide the virtuoso with more ambiguous rewards.

Virtuosity in Question

Much of the music considered above not only celebrates virtuosity but is circumspect about it: that was the nature of the analytical age in which these works were composed, and of the analytical composers who created them. But there are composers who, like Berio, relish artistry, and others who, like Kagel, want to look behind at mechanics and motivations, at the psychological, physiological, and cultural nature of improvisation, its requirements and its costs. *Match*, for instance, is, in addition to a display piece, an essay on the competitiveness of our musical culture, and on the closeness of the concert to the sports event. In later works the questions tend to take over, and Kagel turns virtuosity against itself, either by asking players to take part in musical situations that inevitably deflate the strenuous efforts they demand, or by asking them to devote their skills to quite unaccustomed activities. *Unter Strom* (1969) begins with its three players performing on an electric fan, to which is attached a strip of cloth that strikes the strings of a guitar at each rotation, three children's sirens amplified by a megaphone, and a hard rubber ball in an electric coffee grinder. As so often in Kagel's music, the ridiculousness is partnered by a strange beauty, a beauty all the stranger for being, so it seems, by the way; and a highly formal presentation, not only in the score but in the performance, forbids the piece being dismissed as a joke, or as only a joke. Writing about *Der Schall*, which is similarly scored for a small group using a variety of musical and nonmusical instruments, Dieter Schnebel noted that 'the debilitated or run-down or worn-out sounds, the notes of strange instruments and the noises of non-instruments are employed in a musical progression that radiates the aura of the great classical repertory; a symphony, composed as it were from the wreckage of the old symphonic school.'[4]

As Kagel himself remarked, an essential aspect of his work is 'strict composition with elements which are not themselves pure'.[5] The music is strict in that it is exactly prescribed, as shown in example 39, from *Match*. Kagel, like Cage, was not in the business of improvisation. But he found his material in phenomena that had been overlooked, viewed as secondary, or even spurned: unusual instrumental resources (non-instruments in *Unter Strom*, unaccustomed instruments in *Musik für Renaissance-Instrumente* and *Exotica*), players' gestures, routines of practising. His works of the later 1960s and early 1970s carried thereby a critical charge as much as the contemporary works of politically motivated composers, but with the criticism operating on the cultural plane, and with the object not so much of pointing to a better world as of demonstrating the failures and assumptions of the old one. In Germany, where the power of Adorno's thought was still immense, his works were highly valued and highly influential, and music's ability to express its own deterioration—as well as to structure the ashes, and perhaps thereby claim survival, if not hope—was tested too by Helmut Lachenmann (b. 1935), in a whole series of works initiated by the remarkable *temA* for flute, mezzo-soprano, and cello (1968).

For Lachenmann, a pupil of Nono, the challenge was to reach beyond models of musical practice that were not only outworn but also compromised, in that they had been absorbed by bourgeois culture. The task for composers was to reclaim their materials: to discover new and unsuspected beauty in what, by traditional canons, would be regarded as malformed and inadmissible. What he was after was 'beauty not only through refusing the customary but also through unmasking the conditions of what counts for beauty, such as the suppression of the fundamental physical prerequisites and energies, of the fundamental efforts—if you will, of the concealed labour.'[6] The means by which sounds are combined and connected would have to be rethought, not

---

4. Dieter Schnebel, *Mauricio Kagel: Musik, Theater, Film* (Cologne, 1970).

5. Quoted by Josef Häusler in his article on Kagel for *The New Grove* (London, 1980)

6. Helmut Lachenmann, 'Die gefährdete Kommunikation', *Musik als existentielle Erfahrung*, ed. Josef Häusler (Wiesbaden, 2nd ed. 2004), 102.

taken over from procedures developed in another age for other purposes, and the rethinking would engage the performer—necessarily a virtuoso—in the process. *Pression* for solo cellist (1969–70) is typical of Lachenmann's work of this period in its concentration on irregular techniques, and thereby on the physical mechanism by which the sounds are produced. The score is, as in Cage's prepared piano music, a programme for action, but now requiring new kinds of notation. At the start of the piece, shown in example 45, the directions indicate how the bow is to be held in the right fist while the left hand's fingers produce whispering glissandos of quasi-harmonics; the effect is of quiet respiration or the gentlest breeze, in a *pianissimo* to which the piece often returns.

It is characteristic of the composer that the situation is dialectical, and on several levels. Though the music is produced under pressure (in French, *pression*)—figuratively in the tension any performance is likely to have on account of the unfamiliar techniques, and literally in that it is the pressure of bow and fingers that produces the sound—it is predominantly delicate. A venerable instrument is found to have quite unexpected resources. Things that would be slips under other circumstances are now striven for, and rendered as objects of beauty. Lachenmann's reference to such pieces as 'instrumental *musique concrète*' evokes how this is a music of whole sounds, not of sounds as instances of pitch, duration, and so on, but he has also remarked that the listening experience becomes concrete because 'one hears under what conditions, with what materials, with what energies, and against what (mechanical) resistances each sound or noise is produced'.[7]

As to form, *Pression* reproduces the process of discovery by which it was made: a performance possibility is explored until it leads into, is invaded by, or summons another, in a process of invigorating sonic imagination and drama. Lachenmann's search for new sounds implied new forms, in keeping with his view that any sound comes with formal properties, arising partly from the tradition in which it is being composed, performed, and experienced, and partly from its physical nature. Among the types he has distinguished is the 'cadence sound',[8] of which an example duly appears at the end of *Pression*: a loud pizzicato from which an upward rustle escapes. 'Any object a composer uses,' he has explained, 'any sound, any noise, any movement in sound or connection or transformation—Stockhausen would say: any event—is with all its complexity a point simultaneously on infinitely many straight lines that can be made to course through this point or be pulled through it. Composing means recognizing, at whatever point, the lines on which it lies and from which it derives its meaning in terms of before and

7. Note with Col Legno WWE 31863. See also *Musik als existentielle Erfahrung*, 381.

8. See the composer's essay 'Klangtypen der Neuen Musik', in ibid., 1–20.

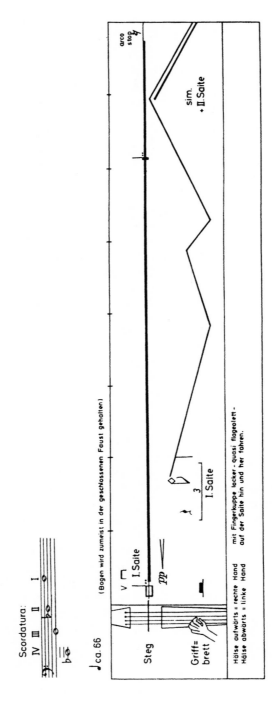

Example 45   Helmut Lachenmann, *Pression*

afterwards as well as its quality in terms of perception. It also means, in deviating from this, drawing other lines through such a point and so discovering new points, reorganizing the first and so ambivalently, polyvalently defining and expressively illuminating both old and new points in what is a newly created connection.'[9]

For Lachenmann at this time the lines could be drawn most freely and richly outside the norms, as in his piano piece *Guero* (1970), named after a percussion instrument and turning the piano into one, which the pianist plays by strumming across the keyboard with fingertips or fingernails (never once depressing a key) and by tactile investigation also of the tuning pins and strings. The piece shows in exemplary fashion how Lachenmann could find a new instrument in the body of the old. 'In its simple coupling of denial and opportunity,' he notes, '*Guero* provides a manual and at the same time psychological study for pianists, who, deserted by their pianistic repertoire, must still hold out as musicians and find themselves—a study, too, for listeners.'[10]

The sophistication and restraint in Lachenmann's thinking are met by simplicity and range, for the eschewal of convention provides access to moments of intense, new brilliance. There may be a sense of exile, but the new world is fresh and waiting to be explored, by listeners as much as by performers. There is no time, here, for nostalgia. Lachenmann accepts from the great tradition the duties of seriousness and weight, but shows how they may be discharged with quite new means. His *Gran Torso* (1971–72) stands, for all the abraded variety of its string effects, in the line of great quartets—indeed, it does so precisely because of the richness, point, and novelty of its materials. Lachenmann did not accept from Nono the need for expressed political affiliation, and yet the exposure of the music (and the musicians) to the listeners is not without social reference, nor is his music's cherishing of the disparaged, weak, and fragile. Extremity is approached with fine care.

Much of Xenakis's music of the period also makes exceptional demands on instrumental soloists, either alone or in combination, and, as much as Lachenmann's, leaves little room for virtuosity as self-presentation. The demands are, though, of a different kind. His solo piano piece *Evryali* (1974), one of the first works in which he created branching 'arborescences' of his 'non-octaving' scales (scales in which the repeating unit is some other interval than the octave), comes as a torrent of sound, as suggested by example 46.[11] (A branch is ending in the top staff as another begins in the lowest.) Such music questions what we mean by accuracy in performance. The pianist Peter Hill has

9. 'Über das Komponieren', in ibid., 76.

10. Note on the piece, in ibid., 383.

11. A page from the composer's graphic representation of the piece, clearly showing the branching scales, is reproduced in the booklet with Montaigne 782 005.

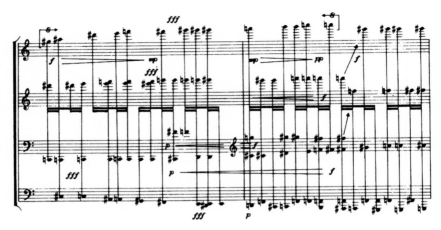

Example 46   Iannis Xenakis, *Evryali*

suggested that in such pieces as *Evryali* the player must decide what can be achieved, what can be omitted, and what can be altered without severe detriment,[12] in which case the performer becomes a co-creator as much as in Lachenmann—but to limit an ideal, not to search it out.

Hill's assumption must be that 'what can be altered without severe detriment' lies open to the performer, but this may not be so, and perhaps is not so in some of Babbitt's music, where in principle every detail is crucial. Example 47 shows the opening bar of his *Post-Partitions* for piano (1966), where a twelve-note aggregate is partitioned into dyads, each struck twice, so that there are twelve attacks. These attacks occur at twelve different time points in six simultaneous metres, a feature that the dynamic levels are designed to clarify, a direct relationship being maintained throughout the piece between dynamic level and time point on the scale *ppppp* = 1, *pppp* = 2, . . . *fffff* = 12, i.e., 0. The 4/4 barring in the example applies only to the triplet quaver units: on the triplet-semiquaver level, there are two notional bars in the example, and on the quintuplet-semiquaver level there are one and two-thirds.

The dynamic levels make it clear that, for instance, the first C in example 47 is at time point one (metre counted in units of a triplet quaver) while the Aβ occurring with it is at time point two (metre counted in triplet semiquavers), and the second occurrence of the same dyad is at time point four (metre counted in quintuplet semiquavers). In this bar two time points are struck in each of the six metrical streams: eight and zero in the semiquaver stream (each a low bass C), for example, or three and seven in that of septuplet semiquavers. These 'time-point dyads' are the rhythmic equivalents of the pitch-class dyads

12. Peter Hill, 'Xenakis and the Performer', *Tempo*, 112 (1975), 17–22.

Example 47   Milton Babbitt, *Post-Partitions*

introduced, if the latter are numbered according to the usual convention that C is zero, C♯ one, and so on; hence, for example, A♭–C has the
numbering eight-zero, and E♭–G is three-seven. There is thus a cohe-
siveness between pitch-class and rhythmic dispositions such as Babbitt
had been seeking since his *Three Compositions.*

However, the ostensible time-point structure cuts against a much
more obvious way of understanding the passage, as an overlapped sequence of two-note repetitions, the staggerings and the repetitions being
at subtly different time intervals. Babbitt's earlier works, such as the
Three Compositions or the streamlined Second Quartet (1954), had suggested a smooth complicity between the composer and performer, performer and audience—a relationship in which the performer presents
and the audience receives what the composer intended. *Post-Partitions,*
like many other Babbitt pieces of this period, testifies to breakdown.
The composer's intentions are not adequately communicated by the
printed music, for all its precision in notation, which, in any event is
utopian (as, for example, in supposing that a difference can be maintained between *ffff* and *fffff*).

Alternatively, and perhaps more optimistically, one can accept *Post-
Partitions* as an exemplary instance of music that performers and listeners have to grasp in ways quite different from the composer's. Just as
one need not be aware of ionic forces and molecular geometries when
admiring a crystal, so the thinking necessary to create such a work as
Post-Partitions may not have to be in the player's mind or the listener's.

One may be impressed more by the pianistic alacrity so vividly placed in evidence, or by the jittery rhythms of slightly uneven repetitions (a Babbitt characteristic), or by the use of extreme registers—the sense that all of the piano's notes remain constantly available (again typical of Babbitt's later music). This perpetual implicitness of the whole pitch repertory—coupled with an unvarying tempo of unfolding, however irregular the rhythmic detail—gives to Babbitt's later music a distinctive quality at once febrile and mechanical. Control is felt, but so is unpredictability.

The Electric Musician

Holliger's *Siebengesang* was a dramatic demonstration of how the virtuoso can find through electronic means a new voice, but the arrival of live electronic music had more profound effects on the nature of performance. Being difficult to predict, because subject to the particularities of the equipment and to fine subtleties of adjustment, live electronic music welcomed indeterminacy and improvisation. The medium seemed almost to demand an empirical choice of means, which in the 1960s and early 1970s would have included conventional instruments or voices with electronic extensions, adapted or invented instruments, and standard electronic devices. Exploration—of timbre, of ensemble relationships, of the interface between composition and interpretation—was primary, largely because the electrification of performance took musicians into a world in which nothing had been standardized. Since little could be foreseen, conditions of performance outweighed what could be written down in advance, and so performing ensembles quickly established their own practices, and normally created their own material. (Something similar was happening in popular music at the time.)

Cage's *Cartridge Music* has already been noted as first in the field; several of his subsequent pieces were prone to electronic performance, even if this was not specifically stated in the score. Stockhausen's first live electronic works—*Mikrophonie I* for six explorers of the sounds of a tam-tam (1964) and *Mixtur* for ring-modulated orchestra (1964)—reveal, not coincidentally, a new experimental feel in his music. According to his own account, he created *Mixtur* as an improvisation: the piece is basically a sequence of textures to be obtained by modulating different orchestral ensembles with different sine tones. (Ring modulation, one of the fundamental techniques of live electronic music in the 1960s and 1970s, takes two inputs and produces sum and difference frequencies from them—an effect somewhat like that of a slightly off-tune radio signal.) One result of the new approach was that works could be achieved very much more quickly, without the long labour on paper that had been necessary to bring about new sounds in *Gruppen*, *Carré*, and *Momente*.

Mikrophonie I also was developed by trial. Here a large tam-tam was activated by two performers using a variety of objects, while two others picked up the resulting vibrations with microphones and a further pair operated filters and volume controls. The score specified the kind of sound to be made (whispering, grunting, trumpeting, and so on), the means of production, the rhythm, the loudness, and the electronic controls to be applied. Moreover, the work was formally determined, for though 'the order of structures may vary considerably from version to version' (and *Mixtur* is similarly a late example of mobile structure), 'a strong and directional form was guaranteed, the composer asserted, by a scheme of permitted connections among the structures.'[13]

That form was enforced not only by the composer's written scheme but also, more fundamentally, by the use of a single instrument, and hence of a connected, if extremely wide, net of resonances. As Robin Maconie observed, 'the process of articulation actually resembles the mechanics of speech, the tam-tam representing the vocal cavity, the various modes of excitation consonants and vowels, and the filters and potentiometers shaping diphthongs and envelope curves',[14] so that there was still here an inheritance from Meyer-Eppler's courses. Heard in this way, the piece was the tam-tam's song or lecture, in which it showed off its vocal repertory. What it said, though, was decisively controlled by Stockhausen, seated at a console to determine the final outcome.

In that respect *Mikrophonie I* was markedly different from much of the work of Stockhausen's U.S. contemporaries, such as the members of MEV or the Sonic Arts Union, a foursome formed by Robert Ashley (b. 1930), David Behrman (b. 1937), Alvin Lucier (b. 1931), and Gordon Mumma (b. 1935). The touring ensemble that grew out of performances of *Mikrophonie I* was devoted almost exclusively to Stockhausen's work, and that work was not about self-projection for the performers, still less about enfranchising the audience. Another difference was that Stockhausen was willing to abandon projects as he moved on to what he perceived as the next stage in a historical process—though to some degree built-in obsolescence was in the nature of the genre. Live electronic music favoured not so much the work as the process, constantly mutating with changes in technology, personnel, and venue, as Stockhausen recognized in moving on from the elaborately prescribed *Mikrophonie I* to *Prozession* (1967), in which elementary signs indicated how the players were to react to one another, starting out from their memories of earlier Stockhausen pieces.

Lucier's pieces show an even greater economy, and a knack for inventing exemplary situations that can be repeated under widely

13. Note with CBS 72647.

14. Robin Maconie, *The Works of Karlheinz Stockhausen* (London, 1976; 1990), 142.

different circumstances. His *Vespers* (1968) has performers exploring a darkened room with click generators and listening to the echoes so that, batlike, they collide neither with each other nor with stationary objects but go about their business of taking what the composer calls 'slow sound photographs'[15] of their surroundings. In his *I am Sitting in a Room* (1970) a spoken sentence is progressively obscured through cycles of playback and rerecording that cover the original sounds with an accumulation of resonances from the room in which the performance is taking place. At the same time, these resonances iron out the composer-speaker's stuttering—an effect dependent, of course, on having Lucier (or a recording of him) involved. There is in any event a tension between the live electronic medium, being fluid and unpredictable, and the finished art work—a tension often resolved, perhaps superficially, by having the composer involved as guarantor of authenticity.

Stockhausen's pieces required him for more than that. Experience with live electronic music encouraged him to use amplification in most of his works from the late 1960s onwards, whether for large resources (*Trans*, *Inori*) or small (*Stimmung* for six singers, 1968), and so to make his presence almost a requirement, to supervise the installation and, often, control the sound in performance, as he did with his live electronic group. In his next work for them, *Kurzwellen* (also 1968), he opened his music's sources from its players' Stockhausen memories to whatever broadcasts might be picked up, each player using a short-wave receiver as well as an instrument. He had been working in radio now for fifteen years, and had often used the imagery of radio, but this was his first work with radios as sound sources, and his admission of quite unpredictable sound material—material which even he could not steer in rehearsal or develop in performance—testified to developments in his musical metaphysics and also to his more general understanding of his role as composer. Instead of trying to embrace the 'music of the world', as he had in *Telemusik* and *Hymnen*, he asked the players of *Kurzwellen* to be always alert to the call of the unknown. This was a work not of integration but of listening; its poise was not to gather but to receive; it was a voyage, in Stockhausen's words, 'to the edge of a world which offers us the limits of the accessible'.[16] The improvisatory *Spacecraft* simultaneously developed by MEV was devised for similar ends, but where Rzewski and his colleagues seem to have been interested in a social journey from self-absorption to group commitment—and where the 'free improvisations' of Globokar's New Phonic Art Ensemble, and of other such groups at the time, were being undertaken partly in liberation from the dictatorship of composers—Stockhausen's intentions for *Kurzwellen* were that it might effect a spiritual unloosening, for both

15. Quoted in Michael Nyman, *Experimental Music: Cage and Beyond* (London, 1974; Cambridge and New York, 1999), 91.

16. Ibid., 69.

players and listeners. Bringing the unknown into dialogue was to be more than a musical procedure.

From this point on Stockhausen became readier to advance spiritual aims. *Stimmung* was a 'winged vehicle voyaging to the cosmos and the divine',[17] and the collections *Aus den sieben Tagen* (1968) and *Für kommende Zeiten* (1968–70), both intended for the composer's live electronic group, consisted of prose poems, couched in oracular language and suggesting meditative exercises in improvisation, or, to use Stockhausen's preferred term, 'intuitive music'.

Improvisation

The nature of improvisation is as hard to pin down as the nature of socialism, with which it had several points of linkage through twentieth-century cultural history—not least in 1968. For Cardew and Rzewski, as was suggested in the last chapter, the linkage was strong, for other composers less so. The impetus to improvise might come out of more general or more specifically musical considerations: for example, Franco Evangelisti (1926–80)—who had been among those at the Darmstadt core, there every year from 1952 to 1961—determined in 1962 that to continue composing would be to repeat himself, and from 1965 onwards his public activity consisted only of improvising, with the variable ensemble he founded in Rome under the name 'Nuova Consonanza'. The heyday of this organization came at the end of the 1960s, and the further coincidence of the May events in Paris and of street demonstrations (especially of students hostile to the Vietnam War) with *Kurzwellen* and the most libertarian music of Berio, Kagel, Globokar, and others is striking. Improvisation was liberation. Virtuoso performers, having taken into themselves the exceptional variousness and the extreme techniques of the music of the last two decades, could now use that stock on their own accounts.

Globokar, who had worked closely with Stockhausen, Berio, and Kagel, enumerated the reasons why performers should engage in free improvisation, and began precisely with 'a need for liberation', followed by 'a search for a new musical aesthetic, a provocation, a wish to work collectively, to develop their instruments, to amuse themselves, a political or social engagement, the wish to belong to an élite capable of improvising, a way of evaluating themselves, a way of expressing themselves not only through sounds but through physical comportment [perhaps because musicians improvising can feel more completely that their instruments are extensions of their bodies, since there is no need to keep track of a score], a need to create a contact (and the most direct possible) with the audience, a need to give free rein to his imagination

17. Ibid., 67.

(without being obliged to spend hours of reflection at a worktable), and many other things.'[18]

This makes a fine manifesto, but most of its points could all too easily be reversed. For example, musicians might consider themselves freer in front of a score than when faced with the fearsome demand to be themselves. Collective work is as much a feature of a traditional orchestra, choir or string quartet as of an improvising ensemble. Evaluation is easier against the standard of a written part. Audiences can be brought into closer contact when there is some shared framework of discourse—and indeed the survival of improvisation (and, like almost everything in music since 1945, it has survived) appears to have depended on the evolution of attunements within ensembles and between ensembles and audiences. Correspondingly the eclipse of improvisation within the art-music tradition (and every survival implies an eclipse) may have come from the recognition that its promises were overoptimistic.

Stockhausen surmounted the problem of the lapsed framework by outlining processes of response, whether to his own earlier music in *Prozession*, specifically to his *Hymnen* in the version of that work with ensemble, or to shortwave signals in *Kurzwellen*, but in the two sets of text pieces he abandoned such moment-to-moment guidance. For example, *Verbindung*, from *Aus den sieben Tagen* (so called because the texts were written during a week-long retreat[19]), asks each musician to 'play a vibration in the rhythm of' his or her body, heart, breathing, thinking, intuition, enlightenment, and the universe. The resulting music, according to the composer, 'comes virtually unhindered from the intuition', through 'joint concentration on a written text of mine which provokes the intuitive faculty in a clearly defined manner.'[20] Where improvisation, in Globokar's terms, is about self-discovery and self-assertion, Stockhausen's stated concern was with finding music outside the self: it is the difference between autobiography and prayer.

His action, therefore, in overseeing and authorizing performances of *Aus den sieben Tagen*—in claiming ownership not only of the prayer text but of the praying—was bound to cause difficulties. During the few years when *Aus den sieben Tagen* was in regular currency, he preferred to give performances with musicians who had had long practice in playing his music; a rare exception was a performance of *Setz die Segel zur Sonne* with the BBC Symphony Orchestra in 1970, but that too was 'rehearsed by the composer'.[21] Moreover, comparisons of different certified performances of the same text suggest that the composer in rehearsal stipulated rather more than is contained in the lines of the

18. Vinko Globokar, 'Ils improvisent . . . improvisez . . . improvisons', *Musique en jeu*, 6 (1972), 14.

19. See Michael Kurtz, *Stockhausen: A Biography* (London, 1992), 160–62.

20. Karlheinz Stockhausen, *Texte*, iii (Cologne, 1971), 123–24.

21. See Stockhausen, *Texte*, iv (Cologne, 1978), 126.

score, and this supposition is borne out by evidence from performers.[22] The gulf between improvisation and his brand of directed intuition produced its emblematic conflict when Globokar disavowed his participation in recordings of *Aus den sieben Tagen*.[23]

But the vulgar interpretation of his motives as megalomaniac is insufficient. There were real problems of formal sameness in improvisation, as Globokar was aware: 'Movements between action-reaction, simple-complex, tension-relaxation are made progressively, rarely in an abrupt manner. The form is often sinusoidal, each situation lasting until it has been exhausted. For the same reason it goes slowly to extinction; brutal conclusions are rare.'[24] Many of these features can be observed in the recordings of *Aus den sieben Tagen* and *Für kommende Zeiten* validated by the composer—especially the slow growths and slow decays. Yet there is variety of structure, gesture, and atmosphere, and the pieces sound different from one another. To that extent, they rescue what Globokar's free improvisation had hoped to obliterate: identity, repeatability.

Free improvisation, as an ideal if not in practice, was a model of the ending of history—the ending that was being expressed simultaneously in the explosion of quotation, in the collapse of the avant-garde, in Cage's virtual abandonment of composition, and in minimalism's reversion to fundamentals. Nothing inherited or learned was to matter, and if traditional instruments too were abandoned or surpassed—as they were by live electronic groups such as Stockhausen's—then each improvisation was a new beginning and a new end, a loop in time that belonged to no continuity. Such nowness had been Stockhausen's explicit aim since *Momente*, and *Aus den sieben Tagen* was, as a project, part of a development that began with *Klavierstück XI*. But the final move, into complete creative abdication, might still be sidestepped by the closet guidance involved in intuitive music. History then could continue. Stockhausen had always seen his role more as an initiator of processes than as a maker of works; *Aus den sieben Tagen* was a particular demonstration of that, and a doorway into a liberation not so much for the performers as for the composer. It gave him permission to trust his own intuition.

22. See Paul Griffiths, *A Guide to Electronic Music* (London, 1979), 81, for a comparison of two versions of *Verbindung*, and Harald Bojé, 'Aus den sieben Tagen: "Text"-Interpretation', *Feedback Papers*, 16 (1978), 10–14, for performance notes by musicians closely associated with Stockhausen.

23. He is mentioned in Stockhausen, *Texte*, iii, 113–28, as having taken part in a sequence of recordings made in the summer of 1969 by members of the Stockhausen group and of New Phonic Art, but the leaflet published with the DG set refers only—and several times—to 'a trombonist (who wishes to remain anonymous)'. See also Kurtz, *Stockhausen*, 174.

24. Globokar, 'Ils improvisent . . . '

14

Orchestras or
Computers

The acceptance of the avant-garde within the wider musical culture, in the years around 1970, enlarged orchestral opportunities for composers at the very time when means of a different sort, digital, were becoming increasingly available. Old or new? As so often, the dichotomy was not so clear.

Orchestras

Pierre Boulez's arrival in 1971 to head both the New York Philharmonic and the BBC Symphony Orchestra is the clearest indication of a match—momentary, as it turned out—between the aspirations of the avant-garde and the needs of leading musical organizations. It was not an obvious marriage: in 1964 Leonard Bernstein's attempt to lead the Philharmonic in Cage's *Atlas eclipticalis* (1961–62) had failed for the players' scepticism with regard to parts drawn from star maps. However, that orchestra had gone on to commission Berio (*Sinfonia*), Stockhausen (Third Region of *Hymnen*), Babbitt (*Relata II*), and Carter (Concerto for Orchestra), and there was a widespread feeling that orchestras would have to engage more thoroughly with new music if they were not to become guardians of a 'museum culture' (which is, for the most part, what happened). At the same time, composers of the 1920s–1930s generation were now in their prime, and most were eager to connect with larger institutions and audiences.

Some came to the orchestra, or returned to it, in response to a generally more active commissioning policy among institutions, and found in the recent music of Berio and Ligeti pointers to new sonic resources. Jacob Druckman (1928–96) was one such. He wrote nothing for orchestra until 1965, but after 1972, when his luminous *Windows* was introduced, was at work on orchestral scores almost constantly. A new kind of new music was emerging here: stimulated by the avant-garde but not set to challenge orchestras' routines. Druckman's music exemplifies this trend with exceptional finesse and beauty.

Other composers of the time remained more intent on innovation. Stockhausen, while continuing to revise his *Punkte*, composed only one more short piece, *Jubiläum* (1977), for a standard orchestra without electronics. Other large-scale projects, such as the 1972 version of *Momente*, would be put together for a tour and recording, and then abandoned, in a realistic response to the orchestral repertory's evident resistance to expansion. Even Boulez, though spending so much of his life now with orchestras, challenged the norms in what he was writing for them. *Domaines* was for six small ensembles, *Eclat/Multiples* for a concertante tuned-percussion nonet with, as it was planned, an orchestra growing from the six soloists of the original *Eclat* (1965), though after the first expansion (1970), with basset horn and a viola section, progress stalled. *Rituel* (1974–75) reseats the orchestra in eight groups. Only with the orchestral recomposition of his *Notations*, begun in 1977, did Boulez start writing again for a regular ensemble. Henze never stopped doing so, though his Sixth Symphony, scored for two orchestras side by side, is unusually heterodox for him, and also belongs, with Berio's *Sinfonia* and Davies's *Worldes Blis*, in the extraordinary repertory of major orchestral scores introduced at the end of the 1960s.

Another from that same period is Carter's Concerto for Orchestra (1968–69), in which the orchestra is reconceived—and repositioned on the platform—as a collection of four ensembles, each focussed on a different register, and each in turn taking the lead in one of the four joined and intercalated movements: the tenor group (cellos, bassoons, piano, harp, marimba, percussion) in the opening of grand but failing gestures; the treble group (violins, flutes, clarinets, metal percussion) in quick, flowing music; the bass group (double basses, trombones, tuba, timpani) in solemn, rousing phrases; the alto group (violas, oboes, trumpets, horns, drums) in fast, affirmative pulsation. These four groupings, and four different sorts of music, are rival winds that blow through the music they bring into being. The metaphor comes from the composer, who related the work to St. John Perse's poem *Vents*, a vision of winds gusting across the United States, and who declared his wish for 'the wind to blow through the music' when speaking of the variations of his First Quartet.[1] Wind—energy without visible substance, movement of great variety in speed, force, and direction, power with no purposes

---

1. See David Schiff: *The Music of Elliott Carter* (London, 1983; 2nd ed., 1998), 161.

or destinations—provides the nearest natural image for the ways and forms in which Carter's music travels.

Many other composers contributed to the orchestral renascence of this period, not least Birtwistle (*The Triumph of Time*, 1972) and Goehr (Symphony in One Movement, 1969; Piano Concerto, 1972). Yet Babbitt's experience adds a cautionary note. The New York Philharmonic had difficulty in finding enough rehearsal time for *Relata II*—a persistent problem everywhere—and the first performance of its predecessor, *Relata I* (1965), was even more disappointing: 'Only about 80 percent of the notes were played at all, and only about 60 percent of these were played accurately rhythmically, and only about 40 percent of these were played with any regard for dynamic values'. Until things could be improved, he concluded, 'composers of such works who have access to electronic media will, with fewer and fainter pangs of renunciation, enter their electronic studios with their compositions in their heads, and leave those studios with their performances on the tapes in their hands'.[2]

Computer Music

A great deal in music since 1945 seems to have been leaning towards cybernetics: the idea of music as sounding numbers, the importance of rules and algorithms in composition, the development of electronic sound synthesis, the concept of the work as a temporary equilibrium of possibilities that could be otherwise realized. Images of the composing mind during this period, as evidenced not only in music but in writing about music, tend to suppose rational selection and combination rather than inspiration. Music created with computers is, therefore, part of a much wider concurrence of music and computing.

As in the early days of musique concrète, the first computer pieces tended to be acclaimed more for primacy than for aesthetic quality, and correspondingly they now figure more in histories, as here, than in performance. The *Illiac Suite* for string quartet (1955–56), programmed by Lejaren Hiller (1924–94) and Leonard Isaacson at the University of Illinois, is widely cited as the pioneer achievement. Xenakis used a computer to handle the manifold calculations his stochastic music had previously required him to make by hand: an early example is his *ST4-1,080262* (1955–62), also for string quartet. And Xenakis's stochastic music, more generally, shows the advent of digital thinking in, for example, the downgrading of the individual event and of moment-to-moment continuity; musical data were now to be assessed globally. Where traditional tonal music had offered time lines hospitable to the listener—lines along which musical processes could be followed—

2. Milton Babbitt, 'On *Relata I*', *Perspectives of New Music*, 9/1 (1970), 1–22: 21–2.

Xenakis was presenting states and unpredictable changes of state. He was not alone: Stockhausen's moment form was explicitly a venture in the same direction. Indeed, the movement towards a new kind of time —a time without reasons and purposes—is the most general and perhaps the most fundamental feature of music since 1945. Reasons and purposes have been displaced into other areas—into the compositional process (which, as in much serial music, may not be laid out for the listening ear), or into political or aesthetic ideology—or else they have been made frankly apparent, not leading the ear but presented to it for monitoring, not communication but structure, as in the early music of Steve Reich (b. 1936). Like the ideals of composing, the ideals of listening were, in the mid-1960s, becoming objective and combinatorial.

This was when the first steps were made in using computers to determine not notes that would be played by natural instruments (as in the *Illiac Suite* and *ST4*) but sounds that would be synthesized electronically. Programs for sound synthesis were developed by Max Mathews (b. 1926) at the Bell Telephone Laboratories in Murray Hill, New Jersey, in the late 1950s and 1960s, latterly with the assistance of James Tenney (1934–2006) and Jean-Claude Risset (b. 1938); those programs were then adapted by composers elsewhere, among whom both John Chowning (b. 1934) at Stanford University and James K. Randall (b. 1929) at Princeton produced their first computer pieces in 1964. As explained by Charles Dodge (b. 1945), another early in the field, creating computer music required the composer to define basic wave forms, virtual instruments whose sounds would be constructed from those wave forms, and 'notes' for the instruments to play, whether these notes were conceived in conventional terms as pitch points in time or in some other way, perhaps, for example, as continuous slides.[3]

Early computer composers naturally fastened on elementary ideas that would have been difficult or impossible to realize without the computer's resources of calculation and control. Tenney combined computer definition with Cageian indeterminacy to create what he called 'ergodic' music (e.g., *Ergodos I*, 1963), in which certain parameters are set but the detail is not, so that events and connections are random within a prescribed musical sphere. Other composers used digital computation to create quasi-instruments that could function over very wide pitch ranges (Randall's *Quartets in Pairs*, 1964), or a process by which irregularly placed chords affect the timbres of continuing contrapuntal lines (Dodge's *Changes*, 1970), or a harmonic system in which the Golden mean ratio of 1:1.618 governs the octave relationship, with timbres made to produce the effect of consonance (Chowning's *Stria*, 1977). But U.S. composers were also impressed—as Babbitt had been when working with the RCA Synthesizer a few years earlier—by the

---

3. See note with Nonesuch H 71245, a record of early pieces by Randall, Dodge and Barry Vercoe.

possibility of making complex music that resisted the performance conditions of the time. (This was another symptom of the age, that so much music should be designed for mechanical, definable performance, though of course there were also economic reasons why university composers—and most professional composers in the United States in the 1960s and 1970s were attached to universities—would find time a commodity easier to obtain on computers than at orchestral rehearsals.) For example, Benjamin Boretz (b. 1934)—like Randall and Dodge, a Babbitt pupil, and editor of *Perspectives of New Music*—rescored his chamber orchestral *Group Variations* (1964–67) as a computer-generated tape in 1968–71.

In Europe, digital technology was introduced at various private and public electronic-music studios in the late 1960s and early 1970s, and used, for example, at Peter Zinovieff's London studio in the creation of Birtwistle's *Chronometer* (1971–72), with clock sounds. Within a few years computer music would become institutionalized, at IRCAM, and a whole new chapter would open, bringing computers into the orchestra.

15

Minimalism
and Melody

'Minimalism', like most terms, is both useful and inexact; it generally refers to kinds of music that emerged in the United States in the 1960s and that wield simple melodic figures in cycles of repetition, the first prominent composers of such music being La Monte Young, Terry Riley, Steve Reich, and Philip Glass, all born in the mid-1930s. Diverse as these four were, they sometimes played in each other's ensembles, and they had common sources in rock and Asian music, as mediated in particular by Young. Their influence was quickly felt by others in the U.S., notably Rzewski, and in Europe.

The term can also be applied to European varieties that arose later and had their origins in chant and sacred polyphony—the work, for example, of Henryk Górecki (1933–2010), Arvo Pärt (b. 1935), and John Tavener (b. 1944)—as well as to Feldman's music of limited means.

New York Minimalism

In 1962, after his early pieces based on few, long notes and his Fluxus text scores, Young founded his own performing group, the Theatre of Eternal Music, to give performances of highly repetitive, drone-based music using carefully chosen frequencies in simple ratios.[1] Ideally, his 'dream music' was intended for continuous performance in 'dream

1. See Dave Smith, 'Following a Straight Line: La Monte Young', *Contact*, 18 (1977–78), 4–9.

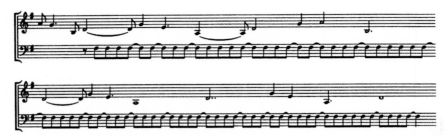

Example 48 La Monte Young, *The Well-Tuned Piano*

houses' as a 'total environmental set of frequency structures in the
media of sound and light.'[2] The frequencies could just be electronically
generated sine tones, drifting very slowly in phase relationship and
hence in perceived volume (*Drift Studies*), or there could be live performers adding further frequencies, while the visual complement would
be the 'ornamental lightyears tracery' of patterned slides and coloured
lights designed by the composer's wife, Marian Zazeela.

In 1964 Young began to concentrate his attention on two projects: *The Well-Tuned Piano*, given as a solo improvisation through various themes and chords on a piano tuned to particular ratios,[3] and *The
Tortoise, his Dreams and Journeys* (so called in honour of a creature having Youngian virtues of longevity and slowness), of which excerpts
were presented by the Theatre of Eternal Music. The members of the
ensemble—among them John Cale (b. 1942), who carried Young's influence to his work with Velvet Underground, and also Terry Riley—
had to be expert in attuning their contributions to the frequency structure in use and, in the case of vocalists, employing different parts of the
vocal cavity to bring forward different harmonics. Young studied the
Indian *kirana* style with Pandit Pran Nath, which perhaps encouraged
a deeper confluence with Indian thought in his conception of music as
environment to be lived in rather than message to be understood, and
in his association of frequency structures with moods. At the same time,
as with Partch, his insistence on just intonation and on his own performing forces had the effect of displacing his music wholesale from
the Western tradition. Example 48, from the five-hour recorded version of *The Well-Tuned Piano*,[4] can only hint at his way of working with
variation in an ambience that is, almost as far as possible, stationary.
The example can only hint also at the tuning. As it affects the notes in
play here, Young's system has the justly tuned F♯ and the B rather

2. Note with Shandar 83 510.
3. See Kyle Gann, 'La Monte Young's *The Well-Tuned Piano*', *Perspectives of
New Music*, 31/1 (1993), 134–62.
4. As transcribed by Gann.

below their positions in the equal-tempered scale, but the G, D, A, and E belong to a different cycle of just fifths, and are all conspicuously raised with respect to equal temperament, the G being above the equal-tempered G♯. So, for instance, the intervals B–D and F♯-A in the example are close to major thirds, the G-A is narrowed, and the F♯–G is almost a minor tenth.

Because Young's music required his presence to tune and play (so that most performances took place in New York), and because no commercial recordings were available until the 1970s, the dissemination of repetitive music was largely in the hands of others. Stockhausen's *Stimmung* (1968)—which, like Young's music, requires singing on resonances and adjustment to a pure consonant harmony, in this case made up of overtones on a low B♭—provided a minimalist experience that was more user-friendly (in that it lasted for little more than an hour), that presented itself more traditionally as a work (having a fixed shape and strong compositorial intentions, in the form both of love poems grafted into it and of statements about its metaphysical purpose as an instrument of meditation), and that was readily available as a score and on record. Riley's *In C* (1964), whose performers play to the same beat while making their own choices from fifty-three different motifs in C major, was another successful and influential simplification of Young's practice and purpose.

Around the same time, Reich and Glass began to combine repetition with process. Both of them, like Young, were influenced by non-Western musical traditions: Glass worked with Ravi Shankar while pursuing more orthodox studies with Nadia Boulanger in Paris, and also studied the tabla with Alla Rakha before composing any of his acknowledged works, while Reich studied African drumming in Accra and Balinese gamelan in Seattle—though only after he had embarked on his career as a composer and performer. In neither case, though, did world-music exploration lead to an abandonment of Western notions of the art work or Western instrumentation and tuning, any more than it did for Stockhausen. As Reich put it: 'One can study the rhythmic structure of non-Western music, and let that study lead one where it will while continuing to use the instruments, scales, and any other sound one has grown up with.'[5]

In Glass's early music the basic principle of rhythmic structure was the simplest possible: that of adding or removing units in a context of repetition and harmonic stasis. For example, each bar of his correctly titled, two-part *Music in Similar Motion* (1969) was repeated over and over again until the composer gave the signal to move onto the next; instrumentation was not specified, for Glass was not interested in having his music played by ensembles other than his own, which generally consisted—during the late 1960s and the 1970s, when the group was

5. Steve Reich, *Writings about Music* (Halifax, 1974), 40.

regularly on tour—of half a dozen players on electronic keyboards and woodwind instruments. Experience together was needed for the method of signalling to work—especially when the music was designed for high speeds and high volume levels, together producing an effect of forward motion at high pressure, jolted by changes of figure and density.

The simple parallel harmony of this composition is characteristic of Glass's 1969 pieces: *Two Pages* is in unison; *Music in Fifths*, again in two parts, is self-explanatory. Later works, including *Music with Changing Parts* (1970) and *Music in Twelve Parts* (1971–74), are much richer, more harmonically varied and, in performance, much longer, with the original rather severe rhythmic processes joined by sustained chordal progressions, so that there are layered textures of musical planes in different but meshing tempos, sometimes very much as in Balinese gamelan music. The nature of the harmony, though, is Western, and has to be in order to establish norms that repetition will estrange.

Reich's first works, like Glass's, have the clarity of a totally fresh approach to musical fundamentals; the two composers were even associated in the beginning as performers, Reich having also played in the initial performance of Riley's *In C*, in San Francisco on November 8, 1964. But Reich had already set out his own independent areas of interest before Glass established himself: in particular, he fixed the scoring of his pieces, because matters of timbre and texture were always integral, and he concerned himself with continuous processes of change. 'I want', he said, 'to be able to hear the process happening through the sounding music.'[6]

This is rather a remarkable statement. For though music from Bach to Boulez might also seem to expose process, it does so, as experience shows, in ways that are ambiguous and that allow other possibilities of interpretation having nothing to do with process, whereas for Reich, at the start of his career, the process, fully disclosed, was the music. As he explained of his first acknowledged composition, *It's Gonna Rain* (1965), created from tape loops of recorded speech: 'Two loops are lined up in unison and then gradually move out of phase with each other, and then back into unison. The experience of that musical process is, above all else, impersonal: *it* just goes *its* way. Another aspect is its precision; there is nothing left to chance whatsoever. Once the process has been set up it inexorably works itself out.'[7] For Reich minimalism was an escape from the embarrassments and unjustifiabilities of choice, just as chance procedures had been for Cage. And in the same way, by what is only a seeming paradox, it opened up a new and personal world.

Reich went on to use 'phasing' processes in another tape piece, *Come Out* (1966), which, like *It's Gonna Rain*, treats the spoken words

6. Ibid., 9.
7. Ibid., 50.

Example 49   Steve Reich, *Violin Phase*

of an African American and delivers a political message by implication, not with the direct force of Rzewski's works of 1972. From here Reich moved in a more abstract direction, adapting his new techniques to live performance in two works of 1967: *Piano Phase* for two pianos and *Violin Phase* for four violins, of which the latter revealed to him 'the many melodic patterns resulting from the combination of two or more identical instruments playing the same repeating pattern one or more beats out of phase with each other'.[8] In example 49, the phase shifting has reached a point where the second violin is two crotchet beats ahead of the first and the third is two crotchet beats ahead of the second (therefore two crotchet beats behind the first); the fourth violin picks out resulting patterns, such as the one shown (three others are also to be projected during the repetitions of this bar). However, from the combination of all four violins the listener may deduce other patterns. The single, objective process is therefore, once again, constantly susceptible to adventitious interpretations, but these are now in the mind not of the composer but of the listener: the music is made by the ear. 'When I say there is more in my music than what I put there, I primarily mean these resulting patterns.'[9]

Similar processes of phasing and pattern enhancement are involved in *Phase Patterns* for four electronic organs (1970), while in another work for the same combination, written the same year and called *Four Organs*, a different sort of process is allowed to run its course: a nine-note chord, jabbed by the organs, has its notes extended one at a time, so that melodic patterns emerge from it and are then obscured again

8. Ibid., 53.
9. Ibid.

as the notes grow to fill all the available time. *Drumming* (1971) was a synthesis of these and other processes, and also a grander public statement, both in its ninety-minute duration and in its scoring for percussion ensemble with piccolo and with female vocalists imitating instrumental sounds.

Glass and Reich reserved their music almost exclusively to their own ensembles and musicians known to them. Since this was true also of Young and Riley, and of others whose work started a little later, such as Phill Niblock (b. 1933), Tom Johnson (b. 1939), Meredith Monk (b. 1942), and Charlemagne Palestine (b. 1945), minimalism went on developing as a bunch of parallel streams quite separate from the regular concert world. Niblock began his musical work in 1968 by assembling long instrumental sounds on tape, choosing frequencies that were close together and slowly changing, to create changing patterns of beats and difference tones. Palestine, a solo keyboard performer, created in *Strumming Music* for piano (1974) a three-quarter-hour stretch of insistent oscillation in which pitch and sound slowly alter as the instrument detunes. Monk also started out as a solo performer, a singer, drawing on vocal techniques from non-Western traditions in music of drones and short phrases repeated in the manner of a mantra. Johnson was the joker in the pack, creating in *The Four-Note Opera* (1972) a Pirandellian comedy for four characters who are melodically limited in the way the title identifies.

Like the circle around Cage in New York a generation before, all these musicians found a sympathetic environment within the art and dance worlds, giving concerts in galleries and collaborating with choreographers. However, an exceptional performance of Reich's *Four Organs*, by Michael Tilson Thomas and members of the Boston Symphony at Carnegie Hall in January 1973, signalled that minimalism could and would enter the mainstream.

Minimalism in Europe

European responses to New York minimalism, especially to Reich and Glass, were most immediate in countries that already had a thriving counterculture open to Cage: Britain, the Netherlands, and Hungary. Among British composers, John White (b. 1936) began in the late 1960s writing what he called 'machines', which he described as follows: 'The sounds tend towards a sort of ragged consonance, the procedures usually involve much repetition with changes happening imperceptibly over large spans of time, and the atmosphere is usually pretty calm and unruffled however fast the pace of the music.'[10] For him the minimalist elevation of consonance reinforced the invitation he had already felt,

10. Quoted in Michael Nyman, *Experimental Music: Cage and Beyond* (London, 1974: Cambridge and New York, 1999), 143.

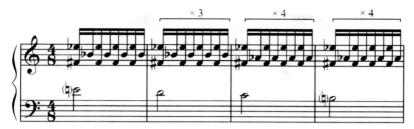

Example 50   Howard Skempton, *One for Martha*

under the impress of Messiaen's *Turangalîla*, to connect not with Asian or African cultures but with masters of the European late Romantic tradition, composers venerated by the mainstream (Scriabin, Bruckner), sidelined (Alkan, Busoni) or spurned (Ketèlbey). Espousing sentimentality as well as system ('systems music' being his term for minimalist process), his work implied a critique of U.S. minimalism as much as a jovial salute.

White implicitly placed himself more solidly against the avant-garde represented by Boulez and Stockhausen, or in Britain by Birtwistle and Davies, and in that respect found common cause with Cardew—though there was nothing political in his thinking, and nothing reflecting Reich-Glass minimalism in Cardew's. He composed the two-hour *Cello and Tuba Machine* (1969) for Cardew and himself to play, following knight's moves across an imaginary chessboard of fourths and fifths. There were also 'machines' around this time among his piano sonatas,[11] of which he was to write several a year for more than half a century. These works, almost all unpublished, unrecorded and unbroadcast, again imply a criticism of the regular musical culture and its demarcations between original and pastiche, serious and nonserious, professional and amateur.

In the light of later events, it may need emphasizing that in the late 1960s Glass and Reich were perceived as experimental musicians, natural heirs to Cage, Feldman, and Wolff, remaining independent of the big musical and academic institutions (thanks to support from foundations and individuals). Early pieces by Howard Skempton (b. 1947), a pupil of Cardew's, suggest how echoes from minimalism and from Feldman—as well as from Romantic piano music, as in White's sonatas, though within tight, small forms—could be sensed behind music at once simple and strange, austere and sensuous. Example 50 shows the first half of his *One for Martha* (1974), one of many short piano pieces he wrote during this period (and later).[12] (The second half is identical,

11. See Dave Smith, 'The Piano Sonatas of John White', *Contact*, 21 (1980), 4–11, available at the online *Journal of Experimental Music Studies*.

12. See Michael Parsons, 'The Music of Howard Skempton', *Contact*, 21 (1980), 12–16, available at the online *Journal of Experimental Music Studies*.

but with the numbers of repetitions shifted to the left, so that the pattern is 3-4-4-1.)

Gavin Bryars (b. 1943) took a different direction from the same starting point, and, like experimental composers in the United States, he found a welcome and a stimulus in the world of visual art. With *The Sinking of the Titanic* (1969) he set out to create a musical project comparable with the conceptual art of the period, in that the 'work' vanishes, there being no space between idea and execution, the execution being a relic or memory or failed attempt. In this case the idea, expressed in verbal instructions, was to recover the sound of the band on the sinking liner playing a hymn tune as they went down with their vessel. Other material brought to the performance might include, as the composer records of one occasion, 'fragments of interviews with survivors, sequences of Morse signals played on woodblocks, other arrangements of the hymn, other possible tunes for the hymn on other instruments, references to the different bagpipe players on the ship (one Irish, one Scottish), miscellaneous sound effects relating to descriptions given by survivors of the sound of the iceberg's impact, and so on'.[13]

With poetic licence Bryars imagined that the tune could, in water, have gone on reverberating for decades, and so *The Sinking of the Titanic* is not only the reconstruction of a sound event from the past but also the realization of one continuing into the present. On both levels, minimalist repetition is not just a possible technique but an absolute requirement, for according to all accounts the band really did play their tune over and over, and the imagined undersea echoing implies manifold repeats—as well as disintegration, which has also been a feature of performances. Bryars's choice of the Titanic disaster has other virtues, answering to how repetitive music can seem to rotate in an eternal present and offering a metaphor for the weight that an audible musical process can generate. The descent of proud magnificence is a metaphor, too, for the state of Western culture at the time—and one may recall that Berio alluded to the same catastrophe in his *Opera*. Moreover, by following the suspect tradition that the band played the hymn tune 'Autumn', Bryars adds further layers of expression and ambiguity to the enterprise. *The Sinking of the Titanic* is based on evidence, but on evidence that may be faulty, and so its grandeur as a musical monument is subverted from within. At the same time 'Autumn', with its phrases of slow descent, effects an image both of the sinking and of the melancholy with which we are bound to contemplate it.

Bryars used repetition again in dignifying a hymn tune in *Jesus' Blood Never Failed Me Yet* (1971), where the source material is a voice recorded on a tape loop, as in Reich's early pieces, except that the voice

13. Note with Point 446 061. This version, released in 1994, was a studio remix based on a performance given in Bourges in 1990.

(of an emphysematic tramp) is singing, and the variation comes in the accompaniment, which again is open to variation in performance, in both length and scoring. As the repetitions go on, so sentimentality gives way to nobility: the tramp's nobility in defying his circumstances (for here, surely, is one who has been 'failed' by the world), the band's nobility in staying with him.[14]

In the Netherlands minimalism became political, as it was for Rzewski. Louis Andriessen (b. 1939), already associated with the radical left in Amsterdam, devoted himself from 1972 to composing and arranging for a wind band that took its name, De Volharding (Perseverance), from one of his minimalist pieces, that included jazz musicians as well as symphony orchestra players, and that preferred nonstandard venues, including out of doors. Minimalism's echoes of jazz and rock were reinforced in Andriessen's strongly pulsed and heavily dynamic scores to create a music of the streets.

Anti-establishment voices had to be quieter in Budapest, where the New Music Studio was founded in 1970 by musicians including the composers László Sáry (b. 1940), Zoltán Jeney (b. 1943), Péter Eötvös (b. 1944), and László Vidovszky (b. 1944). Eötvös soon left to become a member of Stockhausen's ensemble, but the others were more inclined to the new U.S. minimalism, and to the older kind; Sáry was strongly affected by meeting Wolff at Darmstadt and wrote *Sounds* for any instrument (1972) as an immediate consequence, a piece in which notes and chords keep gently recurring in new and unpredictable orders.

Melody

The fact that an older Hungarian composer, Ligeti, could in 1971 give the title *Melodien* to an orchestral piece is a signal that minimalism was part of a wider recuperation of simplicity and definition in music— a recuperation noticeable even in the work of composers explicitly hostile to minimalism, such as Boulez. *Le Marteau sans maître*, in its continuous diversity, offers no encouragement to identify any particular melodic segment as a melody, but in his few works of the 1960s Boulez began to work, if not with themes, at least with figures—a development expressed and announced in the evolution of the orchestral piece *Doubles* (1957) into *Figures-Doubles-Prismes* during the subsequent decade.[15] His next orchestral work, *Eclat/Multiples*, goes further, and

14. See Keith Potter, 'Just the Tip of the Iceberg: Some Aspects of Gavin Bryars' Music', *Contact*, 22 (1981), 4–15; and Richard Bernas, 'Three Works by Gavin Bryars', in Michael Finnissy and Roger Wright, eds., *New Music 87* (Oxford, 1987), 34–46.

15. See Allen Edwards, 'Boulez's "Doubles" and "Figures Doubles Prismes": a Preliminary Study', *Tempo*, 185 (1993), 6–17.

Example 51   Pierre Boulez, *Rituel*

uses the old technique of chord multiplication to establish harmonic fields that remain static for relatively long periods. Then in *Rituel* he based an orchestral work on a single seven-note set (derived from the composition kit he wrote in memory of Stravinsky, '. . . *explosante-fixe . . .*'), and on melody and chorale. The piece is a litany of verses and refrains for homogeneous gatherings ranging in size from a solo oboe to a fourteen-piece brass group, each accompanied by a percussionist beating out time on an unpitched instrument, so that the sumptuous pitched-percussion resonances of *Eclat/Multiples* are replaced by a complex clockwork. Example 51 shows the first verse, and so the first statement of the tritone-rich source set in its melodic form. In succeeding verses, which bring more and more of the groups into heterophonic combination, the melody is extended, reordered, and transposed, but its stable rhythmic character and its limitation to seven notes keep its identity sure. Nor is there any doubt, because of this paucity of intervals, that the same set, though inverted, governs the chordal refrains. The awesome grandeur of the result—its march through time so contrasting with Boulez's normal fluidities, complexities, and ambiguities—appears a curious throwback to the world of Messiaen, and especially to that of *Et exspecto resurrectionem mortuorum*, Messiaen's own liturgy of solos and ensembles with percussion. It also offers a coincidence with current developments in Ligeti and, most strikingly, Stockhausen. But it is neither a celebration of resurrection nor a venturing into new worlds: it is a memorial. In paying tribute to Bruno Maderna, the first of the central Darmstadt band to have died, it seems to throw a wreath over the whole enterprise of the 1950s and 1960s.

Ligeti's recovery of melody was more gradual, and its tone more positive. In several works of the 1960s, including his large-scale Requiem, unaccompanied *Lux aeterna*, and orchestral *Lontano*, he continued his 'micropolyphonic' style, in which, as in *Atmosphères*, clusters glide and slowly evolve. However, there are also more defined features in, for instance, the exaggeratedly dramatic 'Dies irae' from the Requiem, or in *Lontano*, which conveys the sense of a harmonic undercurrent occasionally revealed when the chords thin out towards octaves.[16] Ligeti seemed to confirm this in writing about the harmony of his music from the mid-1960s to the mid-1970s: 'There are specific predominant arrangements of intervals, which determine the course of the music and the development of the form. The complex polyphony . . . is embodied in a harmonic-musical flow, in which the harmonies . . . do not change suddenly, but merge into one another; one clearly discernible interval combination is gradually blurred, and from this cloudiness it is possible to discern a new interval combination taking shape'. As in Boulez's *Figures-Doubles-Prismes* and *Eclat/Multiples*, the restoration of definition was a restoration of harmonically motivated flow.

But of course flow can also erode definition in other areas, and the two textural types of the first pieces Ligeti wrote in the West—the static coloured clusters and the precise, puppetlike movements characteristic of *Aventures* and *Nouvelles aventures*—began to intermingle. Not always. The two are separately presented in his Cello Concerto (1966), where he follows his compatriot Bartók in treating the same material in quite different ways (a characteristic trait found also in his Second String Quartet, for example), first as stillness, then as abstract comedy. In many later scores, however, the two kinds of music are made to combine and to grow out of one another: this is particularly the case in *Clocks and Clouds* for orchestra with female chorus (1972–73), whose title draws attention to the antinomy it will both display and undermine, and in the Double Concerto for flute and oboe (1972). From the interaction seems to come the possibility of a music of notes rather than textures: a music of melody glimpsed first in the last movement of the Chamber Concerto (1969–70).[17]

This work and the Double Concerto also develop those tremulous repeating patterns that Ligeti had introduced in *Continuum* for harpsichord (1968) and *Coulée* for organ (1969),[18] and whose proximity to the world

16. See Helmut Lachenmann, 'Bedingungen des Materials', *Darmstädter Beiträge*, 17 (1978), 93–99, repr. in his *Musik als existentielle Erfahrung*, 35–53.

17. See Michael Searby, 'Ligeti's Chamber Concerto: Summation or Turning Point?', *Tempo*, 168 (1988), 30–34. See also Robert Piencikowski, 'Le Concert de chambre de Ligeti', *Inharmoniques*, 2 (1987), 211–16.

18. For convergent-divergent analyses of these pieces, see Richard Toop, 'L'illusion de la surface', *Contrechamps*, 12–13 (1990), 61–93; Michael Hicks, 'Interval and Form in Ligeti's *Continuum and Coulée*', *Perspectives of New Music*, 31/1

of Reich and Riley is acknowledged in the title of the centrepiece of the two-piano triptych of 1976: 'Self portrait with Reich and Riley (and Chopin is there too)'. The incessant repetition of small fragments brings about a blurring, within which Ligeti's processes of gradual harmonic change can accomplish themselves. An alternative resource is that of microtonal deviation to momentarily confuse the harmony, as in the Second Quartet, *Ramifications* for two string groups tuned a quarter tone apart, and again the Double Concerto, where 'normal' and 'abnormal' harmonies shimmer and merge in glassy brilliance.

All these techniques—the clouding of harmony into cluster, the repetition that obscures, the microtones that infiltrate doubt—are exquisitely calculated to veil the music's underlying processes. Similarly, the bundles of melodies in *Melodien* or *San Francisco Polyphony* (1973–74) defy the effort to take note of them all. Some of Ligeti's works suggest directly that they are portions of things larger: *Lontano* is one that seems not to end but to withdraw beyond hearing, and if the movements of a concerto or a quartet are all variations on each other, then there could notionally be more. But complexity is also a way of showing, within a work's span, how any idea necessarily entails alternatives, variations, and commentaries, that would—were they all present—obliterate it in their concourse. Like Boulez and Berio at the same time, Ligeti was following though the implications of serialism's combinatorial grammar, the limitless possibilities of proliferation and prevarication. What was his alone was the interpretation of musical process as machine. A machine does not sing melodies; a machine manufactures them. And Ligeti was happy to reacquaint himself with melody, harmony, and counterpoint as manufactured composites, as part of the weave.

As with Stravinsky's, his musical mechanisms are sharpest when they come from mechanized instruments: harpsichord, organ, piano. The two-piano work with the self portrait, *Monument-Selbstportrait-Bewegung*, ends with a chorale in the form of 'an eight-voice mirror canon which contracts like a telescope' and which is 'the common coda of all three pieces'.[19] As far as *Bewegung* is concerned, it has that role because it is the apotheosis of the canonic workings trapped amid the earlier lustrous figuration, as in example 52 where the accented notes sound out canons: one of two voices, joined up by the dashed lines, in rhythmic unison (F-E-G-C-A . . . plus its inversion beginning a fifth below), another of two staggered voices. As with Reich's phasing pieces, the cascade of detail gives rise to something simpler, but at the same time the cascade seems to be a rippling out from the simpler fea-

(1993), 172–90; and Jane Piper Clendinning, 'The Pattern-Meccanico Compositions of György Ligeti', *Perspectives of New Music*, 31/1 (1993), 192–234.

19. Programme note for the first British performance, at the Queen Elizabeth Hall, London, on May 8, 1977.

Example 52   György Ligeti, *Bewegung*

ture. Reich provides a ground out of which we derive a figure; Ligeti provides both ground and figure, and leaves us uncertain as to which is primary.

Melody in the context of repetitive figuration was a marked feature of the sound world of the early 1970s, as composers began to respond to New York minimalism: there are examples in Berio's music, for instance in his *Agnus* for two sopranos, three clarinets, and drone (1970–71), included in later versions of *Opera*. In Birtwistle's music of this period, however, melody starts to exert itself unquestioned, retrieving its primitive force as declamation. With reference to his orchestral work *The Triumph of Time* (1972) he has mentioned his interest in working with different rates of change, drawing attention to a cor anglais melody that never alters, and to a soprano saxophone signal that is similarly fixed and insistent until it suddenly flowers near the end of the piece.[20] His melodies often give prominence to groups of neighbouring pitch classes, whether in meandering through small intervals or leaping jaggedly, and often too they unfold as if emerging, in somewhat Varèsian fashion, from a sustained or reiterated note: thus in *Melencolia I* for clarinet, harp, and two string orchestras (1976), the wind instrument seems to summon the music out of a held A, drawing forth both its own fearsome pronouncements and the intricate network of the strings. Example 53 shows the start of the piece, where melody is gradually made possible as the pitch repertory grows out from the initial A, with the addition of G in the falling gesture from the harp, and then of G♯ and A♯ from the low strings, while the harp works over another conjunct chromatic space (from B♯ to F♭). Eventually the clarinet picks up the harp's A–G, and sets out on its own melodic path, which will be interrupted, but never properly concluded. Such a conception of melody as continuing growth, rather than as completed statement, is one of the sources of Birtwistle's continuity, and of the strong sense in each piece that it is creating itself out of the rudiments of sound.

The rhythmic equivalent to this procedure is the evolution of the most complex patterns from a regular pulse, or more usually, from a geared machinery of interlocking pulses. In example 53, the harp's quintuplet quavers prepare—rather in the manner of Carter's metric modulation—the new pulse that enters at crotchet = 112, and every stream in the music proceeds at an even or slightly uneven pulse (the latter in the case of the strings in the crotchet = 44 music, where successive entries follow after intervals of eleven, ten, and eleven triplet quavers). Just as the introduction of a new note is an invitation to melody, so the introduction of a new pulse (quintuplet quavers at crotchet = 44, equivalent to crotchets at crotchet = 112) enables the arrival of others (crotchets tied to semiquavers or to triplet quavers in the faster tempo, in the low string chords which are shown only in rhythmic notation in the example). In this way the music discovers its 'pulse labyrinth', to take up the term Birtwistle used in relation to his *Silbury Air* for chamber orchestra (1977), whose score prints the labyrinth in operation.

Birtwistle's concern with origins and fundamentals is also at the heart of his opera *The Mask of Orpheus*, to which many of his works of the 1970s relate as studies or pendants. It is highly characteristic of him that not only should each work grow of itself but that his output as a whole should do so, with poetic ideas and musical objects repeated

20. Note with Argo ZRG 790.

Example 53 Harrison Birtwistle, *Melencolia I*

from work to work, fulfilling the same function in different contexts, or finding other ways to develop. The first of his Orphic works, *Nenia: the Death of Orpheus* for soprano and five players (1970), was also the first to display a centring in melody, as the voice's invocation of Orpheus at the start cues a long clarinet line. And the prominence of the

Example 54   Karlheinz Stockhausen, *Mantra*

clarinet in Birtwistle's music of this period seems to be not only an autobiographical remnant (this was his own instrument), and not only the fruit of a creative association with the clarinetist Alan Hacker, but also determined by the instrument's powers of vocal forthrightness and flexibility.

Stockhausen, however, was the composer whose restoration of melody was most surprising, most systematic, and most self-conscious. Having steadily opened his notation (if only that) in his works of the later 1960s, he abruptly presented a fully notated score in his *Mantra* for two pianists with ring modulators (1970). Everything in the hour-long work is derived from a melody—or 'formula', to use Stockhausen's term—subjected to variation and to rhythmic expansion and contraction. Example 54 shows the formula as it first appears: the right hand plays its four 'limbs', as the composer calls them,[21] while the left hand plays an inverted variant with the limbs crossed over (i.e., in the order 2-1-4-3). The rhythmic alteration of the formula by regular augmentation or diminution is straightforwardly classical; more unusual is Stockhausen's kind of melodic variation, by which the formula is played in one or other of twelve artificial scales, ranging from the normal chromatic to one in which all the intervals are major or minor thirds, and in which the formula's intervals are correspondingly enlarged, as if it were a design on an inflated balloon. In this maximal expansion,

21. Note with recording on Stockhausen 16.

the upward sixth in the first bar of the formula becomes a leap of nearly three octaves.

The formula also rules the large form of the composition, in that there are thirteen principal sections, based on the skeleton notes of the formula in turn. Each note of the formula has a different character, as shown in example 54 (rapid repetition for the first, sharp final attack for the second, and so on), and the character dominates the respective phase of the work, while the note itself is presented by a sine-wave generator, one for each pianist. Since the piano sounds are ring modulated with these sine tones, the latter serve as omnipresent tonics. At the start, for instance, both sine-tone generators are tuned to A = 220Hz, which is the pitch with which the formula begins and ends; the initial and final notes will, therefore, produce a relatively simple ring-modulated product. In practice the case is more complicated, owing to the inharmonicity of piano sounds; and the effect of ring-modulation to brighten consonant notes (such as those that end each limb) and darken dissonant ones is compromised by equal temperament.

But the effectiveness of the electronically applied tonality is not really the point. The formula is already tonal in itself, with its strong opening suggestion of A minor: it instances the return of the twelve-note modality that Stockhausen had abandoned with *Formel* nearly twenty years before, and hardly requires electronic enhancement. Perhaps Stockhausen needed the ring-modulation system partly to bring the piece (which must have been an extraordinary experience to write, after several years away from staves) into a more familiar world, partly to assure himself of formal integrity, and partly for the sheer joy of new sounds—sounds which often suggest Cage's prepared piano.

It is the joy that seems to propel the music—more powerfully than the sine-tone cantus firmus and the electronic harmony—through its diverse musical phases and through its moments of characteristic humour and wonderment: the moment when the pianists scan massive chords with sweeping glissandos in their sine-wave generators; the moment when they fight for possession of a motif (bars 218–28); the moment when they stand to call to each other in the manner of percussionists in Noh drama (bar 639); the moment when the composition breaks off in its final phase for a résumé of all the formula's melodic transmutations in flurries of even semiquavers. These are exceptional occasions, and the work has more typically a ceremonial continuity; but it is music of moments rather than of symphonic growth, as the composer recognizes in his image of it as a galaxy of different shapes.[22]

Nearly all Stockhausen's works after *Mantra* were based on formula melodies of a similar kind. *Inori* offers a close parallel to *Mantra* in being almost a demonstration of formula composition and transformation: at

22. Note with DG 2530 208.

this point in his career, Stockhausen was widely acclaimed as the outstanding composer of his generation, and the formula style fitted him
in its impression of clarity, logic, and authority, its declaration of its
way of proceeding. Music here draws near to the nature of lecture, and
indeed Stockhausen composed a chanted lecture for soprano to preface
Inori: a lecture on the lecture. His awareness of his status is also revealed in a sequence of works devoted to music as cosmic message.
Musik im Bauch and *Harlekin* both concerned themselves with the figure
of the musician as educator-joker, a thinly disguised self-projection.
Then in 1975–76, Stockhausen used four of the zodiac melodies from
the former work to create a ninety-minute enactment, *Sirius*, in which
four virtuosos—a soprano, a bass, a trumpeter, and a bass clarinetist—
arrive from outer space to instruct the inhabitants of earth, against a
continuous electronic soundtrack. Similar musical resources—and similar dramatic materials, drawn from autobiography, world mythology,
science fiction, and a certain sort of humour—lie behind *Licht*, the
week of operas, on which the composer began work in 1977, and
which is founded on three formulae, one for each of the three principal characters.

Formula composition gave Stockhausen's music something it had
barely had in the 1950s and 1960s: a style. Especially during the decade that began in 1952, he had been able, as he remarked at the time,
to devise a new compositional system for each piece, over a range from
Kontra-Punkte to *Kontakte*, from *Momente* to *Refrain*. Of course, there are
constancies, such as the homemade approach to orchestration and the
concerns—technical, aesthetic, spiritual—with music as voice, but the
differences are still astonishing. By contrast, the post-1970 output is all
of a piece, and distinct (not only in that regard) from what went before. For the composer, however, the operatic projection of his later
music grew out of a sense of drama that had, undeniably, been strong
in his earlier music, and formula composition was a natural outcome
of serialism,[23] not part of the return to tonality that had been one of
the chief features of this muddled period.

23. 'Zur Situation', *Darmstädter Beiträge*, 14 (1974), 19–23, repr. in Karlheinz Stockhausen, *Texte*, iv (Cologne, 1978), 550–55.

16

Ending

The confusion of the late 1960s and early 1970s could engender joy or, equally, despair. There was an abundance of possibility, and a growing abundance of composers, as the first postwar generation started to come of age. On the other hand, music's existence as expressive thought, as the register of inner experience never registered before, was in peril.

Bill Hopkins (1943–81) went to Paris in 1964 in order principally to meet Barraqué, to whose Piano Sonata, in Yvonne Loriod's recording, he 'had listened repeatedly, intently, and with an overwhelming apprehension of living greatness. If music meant anything today, only here was that meaning fully grasped, and it was to a like ideal that my own work falteringly aspired.'[1] What Barraqué's work demonstrated, and implicitly demanded of successors, was 'the meaningful interrelatedness of each single musical decision' within a world where nothing could be taken for granted: 'no witnesses are called, no charades acted out, no authorities invoked, and no restrictive assumptions made.'[2] Pursuing these ideals of total coherence and total independence condemned Hopkins to a creative life less of production than of preparation,

1. Bill Hopkins, 'Portrait of a Sonata', *Tempo*, 186 (1993), 13–14. Nicolas Hodges's essay 'The Music of Bill Hopkins' in the same issue, 4–12, provides a sympathetic introduction to the composer.

2. Review of the Claude Helffer recording in *Tempo*, 95 (1970–71), repr. in *Tempo*, 186 (1993), 2–3.

Example 55 Bill Hopkins, *Pendant*

dissatisfaction, and waiting, which duly became the subject and manner of his music. An extraordinary command of musical resources—especially of harmonic resources—could only begin to operate beyond, around, and in consciousness of an immense blockage compounded of rigour and responsibility.

Under Barraqué's tutelage, Hopkins wrote *Sensation* for soprano and four players (1965), slightly modelled on his teacher's *Séquence*, but going its own way from ecstasy in setting Rimbaud to bleakness in setting Beckett, who was the other great influence on him—an influence that reinforced Barraqué's in demanding ruthless artistic conscientiousness, while also according with a concision, an intermittent simplicity, a fumbling, an irresolution, and a grim humour that separate his music from Barraqué's. Barraqué's music never ends; Hopkins's is ending all the time. His principal achievement after *Sensation* was a set of nine piano pieces, *Etudes en série* (1965–72), which reveal how he was able to develop out of Barraqué a much quieter rhetoric. The music is richly detailed and sonorous in its harmony, and surely propelled by unstable rhythm in a Barraqué-like way, though its movement is much less likely to be towards climax than exhaustion and fizzling out. Two further pieces came out of the long process that produced the *Etudes*: *Pendant* for violin and a *Nouvelle étude hors série* for organ, of which the opening of the former, shown in example 55, may indicate how Hopkins's music finds a fine trail through scattered fragments, and maybe how the music seems to include an awareness that inspects and rejects what comes to it before moving on. The microtonal inflections were apparently suggested by the ideal of birdsong[3] and contribute to the music's freedom, which is the freedom not so much

3. See Patrick Ozzard-Low's review of the recording in *Tempo,* 188 (1994), 38.

of song as of ruminating thought. The only stability arrives at the centre of the piece in a strange dumb tune, which is at once pitifully inadequate and, by virtue of its inadequacy, bang on. It suggests that Hopkins was already seeing in the mentally subnormal a metaphor for the creative artist at a point in history where language seemed to have stopped working.

1975

The fall of Saigon, two years after the signing of the 1973 peace agreement by U.S., South Vietnamese, and North Vietnamese representatives, sends mixed messages through subsequent history. Though the United States had lost the longest and most destructive open conflict of the Cold War, its prestige was little affected, and it was soon to be left without significant enemies, as both China and the Soviet Union concentrated on other problems. Also, though the ending of the war was a victory for the peace movement, whose politics had been predominantly radical and membership predominantly young, the impetus for change evaporated. Liberalization, so rapid in the Western world during the previous decade, went no further, and the way was opened to long periods of conservative government in the United States (1981–93, under Ronald Reagan and George H. W. Bush) and Britain (1979–97, under Margaret Thatcher and John Major).

A certain conservatism also underlines much of the music of the late 1970s and 1980s. Just as the single arrow of progress faltered in the 1960s, so the multifarious subsequent arrows of innovation or reverse began to waver. A new word appeared: 'postmodernism', which rapidly forked in its meanings almost to the end of usefulness. It might imply maintaining the modernist adventure but without constant change, or repudiating that adventure, whether by reviving or evoking the style of some past epoch or by mixing styles, as Berio had done in his *Sinfonia* (or, indeed, Stravinsky in his *Agon*).

Around this same time, the deaths of Stravinsky (1971), Shostakovich (1975), and Britten (1976) brought an end to the era of the composer as public figure, even as the number of professional composers working worldwide started to increase beyond the bounds of summary. Composers are, of course, individuals, and cannot be grouped according to some trend or programme without distortion. Nevertheless, the disintegration of the avant-garde, by now complete, left various cohorts that were, unlike the interest groups of the 1960s and early 1970s, more or less distinct, if all subject to, or participant in, a spirit of recuperation.

17

Holy Minimalisms

Possibly the most striking instance of cultural reprise, harking back to the earliest European musical traditions and yet bound in many ways to its own time, is the calm, repetitive music, often setting Christian texts, of a kind espoused since the mid-1970s by Pärt, Górecki, and other composers, mostly Eastern European. This is not the minimalism of Reich or Glass; it has nothing to do with rock, African, or Asian traditions, and its pulse is almost certain to be slower and gentler. Moreover, where U.S. minimalists essayed the religious, their minds turned to the Eastern cultures with which they had musical connections, Indian (Young, Riley) or Tibetan (Glass). Reich, before scaling religious (or any) texts for the first time in his 'symphony of psalms' *Tehillim* (1981), went to Jerusalem to study chant traditions, just as he had gone to Ghana a decade before to learn drumming on the spot. Pärt and the rest had more in common with Skempton's work, of which they were almost certainly unaware. U.S. minimalism was, by contrast, widely known, but any effect it had on these composers was only as a lens through which to view the medieval and Renaissance music that was being restored to performance around the same time. In that respect 'holy minimalism' was an offshoot of the early music movement of the late twentieth century, and gained some of its force from its association thereby with musical dissidence in Eastern Europe. Volkonsky, an early member of the Russian postwar avant-garde, had gone on in 1965 to found an early music group, Madrigal, in which he played harpsichord. Performing early music allowed him and his

colleagues to voice difference in a way that was irreproachable. To set
sacred texts was similarly to place oneself in contradiction to a state that
had no place for religion. Hence the almost unbroken sequence of sacred works in Penderecki's output, beginning with his St. Luke Passion
(1963–65) and continuing into the 1980s. Holy minimalism, with its
auras of early music and sacredness, was doubly anti-authoritarian.

Pärt

Pärt had begun by following a fairly standard career path for a Soviet
composer of his generation. Young in the early 1960s, a near contemporary of Schnittke, he was the right age to take advantage of the cultural thaw that came in the last years of Khrushchev's rule. He wrote
some baldly elementary twelve-note pieces, then stopped after the
wildly erratic *Credo* of 1968 for choir, piano, and orchestra, with its
extremes of brutality and serenity, its placing of a long quotation from
Bach's familiar C Major Prelude in alien surroundings. For several years
he devoted himself to studies of medieval music while remaining cre-
atively almost silent.

The hoped-for breakthrough came in early February 1976, when
he found something new in ancient musical history. Within the resonance of a low B held by the sustaining pedal and reinforced at the
double octave, a pianist's two hands present a simple melody and its
equally simple accompaniment, as shown in example 56. The performer
is invited by the marking to play as if picking out something recalled
from long ago. And indeed, there is in this music a strong sense of the
distant past—as well as of separation from that past, of loss and absence. The right hand's melody consists of unmeasured phrases that
sound like Gregorian chant, while the left hand's note-by-note accompaniment suggests organum, a way of singing along with chant that
has a history going back a thousand years, to the beginnings of Western musical notation. This tiny piano piece, occupying just two pages
and easily playable by a beginner, thus summons echoes from across a
millennium.

Yet it is by no means medieval pastiche. Its scale is not one of the
classified church modes but B minor, and the left hand's part—what a
medieval musician might want to call the 'vox organalis'—does not
follow eleventh-century rules of voice leading but keeps, with just one
exception, to the notes of the B minor chord. Since these notes are,
more or less, overtones of the bass B hovering in the background, and
since the pedal is all the time bringing forward resonances, the left hand
persistently creates a twinkling effect. What is evoked here is not so
much singing as hearing—not the chanting of monks in some Roman-
esque abbey church but rather the way the ear will glide up and down
in listening to the spectrum of a great bell, as Pärt himself seems to have
recognized in calling what he had discovered his 'tintinnabuli style'.

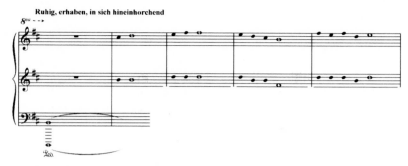

Example 56   Arvo Pärt, *Für Alina*

Within two years of *Für Alina* Pärt had developed its style in works including *Fratres*, originally written, significantly, for an early music group, and *Tabula rasa*, a concerto for two violins with prepared piano and strings that was by far his most ambitious piece of this period. Once more, in *Tabula rasa*, there are echoes of bells (the prepared piano is effectively a cabinet of chimes) and of chant (in the unwavering flux of the melody), along with touches of Vivaldi's 'Winter' concerto. Once more this is white music, fixed in tonality: A minor in the first movement, D minor in the second. Once more, too, the music, though seeming so ageless, is thoroughly modern in conception. Each of the movements is a rhythmic machine, with lines revolving in different geared ratios, and each conveys the experience of a composer who has worked in radio and recording studios. The opening movement, 'Ludus', has the string orchestra repeatedly appearing to fade in and out, as if recorded on a separate track from the soloists, while in the slow finale—'Silentium', music of concentric ripples folding indeed into silence—the orchestral strings sound like an underwater chorus. Such impressions of simultaneous alternative spaces suit the piece particularly to the recorded medium, where not only can the music come from a never-known time (Pärt's remote yesterday that is also today) but also the geometry of its performance is unfixed, left to the imagination.

It was, indeed, through a recording that this work, and Pärt's music generally, became widely known—the first example of a composer making a name in the way that rock and jazz musicians had for decades. Manfred Eicher, whose Munich-based record company ECM had hitherto concentrated on jazz, heard a German radio tape of *Tabula rasa* and decided to release it, together with newly recorded material. The resulting disc, also called *Tabula rasa*, came out in 1984, by which time Pärt had moved in a different direction. Beginning with his seventy-minute St John Passion of 1982, a work scored for solo voices, choir, and a small group of instruments, he devoted himself in his larger enterprises to settings of texts from the Christian tradition—settings which, however, can have little place in contemporary worship by virtue of their language (many of them being in Latin) or their instrumentation. Most of these works were designed as concert pieces, if not, as time went on, as pieces to be heard as recordings. Again past and present are enmeshed, and again the music's strands give an embodiment to absence. Venerable liturgies are invoked, but outside any religious practice. Built with the elegant shadows of the first 'tintinnabuli' pieces, Pärt's sacred settings exist beyond belief. Their church is a church of the abandoned.

Górecki and Tavener

Almost exactly contemporaneous with Pärt's new-old beginning, having been composed in the last months of 1976, Górecki's Third Symphony, with solo soprano, marked a parallel 'return' to a kind of simplicity that never was, but—in distinction from Pärt's pieces—with a weight of sentiment that is announced in the subtitle: 'Symphony of Sorrowful Songs'. The three movements, all of them slow, are all of them laments, and their means are similar: over tonal harmony that slowly rocks back and forth or remains stationary, modal melodies unfold and are repeated, sometimes in canon. Like Pärt, Górecki had earlier been associated with the avant-garde, especially as represented by Penderecki; like Pärt, too, he arrived at his music of 1976 after a period of rejection and reflection. And there is the further similarity of delay followed by exceptional popularity—a process that in the Górecki case went in two phases.[1] Maurice Pialat drew from the symphony for the soundtrack of his film *Police*, whose release in 1985 brought the music some attention, though it was the Nonesuch recording, issued in 1992, that created the storm, selling 700,000 copies within two years. Like Pärt again, Górecki went on to write sacred pieces of unblemished consonance, but did so with a specific religious intention, dedicating his *Beatus vir* for baritone, choir, and orchestra (1979) to the Polish pope, John Paul II.

For Tavener, too, the mid-1970s brought a serious shift. Always a religious artist, he had associated himself hitherto with the liturgy, dogma, and aura of the Roman Catholic church. The strongest musical influence on him, however, came from the hybrid Latin-Orthodox works of late-period Stravinsky, and he joined the Russian Orthodox church in 1977. Setting aside the bold, even garish stylistic clashes of such works as his oratorio *Ultimos ritos* (1972), where a tape of the 'Crucifixus' from Bach's B Minor Mass plays a prominent role, he retrained himself in the modes of Russian Orthodox tradition and developed a purely homophonic and thoroughly consonant style, though with har-

1. See Wilfrid Mellers, 'Round and about Górecki's Symphony No.3', *Tempo*, 168 (1989), 22–24; and Tadeusz Marek and David Drew, 'Górecki in Interview (1968)—and 20 years after', *Tempo*, 168 (1989), 25–29.

monic piquancies that suggest an English-cathedral spirit surviving translation to the gilded domes of Mother Russia. He became hugely productive, especially of choral music, much of it for the Orthodox liturgy. *The Protecting Veil* (1988), a three-quarter-hour cello concerto, brought a change of medium but not of essential voice, as this haunting work is a chant for the soloist, largely in the soprano register, with support and resonance provided by a string orchestra. Here again, although the subject is Orthodox—an appearance made by the Virgin Mary, descending into the Blachernae Church in Constantinople in the early tenth century and spreading her veil over the congregation—there are echoes back through British musical history, the ranks of pillarlike concords recalling Vaughan Williams's Tallis Fantasia.

(Messiaen)

Messiaen was by no means a minimalist, but he certainly believed in holiness, and his progress through the 1970s and 1980s offered interesting points of similarity and contrast with the paths taken by Pärt, Górecki, and Tavener. For one thing, he was a working church musician, taking his place regularly at the organ of La Trinité in Paris and continuing to write organ pieces that could be used in a liturgical context: a compendium appeared in 1984 as *Livre du Saint Sacrement*. But most of his pieces were, as they had been in the 1930s, sacred compositions for the concert hall—or, in the case of *Saint François d'Assise* (1975–83), the opera house. His return to the sacred concert in 1963 with *Couleurs de la Cité Céleste* had soon brought forth a grand resuming of his creative life, presented in a sequence of full-length works: *La Transfiguration de Notre Seigneur Jésus-Christ* for choir and orchestra with seven instrumental soloists (1965–69), *Des Canyons aux étoiles . . .* for piano and orchestra (1971–75), and *Saint François*. Along with innovations— chantlike vocal writing, whether choral or solo, and an episode of uncoordinated birdsongs in the scene in *Saint François* where the saint preaches to his avian cousins—these works show a capacity for resumption that was startling in an era of rapid and irrevocable change. In his opera Messiaen wrote for the ondes martenot for the first time since his *Turangalîla*, and went back still further, to the 1930s, to recapture a wild scherzo style for the dance for the leper whom Francis heals. He also revisited the musical machinery of the *Mode de valeurs* for the scene in which the protagonist receives the stigmata.

It is partly the exultant range of Messiaen's music—from unaccompanied chant to hurtling heterophonies of orchestral blocks, or scintillant piano writing, or plush string harmony, all within *La Transfiguration*, or, in that same work, from transformations of birdsong to evocations of Himalayan as well as Balinese traditions—that separates it from that of the holy minimalists, but there is another factor: the relative scarcity of simple triads, which in Pärt, Górecki, and Tavener are an overt mark of the serene as much as they are in Fauré's Requiem and also a more covert mark of pleasant familiarity, even comfort. With his wider and more complex harmonic vocabulary (often related to resonance phenomena)—and with a melodic style, in benign coexistence with it, still related to the modes of limited transpositions—Messiaen sets his music in a world apart. Its apartness, defined perhaps principally by the modes and how Messiaen uses them to transmute, or to receive, his sources (as with the birds of *Réveil des oiseaux*), may be what makes possible the extraordinary achievement of coherent heterogeneity. And the fact of apartness changes everything. Even the grandest affirmations of consonance—and they are spectacularly grand in the closing sections of both *La Transfiguration* and *Saint François*—seem, however resolute, still ungrounded, homecomings not to any place on this earth.

One of the challenges of the sacred concert, or the sacred opera, is that it confuses what are normally very different kinds of public gatherings, which people join through different routes and with different expectations: the audience and the congregation. Messiaen's intention was not to manifest his faith—though his music could not have been made without it—but to make possible a religious experience for his listeners. Personal expression is ruled out by the multifariousness of means: the music has no consistent voice. But exactly that multifariousness, contributing to a disorientation attained in another way by the music's apartness, is necessary to bring about what Messiaen on many occasions called 'dazzlement',[2] the condition under which the auditor could experience flashing visions of the beyond, to quote the title of the composer's last completed work, scored for what was by this stage a characteristically expanded orchestra: *Eclairs sur l'Au-delà* (1988–92).

Another paradox, or nest of paradoxes, is in the combination of sacredness and showmanship, of grace and grandiloquence, for which such expanded resources were necessary. In addressing his indeterminate audience-congregation, Messiaen acts in a very public, even theatrical way, especially in these late works, all of which are conceived in scenes expanding on some moment or image of sacred narrative or natural observation: tableaux vivants in sound. These works are made to be heard communally, among people sharing exposure to their tactics of awe, whereas the dissemination of the works of Pärt, Górecki, and Tavener has been largely, as already intimated, by way of recordings, especially during the two decades from 1983 when the compact disc was the dominant medium. Excess, outburst, embrace: these make the measure of Messiaen's creative gestures, and indicate a very different understanding of the holy.

2. For a provocative exploration of dazzlement, see Sander van Maas, *The Reinvention of Religious Music: Olivier Messiaen's Breakthrough Toward the Beyond* (New York, 2009).

Ustvolskaya

Messiaen was a public figure not only in his art but also in his life, especially after his retirement in 1978 from his teaching position at the Paris Conservatoire had freed him to travel the world to attend performances and receive honours. Pärt and Tavener, too, have exerted themselves in the public arena, giving interviews for written and video media. And if Górecki was more reticent, he appears positively extrovert beside the extraordinary case of Galina Ustvolskaya (1919–2006), who resisted journalists and photographers, who travelled only once outside her native Russia (for a concert organized by Reinbert de Leeuw at the Concertgebouw in Amsterdam in January 1996), and who went on composing in the face of almost total neglect.

From her twenties to her fifties she supported herself by teaching in the junior department of the Leningrad Conservatory and writing music for immediate consumption: cantatas, light orchestral pieces, songs, and film scores, all of which she disavowed. Meanwhile she wrote the music she wanted to write, almost none of it performed at the time. In the 1960s she virtually gave up creating her 'real' music, to start again in the 1970s when she was beginning to get performances (often of pieces that had been waiting two decades)—though still her work was heard only rarely, and only in the Soviet Union. She was virtually unknown abroad until the late 1980s, by which time she had almost ceased composing for good.

All the larger works she produced during her last two creative decades have sacred subtitles (in the case of the three Compositions of 1970–75, tagged with words from the Latin liturgy) or texts (in that of the four Symphonies of 1979–90), and all are for unusual ensembles, the irregularity being essential to each work's nature as outside genre (for the title 'Symphony' is negated by what hers are), even outside history. The words of her Symphony No. 5, her final work, are those of the Lord's Prayer ('Our Father'), spoken in Russian by a man who 'must recite the text as if he were fervently praying to God!' Ustvolskaya expects intensity, too, from her instrumentalists, on violin, oboe, trumpet, tuba, and wooden cube (struck with mallets), this last a device she had introduced in her Composition No. 2. The violinist, who keeps repeating the same brief phrase, is asked to play 'forcefully, imploringly and *espressivo*, like a "voice from the grave"', while the others have the simple direction *espressivo* for their more varied but still limited repertories of gesture.

Since the musical style is the same in the two piano sonatas (Nos. 5 and 6) that were her only other works of this period, the powerful invitation is to consider them, too, as in intention addressing or even enunciating the sacred. The style is certainly minimal (though maximal in force, with the wooden cube of Composition No. 2 and Symphony No. 5 a present emblem of the hammer blows Ustvolskaya conjures

Example 57   Galina Ustvolskaya, Piano Sonata No. 5

elsewhere with her frequent *fortissimos*), but not at all in the Pärt sense, as may be gauged from example 57, the opening of her Piano Sonata No. 5.

This sixteen-minute composition is in ten linked sections, of which the last repeats the first (including its *espressivissimo* indication), while a further four (including one that consists of intensive clusters) are marked *espressivo*. The music may be bare, retracted to the fundamental —a repeating figure, lapidary two-part counterpoints across a yawning gap, clusters driven in again and again, or sometimes softer linkages of chords—and yet it speaks with its own huge force, its own stark contrasts, its own almost vacant simplicity. It needs, of course, performers who can project—through its hugeness, its starkness, and its vacancy— the elemental.

Contradicting the affirmation that the texts might seem to presuppose (notably that of Symphony No. 5), this music's posture is interrogatory. The opening of example 57 seems to be asking the same question three times over—or perhaps not so much asking the question as stating it, since there is no voice here that one could imagine to be asking. The very first note survives the question, and indeed survives the sonata, for it is repeated alone numerous times and is there at the end, when the threefold question returns. It is not a tolling bell, like the recurrent note of Ravel's 'Le Gibet'. Its meaning is at once infinitesimal—conveyed, perhaps, by the subtleties of colour and even of apparent pitch it acquires from its changing surroundings—and cosmic. We are a long way from reassurance, and from joy.

18

New Romanticisms

Perhaps it was all a search for expression. Much of the music of the 1950s and 1960s is hard to place in expressive terms; to ask what *Kontakte* conveys, beyond an exhilaration in discovery and a continuing sense of encountering the strange and powerful, feels like an empty question, and the general eschewing of opera (even of vocal music altogether in Carter's case) may have come from a hesitation as to meaning. Now, in the mid-1970s, expression seemed to matter again, and the rise of religious music was just one symptom.

As to the cause, not the least factor was the arrival of a new generation, born after the war—composers who had grown up with the music of Boulez, Stockhausen, Nono, Ligeti, Babbitt, and the rest, who very likely had studied with one or other of these seminal figures, and who felt the urge to do things differently. Wolfgang Rihm (b. 1952) would be an example: a composer who studied with Stockhausen in 1972–73 and later learned a lot from Nono's music.

At the same time, the increasing permeability of the Iron Curtain brought to the West the music of Eastern European composers who had not experienced the absolute zero of total serialism or chance operations but had been brought up within a culture where the post-Mahlerian expressive voice—a voice that, however ironized, could still communicate emotional force—was alive and well in the music of Shostakovich.

Then again, within the West some composers, hitherto adherents of the avant-garde, began to interpret their creative dissatisfaction as stylistic disaffection, and so to make strenuous efforts at retrieval. George Rochberg (1918–2005) gained much attention at the time for his Third Quartet (1972), in which music that was relatively conservative for its period, connecting with the quartet writing of Bartók, Shostakovich, Berg, and Schoenberg, astonishingly opens (or closes) to reveal a slow movement in late-Beethoven manner. Rochberg had come to realize, as he wrote, 'that the music of the "old masters" was a living presence, that its spiritual values had not been displaced or destroyed by the new music'.[1] But though one might well want to agree, it by no means follows that spiritual value can be reattained by imitation; indeed, imitation could be interpreted as an assault on the uniqueness of style and personality on which spiritual value might be thought partly to depend. If an imitation can be taken as genuine, then the genuine truly is, if not displaced or destroyed, ineluctably degraded.

There were, moreover, other ways to maintain the dynamism and the expressive potency of the great tradition.

Rihm

A quick starter and prolific, Rihm began to gain attention in Germany and even beyond when he was still in his early twenties. The first performance of his orchestral piece *Morphonie-Sektor IV* at the 1974 Donaueschingen Festival seems to have been crucial, for reasons similar to those that had made Ligeti a talking point after the première of *Atmosphères* at the same place fourteen years before: here was something that appeared to undermine the foundations of new music. Rihm's daring move was to reintroduce an expressive rhetoric widely felt to be unavailable following World War II. Indeed, this was what the whole thrust of music since 1945 had been against. For some years afterward, Rihm was lumped with other German composers of his generation—such as Manfred Trojahn (b. 1949), who had also caused a stir, with his frankly retro First Symphony (1973–74), and Wolfgang von Schweinitz (b. 1953)—as manifesting a revolt against the aging avant-garde in favour of a return to traditional genres and traditional notions of gesture and expressivity. It was not an unjust view. Rihm rapidly produced three symphonies, and his music emphatically asserted an expressive immediacy and power rare in music since Mahler and the expressionist Schoenberg.

However, his message was not comfortable. His choice of song texts from the work of the clinically insane—Hölderlin, Ernst Herbeck, Adolf Wölfli—acknowledged that musical expression now was in an extreme situation, that the direct voice was necessarily a deranged voice, if a voice more dislocated and infantile than hysterical in the manner of Maxwell Davies. The spokespeople of Rihm's early songs and operas

1. Note with Nonesuch H 71283.

(two genres not so separate in his output, since each of the song cycles is voiced by a character: the poet) have a madman's licence to transgress: 'I loved you once! I love you no more. I shit in your eyes!' begins the *Wölffli-Liederbuch* (1980–81). The violence done on musical language is fierce and cold. Often it is a matter of abrupt shift, or of dismantling models of simpler, more innocent musical times: Schubertian lied or nursery rhyme.

Of course, Schubert's music might not be so innocent. The 150th anniversary of his death falling during this period, Schubert was a ready emblem of expression as deviation from established norms, invoked by two composers in the sesquicentenary year: Rihm in his *Erscheinung* for string nonet with or without piano and by Schnebel in his *Schubert-Phantasie*,[2] one of his *Re-Visionen*. The latter has elements from Schubert's late G major sonata brought forward by a symphony orchestra with reduced strings, behind a veil of slowly changing harmonies from the bulk of the string section. Schnebel's typical scepticism and quizzicality freeze here in a moment of rare beauty. Riehm's *Schubert Teilelager* for string orchestra (1989) offers a telling and poignant postscript, based on the arpeggiation of the piano accompaniment to the song 'Der blinde Knabe', surely chosen not only for this feature but also because the poem tells of a faculty that has been lost. 'Today', Riehm writes, 'authentic "romantic" feeling can only be experienced vicariously through the telling about it, about the hopes that were enunciated in this era, which have since then worn out'—those hopes, one may point out with reference to the composition's date, as much political as artistic. 'One can at best show where the markers point toward something,' he concludes, 'but the carrier itself is gone.'[3] However, the music itself is not so pessimistic, for some hazardously won wisps of melody begin to draw around the ongoing arpeggios.

Rehearing Schubert was exceptional for Riehm, but not for his near namesake Rihm, who took the freedom to quote and imitate from his age—though there is nothing playful in his practice, and nostalgia is more a waking nightmare than a dream, for always the gap between past model and present reality is evident and disquieting. The second movement of his Third String Quartet (1976), for example, settles into a Mahlerian adagio, but one tugged and strained, so that it appears to be unfolding both in its own time frame, coherently, and in a new one, incoherently.

Whether as cause or effect of his music of ruination, Rihm conjured the ruined mind not only in his songs but also in his widely performed chamber opera *Jakob Lenz* (1977–78). His subsequent theatre works absorbed ruin, showing it not as a protagonist's condition but as the

2. See his 'Auf der Suche nach der befreiten Zeit', *Musik-Konzepte,* Sonderband Franz Schubert (Munich: text+kritik, 1979), 67–88.
3. Note with Cybele 860.401.

nature of the world. Of *Die Hamletmaschine* (1983–86), based on Heiner Müller's simultaneous deconstruction and reconstruction of the play, he wrote that 'the whole thing sings of extensive destruction', and noted that the action takes place 'in front of the "ruins of Europe" whose dust is still the best nourishment for anyone who wants to confront things or wants to know where we come from'.[4] However, he has also said that he is interested less in where he has come from than in where he is going,[5] less in connection and memory than in breakage and freedom. 'Freedom must be *seized*. . . . This is only possible through free *displacements*—initially in breaks and interruptions (on the stylistic level as well)—which can crowd themselves together to create a total consistency of sound activity. The connecting potential of music is enormous and often a bother for me, since I would like to break out of general contexts. . . . I and my work are animated by the search for "dis-connection" (parataxis as a form of thought and imagination).'[6]

It is perhaps because 'dis-connection' implies connection (in that there has to be an evident something that has been broken, or—better —that is in the process of being broken) that Rihm's music maintains a hold on pitch, and especially on the precarious extreme high treble. A tenuous, pressured progress from one dangerous high note to another, with fallings into noise, the equally extreme bass, or the banality of more ordinary registers, is a characteristic of his music, and one that reflects his admiration for Nono: the 1988 ensemble piece *Kein Firmament*, of which an excerpt is shown in example 58, provides a remarkably sustained example of fragility become force. The far treble is perhaps for Rihm the last wilderness of music, the last place where there are no maps, and where it might be possible to depart, to quote the last line of the brief Rimbaud illumination he set in *Départ* for chorus and small orchestra (1988), 'in affection and noises that are new'. 'Dis-connection' is often projected, too, through space, with instruments placed at distant points in the auditorium, as when two trumpets sound out from behind the audience in the piano concerto *sphere* (1992–94). As he has recalled, his experience of singing in oratorio performances as a boy gave him this feeling of sound as happening all around.[7]

Music that is, in all senses, spaced out has tended to displace the more heavyweight wreckage on which much of the power of *Die Hamletmaschine* was based: the wreckage of Beethoven-Wagner funeral march, of Handel aria, of dramatic-soprano scena, of the expressionist music dramas (*Erwartung*, *Die glückliche Hand*, *Wozzeck*) Rihm had needed in order to discover that piece. His later opera *Die Eroberung von Mexiko* (1987–91) finds destruction imminent rather than achieved: the work's

---

4. Note with Wergo 6195.
5. See Dieter Rexroth, ed., *Der Komponist Wolfgang Rihm* (Mainz, 1985).
6. Note with Wergo 6195.
7. See Rexroth, *Der Komponist Wolfgang Rihm*.

Example 58   Wolfgang Rihm, *Kein Firmament*

essential point is the moment of confrontation between Montezuma and Cortez, which—repeating and intensifying one of the themes of *Die Hamletmaschine*—is a confrontation between female (Montezuma is a soprano) and male. Accordingly, the text is not a catastrophic 'afterwards', like Heiner Müller's treatment of *Hamlet*, but a tense 'not yet': Rihm adapted his libretto from a dramatic project by Artaud.

That Artaud should have returned to relevance (Rihm had already based his full-length ballet *Tutuguri* of 1980–82 on Artaud) is a signal of how composers in the 1980s wanted to draw again on a spontaneity and a nakedness that had been Boulez's in the late 1940s, and that subsequent European modernism had compromised by system. For Rihm, system is anathema. Even words can be too binding: he has done without them in several vocal works, including the music-theatre piece *Séraphin* (1994). The only syntax is internal need, in a ratcheting-up of Romantic subjectivity. 'The whole thing free, without scaffolding. The grid work which arises has not been knitted together previously or painted on afterwards. It exists in what happens. The consistency, when it arises, belongs to the music as something entirely its own and not the result of an analogy, a reference to some level of planning. What is—is.'[8]

Schnittke, and the Hectic Present

After Shostakovich's death, in 1975, Schnittke looked to be his most likely heir, but remained poised on the threshold as Soviet culture entered a period of uncertainty that would lead, within a decade and a half, to its demise. This was Schnittke's fate, perhaps wished-for fate: to be on the brink. He had shown his fitness for Shostakovich's mantle not just by pursuing standard genres (symphony, concerto, quartet, sonata) but also by escalating the most distinctive modes of post-1936 Shostakovich: anxiety (when we might feel we are hearing the composer's voice directly), irony (when we know we are not), and anxious irony or ironic anxiousness (when we cannot be sure). He had even used Shostakovich's personal motto, the D–S–C–H motif (D–E♭–C–B), in, for example, his Third String Quartet (1983) and Seventh Symphony (1993).[9] It may even be that a sense of writing someone else's music is part of the desperation his works convey, and in which they seem to have been created—a desperation whose symptoms include a startling productivity, especially from the mid-1980s onwards. The sources of that desperation must include the composer's persistent ill-health, but they would also have to involve his artistic alarms: panic at the collapse of history into a meaningless simultaneity, and the trepidations of a man belonging to and reporting from a culture passing from tight constraint into unchecked freedom.

As in the music of his contemporary Davies, overt, exuberant parody receded during this period, but what was left behind, in Schnittke's case, is often a disconcerting skeleton. Long stretches of the opening allegro of his Sixth Symphony (1992), for example, are occupied by just a few brass instruments, or by the low strings, and much of the material is abrupt: idea, silence, idea. The absence of phrasing marks and dynamic gradations also suggests something bare. Other works to show a rampageous and partly humorous, partly despairing medley of historical references include the Concerto Grosso No. 1 for two violins, harpsichord, prepared piano, and strings (1977), which includes 'formulae and forms of Baroque music; free chromaticism and micro-intervals;

8. Note with Wergo 6195.
9. See Paul Griffiths, 'Schnittke's Seventh', *The New Yorker* (7 March 1994), 91–93.

Example 59   Alfred Schnittke, String Quartet No. 3

and banal popular music which enters as it were from the outside with
a disruptive effect.'[10]

The Third Quartet begins with three quotations marked as such
in the score: a double cadence from Lassus's *Stabat mater* and the head
theme of Beethoven's *Grosse Fuge*, as well as the D-S-C-H motif. As the
slow first movement continues, it remembers these ideas fairly closely,
though there are interpolations that seem foreign, and that sometimes
enter to dramatic effect, as well as passages that appear to grow from
general features of the opening material, including a long stretch of
what is initially white-note canon (though the disturbing vision of
innocence soon characteristically clouds and distorts). The second,
scherzolike movement has an obsessive first theme that looks back to
the canon, and through that to the Lassus and the Beethoven, both of
which are soon recalled more directly. Like Hamlet rushing from place
to place in order to escape his spectral father, the scherzo theme
keeps being rattled by the ghosts of Lassus and Beethoven, and jump-
ing from one harmonic position to another: example 59 shows a passage in which a Lassus variation introduces a counterpoint between the
scherzo theme in the viola and the Beethoven in the first violin. The

10. Preface to the score. See also Ivan Moody, 'The Music of Alfred
Schnittke', *Tempo*, 168 (1989), 4–11.

movement continues into fierce drama and parody, and is followed by a slow march finale. Here the conflict is not resolved: it ends in exhaustion.[11]

Schnittke's vivid expressivity demands a traditional musical milieu of means and form, for it makes its points through contortion, parody, and extremity: bizarre thematic transformation, guying by misappropriation, a venturing towards the far edges of register or dynamic. The traditional role of string instruments as expressive agents is also strongly implicated. In his comparatively few vocal works—comparatively few, that is, until the flood of operas from him in the 1990s—the singers often seem, in contrast, generalized, taking part in some ceremonial. The ceremonial may be explicitly Christian, as in the Second Symphony (1979), based on the composer's visit to Bruckner's church of St Florian and incorporating an 'invisible mass', or in the Concerto for chorus (1984-5), with its radiant restorations of traditional Orthodox music gesturing towards holy minimalism. Alternatively, in the Fourth Symphony for four singers and orchestra (1984), the music is based on four different styles of chant: Russian Orthodox, Gregorian, Lutheran, and Jewish, all sung wordlessly. There is also often an atmosphere of chant in the dislocated litanies of the Sixth Symphony. In both the vocal symphonies, the Second and the Fourth, the muted voices suggest a mummed worship. Part of the point may have been to make a protest against the persecution of religion in the Soviet Union, but equally the music laments the loss of divine community, of the social order that sustained the individuality that all Schnittke's music pursues through labyrinths of intensity, disaffection, and black comedy.

Gubaidulina, and the Visionary Future

Belonging to the same time and place as Schnittke, Sofia Gubaidulina (b. 1931) similarly emerged from the school of Shostakovich, through serialism, to create works whose intensities depend on multifarious references. She did not, though, embed those references in standard genres, except in her string quartets. Her single symphony, 'Stimmen . . . Verstummen' (1986), has twelve movements; her violin concerto, *Offertorium* (1980), plays continuously. Many more of her works set up conditions pertaining to them alone: *The Hour of the Soul* (1974), in which a percussionist stirs up an orchestra, out of which a mezzo-soprano eventually arises; other works that place percussion instruments to the fore; still others with a prominent part for the bayan, the Russian accordion; *Perception* for soprano, baritone, string septet, and tape (1983), one of several pieces concerned with an antinomy between female and

11. On this work, see also Hugh Collins Rice, 'Further Thoughts on Schnittke', *Tempo*, 168 (1989), 12–14.

male sensibilities. *The Hour of the Soul* was written for a male percussionist, Marek Pekarski, and in the composer's words: 'only at the end does the truly feminine nature appear'.[12]

This femaleness is, however, a theme subsidiary in most of her music to matters of spirituality and belief, which she assails by means quite different from those of her minimalist contemporaries. Adhering to a Russian tradition that goes back to Scriabin and some of his followers, such as Nikolay Obukhov, she works with musical events and processes as symbols. In *Offertorium*, for instance, the subject from Bach's *Musical Offering*, which is first dismembered in the manner of Webern's orchestration, stands for the composers 'who have produced . . . the greatest impression on me'; more importantly, its progressive curtailment, lopped from both ends, is the realization of her germinal idea that 'the theme would offer itself up as a sacrifice'.[13] No material that could be used in such a symbolic drama is ruled out, and since the music has its meaning through representation, through a language in which mental states and transformations are to be understood as figured in sound hieroglyphs, a purely musical integrity is beside the point, and might even be misleading, if it were to divert attention from the symbolism. This is where Gubaidulina differs from Messiaen, whose proclamatory harmonies her music sometimes encounters. In her music there is no commitment to *écriture*, or to symmetry. The characteristics are instead abrupt, ripped change, a finish that is often rough, raw, and ragged, and a variety equalling Schnittke's.

Gubaidulina, again like Schnittke, earned her living during the Soviet years as a composer for films, though in her case for animated films, and her concert works may suggest—because their intention is always towards something beyond what is heard—a cartoon music of the soul. *'Stimmen . . . Verstummen'* is a case in point. The angelic rapture with which it begins, and to which it keeps returning, is a febrility of high D major triads—an image of childlike simplicity. Another such image is threaded through her Second Quartet (1987) in the form of a unison G. In asking us to accept the elementary as part of a vastly ranging soundscape—and not only as part but by implication as the highest part—Gubaidulina offers no intrinsically musical motivation but only an invitation to stay the course.

Sex and Sexuality

Gubaidulina's distinction of specifically male and female personalities raises questions. The writings of the great modernist pioneers, from Varèse to Boulez, are indeed full of sexual imagery of a traditionally male cast—the imagery of action, seizure, impregnation. Similarly, the

12. Claire Polin, 'Conversations in Leningrad, 1988', *Tempo*, 168 (1989), 19.
13. Quoted in note with DG 427 336.

great rotation that occurred in music in the early 1970s, involving everything from issues of language and general practice to matters of individual sensibility, could be construed as a turn to the female's conventionally more accepting and inclusive attributes. However, music could also be a means to question difference.

For example, the appearance on the operatic stage of sexually ambivalent voices, notably the countertenor, and cross-dressers is no more a particularly homosexual phenomenon in the modern period than it was in the eighteenth century (and perhaps no less). In many instances, the construction of artificial or equivocal sexualities may have a strong homoerotic charge—as in the countertenor Oberon of Britten's *A Midsummer Night's Dream* (1960), or the principal character of *The Intelligence Park* (1981–88) by Gerald Barry (b. 1952)—but the possibility of such characters seems to be in the nature of the art, subcutaneously gay in its lack of straight speaking, as much as in that of the composer.

The work of women composers, Gubaidulina included, also argues against difference. The sly comedy of Judith Weir (b. 1954), for instance, is parallelled in the music of Franco Donatoni (1927–2000); Gubaidulina's religious intensity finds echoes in Schnittke; Saariaho's exploration of timbre is not uncommon among composers of her place (Paris) and time; and the work of Pauline Oliveros (b. 1932), a pioneer of electronic music who became most active as an improvising musician and instigator of creativity in others, shows preferences shared with Riley or Wolff.

Silvestrov, and the Reverberating Past

Like his contemporaries Schnittke, Gubaidulina, and Pärt, Valentyn Silvestrov (b. 1937) found that new impulses from the West—most conspicuously Webern in his case, absorbed in his *Quartetto piccolo* of 1961—did not after all replace but remained alongside, in critical dialogue and balance with, the Romantic-diatonic-symphonic tradition that was being maintained in the Soviet Union, perhaps for reasons as much cultural and political. It may be significant that all these composers came from outlying areas of the country: Schnittke from the Volga basin, Gubaidulina from Tatarstan, Pärt from Estonia, and Silvestrov from Ukraine. What is equally striking is that they all went through a decisive period of readjustment in the mid-1970s.

With Silvestrov the major immediate outcome has come to seem his *Quiet Songs* (a title also translated, erroneously if more poetically, as *Silent Songs*), a cycle of twenty-four settings for voice and piano of mostly classic Russian poems, put together between 1974 and 1977. Evoking the musical world of a century earlier, the work is thoroughly old-fashioned in genre and style, and yet unlike anything one has heard before, since Silvestrov has his own kind of slowly falling, slowly clos-

Example 60 Valentyn Silvestrov, *Quiet Songs*

ing melody, tender and melancholy. In the nineteenth-century song literature such a phrase would be expected at the end of a touching or reflective number, but Silvestrov commonly starts this way, as shown in example 60, from a Pushkin setting, where this imminently closing music might also suggest, if in simplified form, a parallel with the exactly contemporary spectral music happening in Paris, except that the resonances here are as much historical as acoustic. Silvestrov's songs are on the point of ending as soon as they begin, and they go on ending. Coupled with the *sotto voce* requested of the singer, the fine differentiations of tempo and dynamics (as if this were not the music itself but a transcription of a pre-existing performance), the choice of staple Russian poems and the piano's gentle, enfolding support, the effect is to make these songs slide into consciousness like memories, faint and incomplete but no less affecting for that—indeed, affecting in being faint and incomplete. This is music that is largely lost even before it has come to be heard. As much may be said of the composer's Fifth Symphony (1980–82), where again, but on the much larger scale of an unbroken three-quarter-hour orchestral movement, the music is continuously coming to an end even as it rolls reluctantly on.

Symphony?

Beyond the Soviet Union, where the example of Shostakovich carried so much weight, the reappearance of the symphony in the mid-1970s came as bizarre, almost scandalous. Berio's *Sinfonia* was firmly not a symphony, the title teetering on the edge of a transgression not made, and the same may be said of Carter's *A Symphony of Three Orchestras* (1976–77), or even of his later and rather deliberately named *Symphonia* (1993–97). In any case, an isolated symphony scarcely represents a commitment to the symphony as a genre, and it was perhaps to abstain from such commitment, to make the symphony a special case each time, that Goehr followed Stravinsky in giving his symphonies other

identities than a number: Little Symphony (1963, for chamber orchestra), Symphony in One Movement (1969, revised 1981), Sinfonia (1979,
again on a Haydn-Mozart scale), Symphony with Chaconne (1985–86).
Goehr was yet another composer for whom the mid-1970s marked a
fault line, for in 1976 he stopped using twelve-note rows consistently
(though he remained very much a Schoenbergian) to explore a sort of
fully chromatic modality that had emerged from within his serial practice. And yet his was a smooth trajectory that took him progressively
(or regressively?) away from a youthful closeness to Boulez, with
no great repudiation: 'I recognised in myself, on the one hand, a desire
for abstraction, for formal innovation and for systematisation, and on
the other a wish to express human feeling in a realistic manner as it
has existed from Monteverdi to Janáček.'[14] The motivation of a new
Romanticism—or, rather, of an old Romanticism newly thought—could
not be outlined more clearly.

Composers outside the Soviet Union who, unlike Goehr, Carter, and
Berio, had set themselves to writing numbered symphonies before the
mid-1970s did so in distinction, perhaps in challenge, to the avant-garde.
Henze's Seventh (1983–84), coming after a gap of a decade and a half,
was explicitly a return to symphonic normality and an acceptance of a
place for itself and its composer in the Austro-German tradition. In the
United States, William Bolcom (b. 1938) had written his First Symphony
at the age of nineteen, emulating Barber, and not only in precocity.
Evidently enamoured, as Henze was at the same age, of everything in
earlier twentieth-century music from Berg to Stravinsky, not excluding
rambunctious march and popular song, he went on to encourage versatility within a style rooted in older practice. His Third Symphony
(1979) has a scherzo whose kaleidoscopic motifs keep fusing into a
slow foxtrot, fashioned with great affection; the slow movement of his
Fourth (1986) sets a Roethke poem in the style of his cabaret songs.

Oliver Knussen (b. 1952) got going as a symphonist in his teens,
and proved in his Third (1973–79) that Carterian principles of harmonic-
rhythmic differentiation—coupled with orchestration on a Ravelian
level of imagery and expertise, as well as a personal style on an edge
between the childlike (the images as musical toys, suggesting fanfares
or dances or even children's songs or skipping games at different times)
and the exquisitely sophisticated—could produce compelling symphonic
dynamism, not to speak of aural magic. The work is in three parts playing continuously: an introduction that, having slipped into being, is
soon pressing forward, an allegro of four distinct but interpenetrating
musical states borne by the sections of the orchestra (strings, woodwinds, tuned percussion with harp, brass), and a slow finale arising
from out of the sustained, clamorous chord towards which the allegro

---

14. Derrick Puffett, ed., *Finding the Key: Selected Writings of Alexander Goehr*
(London, 1998), 19.

has driven. Ideas from before are now recollected in repose, before the music dissolves, sliding away with the clarinet gesture that opened it. This turned out to be a one-off, however, for a long-promised fourth symphony failed to materialize, and when Knussen returned to large-scale orchestral music, following a pair of fantasy operas, his chosen genre was the less fraught, less weighted concerto.

It was the whole symphonic cycles of others, of composers who had more thoroughly identified themselves with radicalism, such as Penderecki and Davies (another skilled at foxtrots), that caused the surprise. Penderecki's First Symphony (1972–73) opened the way towards a restitution of late nineteenth-century tonal means and progressiveness that he took much further in his Second (1979–80), with its shades of Bruckner, and that he interpreted in his own pronouncements, quite lacking Goehr's subtlety, as a retraction: 'The musical world of Stockhausen, Nono, Boulez and Cage was for us, the young—hemmed in by the aesthetics of socialist realism, then the official canon in our country—a liberation. . . . I was quick [sic] to realize however, that this novelty, this experimentation and formal speculation, is more destructive than constructive,' but he was able to be 'saved from the avant-garde snare of formalism by a return to tradition'.[15] The explanation echoes Rochberg's of a few years before.

Such was by no means Davies's rationale in embarking on a symphonic cycle with his No. 1 (1973–76) and continuing it with seven more by the end of the century. He persuasively defended his move into a traditional genre as prepared and even necessitated by the quasi-symphonic manner of his orchestral works of the preceding decade, especially his Second Taverner Fantasia and *Worldes Blis*, and as justified by the condition his harmony had now achieved, after twenty years as a professional composer. For example, in a note on a work that came straight after his First Symphony, his chamber symphony *A Mirror of Whitening Light* (1976–77), he remarked how he had endeavoured to create 'functional harmony operating over and relating large spans of time',[16] and from this point onwards his analyses of his own pieces make free with such terms as 'introduction' and 'recapitulation' (though in place of 'development' he prefers 'transformation processes'), or 'dominant'.[17]

The questions these works propose are those of how deeply, firmly, and fully new kinds of symphonic architecture and force can be imposed. They are questions of authenticity that absorbed this composer

15. Note with Naxos 8.554491.

16. Paul Griffiths, *Peter Maxwell Davies* (London, 1981), 164. For analytical comments on the work, see David Roberts's review in *Contact*, 19 (1978), 26–29.

17. See, for example, his note on his Second Symphony in Griffiths, *Peter Maxwell Davies*, 171–74, and other notes published with recordings.

from the beginning, and that are implicit in any effort at Romantic renewal. Gestures of pronouncement, of dialogue, of climax can be brought about, and Davies's climaxes, with great ringings of bell sounds or swirls of high woodwind or eruptions of brass, are highly effective. But are these things compelled by the whole nature of the whole piece or are they adventitious, simulacra playing on the surface?

Feldman and Loss

Like Scelsi and Nono, Feldman began to loom much larger in the musical world a few years before his death—and for similar reasons. His lack of an ideology had relegated him to the second rank in the ideological 1950s, when even Cage had had an ideology: the ideology of having no ideology. Also, as a big man, and a man of humour, he perhaps fitted too well the role of comfortable clown. But in the 1970s, when trust in ideologies faltered, here was a waiting hero: a composer who had been quietly making music by, as it seemed and seems, unaided intuition—a Romantic. According to a story of his own: 'My past experience was not to "meddle" with the material, but use my concentration as a guide to what might transpire. I mentioned this to Stockhausen once when he had asked me what my *secret* was. "I don't push the sounds around." Stockhausen mulled this over, and asked: "Not even a little bit?"'[18]

Using 'my concentration as a guide', Feldman had quickly gone on from the graph scoring of his *Projection* series, for the reason that he was interested in freeing sounds, not performers. (He did, however, return to graph scoring for works on a larger scale: *Out of "Last Pieces"*, *Atlantis*, and *In Search of an Orchestration*.) Before they could be freed, sounds first had to be identified—and he excelled in identifying harmonies that would, under the *pianissimo lentissimo* conditions of his music, sound delicate and detached. So he had begun to notate pitches, but to leave them just as note heads, with no rhythmic indication, as Cage did in the *Music for Piano* series. Different players, or groups of players, would then proceed through their parts independently: this was the case in, for example, the *Durations* series for various ensembles (1960–61) or *Between Categories* for two quartets, each of tubular bells, piano, violin, and cello (1969). Such a rhythmic loosening would not have been possible in music for several performers without the assumption, always present in Feldman, that the music must be slow, so that there is never any question of linking a sound to what had gone before. Each must exist for itself, and in order to accommodate so

18. Morton Feldman, 'Crippled Symmetry', *RES: Anthropology and Aesthetics*, 2 (Cambridge, Mass., 1981); reprinted with Hat Art 60801/2 and in B. H. Friedman, ed., *Give My Regards to Eighth Street: Collected Writings of Morton Feldman* (Cambridge, Mass., 2000), 134–49.

many diverse existences, none must dominate: hence the second requirement almost constant in Feldman's music, that it be quiet. In the composer's words: 'the music seems to float, doesn't seem to go in any direction, one doesn't know how it's made, there doesn't seem to be any type of dialectic, going alongside it, explaining it. They [the audience] are not told how to listen, that is the problem. Most music listens for the public.'[19]

By the end of the 1960s, Feldman had restored conventional rhythmic notation, and in the series *The Viola in My Life* (1970–71)— especially in the viola concerto that is its fourth and last member—had also restored melodic gestures, but within music that drifts, circles, and loses its way (but finds it exactly in that loss).[20] Most of his subsequent works, though fully notated, maintain the instant-by-instant unfolding —as well as the quietness and the slowness—that had defined his world since the early 1950s. Asked by Heinz-Klaus Metzger if his gentle music was in mourning for the victims of the Holocaust, he came close to agreeing, but wanted to widen the question to include 'say, for example, the death of art'. 'I do in a sense mourn something that has to do with, say Schubert leaving me. Also, I really don't feel that it's all necessary any more. And so what I tried to bring into my music are just very few essential things that I need. So I at least keep it going for a little while more.'[21]

If this suggests threads of music squeezed out against finality, the image is borne out by his output up to this point, since, though numerous, his works had tended to be brief and for small ensembles: many are for piano (or multiple pianos), whose sound—chordal, resonant, reducible to an extreme *pianissimo* without danger of breaking or fraying— particularly suited his purposes; others are for choice instrumental groupings; very few involve voices, and those few are mostly wordless. But in the early 1970s the pattern began to change, in dimensions of both size and scoring. There were suddenly more orchestral works, characteristically titled either with their instrumentation (*Cello and Orchestra, Piano and Orchestra, Oboe and Orchestra*, even just *Orchestra*) or with some pregnant semiabstract phrase (*Elemental Procedures*). Partly this was a matter of opportunity. In 1971–72 Feldman had been resident in Berlin, and from that time onwards he was frequently commissioned by European orchestras and radio authorities.

But the other growth in his music—the growth in length—cannot be explained by market forces. At the end of the 1970s his works became immense: *Violin and Orchestra* (1979) plays for over an hour, *String Quartet* (also 1979) for over an hour and a half, *String Quartet II*

---

19. Conversation with Heinz-Klaus Metzger and Earle Brown. A recording and a transcription are supplied with EMI C165 28954/7.

20. See note with ECM 1798.

21. EMI C165 28954/7.

(1983) for up to five and a half hours. The possibility of great length
may have been opened by his soprano monodrama *Neither* (1977), to a
sixteen-line text written for him by Samuel Beckett, the only text that
writer created for musical setting. However, a seventy-minute stage
piece is not unusual (though one with so few words may be), whereas
a string quartet that goes on for hours without pause quite definitely is.
So is the other genial monster in his output, the four-hour *For Philip
Guston* (1984), which was one of several pieces he wrote at that time for
a touring group that included the flautist Eberhard Blum, the percussionist Jan Williams, and the pianists Yvar Mikhashoff and Nils Vigeland.
(Works of this period, demanding dedication, were often written for particular musicians, who included also the pianists Bunita Marcus, Aki
Takahashi, and Roger Woodward, the singer Joan LaBarbara, and the
violinist Paul Zukofsky.) 'My whole generation', he said, 'was hung up
on the 20 to 25 minute piece. It was our clock. We all got to know it,
and how to handle it. As soon as you leave the 20-25 minute piece behind, in a one-movement work, different problems arise. Up to one hour
you think about form, but after an hour and a half it's scale. Form is
easy—just the division of things into parts. But scale is another matter.'[22]

Feldman spoke of 'the contradiction in not having the sum of the
parts equal the whole: The scale of what is actually being represented
. . . is a phenomenon unto itself.'[23] At the beginning of his career he
had, even more than Cage, been influenced by the New York painters
of his generation and the one before,[24] and in his late works he may
have wanted to achieve—as he did achieve—the kind of presence a
large Rothko has by virtue of its scale: the grandeur and the strangeness that come simply from there being so much of it manifested with
so little rhetoric, almost none, a quality of vast unimposing being. Another influence on Feldman's late music—or 'permission' for it, to use
his own word—came from Islamic rugs, which he collected. On his
floor there was, for instance, an Anatolian chequerboard piece 'with
no systematic color design except for a free use of the rug's colors re-
iterating its simple pattern.'[25] Symmetry on one level, of geometry, is
combined with asymmetry on another, of colouration—an asymmetry
subtly complicated by the fact that the colours of rural rugs are uneven, because yarn was dyed in small quantities. According to his own
account, it was out of such observations, rather than by glancing aside
at the minimalism of younger New York contemporaries, that he began
to work with repetitive pattern at the time his music grew.

And certainly the works of his last eight or nine years (works that
must, in terms of duration, account for fully half his output) have little

22. Universal Edition brochure (1994).
23. Feldman, 'Crippled Symmetry'.
24. In ibid., for example, he refers to Rauschenberg, Pollock, and Rothko.
25. Ibid.

Example 61   Morton Feldman, *Three Voices*

beyond repetition in common with those of Reich and Glass. Pulse, where it exists, is slow, and the music remains quiet. Most decisively, there is no process, but still a drifting. Tonal features return: they can hardly be avoided when there is so much repetition, and in some pieces—such as *Triadic Memories* for solo piano (1981), which can play for up to an hour and a half—Feldman made a feature of them. But the progressive implications of common chords are resisted. 'Chords are heard repeated without any discernible pattern. In this regularity (though there are slight gradations of tempo) there is a *suggestion* that what we hear is functional and directional, but we soon realize that this is an illusion.'[26]

Feldman's repetitions also differ from most in his creation of a symmetry 'crippled' by asymmetry, whether from 'slight gradations of tempo', from changes of orchestral colour (in *The Turfan Fragments*) or from rhythmic notations that look exact but will inevitably be performed a touch inexactly. For instance, at the start of *Three Voices* (1982), shown in example 61, the coordination of the top part with the other two is unlikely to be precise, and the imprecision—suggesting life, suggesting failing—seems to be wanted. Composing the piece shortly after the death of his closest painter friend, Philip Guston, Feldman had in mind a singer with two loudspeakers behind her. 'There is something kind of tombstoney about the look of loudspeakers. I thought of the piece as an exchange of the live voice with the dead ones—a mixture of the living and the dead.'[27] The dead would have to include the metrical regularity and the harmonic directedness that the music can no longer operate—'something . . . to do with . . . Schubert leaving me.'

Lachenmann and Regain

A composer whose catalogue begins with a reminiscence of Schubert, in a set of five variations for piano he wrote in 1956, could never feel totally deserted, even if that might at one stage have been his wish. The period of avoiding the conventionally beautiful sounds of music was

26. Ibid.
27. Quoted in note with New Albion 018.

brief, just a few years around 1970, after which Lachenmann found himself by the logic of his own method—considering musical points and the lines of energy and reference running through them—faced with the former: 'Working thus we encounter not only other, new shapes resulting from the initial idea but sometimes also, surprisingly, old acquaintances, which in a new context show themselves in a new light, and we come to shapes that probably we would never have accepted willingly.'[28] Pitched tones rushed back into his music, even triads, but sounding fresh because freed from their usual functions—and freed, too, from any requirement to shock or seduce by their familiarity, as in so much music of the time, since they are defamiliarized by the strength of the new context. He could now, as he put it, deny denial. Instead of being separated from traditional repertory, on the margins, however fruitful those margins had shown themselves, the thinking of instrumental *musique concrète* could be taken into the citadel, and even into some of its holiest places, for Lachenmann was to compose works after Mozart's Clarinet Concerto (*Accanto* for clarinet and orchestra, 1976–77) and Beethoven's Ninth Symphony (*Staub* for orchestra, 1985–87).

More was involved here than an extension of compositional technique. Writing about *Accanto*, Lachenmann observed how composers were doubly paralysed by society, experiencing 'speechlessness with regard to our real anxieties and threats' and 'the false articulacy in which we are led to believe by the mess of media and the culture industry'. Thus 'traditional works, which we indeed love, which have stamped us and which engage our commitment are often disastrously made to seem strange and hostile creatures'; works that were 'originally historic examples of humanity's spiritual awakening' were now used to put people to sleep.[29] To quote from such a work in a new and thoroughly integrated context, to find new lines of force linking it to the present and the present to it, was therefore not just a creative but a moral act. So was it to reinvigorate—and newly feel the vigour of—the small currency of tonal music.

Several of Lachenmann's works of the later 1970s and 1980s take up these challenges with no hint of regression, still less of postmodern repro. His Romanticism, quixotic by his own smiling admission,[30] was to believe that new beauty remained possible and that it mattered. A favourite image was that of the composer as organist,[31] working on the keys that were the materials for the composition, constructing the keyboard all the time; now chords, gestures, rhythms, and even forms from

28. Helmut Lachenmann, 'Über das Komponieren', *Musik als existentielle Erfahrung*, ed. Josef Häusler (Wiesbaden, 1996; 2004), 80.

29. Ibid., 168.

30. See ibid., 80.

31. See ibid., 78–79

Example 62   Helmut Lachenmann, *Allegro sostenuto*

older music would have a place there. Underlying *Tanzsuite mit Deutsch-landlied* for orchestra with string quartet (1979–80) is indeed a succession of dance types, including waltzes, siciliano, and gigue, as well as the German national anthem. The fifty-minute piano concerto *Ausklang* (1984–85) contains tonal chords and arpeggios, along with a plethora of stuttering monotones, but so far from representing visions of stability, these features are fractured, and the music's progress depends not at all on old syntax but, characteristically, on sparkings of energy from one place to another and on indwellings in the one place. By focussing on reverberation (which is one meaning of the title)—especially on the reverberation of the solo piano, which the orchestra so often extends, transforms, colours or abuses—*Ausklang* deprives itself of the fiction that music can reinvigorate itself by returning to methods and principles of the past. Every gesture here is fading. But the rich variety of fadings becomes a new kind of musical optimism erupting in bursts of humour, a demonstration of the possibility of recreating, out of an entirely modern sensibility, music on the grand scale, for *Tanzsuite* and *Ausklang* are both quasi-symphonies in matters of extent, density, and (concealed) multimovement form.

The principle of reverberation also operates in *Allegro sostenuto* for clarinet, cello, and piano (1987–88), whose title, borrowed from the marking Chopin gave his 'Aeolian Harp' étude, provided the composer with a stimulating antinomy of speed and stasis. Right at the start, shown in example 62, resonance effects are explored, not only in the piano writing but also in how piano tones can be sustained by the companion instruments, and yet an allegro dash is already implicit. 'The musical material,' Lachenmann notes, 'is determined by the mediation between the experience of "resonance" . . . and "movement". These two aspects of the sounding substance meet in the display of structure as a multifariously ambivalent "arpeggio".' On the most local scale, the arpeggio might be a musical figure, whether in one of the instruments or bouncing between them. Over larger stretches of time, erratic movement in one direction or another may be the guise of an underlying stasis, or stasis may be a momentary arrest, encapsulation, of movement.

Lachenmann's output during this period was divided largely between chamber pieces (including a second quartet) and orchestral scores, each of the latter conceiving the orchestra in a different way by virtue of a solo part (or group in *Tanzsuite*) that could be focus or foil and also in terms of character, of how its keyboard of sounds and principles was made up. There was, too, the composer's first contribution since his student days to the repertory for modern ensemble: *Mouvement (—vor der Erstarrung)*, commissioned by the Ensemble Inter-Contemporain and dating from 1982–84. As is implied by the bilingual title—'Movement (—before Paralysis)'—this is another on-the-edge exploration of mobility under strained circumstances.

The composer called it 'a music of dead movements, almost final spasms',[32] but we should note that 'almost'. Music here is in an acute condition, but not a hopeless one. The old harmonic means have been outworn and their twentieth-century replacements exhausted. Those paths along which earlier music travelled have become polished shiny-smooth, so that there is now no purchase on them. Yet still there is action, if flailing in the air. Still there is a coursing rhythmic energy, often in insistently pulsed patterns. Still, there are gestures of beginning, of challenge, of upward sweep through the orchestra, of disintegration. And these things, miraculously, create a new kind of movement, in both senses. Avoiding what he calls an 'exoticism of the alienated', Lachenmann as usual makes unusual effects sound fresh, beautiful, and inviting, as well as meaningful. We may have the impression at times of the strong propulsive force of a symphonic allegro, the strenuous conflict of a development, the liveliness of a scherzo, the calm and consolation of an adagio. Towards the end, the movement becomes one of rapid triplets, perhaps to suggest a kind of finale going back to Bach's gigues, except that this is only the penultimate section, giving way to the work's luminous close.

Lachenmann's Romanticism does not reside primarily in his reactivation of traditional materials but rather in his insistence on music's duty to address questions of human existence, despite all the cramps and constraints imposed on it by present-day society: to continue music's programme of freedom, and thereby to add to the means by which people can free themselves. 'Above all', he wrote soon after *Mouvement*, 'is the vision of freedom. . . . I would like to "sing as the bird sings, living in the branches" (Uhland), but we live in the branches of a ruined forest.'[33]

32. Note on the work, ibid., 396.
33. Lachenmann, 'Über das Komponieren', ibid., 82.

19

New Simplicities

Retrospection, so much a dominant aspect of music in the 1970s and 1980s, could be a matter not of turning back the clock to the Middle Ages or the nineteenth century but of finding a new simplicity to replace the old, in whatever way.

Cage, or Innocence

There is no more powerful demonstration of the inexorability of progress in the 1950s and 1960s than its effect on an artist devoted to non-intention. Cage had accepted that new music demanded new ideas, and in his *Concert for Piano and Orchestra* he had spent them prodigally. His relatively few pieces after that had, almost every time, introduced new procedures, new means, new notations. Then in 1969 came a return: *Cheap Imitation*—originally a piano work, later orchestrated and adapted for solo violin—was his first fully prescribed composition since the time series of the mid-1950s. (The coincidence with Stockhausen's *Mantra* is striking.) This might have been a special case: Cunningham had choreographed Satie's *Socrate*, but could not get the rights to use Cage's transcription of the score; hence this 'cheap imitation', repeating Satie's rhythmic structure so that the dance moves Cunningham had prepared could be retained, but transposing each phrase by chance. However, far from being an isolated exercise in musical economy, *Cheap Imitation* turned out to be the key to the manifold production of Cage's last two decades, for it embodied a truth that became inescapable as the

1960s receded: the truth that new ideas were no longer going to be so easy to find. Cage mentioned with approval Gunther Stent's conclusion that 'everything has been thought; all the fundamental discoveries have been made', and added: 'That doesn't mean that we don't need to compose new music, but new ideas on music are no longer necessary.'[1]

His choice of the word 'necessary', rather than 'possible', suggests how for him the postmodern condition was not a cause for anxiety but another liberation. 'I have been talking about abundance. I believe that what we can reasonably expect, within this state of stasis, is the interpenetration of . . . arts and . . . sciences . . . in a climate very rich with joy and—I am purposely using an expression frequent in Japanese texts—bewilderment.'[2] In his own work, the interpenetration resulted in a flowering of writings, prints, drawings, and watercolours, all based at root on principles of chance composition he had developed in music, while the release from the necessity of new ideas enabled him to return to the musical productivity he had known in the decade before *4' 33"*. In *Song Books* (1970) he created a vocal complement to the *Concert*: a collection of ninety *Solos for Voice* that covered a great variety of notational forms and could be performed individually or assembled in any way for a choral performance. In keeping with his professed belief, the ideas were not new, for the *Solos* repeated compositional methods he had introduced during the previous thirty years; but undoubtedly the music was.

Now that he was composing again, new ideas inevitably came despite their unnecessariness, and by the mid-1970s he was at work in several different areas. There were pieces for natural instruments— amplified plant materials in *Child of Tree* (1975), water-filled conch shells in *Inlets* (1977)—chosen partly because their acoustic properties would be unpredictable: 'In the case of *Inlets*, you have no control whatsoever over the conch shell when it's filled with water. You tip it and you get a gurgle, sometimes; not always. So the rhythm belongs to the instruments, and not to you.'[3] There were pieces for conventional instruments requiring extraordinary virtuosity: the *Etudes australes* for piano (1974–75), the *Etudes boréales* for cello and piano played as percussion kit (1978), and the *Freeman Etudes* for unaccompanied violin (1977–90). For all these pieces, pitches were chance-selected with the help of star charts (hence the titles of the first two sets), and Cage used chance operations also to determine—sometimes deliberately over-determine—other aspects: 'I had become interested in writing difficult music, etudes, because of the world system which often seems to many

1. John Cage and Daniel Charles, *For the Birds* (Boston, Mass. and London, 1981), 219.

2. Ibid., 220.

3. Cole Gagne and Tracy Caras: *Soundpieces: Interviews with American Composers* (Metuchen, N.Y., 1982), 77.

of us hopeless. I thought that were a musician to give the example in public of doing the impossible that it would inspire someone who was struck by that performance to change the world.'[4] There were composed musicircuses, most notably *Roaratorio* (1979), which combined his own reading of mesostics extracted from *Finnegans Wake* with tapes and performances by Irish folk musicians. There were disintegrations of existing music, created by omitting notes and extending those that remained: generally he used old American music—hymn tunes in the case of *Hymns and Variations* for twelve amplified singers (1979)[5]—a source to which he seems to have been drawn in making *Apartment House 1776* for the bicentennial of the United States. There were works that were musicircuses and disintegrations at the same time: the *Europeras* composed out of the traditional operatic repertory. There were one-off events, such as *Il treno* (1978), three happenings on 'prepared trains'. There were efforts at making the orchestra a model of calm anarchy: the orchestral versions of *Cheap Imitation* (1972) were to be played without a conductor; *Etcetera* (1973) offers twenty players the choice of playing as soloists, on cardboard boxes, or joining any one of three conducted ensembles; *Quartets I-VIII* (1976), another hymn tune piece, puts forward a different ensemble of four musicians for each phrase; *Thirty Pieces for Five Orchestras* (1981) again features small groups, but this time overlapping, as the five orchestras proceed independently.

Thirty Pieces for Five Orchestras is, as James Pritchett has pointed out,[6] one of the first compositions to profit, by reverse interpenetration, from the work Cage had begun to produce as a printmaker in 1978. Not only did he repeat, in making scores, a method he had used in making prints—that of placing marks through chance-placed holes in cardboard templates—but there is a similar effect of fragile straying designs, achieved partly in the music by a new technique of placing each piece only loosely within a bracket of time, giving the period during which it must begin and the period during which it must end. He repeated this idea in *Music for* (1984–88), a set of parts to be put together as required (so that, for example, a string quartet might make *Music for Four*) and in the profusion of 'number' pieces that followed, each with a title that just states the number of parts, with a superscript if that number has already been used: hence *Four* for string quartet (1988), *Four²* for SATB chorus (1990), *Four³* for one or two pianos, twelve rainsticks, violin or oscillator, and silence (1991), and so on. Cage's comments on his late pieces imply, whatever else, an objective delicacy: he spoke of sounds being 'brushed into existence'[7] and of music now con-

4. Note with Etcetera KTC 2016.

5. See William Brooks: 'John Cage and History: *Hymns and Variations*', *Perspectives of New Music*, 31/2 (1993), 74–103.

6. James Pritchett, *The Music of John Cage* (Cambridge, 1993), 185.

7. Quoted ibid., 200.

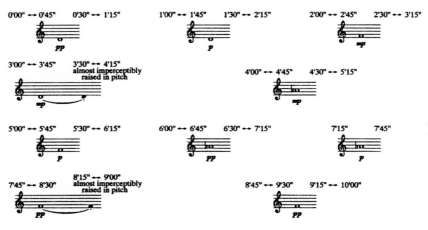

Example 63   John Cage, *Two*

veying 'a feeling of not knowing where you are in sound, but rather floating'.[8]

Example 63, the flute part from *Two* for flute and piano (1988), shows how the time-bracket notation works. Each note could, at the maximum, endure for a minute and a quarter, or, at the minimum, be a *staccatissimo* some way between thirty seconds and forty-five seconds into the bracket; each could also be silent, if the player decided to end it before it had begun. Typical of the series is the reduction of events to single tones. Cage had been working with reduced compasses since *Hymnkus* (1986), for instruments playing notes within the ambit of a fifth; during the whole of *Two*, which lasts up to ten minutes, the flautist plays no more than these ten notes at three different pitches. The piano part, of course uncoordinated, is not much more active.

After the speed of the *Etudes* and the exuberance of *Roaratorio*, there is this predominant stillness in Cage's late music: a stillness of single sounds simply existing. So detached from flow, any sound—even a traditional chord—seems to be waiting and new.

Denyer, or Outsiderness

As already noted in the cases of Ustvolskaya and Scelsi, outsider voices found a wider hearing in the late 1970s and 1980s as the rush of progress became becalmed. For Ustvolskaya recognition arrived too late for any change, but Scelsi's last works move from their intense otherness to recognize liaisons, whether with ancient or exotic traditions in their

8. Quoted in David Revill, *The Roaring Silence: John Cage: A Life* (London, 1992), 278.

modal melodies or with Feldman in their slow reiterations (as in *Aitsi* for amplified piano, 1974, recreated in 1985 as the composer's Fifth Quartet).

The British musician Frank Denyer (b. 1943), a noted performer of Ustvolskaya and Scelsi (and Cage, whose *Two* he has recorded), also chose a path well away from the mainstream. Following visits to India and Japan he did academic work in Nairobi (1978–81), then moved to the arts college at Dartington. He did not publish his music, and none was recorded until 1984. Many of his works resist the normal concert format in their scoring: *After the Rain* for shakuhachi, violin, three ocarina players, and percussion (1983), for example. This is music, too, that, while fully notated, exists at a remove from the standardization of Western music. The word 'vulnerable' recurs in the composer's programme notes and is apt, for he prefers not only hazardous combinations but also what sound like natural materials: untrained voices, instruments found or constructed, wind instruments that do not disguise the noise of breath (the shakuhachi being a favourite), in which regard there is a connection with Lachenmann. Like musicians with whom he came into contact in Asia and Africa, Denyer works with the fundamental elements of mode, repetition, and pulse, often assembled in layered textures, but there is no exoticism here for the reason that the creative persona is remarkably quiet. This is music that seems just to have arisen, to be arising. In the haunting violin solo *A Fragile Thread* (1979) there is only the instrument and the performer, moving along a hair-thin (nonvibrato) line in each of two short movements, both wavering (sliding towards and away from often microtonally inflected pitches) but taut as they circle in different paths through the small compass of their particular melodic terrain. Since the same piece can be sung, hummed, or whistled, we can do without the instrument and performer and all have this terrain for our own.

Kurtág, or Immediacy

In some ways Kurtág was another outsider, scarcely known outside Hungary until the later 1970s, when his insistence always on the expressively forceful gesture gained wider relevance. An important role in disseminating his work was played by Boulez, who came upon the score of *The Sayings of Péter Bornemisza* and commissioned a work for the Ensemble InterContemporain, *Messages of the Late Miss R. V. Trusova* for soprano and thirteen players (1976–80). Meanwhile, the completion of the Bornemisza piece had been followed by two shorter song sets, a failed orchestral project (*Twenty-Four Antiphonae* Op.10 for diverse groups—though the failure may not be permanent, since other remnants have eventually found completion, sometimes after many years), and then a further period of silence, relieved by Kurtág's recognition, prompted by the younger composers of the New Music Studio,[9] that silence might be broached through serious playfulness. Like Stravinsky and Bartók at points of crisis, he tested a new way forward in music for children, and in 1973 began writing pieces for what were to become several volumes of piano pieces: *Játékok*, or *Games*—games played with notes, whether games of formal and technical device, or games of imitation. (Other composers found this source of renewal a little later, Lachenmann in his piano album *Ein Kinderspiel* of 1980, which he described, quoting Adorno, as being 'even more about pointing toward a childlike model than conjuring up childhood',[10] and Berio in his *Duetti* of 1979–82 for junior violinists and their teachers.) From this point onward his music is full of arrangements and homages, covering everything from Machaut to the present, in every mood except the nostalgic, and including reworkings of his own discoveries: example 34 has its derivatives in *Játékok*. The many works that have come since Kurtág began his piano games might be considered *Játékok* for grown-ups: the significantly titled *Twelve Microludes* for string quartet (1977–78)— fragments, as always with Kurtág—provide an example. Like Bartók's *Mikrokosmos*, *Játékok* is educational music in the widest sense, in that it provides an education in a composer's sources, sympathies, and techniques, an education valid for large further areas of his output.

One great difference, however, between *Játékok* and the 'adult' music of 1973–87 is that nearly all the latter is vocal, and much of it, following their work together on *Trusova*, was written for Adrienne Csengery, whose reminiscences[11] provide abundant testimony to the intensity of their preparations and rehearsals: the composer's experience in teaching chamber music was not, after all, peripheral, but central to his ideal of making musical communication maximally responsive and responsible, as other performers he has coached have avowed.[12] It may be that the comparative dearth of instrumental works during this period, by contrast with the pattern of his output before the Bornemisza piece, came from a need he felt to discover, in composition and rehearsal, another person, whether the person of a singer or of a poet. In *Trusova* and two companion works, *Omaggio a Luigi Nono* for chorus (1979) and *Scenes from a Novel* (1979–82), that poet was Rimma Dalos, a Russian writer living in Hungary. During this time Russian became

---

9. See Bálint András Varga, *György Kurtág: Three Interviews and Ligeti Homages* (Rochester, N.Y., 2009), 9.

10. Note on the work, Helmut Lachenmann, *Musik als existentielle Erfahrung*, ed. Josef Häusler (Wiesbaden, 1996; 2nd. ed., 2004), 394.

11. See István Balázs, 'Portrait d'un compositeur vu par une cantatrice: entretien avec Adrienne Csengery', *Contrechamps*, 12–13 (1990), 184–94.

12. See, for example, the video recording (on Bridge 9270A) of a rehearsal with Tony Arnold and Movses Pogossian.

for him 'almost a sacred language'[13]—sacred, perhaps, in having been rescued, in Dalos's compact and highly charged poems, from the laziness and cynicism of its daily use during the dying phase of Soviet hegemony.

In *Trusova* Kurtág wrote for a larger ensemble than hitherto: an expansion of the twangy formations of his Four Capriccios and Four Pilinszky Songs, and curiously—perhaps deliberately—close to the instrumentation of Boulez's *Eclat*, though sounding so different. Kurtág's music proceeds in spidery counterpoint, exerted at every turn, rather than in waves and splashes, and normally it uses just a small number of the available forces, focussing increasingly on the combination of voice and solo string instrument that had been a recurrent ideal since *In Memory of a Winter Sunset* (1969). Not only did this combination provide a model of the interaction of music and verbal language, but it made possible a close interdependence and a fluidity of roles: the voice may seem to accompany the instrument.

It was for soprano and violin that Kurtág wrote his longest work so far, the *Kafka-Fragmente* (1985–86), in which forty extracts—chosen chiefly from the letters and diaries, and ranging from apophthegm to anecdote—are assembled in four sequences, lasting altogether for seventy minutes. Kafka's paradoxical edges—between irony and anxiety, between withdrawal and explosion, between creative potency and indecision—are Kurtág's too, and in this collaboration the composer was perhaps closest to standing before a mirror, of challenging clarity. The work was a culmination, and after it came just two small collections for soprano and piano before a return to instrumental composition, for larger forces than hitherto, in . . . *quasi una fantasia* . . . for piano and instrumental groups (1987–88).

By dispersing the instruments—in a way perhaps opened to him by Nono—Kurtág discovered a fragmented orchestra suited to his fragmented form. Ideally the pianist is to be on stage with only timpani and drums; other percussion—an unpitched metal group of cymbals, gongs, and triangles, a smaller 'echo' ensemble of them, and a number of tuned instruments, including the composer's much-favoured cimbalom —are to be on a middle gallery, with mouth organs; teams of five woodwind, four brass, and five strings are then to be placed on the highest level. Drama, which had previously been justified and described in the music by words, was now implicit in the resources, and the composer's relationship with a poet became the relationships his music could build in space: relationships of echo, nonrelationships of concurrent dissimilarities (especially in the third of the four short movements, a wild 'Presto minaccioso e lamentoso'). The work also echoes earlier

13. As quoted in István Balázs, 'Dans la prison de la vie privée', *Contrechamps*, 12–13 (1990), 198–210.

Example 64a   György Kurtág, *Twelve Microludes*

pieces, in a way by now characteristic: once a reality had been built, it remained a reality for other circumstances. Example 64a shows the ending of the fifth of the *Microludes*, and example 64b the corresponding passage from the finale of . . . *quasi una fantasia* . . . . The material is expanded in time, by echoing, as well as in texture, but it is arguably also intensified, particularly when the tonic E is repeatedly undershot. Once again, with the simplest materials, hardly more than a descending scale, Kurtág creates an original gesture and an immediate meaning.

Holliger, or Extremity

Already in the early 1970s Holliger's exploration of extreme possibilities, in his work as a performer, had become crucial also to his creative activity, when writing for himself and for others. Extreme possibilities suggest that language is being expanded, through the addition of non-standard timbres, microtones, far registers—and the thrill of discovery is there in such early works as *Siebengesang*. But Holliger's later music reveals another implication in radicalism, of minimization and constraint, as in Nono, Kurtág, and Rihm. Music seems destined to move onto what had been neglected as unpromising wasteland: this is the imperative if one is to avoid quoting the styles and materials of past music, and if one is to avoid—as may be a still more commanding injunction—the rhetoric of certainty. Holliger's music breathes uncertainty in its choice of marginal vocal and instrumental techniques, and refuses the directive first person singular of the composer's voice by dealing with materials and forms that are so simple as to be impersonal.

Taking his way along this arduous but fruitful path, Holliger went in the later 1970s and 1980s with two guidebooks. One was provided by the late dramas of Beckett, which supported him in his attention to tight structure, bareness, and a sense of the performer as a body and a voice: out of this collaboration came settings of *Come and Go* for three trios of female singers with trios of flutes, clarinets, and violas (1976–77), *Not I* for soprano with a tape created at IRCAM (1978–80), and *What Where* for four male singers with four trombones and percussion (1988). Holliger's other vade mecum was Hölderlin, whose poetry has

Example 64b György Kurtág, *. . . quasi una fantasia . . .*

challenged and fascinated composers throughout the post-1945 period, so that one might almost write its musical history through responses by Nono, Britten, Henze, Maderna, Kurtág, Ligeti, Rihm, and others.

The attractions of Hölderlin must include the musicality of his syllables and images, as well as his evocation of another world, created by sound almost before it is created by words, and the fragmentary nature of much of his work, apt to a time and a musical climate in which the definitive statement is hard to sustain. But Holliger, like Rihm, was drawn also by the late poetry written under the pseudonym 'Scardanelli'—the 'mad' poetry, whose escape from rules of sense, taste, and cultural nobility makes it unusually relevant in a musical world similarly loosened from agreed ideals. Between 1975 and 1979, came three seasonal cycles of settings for sixteen voices, to which the composer then added instrumental paraphrases, commentaries, and interludes—*Übungen zu Scardanelli* for small orchestra and tape (1978–85), *(t)air(e)* for solo flute (1980–83), and *Ostinato funebre* for small orchestra (1991)—to make an entire concert.

That Holliger should have made his Hölderlin settings for chorus rather than for solo singer may have to do with his wish for an impersonal voicing, with the relationship he had formed with Clytus Gottwald and the Schola Cantorum Stuttgart (who had performed his earlier *Dona nobis pacem* and Celan setting *Psalm*), and perhaps also with a certain Swiss veneration of Bach: the *Scardanelli-Zyklus* is a secular Passion, slowly oscillating between homophonic and canonic movements, and inviting contemplation of a solitary and exemplary figure, that of the poet, confined in his tower at Tübingen but with his mind wandering.

The chorus is not, though, the unified community it was in eighteenth-century Leipzig, and Holliger's choral writing takes traces through disintegration. In 'Der Frühling (I)', for example, the singers have to deliver root-position triads breathily, or with almost emptied lungs, or humming. 'Der Winter (III)' is a four-part mirror canon in triads moving through intervals between a tone and a quarter tone. 'Der Winter (II)', also a four-part canon, has all the performers singing *ppp* in a narrow 'dummy bass' register (between A and E♭ at the bottom of the treble stave for the sopranos, for instance). The soprano, alto, and tenor parts of 'Der Herbst (I)' have sudden shifts of register from chord to chord, sometimes by more than two and a half octaves, as these singers project dissonant overtones on a bass line plummeting to A below the stave. 'Der Sommer (III)' is a chain of three canons for seven female voices (number symbolism recurs here as in *Siebengesang*, and indeed as in Bach: the tempos of 37 and 73 in 'Der Herbst (II)' relate to Hölderlin's age when he entered the tower and his age when he died), the first canon in semitones, the second reducing each interval by a half, and the third halving the intervals again. Example 65 shows the melody of this last canon; the arrows on the accidentals indicate a quarter-tone rise, and those on the note heads an eighth-tone rise. As

Mit   neu - en   Far - ben   ist ge - schmükt der   Gär - ten   Brei - te,

Example 65   Heinz Holliger, *Scardanelli-Zyklus*

in the other two summer pieces, each singer sings to the tempo of her pulse, which not only manifests the physiology of performance, as in earlier Holliger pieces, but makes the chorus—even in a unison canon—into a collection of errant individuals. One of the *Übungen*, 'Sommer-kanon IV', is an orchestral version of the same piece; others are images that relate more tangentially and metaphorically to Hölderlin: 'Eisblu-men', or 'Ice Flowers', a string septet in harmonics; 'Schaufelrad', or 'Paddlewheel', in two slowly rotating six-note chords; 'Ad marginem', where the instruments move towards, but do not reach, the extreme registers represented on tape throughout.

Sciarrino, or Intimacy

Proudly self-taught, though stimulated by Nono's example, Salvatore Sciarrino (b. 1947) developed through the 1970s and into the 1980s a music of murmurs and stammers, of sounds at the edge of silence, of quiverings and faint pulsations. Like Nono, and like Nono's pupil Lachenmann, he savoured marginal sonorities: breathy sounds and multiphonics on woodwinds, harmonics, and all kinds of rustlings from string instruments, microtonal waverings, the vast possibilities of a hushed vocalism. Like those colleagues, too, he had no interest in pre-senting such materials as effects within a traditional discourse. In his music, rather, 'structure and sound event arise from the same needs and grow towards or tend towards a common perspective, a new image'.[14] Sound for him is a living substance, and in much of his music of this period it is tremulous as if with its own vital signs. At the same time, it bears the traces of human corporeality. Bodily rhythms of walking, pulse, and respiration are often audible; the tremulousness may also suggest the scratching of a pen on paper, as if the music partly con-veyed the sound of its being composed. Moreover, the musician's ac-tion in performing it is brought into play, not least in a whole series of pieces for the musicalized breath of an unaccompanied flute: *All'aure in una lontananza* (1977), *Hermes* (1984), *Come vengono prodotti gli incan-tesimi?* (1985), *Canzona di ringraziamento* (1985), *Venere che le Grazie la fioriscono* (1989), *L'orizzonte luminoso di Aton* (1989), *Fra i testi dedicati alle nubi* (1989)—all these in addition to accompanied pieces, such as the charming *Fauno che fischia a un merlo* for flute and harp (1980).

14. Salvatore Sciarrino, *Carte da suono (1981–2001)*, ed. Dario Oliveri (Rome and Palermo, 2001), 139.

Three further things are evidenced by this list: Sciarrino's productivity, the ease with which his music forms itself along a single line (a
simplicity pregnant with sophistication and also implicit in his view of
sound as living, the single line a single life), and his often poetic titles,
which suit his often poetic music, rich in allusions to Mediterranean
mythology as mediated by literature and visual art ('Faun whistling to
a blackbird' is a painting by Böcklin), to meteorological phenomena
('From texts dedicated to the clouds'), and, though not here, to night-
time and darkness. Music that speaks from the human body and even
seems to have a body of its own is thus also dematerialized—'such stuff
as dreams are made on', to pick up an analogy the composer himself
has put forward: 'For me music inhabits a borderland. Like dreams,
where something both is and is not, and is something else—and where
these feelings, the most unstable, slip across the wonder of a single bat-
ting of the eyes.'[15]

Instability, fragility, softness of contour as of dynamic: these are
some of the conditions for his music's suggestive power. Ideas flicker
into existence and are gone; more often we seem to be hearing only
their traces: draught from a departure or a stirring of dust. A quotation
may be evoked by a wisp of melody, or by a chord, or by a rhythm.
In *pianissimo* trembling—its most characteristic state—the music finds
the means for associative abundance even though the texture be thin,
the haze being thus a virtual polyphony (for which the composer once
found a humorously clear model in transcribing Bach's imposing D
minor Toccata and Fugue for his favoured solo flute). Quiet rumblings
may suggest distant thunder, or gunfire. The music's whisper is that of
grave confidences being vouchsafed. We may feel ourselves too close
for comfort, and at the same time not quite close enough.

Much of the above may be suggested by example 66, showing
the opening of the second (and first to be written) of his *Sei capricci* for
solo violin (1975–76), all of which play in the upper air of harmonics,
'normal' sounds being here abnormal. No. 2 is the only slow piece in
the set—the only one, therefore, that could (and does) fix itself to an
inhalation-exhalation rhythm, while its companions are concerned
more with a bodily tempo that is actualized in the performance rather
than present as metaphor, that of the player's busy left hand. The display element, for which a precedent is found in the appeal to Paganini's
caprices, is by no means inimical to intimacy. Pressed thus hard, the
violin agrees to release confidences it has hitherto kept under wraps,
especially in the vertiginous territory of its harmonics.

Sciarrino's exploration of instrumental possibilities was helped by
longstanding relationships with performers, notably the flautist Roberto
Fabbriciani (who was providing the same service for Nono, among
others), the string players Aldo Bennici and Salvatore Accardo, and the

15. Ibid., 53.

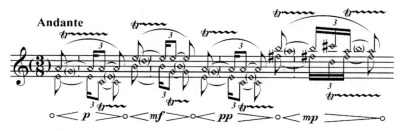

Example 66   Salvatore Sciarrino, *Sei capricci*

pianist Massimiliano Damerini. In the case of the piano, whose sounds are more or less fixed (for a composer not inclined to look beyond the keyboard), Sciarrino achieved uncertainty and impalpability—the qualities of his intimacy—by using the extreme registers, by drawing on a chosen heritage of rapid figuration going back through Ravel and Liszt to Bach and Scarlatti, by formal intrigue (as in his Second Sonata, dating from 1983, which grows as a sequence of responses to an insistent high chord, intermittently repeated, gradually ignored by the increasingly varied music it has brought forth, eventually lost or silenced or sulkingly mute and finally restored with new, charier consequences) and, as so often, by slipped-in semiquotations. They were full quotations in one of his earliest pieces, *De la nuit* (1971), which weaves garlands with, around, and among vestiges of Ravel's *Gaspard de la nuit*, and they were full again in another piano solo that once more shows his highly cultivated humour: his embrace of Ravel's *Jeux d'eau* together with Nacio Herb Brown's 'Singin' in the Rain' under the umbrella of his *Anamorfosi* (1980). Much more often, though, the reference is not quite defined and gone before it can be named. Sciarrino's piano music, like his music generally, may also be self-referential, conjuring what has gone before, its process so often pointing toward the movement of memory, or calling across to another work, as the Third Sonata (1987) calls across to the Second.

20

New Complexities

The term 'new complexity' arose in the late 1980s[1] to describe the music of Brian Ferneyhough (b. 1943) and others felt to be advancing again from the complexity of the early 1950s, and so countering the general regression toward the simple, normal, or merely old. Such music established itself most fully and freely in the United States, thanks partly to the continuing example of Babbitt, in Britain, thanks to the impression made not only by Ferneyhough but also by Michael Finnissy (b. 1946), and in Germany, thanks perhaps to the failure of the Darmstadt flame quite to extinguish itself, and to the goad of Germanic musical history. However, it is the British group, if group it be, that has been most conspicuous since the early 1980s, in terms of teaching, of influence, and of the dissemination of their music.

Ferneyhough

Born in England, but trained in the Netherlands and Switzerland, and subsequently active as a teacher in Switzerland, Germany, and the United States, Ferneyhough was an international figure before he was a national one: his big break came at the 1974 Royan Festival, and for some years he was more performed and more influential in continental Europe than in Britain. As with Hopkins, his critical attitude to the

1. See Richard Toop, 'Four Facets of "The New Complexity"', *Contact*, 32 (1988), 4–50. The quotation marks indicate the term was current by then.

music of the 1950s was sharpened by the intensest appreciation of the lessons that could—and the challenge that must—be drawn from that music. There was no going back. He took over the role of intellectual and creative combatant that most of the leading composers of the 1950s had abandoned, and he brought excitement back to Darmstadt.

The importance to him of the earlier Darmstadt adventure is evident in his first scores—in, for example, the highly sophisticated rhythmic notation suggestive of the first book of Boulez's *Structures* or of Stockhausen's first *Klavierstücke*. But he may have identified more in his early twenties with the music Boulez was writing at the same age. He similarly concentrated on small instrumental forms, always including the piano, and similarly achieved a wild, fresh energy that would, in his case, remain characteristic. The sources of that energy, though, were different. Where Boulez was in arms against the past, crashing through the models of Beethovenian sonata or French good taste, Ferneyhough's intensity is typically more creative than destructive. System is not in the way of expression: expression happens by, through, and in system—or rather, by, through, and in the entrammelling of a human being (first the composer, later the performer) with system. As Ferneyhough said, for example, of his *Four Miniatures* for flute and piano (1965), 'the flute part contains several very specific rhythmic configurations whose purpose is to focus the performer's mind on that particular dimension at very precise junctures.'[2] Similarly, the purpose of complex musical architectures is to focus the composer's mind at the very precise juncture of inscription.

Another difference is that Ferneyhough never emulated Boulez and Stockhausen in projecting his works as models for the future. Also, his few references to the past have concerned somewhat distant prototypes: Webern and the fantasias of Purcell in the case of his first major work, the Sonatas for string quartet (1967), or the polychoral music of sixteenth-century Venice and England. (The English references are poignant, coming from a composer who found his training and his opportunities largely in continental Europe, where radicalism survived.) His method appears to have been to assemble so many strategies— strategies of quantification and transformation having their roots in 1950s serialism—that his creative options were, to use his own word, 'focussed': hence the characteristic impression of musical figments of extreme articulacy and force, such as began to arrive particularly in the solos of *Prometheus* for wind sextet (1967) and the duo for two violins in the Sonatas, composed, like other works of this early period, of discrete fragments (twenty-four in this case). Like other early works, too, this first quartet was unheard for several years, receiving its first complete performance at Royan in 1975.

---

2. Interview with Philippe Albèra in *Contrechamps*, 8 (1988), 9.

Meanwhile Ferneyhough went on to pieces that model his relationship with his material in the act of composition: solos, in which
the performer, like the composer, has to operate at a level of extreme
awareness while negotiating a way through a multitude of rivalling
and even conflicting demands, and *Transit* for vocal and instrumental
ensembles (1972–75), in which imaginative perception is both the goal
and the constant mode of being. If the earlier works had looked towards Boulez and, to a lesser extent Stockhausen, those of the early and
mid-1970s move on to the sites of the second-generation avant-garde:
the unaccompanied chorus, swarming with new vocal techniques, in
Time and Motion Study III (first performed by Clytus Gottwald and his
Schola Cantorum Stuttgart, who had gone this way, though never quite
so arduously, with Kagel, Schnebel, and Holliger[3]), and the solo flute
and cello, the bearers of so many new musical messages during the late
1950s and 1960s, in *Unity Capsule* (1975–76) and *Time and Motion Study
II* (1973–76).

The opening of *Unity Capsule*, shown in example 67, may suggest
the problems, even in what is a relatively simple passage.[4] Ferneyhough's use of short note values, which gives his scores a characteristic
scarified look, makes it possible for him to indicate continuity in the
beaming, and may also sharpen the player's zest for speed—for speed
quite deliberately dangerous when there is so much to be considered
and done. Not only are the judgments of pitch, duration, and dynamic
exceedingly fine, but Ferneyhough adds many further levels of demand
and distinction. To paraphrase his own explanation of the notation,[5]
the half-rhomb note heads in the first bar indicate sounds with a great
deal of breath noise; the block note head on the voice line in the second bar indicates 'play with the mouth open and with full but diffuse
respiration—as if your breath were cut off', while the circle in the next
bar stands for a plosive produced by the tongue without breath. The
inverted T shapes above the stave mean 'without tongue attack'; the
rotating U shapes show the angle at which the instrument must be held
to the lips; and the plus signs indicate percussive but silent depressions
of the keys. There are also more conventional indications of fingering.

Not only all this (and later much more), but the piece also com-
presses into its capsuled unity a great many cross-references: for example, the 4-3-2 pattern of the opening bars is echoed in the numbers

3. See Clytus Gottwald, 'Brian F. oder Von Metaphysik der Positivismus',
Melos, 44 (1977), 299–308.

4. For a performer's view, see Kathryn Lukas, 'Cassandra's Dream Song &
Unity Capsule', *Contact*, 20 (1979), 9–11. See also a fascinating account by Steven Schick in his 'Developing an Interpretive Context: Learning Brian Ferneyhough's *Bone Alphabet*', *Perspectives of New Music*, 32/1 (1994), 132–53.

5. Brian Ferneyhough, 'Unity Capsule: un journal de bord', *Contrechamps*,
8 (1988), 140–48.

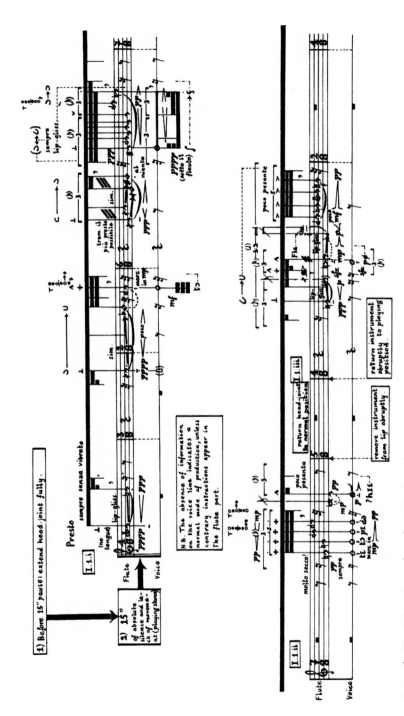

Example 67 Brian Ferneyhough, *Unity Capsule*

301

of subsections within the first section (new subsections begin, as shown, with the fifth and seventh bars), and in the number of sections within the piece. Of course, the status of the information is in doubt, partly because there is so much of it, partly because some bits of it will cancel out others, and partly because it cannot be projected: for instance, the only bar in example 67 likely to be definable as a length is the sixth. But the music is surely aware of its condition. Ferneyhough's hint that a bar can be measured only by means of an ungainly physical gesture is one of his black ironies, and his often-quoted statement that his concern is with 'the positive nature of doubt' may be understood as a declaration that his music exists precisely in its imprecision—in the failures and the overabundances of its performance.

Support for that would come from his preface to the earlier and far less intensively notated flute solo *Cassandra's Dream Song* (1970): 'The notation does not represent the result required: it is the attempt to realise the written specifications in practice which is designed to produce the desired (but unnotatable) sound quality. A "beautiful", cultivated performance is not to be aimed at. . . . Nevertheless, a valid realization will only result from a rigorous attempt to reproduce as many of the textural details as possible: such divergencies and "impurities" as then follow from the natural limitations of the instrument itself may be taken to be the intentions of the composer.' The difference in *Unity Capsule* is that the 'divergencies and "impurities"' will come not only from the instrument but from the frantic nature of the task. As the composer has pointed out, the density of instructions 'often stops performers "remembering" too far ahead, and leaves them in a constant state of "surprise attack", as the horizon of memory closes around them'. For listeners, too, this may happen. Though Ferneyhough has protested that his 'structures, as linear entities, *can* be heard individually',[6] it may be that 'a "beautiful", cultivated' appreciation is less to be hoped for than a constant grappling, and that the only form will be the drive to understand—or at least to keep pace with—the drive immanent in the performance.

The flute was Ferneyhough's own instrument; it provided him with a great variety of effects; and, as a monodic source, it added a further level of useful constraint on a composer for whom 'texture and structure . . . are the two vehicles of expressive form.'[7] But he also found possibilities of highly charged virtuosity in the dramatic persona of a cellist wired-up so that vocal and instrumental sounds could be amplified and recorded: hence *Time and Motion Study II*, part of a series whose title is a pun on the efficiency tests to which British workers were subjected in the 1960s. This was Ferneyhough's nearest approach to Kagelian borderlands of instrumental theatre and social criticism. Similarly,

6. Albèra interview, 38.
7. Ferneyhough, 'Unity Capsule: un journal de bord'.

Transit is unusually concrete: unusually generous with an almost Beri-oesque or Birtwistlian sonorous appeal (in the chattering together of voices and instruments, or in the eruptions of brass), and unusually acknowledging of a world outside itself. Part of what made Ferney-hough so problematic a pioneer was the close centring of each of his works on materials and issues proper to it alone. *Transit*, one of his very few vocal pieces, looks out. In its texts, in its layout (in concentric semicircles of instruments around the singers), in its form and in its imagery, it concerns itself with the mind's penetration of the objective universe, even if this is perhaps only a metaphor for the mental and physical agilities working at pressure in the more abstract pieces.[8]

Funérailles for string septet and harp, completed in 1980, ends a pe-riod in Ferneyhough's output with a memorial that also has elements of the illustrative (foretastes of the 'cathedral-under-the-sea' sonorities of his *Mnemosyne* for bass flute and tape[9]), and which may evoke 'a rite taking place behind a curtain',[10] but which stands by and for itself—or rather, itselves, since its dual character absorbs any external refer-ence into a force field between the two panels, which are to stand sepa-rately in a programme, like two matching doors. Matching, but not equal. *Funérailles II* surely has to be played second, since not only does it heighten the experience by dearth, but it ends with a desperate, conclusive gesture as some of the string players take up percussion instruments.

Ferneyhough's next two works, the Second String Quartet (1980) and the quasi-sonata for piano *Lemma-Icon-Epigram* (1981), exude a supreme confidence, not least in removing themselves from the blasted, withered soundscapes of *Unity Capsule* and the *Time and Motion* series (busy deserts though those are) and from the associated notational com-plexity. This may have been a fruit of the composer's success. It may have come, as he has suggested, from the discovery that closings of the memory horizon could be engineered more subtly. It may have been stimulated by work on what was for long his only piece for full orches-tra, *La Terre est un homme* (1976–79), whose complement of a hundred and one players effectively precluded—for reasons of time in the com-position if not practicality in the performance—the wealth of detail found in the immediately preceding compositions. The Second Quartet is a quartet on silence: not only the gaps that break up events and pro-cesses in the early part of the single movement, but perhaps also the silencing of differentiation that takes over as whistling high glissandos—magical sounds that had appeared in the Sonatas—come to dominate.

8. A valuable essay by James Erber accompanies the recording on Decca HEAD 18.

9. Interview with Richard Toop included in the publisher's brochure for the *Carceri d'invenzione* cycle (London, 1993), 11.

10. Note with Erato 88261.

The piece also enacts, as it grows from an opening violin cadenza, the move in Ferneyhough's output from the essentially solo music of the 1970s to the later solo-plus-ensemble formats.

The Second Quartet marks a new clarity of utterance, with respect to how easily the memory horizon can be pushed back so that ten minutes can be perceived as a logical span. It may be significant that the composer, not prone to explications of technique, published an analysis of this piece,[11] for in a sense the music here is what can be analysed, whereas in *Unity Capsule* the music is what cannot be. Going into more detail than the composer, Richard Toop's analysis of *Lemma-Icon-Epigram*[12]—an analysis that belongs with Ligeti's of *Structures Ia* as a modern classic of the genre (or classic of the modern genre)—indicates how the logic may be laid bare in terms of transformations (of note sets, durations, durational successions, time signatures, dynamics—all the usual quantities of 1950s serialism) that are individually quite simple but complex in their interworkings.

These two works, the quartet and the piano piece, fit appropriately into repertories not short on masterpieces, whereas their predecessors are more difficult to programme: it is hard to imagine, for example, a cello recital that could accommodate—withstand—*Time and Motion Study II*. Such considerations may have led Ferneyhough to the idea, adumbrated by *Funérailles*, of creating a whole concert of his own, the *Carceri d'invenzione* cycle (1981–86), named after Piranesi's engravings of 'imaginary dungeons'—or 'dungeons of imagination', to posit a pregnant secondary interpretation. What Ferneyhough admired in these architectural capriccios was a content 'hyper-loaded with expression, with explosive and implosive energy', generated by 'the tremendous multiplication of sometimes quite contrary perspectival lines'.[13] His assumption here that 'expression' has to do not with parallelling or eliciting emotions but with 'energy' is significant for his whole output: his writings and interviews are full of metaphors of force and tension, as in his suggestion that the first idea for a piece might come in the form of 'baroque constructions of levers and pivots which shift the coagulum of time to one side or the other'.[14] On this idea of music as energy moving time, he has suggested that the finale of the *Carceri* series conveys 'situations in which alterations in the flow of time through

11. 'Deuxième quatuor à cordes', *Contrechamps*, 8 (1988), 149–62.

12. 'Brian Ferneyhough's *Lemma-Icon-Epigram*', *Perspectives of New Music*, 28/2 (1990), 52–100.

13. Toop interview, 6; see also Richard Toop, '"Prima le parole . . ." (on the sketches for Ferneyhough's *Carceri d'invenzione I-III*)', *Perspectives of New Music*, 32/1 (1994), 154–75. For a painting of his own, similarly replete with contrary geometries, see the cover of Etcetera KTC 1070.

14. Albèra interview, 34.

and around objects or states become sensually (consciously) palpable'.[15] Piranesi's designs may have looked to him like such musical embryos: 'baroque constructions' of stairways, vaults, towers, bridges.

The Piranesian heptalogy consists, in order, of *Superscriptio* for piccolo,[16] *Carceri d'invenzione I* for sixteen players, *Intermedio alla ciaccona* for violin, *Carceri d'invenzione II* for flute and twenty players, *Etudes transcendentales/Intermedio II* for soprano, flute, oboe, cello, and harpsichord, *Carceri d'invenzione III* for fifteen wind and three percussion, and *Mnemosyne* for bass flute and tape. It is a sequence that can, characteristically, be understood in several ways. There is an alternation of orchestras, in the three *Carceri d'invenzione*, with smaller formations. There is a flautist's descent, from thrilled solo initiation on the piccolo, through quasi-concerto (in *Carceri II*) and semi-concealment in a chamber group (playing flute, piccolo, and alto flute in the *Etudes transcendentales*), to solo memorializing, when this player is the last on the field of action—a field whose final emptiness is accentuated by the fact that it echoes with recordings only of the player's own voice. There is a symmetry around the flute concerto. But there is also a stronger symmetry around the *Etudes transcendentales*, which are much longer than any of the other works, occupying almost a third of the total ninety-minute length.

These *Etudes* claim a high position, after *Pierrot lunaire* and *Le Marteau sans maître*. Like the Schoenberg work, they set poems in German, by Ernst Meister and Alrun Moll; Ferneyhough has also drawn attention to the connection in saying that he was tired of 'the rather white sound' of the *Pierrot* ensemble (though later, in *On Stellar Magnitudes*, he was to write precisely for that ensemble) and wanted 'a hard-edged metallic quality'[17] The relationship with Boulez's piece is more implicit, though marked by there being similarly nine movements in three interlocking cycles. Also, just as Boulez paid homage to Schoenberg in including a piece for voice and flute, so Ferneyhough does the same to place his work further along the line.

Another connection with Schoenberg and Boulez is in the reformulation of the ensemble from movement to movement—a reformulation to which Ferneyhough adds a redefinition of character. For example, the *pianissimo adagissimo* of the fifth number, shot through with regular rhythms, moves dramatically, through a sustained note on the cello, into the most songlike movement. Around this lyrical centre are pieces in which the vocal line is splintered or drawn into elaborate melismas, and the symmetry is enhanced by the location of movements

15. 'The Tactility of Time', *Perspectives of New Music*, 31/1 (1993), 20–30.

16. For an analysis see Richard Toop, '*Superscriptio* pour flûte piccolo solo', *Entretemps*, 3 (1987), 95–106.

17. Toop interview, 7.

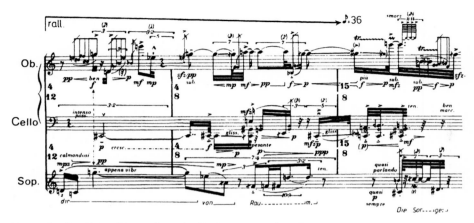

Example 68   Brian Ferneyhough, *Etudes transcendentales*

in which the silence of the woodwind brings the harpsichord into re-
lief: the third, in which the addition of pizzicato cello heightens the
guitarlike nature of the harpsichord's broken chords and tremolos, and
the eighth, for voice and harpsichord alone.

But the work's stature depends not on generalities but rather on
the high density of significant incident. Beginnings and ends of movements are often brilliant: the cello cadenza at the end of the second
song, the alarm call for piccolo, oboe, and cello in unison at the start of
the last, the already mentioned link between the fifth and the sixth,
and, most startling of all, the guttering close of the final song, as tiny
instrumental fragments trail off into—or protest against—silence. What
Ferneyhough might want to call 'energy' so often communicates itself
as drama, or, one might simply say, as beauty: the supple vocalise on
vowel sounds in the last movement, following a passage in which the
singer has only been able to enunciate consonants. Also, though so
much that happens must remain as wonderful bewilderment, threads
of explicability are constantly working through to the surface, as in the
passage from the second song shown in example 68, where the oboe
takes over the soprano's G, pushes it up a quarter tone, and then, after
another thought, pushes it on up another. Part of the point, not just
in this piece, seems to be to have us oscillating between interpreting
quarter tones in this way as inflections (hence the importance of the
glissando in Ferneyhough) and understanding them as distinct entities.
On the larger scale, we may wonder how much the separate songs—
and the separate pieces of the whole *Carceri* cycle—are inflections of
one another, how much discrete.

Example 68 provides a simple instance of a gesture—the transferred and interrupted upward slide—existing not alone, as in the solo
pieces of the 1970s, but within a context, whether in opposition to it,

nascent from it, or declining into it. This shift may have to do with an alteration in how the composer has been able to view himself: not as a voice crying in the wilderness, but as an active, engaged participant in the musical world. On a less metaphorical plane, it is through embedded gesture that, for Ferneyhough, the work speaks, and declares its difference from the un-gesturing crystallinity that is the potential peril of an organization as ramified as his: 'Music is not dead material, nor yet abstract form. Still less is it meaningless maneuvering in an uncaring, arbitrary void. The idea of the figure seen as a constructive and purposive reformulation of the gesture should clear the path for aura, the visionary ideal of a work entering into conversation with the listener *as if it were another aware subject*'[18] (italicized in the original). Especially in a period of so much musical dumbness, Ferneyhough's works may indeed appear, in their rich networking, to have taken on life and consciousness. They have the recognizable familiarity and the unfathomable strangeness of other people. And his search for gestures and contexts for gestures may have something to do with the preponderance of the solo-ensemble contrast, within the *Carceri* cycle and in the works that followed: the Third Quartet (1987), which, like the Second, has solo incursions; the Fourth Quartet (1989–90), in which a soprano joins the ensemble;[19] and a sequence of chamber concertos that began with *La Chute d'Icare* (1988).

The notation in example 68, typical of later Ferneyhough, is less fraught than in *Unity Capsule*, even though the composer compounds temporal complexity by introducing novel time signatures (2/10 earlier in this movement), which—along with the speeds, the irrational rhythms, and the quarter tones—ensure that the work lives up to the difficulty of its Lisztian eponym. Difficulty is intrinsic to the music: Ferneyhough is writing under extreme conditions (the advanced development of notation and performance in western culture, the neglect of that development in so much new western music), and his music necessarily reflects and embodies the extremity. Also, as with Liszt, the strenuous may be seen as a route to the transcendent. For that is the music's ambition. Its concern with edges—not only the edges between movements but perhaps also the edge of the high treble, the edge between sound and word, the edge of achievable speed—has to do with achieving that '*salto mortale* . . . over the end . . . of a composition, in such a way as to be able actually to modify, to change, to show in a different light the world outside the object itself.'[20] The work's fragmenting end may be an image of this leap by which it would enter the world,

---

18. 'Il tempo della figura', *Perspectives of New Music*, 31/1 (1993), 10–19.

19. For his high regard for Schoenberg's Second Quartet, see Paul Griffiths, *New Sounds, New Personalities* (London, 1985), 81.

20. Toop interview, 6.

would attain 'a certain permanence'[21]—the permanence that led to the choice of poems having to do with death and survival.

Finnissy

The first full performance of the *Carceri* cycle, at Donaueschingen in 1986, came little more than a decade after the composer's debut at Royan, during which time other kinds of new British complexity had came to the fore. Unlike Ferneyhough, Finnissy made his life in Britain, as did James Dillon (b. 1950), while Chris Dench (b. 1953) settled in Australia and Richard Barrett (b. 1959) moved between the two countries, both these latter composers working often with the Elision Ensemble, whose individual virtuosities and splendiferous range of colours (with a prominent tuned percussion centre, including anklung, mandolin and guitar, as well as full stretches of winds and strings) produced a kind of sensuous complexity that may be uniquely Australian.[22]

Finnissy's output—in another contrast with Ferneyhough (and there are more)—became prodigious and diverse, comparable with Rihm's in that respect, and similarly prompted by a driving subjectivity. In his numerous piano works—most of them written for himself to play, and including several concertos as well as whole books of what he called 'transcriptions' and other solo pieces—complexity is often a fair enough statement of the pressure of events within the music, and of the pressure of histories behind it. These histories would include the history of keyboard virtuosity, and its associate histories of wildness matched but not tamed by determination (Alkan, Grainger, and Ives are among the heroes Finnissy has celebrated in piano portraits) and festooning elaboration, as shown particularly, but not only, in his transcriptions, of music from Verdi to Gershwin—versions that often bury the original within the turmoil of following through what had been implicit or undecided or underachieved. But not all Finnissy's music was like this. His String Trio (1986), based on material from Mahler's Ninth Symphony, is remarkable for its sustained stillness, its seeming hold of a waiting frenzy in tense check, unless this is a fastidious dispassion violent in itself. Utterly different, his cycle of *English Country-Tunes* for piano (1977) wields immense power against a Merrie England interpretation of past reality, as suggested by example 69; the work was composed 'in celebration of the Silver Jubilee of Her Majesty Queen Elizabeth II'. Frenzy in such works may express dissatisfaction with the

---

21. Ibid., 8.

22. These four composers are the subject of Richard Toop's 'Four Facets of "The New Complexity"', *Contact*, 32 (1988), 4–50. For a response to this article, see Arnold Whittall, 'Complexity, Capitulationism and the Language of Criticism', *Contact*, 33 (1988), 20–23.

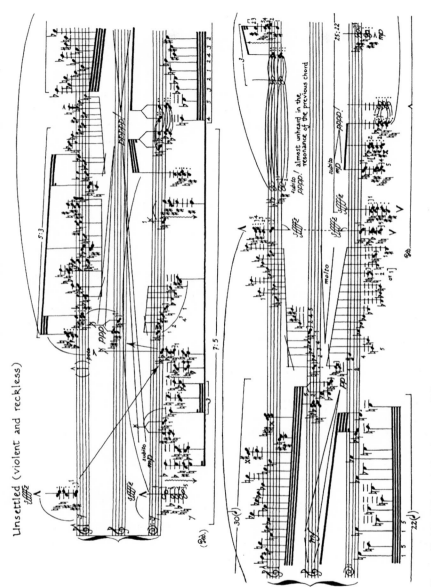

Example 69 Michael Finnissy, *English Country-Tunes*

culture the composer found around him—musical, social, and political
—but it comes, too, from a corporeal engagement with the piano. String
or wind instruments allow a different voice to come forward in slow
music, an intensity—sharpened, as it were, by quarter-tone tuning—
on a knife edge between melancholy and rage. Disenchanted with contemporary England, Finnissy found images of better societies in folk
music from a range of sources and, during teaching stints in Melbourne, among Australian aboriginal people. From this last encounter
came a sequence of pieces, evocative of raw nature but also of displacement, that led up to his orchestral composition *Red Earth* (1988), for an
ensemble resting unquietly on two didjeridus.

Charged Solos

In Dillon's music, as in Finnissy's, complexity is mitigated by a kind of
rude energy having parallels in Xenakis and as far back as *The Rite of
Spring*; his orchestral piece *helle Nacht* (1986–87) exemplifies this,
though unusual in his output of this period for its scale. Partly for lack
of bigger commissions, partly because their music called for an intense
engagement from performers, on account not only of its notation but
also of its expressive thrust, composers associated with 'new complexity' tended to work with soloists and small groups with whom they
were familiar. That was true also of others, such as Babbitt, many of
whose small-scale pieces of this period have an ease and wit reflected
in their titles: *Playing for Time* for piano (1977), *Sheer Pluck* for guitar
(1984), *The Joy of More Sextets* for violin and piano (1986). But demanding as it is in terms of poised agility, Babbitt's music makes little use
of the new sonorities—and none of the pitch bendings—found in the
work of his younger British contemporaries, or in that of Pascal Du-
sapin (b. 1955), a Xenakis pupil who produced a sequence of high-
energy pieces in the 1980s.

Most of these European composers wrote for solo flute, possibly
spurred by Ferneyhough's example, but profiting also from contact
with virtuosos. Dillon conceived *Sgothan* (1984) for Pierre-Yves Artaud,
who had given the first performances of *Cassandra's Dream Song* and
Unity Capsule, and in the same decade Dench produced a whole series
of solos for flautists including Roberto Fabbriciani, Ferneyhough's preferred soloist for the *Carceri*. There is something solitary about the unaccompanied flute—as Babbitt was to recognize in *None but the Lonely
Flute* (1991), with musical as well as titular allusion to the Tchaikovsky
song—and Dench's skill with looping, self-similar melody fits with the
concomitant pensiveness. His *Sulle scale della Fenice* (1986) comes back
occasionally, and wittily, to a figure of downward steps, reinterpreted
with microtonal inflections towards the end; it has almost nothing in
common with Dillon's zigzag of moments rich in glissandos, breathy
tones, wild leaps, and trills, or with the struggle for expression that char-

acterizes Ferneyhough's writing for the instrument (or, perhaps, any instrument). The comparison is instructive for any judgment of 'new complexity' as a movement.

So would be a comparison of the late Romantic flamboyance and sweep often found in Finnissy's piano music with the pulsed, iterative energies of Barrett's *Tract I* (1984–89), even if characteristic of both is an atmosphere of search and a bedrock of anger.

21

Old Complexities

The dream of Darmstadt in the 1950s, or at least the stated purpose, was to develop a new musical language that would nurture any number of idiolects, as the languages of Renaissance polyphony or common-practice tonality had done. Out of it, of course, came a babble of more or less independent, and in some cases rudely conflicting tongues, being elaborated by former revolutionaries become mature masters, now in their fifties and sixties (or seventies and eighties in Carter's case). Almost all those who had been at the forefront at the beginning of this story remained vigorously active; the death in 1973 of Maderna was a first blow, to which both Berio and Boulez responded with memorials. Almost all, too, experienced the common change of direction in the mid-1970s, after the dream or the purpose had vanished.

Carter and the Poets

With age Carter did not slow down but speeded up. Big instrumental compositions were coming now not every three or four years but almost annually, still pursuing diverse movements and characters in polyphony. In *A Symphony of Three Orchestras* each of the groups has four different types of music, the twelve being entwined together. Other works explore diverse alliances on a smaller scale: the Triple Duo (1982) is a comedy of partnerships for flute and clarinet, violin and cello, and piano and percussion, *Penthode* (1984–85) a drama for five mixed and dissimilar quartets. *Night Fantasies* (1978–80), a piano work of sonata

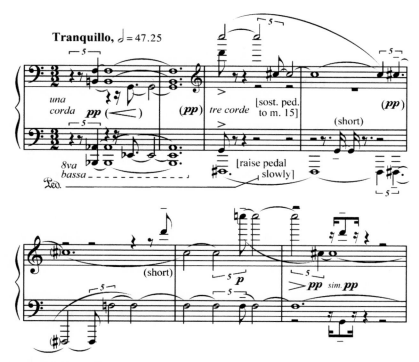

Example 70   Elliott Carter, *Night Fantasies*

length and weight, regained a Schumannesque instrumental poetry while hewing to characteristic Carterian harmonic regions, each a twelve-note chord in which all the intervals from a minor second to a major seventh are represented. Relations of closeness or contrast among these regions are played out as the work proceeds, and there is an equally characteristic rhythmic structure, based on simultaneous regular pulsations every twenty-seven quintuplet quavers (divided as nine plus eighteen) and every thirty-five semiquavers.[1] Example 70 shows the opening of the piece, where this rhythmic structure starts after the low introductory chord, all the attacks belonging to one or other of the slowly pulsing layers. Only six of the potential twelve notes are in play here, three of them shared with the initial chord. This kind of allusive movement, and the brilliant darkness, are typical of the piece, through its turmoil of diverse speeds and shapings, and the all-interval chords went on to determine the composer's subsequent works, which included further contributions to the two classical genres

1. See John F. Link, 'The Composition of Elliott Carter's *Night Fantasies*', *Sonus*, 14/2 (1994), available online at http://www.wpunj.edu/coac/music/link/ JohnLinkSonusPaper.pdf.

predisposed to his kind of musical discourse: a Fourth Quartet (1985) and concertos for oboe (1987) and violin (1990). There was also a cascade of instrumental miniatures, following the early splash that was *Riconoscenza* for solo violin (1974), a homage to Carter's contemporary Goffredo Petrassi (1904–2003).

The more surprising Carterian innovation, however, was the introduction of the solo singing voice in a triptych of chamber cantatas, collaborations with U.S. poets close to the composer in terms both of time and of mentality: Elizabeth Bishop in *A Mirror on Which to Dwell* for soprano (1975), John Ashbery in *Syringa* for mezzo (1978), where a bass-baritone adds an audible substratum of ancient Greek verse in the original, and Robert Lowell in *In Sleep, in Thunder* for tenor (1981). What was surprising here was not only the return to vocal composition, after a lapse of more than thirty years, but also the interposing of a lyric voice in the work of a composer whose voices had been manifold and mutable—the introduction, too, of a sensibility, not only in these vocal works but also in the concertos and in *Night Fantasies*, that might almost put the composer among the new Romantics. The polyphony, however, remains. Carter's choice was of poets whose works are themselves polyphonic: self-questioning, spinning with references, sliding among different sorts of rhetoric. What he creates in his sung lines is, too, a constructed sort of lyricism, not unlike Stravinsky's in his Shakespeare settings and later songs—a sort of lyricism in which one hears both the voice and the assembly of the voice. There is also the sense of the singers as slightly apart from the musical action, which they hear a moment before the audience, and comment upon. Then in *Syringa* there is the real polyphony of two singers who not only come from two different times but spearhead—like the soloists of the Double Concerto—two different understandings of musical time: incantatory in the case of the bass-baritone, whose line often oscillates across wide intervals, and conversational in the case of the mezzo. The ostensible subject of *Syringa* is the story of Orpheus, which is patched together in the bass-baritone's anthology and mused on by the mezzo. But the story of Orpheus is also the story of time: the striking nearness of the past and yet the impossibility of return, the constant onrush of moments and yet the eternal present of love, the vanishing of music that can yet always be performed again. The two voices, those of oracle and dinner-party guest, sing mostly about the busy world in which they both astonishingly exist.

Carter's fecundity in his seventies and eighties was a measure, of course, of his mental alertness and gaiety, but may also reflect how the works of his forties, fifties, and early sixties—works that each required a hefty stretch of time in the composing—were needed to launch him into a more rapid creativity. Alternatively (or additionally), the condition of music since the early 1970s, with the decline of modernism as a progressive force, may perversely have stimulated a composer for whom the modernist achievement was something to be celebrated rather than joined. There was always this posteriority. For Carter, coming of age at a time when the early modernist advances of Stravinsky, Schoenberg, and Ives were recent history, the great need seems to have been one of clarification and triumphal commemoration: one could compare his historical position with Bach's, as a master of order (despite the fact that what he was ordering was dynamic movement) after a period of wholesale musical revolution. Change may be his principal subject, but the elation in his music is the elation of arrival.

Xenakis and the Arditti Quartet

Unlike others of his generation, Xenakis stayed as raw after the mid-1970s as he had been before, though there was a notable change at that common point of rethinking in his occasional use of 'non-octaving' scales to create not long ribbons, as in *Evryali*, but abrupt motifs, and his corresponding reduction of rhythm to regular pulsation, allowing him to evoke folk music: perhaps the folk music of his Balkan childhood but also, clearly, folk music as mediated by Stravinsky. His orchestral piece *Jonchaies* (1977) vividly recalls *The Rite of Spring*; *Ikhoor* for string trio (1978) begins by almost quoting the 'The Augurs of Spring' from that work. Where elements appear out of the central tradition—an E♭ major chord suddenly in *Echange* for bass clarinet and ensemble (1989), some struggling polyphonic imitation in *Akea* for piano quintet (1986), and of course the conventional chamber media of this and several other pieces—the effect is to emphasize difference rather than assimilation, and certainly not postmodern playfulness.

A second shift in Xenakis's music at the mid-1970s was one of gear, for, like Carter, he became more prolific, especially of orchestral pieces and repertory for what was becoming fixed, around the example of Ligeti's Chamber Concerto, as a standard mixed ensemble of fourteen or so players: the founding of the London Sinfonietta (1968), the Ensemble InterContemporain in Paris (1976), Ensemble Modern in Frankfurt (1980), Klangforum Wien (1985), and other groups encouraged this process. As for the striking resurgence of the string quartet during the same period, that was led by two groups: the Kronos Quartet, founded in Seattle in 1973, and the European-based Arditti Quartet, which started up the following year. Each soon established its own aesthetic, the Kronos favouring U.S. composers with minimalist roots and others from around the world drawing on folk traditions, the Arditti taking on those who kept faith with the post-1945 avant-garde, including Lachenmann, Ferneyhough, and Carter.

Nancarrow was another. Discovering that such musicians as the Arditti had, during the three and a half decades he had been with the player piano, learned to cope with the rhythmic complications of Carter or Boulez, he returned in 1983 to writing for performers. His Third

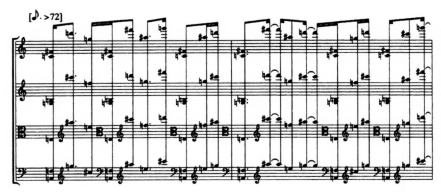

Example 71   Iannis Xenakis, *Tetora*

Quartet (1987) is, like much of his player-piano music, composed of canons whose voices move at different speeds, here related in the ratios 3:4:5:6, but ending with an acceleration canon in which the instruments have to get faster at different rates (3%, 4%, 5%, and 6%) to land up with a justified sense of achievement on C in octaves.

Xenakis, too, was of this group, and wrote several pieces for the Arditti. Example 71, from *Tetora* (1990), illustrates his distance from canonical respectability in the most canonical form. It is not only that the close harmonies, played without vibrato, create a quite new quartet sound, one suggestive more of the wheeze of a mouth organ, but also that the irregular circulations of a small number of chords, set to an even smaller number of durations, produce a static band in music whose impulse depends on a constant refreshment of such images. Xenakis's ability to forget—within a composition, or within his work as a whole, with his disregard for traditional criteria of sound, form, and appropriateness—was startling in an age so much of allusion and retrieval. From mismatched timbres and abrasive sound came his music's power—from that and from the paring of materials to the bare essentials of pulsation, insistent note repetition, and textural contrast.

Nono and Listening

According to Nono's own account, he was set on a new path in the wake of his second opera, *Al gran sole carico d'amore*: 'After that complexity I felt the need to begin again from the beginning, to put myself back to study, starting out just with the most constrictive and demanding of instruments, the piano.'[2] The result was a solo piece for Maurizio Pollini, . . . *sofferte onde serene* . . . (1974–76), exploiting again the strong bass of Pollini's style that had been prominent in the concertolike *Como*

2. Laurent Feneyrou, ed., *Luigi Nono: Ecrits* (Paris, 1993), 104.

una ola de fuerza y luz just a few years before, but now without political explicitness, and with a lessening of the drive that had been just as much a Nono characteristic. Tape, hitherto a resource for documentary realism or sonic power, becomes a medium of exploration, as the pianist plays against manipulated recordings of chords and of the instrument's mechanism. 'Sometimes I cut off the attack, so that the sound manifests itself as resonance without time . . . It's like listening to the wind, you listen to something that passes, but you don't hear the start, you don't hear the end: you perceive a continuity of distances, of presences, of undefinable essences.'[3]

The wafting passage of the piece seems bound up with its means, with the slow movement of reality (the live performance) over memory (the recording)—or perhaps of memory (innate) over reality (external). All is echo. The pianist echoes events on tape, turns chords that emerge from the recording; the tape, with its reverberation, places the music in a widened space. The piece also finds the composer attending not to global events but to his immediate location and tradition—and then through them to the distance. At a time when media of communication have become subject to the interests of profit, direct sensual experience offers the only guarantee of truth, and from this moment onwards the composer is first of all a listener, listening to the sounds he puts on paper, listening to other sounds in the electronic studio, listening to the world. 'In my house on the Giudecca in Venice, one constantly hears the sound of bells, coming day and night, through the mist and with the sun, with different resonances, different meanings. They are signs of life on the lagoon, on the sea. Invitations to work, to meditate; announcements. And life goes in the suffered and serene necessity of "the balance at the bottom of our being", as Kafka says. Pollini on live piano is amplified with Pollini on piano elaborated and composed on tape. No contrast, no counterpoint. . . . Between these two planes there is the study of the formative relationships of the sound, notably in the use of the vibrations of pedal strokes, which are perhaps the particular resonances "at the bottom of our being". These are not "episodes" which expend themselves in succession, but "memories" and "presences" that superimpose themselves on each other.'[4]

After this there was, most unusually, a gap in Nono's output. He revised *Al gran sole* for return performances at La Scala in 1978, in which year was broached the prospect of a third opera, after Aeschylus's *Prometheus*. But there was nothing new until 1979, when he wrote *Con Luigi Dallapiccola* for six percussionists with electronics and began *Fragmente-Stille, an Diotima* for string quartet. Still no voices; still muffled sound worlds, for *Con Luigi Dallapiccola* has the alert quietude of a piece whose musicians must listen to their instruments as much as play

3. Ibid.
4. Note with DG 2531 004.

them, and *Fragmente-Stille* unfolds on the edge of sense, being, as the title indicates, a sequence of fragments and silences.

The address of the piece 'to Diotima' is explained by the presence throughout the score of quotations from Hölderlin, and especially of phrases from his poem 'An Diotima'. These quotations are meant as stimuli and indications for the performers; they are, according to the composer, 'diverse moments, thoughts, silences, "songs", from other spaces, other heavens, for rediscovering in other ways the possibility of not "decisively bidding farewell to hope"',[5] this last phrase coming from a letter Hölderlin wrote to Susette Gontard in 1799. Hope is always in Nono the hope for a just society: the political intention in *Fragmente-Stille* is as vital and actual as it was in the revolutionary frescoes of a decade before. But the manner has changed from rhetoric to silence, from persuasion to listening. Good listening was, for Nono in this last decade, a political act—good listening that would be searching for the other, and not only for echoes of the self. As he said in a lecture in 1983: 'When one comes to listen, one often tries to rediscover oneself in others. To rediscover one's own mechanisms, system, rationalism, in the other. And that: that's a violence that's thoroughly conservative.'[6] By its use of quarter-tones, of high registers, and of silence, *Fragmente-Stille* invites the minutest observation—the kind of observation that must go into its performance and that went into its making, for Nono seems to have written the piece as a kind of diary, waiting for time alone to tell him what to place next.[7] Occasionally there are coded messages, as in the viola's quotation, towards the end, of the tenor from a song, 'Maleur me bat', that was printed in Venice with an attribution to Ockeghem, and that Nono had studied with Maderna. (The Hölderlin fragment here is 'Wenn ich traurend versank . . . das zweifelnde Haupt': 'When I grieving went down . . . the doubting head'.) Messages of regret, then, exist along with the push of hope, but the hope is unsparing and transpersonal.

Playing continuously for around forty minutes (the duration is unspecifiable because there are so many variable pauses), the quartet has its players for the most part in rhythmic unison. Once more there is 'no contrast, no counterpoint', but rather a single slow line that travels through quarter-tone discrepancies and is perfused, melodically and harmonically, by tritones. These tritones—and the fragmentary presentation, one breath or one chord at a time—give the work its consistency, while the journey presses on from the opening unsupported treble through the gains of the lower register, of quarter tones and eventually of harmonics.

5. Preface to the score.
6. Feneyrou, ed., 'L'Erreur comme necessité', *Ecrits*, 256.
7. See Wolfgang Rihm's reminiscence of a conversation with the composer, in Josef Häusler, ed., *Brennpunkt Nono* (Salzburg, 1993), 55–56.

Where . . . *sofferte onde serene* . . . had been residually dramatic, and thereby effective in quite a conventional way, the quartet appears to shun overt success: central to its hope is the hope for something that is not yet available, that cannot yet be heard, that goes on being searched for—the hope for another world. In its fragmentation and its stillness (stillness of dynamic and stillness of motion), as well as in its intimate appeal to the intent ear and in its turn from the all-interval series to the scala enigmatica of Verdi's *Ave Maria* (C–D♯–E–F♯–G♯–A♯–B–C, returning downwards C–B–B♭–A♭–F–E–D♭–C, and so providing three of the six possible tritones), the work announced what were to be the dominant features of Nono's abundant last decade, and in particular prepared the way for *Prometeo* (1981–85), which emerged not as an opera but as a 'tragedy of listening', in which the drama takes place between sound and ear. There is no staging, no action. Instead, everyone concerned, whether musician or auditor, was to have a place in a wooden boatlike construction designed for the piece by Renzo Piano. This provided Nono with something on which he repeatedly insisted during his last years: space—the space, the emptiness, to which music could bring a purpose, if sound sources were to be dispersed within it, and if the sound were to be such as would explore and vivify what it came into. At the Sudwestfunk studios in Freiburg, he worked, during the period of *Prometeo*, on techniques of sound modification and projection with Hans Peter Haller (with whom Boulez had worked in the early 1970s on versions of '. . . *explosante-fixe* . . .' for electronically transformed instruments) and on instrumental possibilities with a circle of dedicated musicians, among them the flautist Roberto Fabbriciani, the clarinetist Ciro Scarponi, and the tuba player Giancarlo Schiaffini. He was particularly interested in sounds that do not disclose their origins, as he had been in *Fragmente-Stille*, where violin, viola, and cello are so seldom heard as distinct voices; in the new pieces he worked with tones from registers in which the instruments produce almost pure frequencies, and also with unusually low and unusually high registers, and with sounds achieved by irregular playing techniques. Often his material would, too, be microintervalically inflected, representing by other means another world. Such sounds would, for the listener, slip out of the carapace of timbral and harmonic taxonomy: unnameable, they would be invitations to think in new terms.

The first tentatives towards *Prometeo* came in *Das atmende Klarsein* for small chorus, bass flute, and electronics (1980–81) and *Io* for three sopranos, small chorus, bass flute, contrabass clarinet, and electronics (1981), both of which formed part of the full work when it had its first performances, in the disused church of San Lorenzo in Venice in 1984. Another step came in 1982, when Nono wrote a second 'Polish diary' in answer to a commission from the Warsaw Autumn festival, which in the event did not take place that year, because of the imposition of martial law and the country's economic catastrophe. *Quando stanno morendo*

—not a big orchestral piece as the first *Diario polacco* had been at the time of the late 1950s thaw, but small and quiescent—takes its title from the words by Velimir Khlebnikov with which its anthology of Eastern European poetry ends: 'When they are dying men sing'. Once again, hope has to be realized out of a context of despair, voiced here for the most part in a slow interweaving of four female singers over flute, cello, and electronics. By this point in history it was time to sing requiems over the revolution; resistance and progress, both human and musical, demanded a departure—and it would have to be a sorrowful departure—from cherished systems, Marxist and Schoenbergian, that had outlived their usefulness as beacons of a better world.

The circle of works around *Prometeo* includes not only preparations but re-echoings, as in the pieces Nono went on composing with and for Fabbriciani, Scarponi, and Schiaffini, such as *Omaggio a György Kurtág* (1983–86) or *A Pierre* (written for Boulez's sixtieth birthday, in 1985, and renewing the friendship that had been broken when, as Nono saw it, Boulez had failed to take up the political implications of radical music: in an echo of Beethoven's gesture, he had withdrawn the dedication of *Canti per tredici* to 'Pierre Boulez, for his humanity'). The *Prometeo* sound world—rarely assertive, much more usually slow, quiet and invitatory—is one of keening high voices (the solo singers are the same quartet as in *Quando stanno morendo*, with the single addition of a tenor), of electronically modulated instruments often going further into the as-if-underwater reverberations of . . . *sofferte onde serene* . . . , and of orchestral textures made strange by quarter tones. This last aspect of *Prometeo* took on separate life in the short orchestral piece *A Carlo Scarpa* (1984–85), whose prickling near-unisons and near-octaves suggest Scelsi, though in a context not of steady movement but, as in *Fragmente-Stille*, of event laid after event.

After *Prometeo* had been revised, for its 1985 revival, Nono moved on to a group of works written under the sign of an inscription found on a cloister wall in Toledo: 'Caminantes, no hay caminos, hay que caminar' ('Wayfarers, there are no ways, only faring on'). This had been the belief enshrined in his music at least since *Fragmente-Stille*: the belief, as musically expressed, that what absorbs all importance is the next step, not some hoped-for destination—the belief, as much political as musical, that freedom moving under contract is freedom limited. But the belief in freedom—in a pure freedom under which liberty of individual thought and action would be boundless—had always guided him, and his creative life had repeatedly shown a willingness to jettison what he had learned for what was unknown, the 'caminos' for the 'caminar'. (*Il canto sospeso* and *Intolleranza* were watersheds as critical as *Al gran sole*.) In these last works, however, the intimation of freedom— the hope—is even more than before expressed by musical means that are themselves intimations, pointers, and trajectories: the use of space, looking towards a potential omnipresence of sound; the soaring into an extreme high treble; the involvement of the performer as a companion traveler, presaging a collectivity of creative endeavour.

The last two large-scale works, *Caminantes . . .* (1986–87) and *No hay caminos, hay que caminar . . .* (1987), both require orchestral musicians to be disposed in various groups: *Caminantes . . .* was written for the Munich Gasteig, one of the modern halls the composer approved as extrapolations from San Marco in terms of polychoral possibility (once more the composer listens out in his music from his home base in Venice); *No hay caminos*, which is, with *Fragmente-Stille* and *A Carlo Scarpa*, one of his few works since the early 1960s without electronics, extends the sound-searching manner of the quartet to a collection of seven groups. During the busy time of these two works he also formed a plan for a series of small pieces with electronics, still exploring space. For example, in *Post-prae-ludium no.3* for piccolo, the player was to walk around the hall, sometimes drawing near to one or other of four microphones that would capture the sound for different kinds of electronic treatment. But the idea was never fully developed: at the only performance, in 1988, 'Fabbriciani and his piccolo "walked"—guided by Nono's gestures—through the hall, freely improvising, with live electronics but no written score'.[8] To some degree, opening the work to the performer was a way of freeing it, or at least of showing how it might be free. As Nono wrote of *Post-prae-ludium no.1*, for tuba, of which he did produce a final score: 'The course of this composition is fixed in all its details, but the score is intended only to be a basic guide for the performer. . . . The given notation, new performing techniques and live electronics all unite to supplant any interpretation on my part.'[9] Nevertheless, there had to be something to interpret. In the 1950s, Nono had reacted violently against Cage, in whose music he saw an image of the disconnected individuals of a failed society. And though the fragmentation and the looseness of his late music might seem implicitly to rescind that dispraise, what stays is the quite un-Cageian progressive urge: from sound to sound, from place to place, from notation to realization. However disintegrated, the music is looking for another harmony.

In his last two years Nono found a new collaborator in Gidon Kremer, who was for him perhaps not just a supreme violinist but also a representative of Russian culture—the culture in which, for Nono, the political and artistic questions of the twentieth century had been felt and fought most intensely. (In *Al gran sole* he had worked with the stage director Yuri Lyubimov; *No hay caminos* was a memorial to the film director Andrey Tarkovsky; and Russian texts are sprinkled through many of his works.) The departure was not new: the title *'Hay que caminar'*

8. Hans Peter Haller, in *A proposito di* Découvrir la subversion: hommage à Edmond Jabès *e* Post-prae-ludium n.3 'Baab-arr' *di Luigi Nono* (Milan, 1993).

9. Note with Ricordi CRMCD 1003.

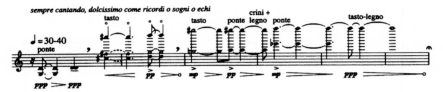

Example 72   Luigi Nono, *La lontananza nostalgica utopica futura*

soñando indicates the link Nono's last composition, for two violins, has with preceding works, and *La lontananza nostalgica utopica futura* for violin and tapes (1988–89) takes up the live-recorded interplay of . . . *sofferte onde serene* . . . , under a title suggesting how, for Nono, utopia was both a long way ahead ('the future utopian distance') and, in feeling, a long way behind ('nostalgic'). Also, both pieces continue the idea of the ambulant musician, moving between music desks in different parts of the hall. But these final works are distinguished from their immediate predecessors by the colour and, in particular, the range of the violin, from open strings (recurrent, rooting the sound in the nature of the violin) to notes way above the treble staff, as shown in example 72. The music can look back, perhaps nostalgically, to *Fragmente-Stille* by way of string scoring, tritones, and changes of colour (nostalgically, for the years between 1980 and 1988 had seen the hardening of market capitalism in the West and a repudiation of socialism in Eastern Europe and China), and at the same time, however slowly and labouredly, onward and upward.

Stockhausen and Licht

Stockhausen's status as an originator, from the early 1950s to the early 1970s, has been amply documented earlier in this book. Then things changed. There was the general lapse of belief in origination, and as a result the composer's self-belief—never in any doubt, to judge from all appearances[10]—increasingly had to express itself in a personal mythology, and by personal means: he became his own publisher and his own record producer, and, continuing as his own performer, from 1975 he concentrated his attention on a group consisting of his children and regular members of his household, including his sons Markus (trumpet) and Simon (saxophone and synthesizer), his daughter Majella (piano), and his companion Suzanne Stephens (bass clarinet), with the flautist Kathinka Pasveer joining the central team in 1983.

10. See, for example, Karlheinz Stockhausen, *Texte*, v–vi (Cologne, 1989), which cover the first three *Licht* operas, and the material published with the recordings.

To some extent this resort to an intimate circle was a continuation of the group work he had undertaken in the late 1960s and early 1970s; it was also a practical solution to the problem of rehearsing complex music—music that generally demands a partly mimed presentation, often in costume, and that therefore has to be played from memory. Close contact with these players resulted, too, in unlikely encounters with music of the classical period, in a sequence of cadenzas that treat themes by Haydn and Mozart as post-*Mantra* formulae,[11] and that have a singular tone by virtue of the humour, craziness and awesomeness characteristic of *Licht*. However, the Stockhausen 'family' served to isolate the composer from wider musical culture—or perhaps rather to compensate for an isolation he would have experienced anyway. Avant-gardes were now out of style; avant-garde leaders even more so.

The seven-opera project *Licht* can be seen as a strategy of creative survival in an age sceptical of the forging genius and inimical to innovation. Begun in 1977, the work effectively released Stockhausen from the need to have any new ideas for the next quarter century. As he put it himself, after twenty-five years of discovery would come twenty-five years of integrating what had been discovered,[12] and, indeed, most of his earlier preoccupations continued on into *Licht*: setting music in space; finding new timbres, both electronic and instrumental; mixing vocal and instrumental categories; creating images of divine order; making the concert a ritual act. *Licht* can be understood too as a response, in shallow times, to the call to greatness—a call coming not only from the composer himself but from his public.

While the scale of the enterprise would appear to imply the highest ambitions (Wagner's *Ring* provides the inevitable comparison), the working-out seems designed, by its deficiency, its comedy, and its inconsistency, to contradict any such claims. By offering individual scenes as responses to commissions, the composer ensured that each opera became a ragbag: *Montag* (1984–88), for example, includes a girls' chorus, a keyboard intervention (*Klavierstück XIV*), trios for sopranos and tenors, a ballet of perambulators, various solos and ensembles for wind instruments (especially Stephens's basset horn and Pasveer's flute), an enactment of the Pied Piper legend, and much else washing in on tides of sound from synthesizers and percussion, which Stockhausen used as a 'modern orchestra', a replacement for the standard orchestra, with which he did not work for almost two decades after *Donnerstag* (1978–80), the first *Licht* opera to be composed. Of course, the multifarious elements of *Montag* are connected by their dependence on the three

11. For a discussion of these cadenzas, especially those for Haydn's Trumpet Concerto, see Glenn Watkins, *Pyramids at the Louvre: Music, Culture, and Collage from Stravinsky to the Postmodernists* (Cambridge, Mass., 1994), 433–38.

12. See Tim Nevill, ed., *Towards a Cosmic Music: Texts by Karlheinz Stockhausen* (London, 1989), 102.

Example 73a   Karlheinz Stockhausen, nuclear formula for Eva

ground formulae of *Licht*—one for each of the principal characters—but the elaboration of those formulae into multilayered textures produces, in almost all cases, an extremely slow harmonic rhythm, and Stockhausen's formal ideal remains that of *Momente*: not an impelled continuity but a succession of diverse moments.

Example 73a presents one of the formulae in its basic state, and example 73b shows an extract from one of the moments: *Pietà*, from the second act of *Dienstag*[13] (1987–91, but incorporating *Der Jahreslauf*, which was written in 1977 for Japan, where Stockhausen formed the plan for *Licht*). The formula, as usual with Stockhausen, includes all twelve notes, parcelled into strikingly characterized motifs that by no means eschew tonal echoes. Among these motifs, that of the fifth bar occupies the soprano in the example, while the flugelhorn considers and reconsiders the immediately preceding octave fall. At the same time, both lines are locked into formula expositions proceeding at much slower tempos: Stockhausen's basic scheme for the piece[14] shows seven simultaneous, slow-motion formulae.

A short example cannot communicate the immensity of *Pietà* as a flugelhorn showpiece, covering a range of almost five octaves, continuing for almost half an hour, requiring the production of quarter tones and approximate eighth tones by means of chosen fingerings and rustling breath (notated by a diagonal stroke through the note head), and introducing 'vowel sounds and vowel transitions . . . which sometimes resemble a movingly "weeping" human voice . . . , kissing-noises into the mouthpiece, new kinds of tremoli, tongue-trills, soft tonguing technique, use of plunger mute'.[15] The piece is, on this level, a testimony to Markus Stockhausen's prowess. Nor can the example adequately convey the power of one of the most affecting episodes in *Licht*, where, during the course of a combat between Michael trumpeters and Luzifer trombonists, one of the former is wounded. 'A woman—the soprano—appears, and sits down. The trumpeter is laid across her lap in a way similar to that in which Christ is seen on the lap of his mother Mary in Pietà paintings and sculptures. The soul of the trumpeter then rises out of his body, hovers behind the soprano, stands very large as a

13. For a note on the tape that runs through this act, together with six pages from the score, see Karlheinz Stockhausen, '*Octophony:* Electronic Music from *Tuesday from Light,' Perspectives of New Music*, 31/2 (1993), 150–70.

14. Reproduced with the recording on Stockhausen 43.

15. Note with recording on Stockhausen 43.

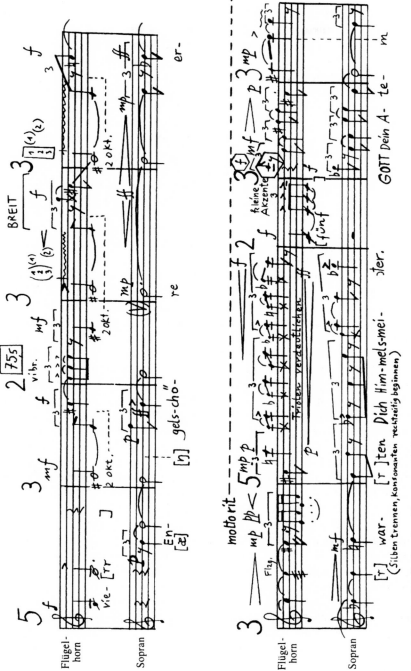

Example 73b Karlheinz Stockhausen, *Pietà*

spirit behind her and plays—on flugelhorn—the duet with her, while she constantly looks at the body on her lap or sings upwards to Heaven.'[16] However, even a short extract may be enough to show how Stockhausen's *Licht* music is a constant, fluid reiteration of selected notes and patterns.

The prevalent musical qualities—the slowness, the lack of dynamism, and the stasis and repetitiveness implicit in the formula method —are appropriate to the ritual nature of the work, given that Stockhausen's conception of ritual is conditioned by his European background and by his keen response to Japanese temple practice. *Donnerstags Abschied*, for five trumpets sounding from high positions as the audience leaves the first opera, belongs to a German tradition of tower music, and *Mädchenprozession*, a *Montag* episode for girls singing and bearing candles, has parallels in Catholic liturgy, while the final scene of *Samstag* (1981–83), *Luzifers Abschied*, recalls the composer's reminiscences of the Omizutori ceremony, which he witnessed during his 1966 visit to Japan.[17] And then, besides reproducing other rituals, *Licht* is a ritual itself. One normal feature of rituals, however, is that they present beliefs and actions in which there is a common consent, and this cannot be imagined to be so of *Licht*. Just as each opera is a collection of assorted musical items, so the heptalogy's myth is a synthetic mix of occult lore (for which *The Urantia Book* was an important source), Christianity, and autobiography. Miscellaneity, though, need not disqualify. On the contrary, the variety is a remarkable achievement, when so many of the musical numbers are scored for similar ensembles, with trumpet, basset horn, flute, piano, and synthesizer at the nucleus, and when everything is guided by the three generative formulae. *Licht* may be regarded, too, as a creative contribution to the questioning of wholeness that was going on at the same time in—to pursue the obvious analogy—stagings of Wagner's operas and the revival of piano transcriptions of episodes from them. Stockhausen's work positively embraces contradiction and variation, and disputes the primacy of the whole by proving the self-sufficiency and mutability of the elements. Moreover, the deliquescence progressed.

Donnerstag has a certain integrity of means and subject matter, marked by its steady accumulation of musical resources (the first act is for vocal and instrumental soloists plus tape; the second is a concerto for stage trumpeter and pit orchestra, with occasional secondary soloists; the third brings on full choral and orchestral forces) and by its portrayal of the hero's formation, journey around the earth, and return to the heavens. This hero is Michael—part angel, part Christ, part cosmic messenger, part self-image on the part of the composer—who is represented in this opera by a trumpeter, a tenor, and a male dancer.

16. Ibid.
17. See Stockhausen, *Texte*, iv, 443–47.

His father-antagonist, Luzifer, also has three embodiments, as trombonist, bass, and male dancer; so does the third main character, Eva, who is the eternal female, Michael's mother, guardian, and consort, appearing as basset hornist, soprano, and female dancer. In later operas, these associations were somewhat modified: in *Montag*, for instance, the manifestations are often tripled, and the arrival of Pasveer encouraged the composer to create large roles for flautist as Eva figure in *Samstag* and its sequels. In parallel, the partial but real wholeness of *Donnerstag* has disintegrated by the time of *Samstag*, which is a sequence of four quite separate acts, and disintegrated further in *Montag*, where the unit is the scene within an act. (The order of composition was logical, beginning with the three operas spotlighting the central characters in turn, and continuing with the three concerned with pairs of characters —Michael and Luzifer in *Dienstag*, the day of war; Luzifer and Eva in *Freitag*; and Eva and Michael in *Mittwoch*—before the composer arrived finally at the concelebration of all three in *Sonntag*.) After *Montag*, too, Stockhausen often went back to earlier parts of the cycle in a potentially limitless process of arrangement and expansion. Whole scenes and acts of *Donnerstag* and *Samstag* were adapted for different formations, sometimes more than once, or quarried for new smaller pieces, as when a soprano-bass duet from the first act of *Donnerstag* emerged in 1993 as *Bijou* for alto flute and bass clarinet with tape. Just as Stockhausen's librettos ululate with metamorphosis ('fraitak mahakdak mähäkdok frakfrik frigga venusik nikkelfik a-haintselfrik venuspik fridach venuschelmuschel frigigapuschel', to quote from *Montag*) so *Licht* became a perpetually self-generating, self-regenerating network.

The grandeur of the project is inseparable from its bathos. By its absurdity and by its mess, the work testifies to the impossibility of a real drama of the world and time being achieved at the end of the twentieth century. Its destiny is to be at once magnificent and ridiculous.

Birtwistle and Ritual

The process illustrated in Birtwistle's *Melencolia I*, by which a single note gradually gives rise to a whole musical world, was the process of such immediately subsequent works as *Silbury Air* and *. . . agm . . .* for chorus and three instrumental groups (1978–79). This latter, though based on fragmentary verbal phrases (the broken relics of Sappho's poetry) and written for fragmented ensembles, is music of unusual spaciousness and continuity in Birtwistle, and may have been both consummation and dead end. During the next year or so, he produced only the Clarinet Quintet, perhaps his most inscrutable piece, and a choral item related to the Orpheus project, which had been interrupted in 1975, when it seemed the large-scale opera might never be staged. But in the summer of 1981 a relatively small piece, *Pulse Sampler* for oboe and claves, opened new possibilities for him in the combination of melody and rhythm as independent but knocking entities, and soon afterwards he took up *The Mask of Orpheus* again: an examination of the work might well reveal how, as with *Siegfried*, the third act implies much more than an interval separating it from the other two.

After finishing *The Mask of Orpheus* in 1984, Birtwistle took the basic principle of *Pulse Sampler* onto a wider plane in *Secret Theatre*, which is scored for roughly the same ensemble as *Silbury Air* (the regular lineup of solo woodwind, brass, and strings, with piano and percussion), but which exists in quite its own world, partly because it starts boldly rather than with a slow birth, partly because of the intricate, constant play between an essentially melodic 'cantus' and an essentially rhythmic 'continuum' that is a clockwork of ostinatos (though in Birtwistle mechanical repetition is nearly always subject to a bit of shove, so that regularity is offset by distortions that make each new element different and interesting). Though the composer introduced these terms with *Secret Theatre*, the opposition goes back deeply into his output, and may be found, for example, in *Melencolia I* (see example 53).

Birtwistle has described the orchestral scores of his operas as musical dramas without voices, saying of *The Mask of Orpheus* that 'the orchestra, even though it responds to the events on stage, has a life of its own',[18] and *Secret Theatre* is maybe the accompaniment to an opera we cannot see and have no need to. But it also, like *Verses for Ensembles*, makes the concert platform into a stage. The 'cantus' is played by one or more soloists standing aside, the 'continuum' by the rest of the ensemble—though of course the two categories are not held separate: the 'cantus' is always in danger of devolving into faltering repetition, while the threat to the 'continuum' is that it become impressed too much by the free flow and largeness of the melody. The grand *Earth Dances* for large orchestra (1985–86) then moves the idea onto a further level of possibility, with multiple strata of both 'cantus' and 'continuum'. Both works introduce new textures (the rich low register of *Earth Dances*) and new gestures (such as the rippling downward staccato scale with which, in both works, a long expansion seems to deflate) that look towards a new opera, *Gawain* (1990–91), which was to work with continuous growth and continual repetition over a larger span.[19] Further steps were taken in a surprising turn to lyric music (always featuring the high soprano voice, and usually with a mixed ensemble) in settings of Rilke, haiku, Celan, and the composer's own poems—verse whose pregnant images and fracturings could be exacerbated by music.

18. Note in the programme for the 1986 English National Opera production.

19. See Rhian Samuel's note on the music in the programme for the 1991 Covent Garden production and its 1994 revival.

Meanwhile, the first performances in 1986 of *The Mask of Orpheus*, *Earth Dances*, and the 'mechanical pastoral' *Yan Tan Tethera* brought the composer belated recognition, and perhaps satisfaction. His next major work, *Endless Parade* for trumpet with shadowing vibraphone and accompanying string orchestra (1986–87), is effulgent, exultant, and therefore simpler, with the trumpet's melody repeatedly returning to an initiatory signal before going off on new trajectories, and with the different roles more firmly and permanently established than had been the case in *Secret Theatre*. The next piece he wrote for the soloists of the London Sinfonietta, *Ritual Fragment* (1990), strikes a different tone—it was written as a memorial to Michael Vyner, the ensemble's long-serving artistic director—but its public address is no less direct, perhaps because again it presents melody not as communal chant, as in *Secret Theatre*, but as solo declamation.

This time there are ten soloists, who take their turns to stand and enunciate at the focus of the semicircle in which the others are placed, then return. According to the composer, what they play as soloists is 'a continuous line',[20] though where the 'cantus' of *Secret Theatre* had welded disparate instrumental voices into a unity, *Ritual Fragment* makes it possible for each instrument to make its statement in its own way, with its own rhetoric of gesture and motif. In example 74, which shows most of the horn's eulogy, the solo instrument begins by echoing the stentorian rising tenth that has just been announced by the bass trumpet (which, in its own solo, will majestically reclaim the gesture) before going on to the emphatic D that is properly its own. The bassoon has one of Birtwistle's de-characterized melodies in even values and narrow intervals—the kind of line that could go on forever, always the same and always different (cf. example 53)—while the trumpet and the viola, at the final climax, jump out with memories of highly characterized ideas from their solos. The piano and bass drum are, as is clear from this example, signalling instruments; the cello and the double bass, also unable to move, occasionally seem to converse with the soloist (the cello here could be recalling the horn to its correct path), but more generally underpin the harmony. And it is now sustained harmony, rather than rhythmic ostinato, that provides the 'continuum'—harmony that tends to underrate rhythmic precision, just as the percussed and pizzicato rhythms of earlier Birtwistle scores had underplayed harmony. In placing melody against melody in a harmonic echo chamber, *Ritual Fragment* has a new ease, and yet its gestures—the signals, the solo pronouncement, and the memories all observed in example 74—are keenly asserted. The move from a rhythmic to a harmonic background provided the last fundamental necessity for the composition of *Gawain*.

20. Preface to the score.

Example 74   Harrison Birtwistle, *Ritual Fragment*

Berio and Memory

Berio was the great rememberer. So perhaps were all composers—especially at a time when sudden acts of forgetting (such as occasioned total serialism or minimalism) were very much less likely than exhaustive recollections, and when music had to adopt extreme measures (as in Ferneyhough) if it was not to remind us of anything outside. What Berio remembered, however, was not the substance of the past but rather the whole subtending language, culture, and history. And his remembering goes on not before the music is composed but as it proceeds, as if the music itself were remembering—remembering what the flute meant to Debussy, remembering what a major third has been in a universe of melodic and harmonic languages, remembering forms and textures, remembering possibilities of narration, from elementary signalling to unfolding complex stories in the theatre. The chamber-orchestra piece *Requies* (1984–85), a beautiful memorial to Berberian, seems to mimic the process of remembering a melody: recalling snatches, trying them out in different ways, finding its conclusion in a question. Music remembering, even conscious of itself remembering, posits a relation between past and present. To quote a phrase from Dante that Berio and Sanguineti used in *Laborintus II*, and that the composer further recalled in interview:[21] 'Music is all relative'. It asks 'the ever-open question of how man relates to the world',[22] and as it does so, its answers become themselves part of the world, so that every new work enters a widened field of relations, and widens it still more. Such was Berio's all-embracing inclusivity by this period.

Because his concern was with relations—with processes rather than objects—his music is unusually difficult to excerpt. The objects, as already mentioned, may come from different sources, and Berio welcomed them arriving with the aromas of their origins; specific in his music are the processes—both the processes we infer from how the objects appear (processes of transcription) and the processes executed within the music (processes of transformation). But some of this may be evident in example 75, a short passage from the middle of his orchestral piece *Formazioni* (1985–87), where the horns introduce a nineteenth-century Romantic curve, echoed by the strings, and then the oboe enters with something like a folk song. The connection between these two comes most of all, perhaps, in the ocean swell of the harmony, which very often in Berio remembers the melody—keeps notes in store, and as it re-selects them, forever makes possible new melodies. (This was a technique that went back to Berio's *Sinfonia*, at least, and may be found in an exemplary fashion in Ligeti's *Melodien*.)

21. Rosanna Dalmonte and Bálint András Varga, *Luciano Berio: Two Interviews* (London, 1985), 23.
    22. Ibid., 21.

Example 75 Luciano Berio, *Formazioni*

One may note Berio's concern with harmony in the *Sequenza* compositions of this period, even those for exclusively monodic instruments: *Sequenza IX* for clarinet (1980) and *X* for trumpet (1984). The former originally had responses from a computer (though the idea was abandoned, and surely the work's quasi-Bachian implicit harmony is enough —together with the harmony of clarinetish histories it brings about, from Mozart to Stockhausen by way of Brahms and jazz, while *Sequenza X* requires an undamped piano into which the trumpet can be blown to set off sympathetic vibrations. In *Sequenza VII* the harmonic tracking was by means of an omnipresent monotone, and *Formazioni* again has a drone, a middle-register E, that only very slowly dissolves during the course of the piece (it is still intermittently there in the example). Music remembers its most primitive past—drone, pulsation, repetition—as integral to its present sophistication.

Within the narrower history that is Berio's output, *Formazioni* has a notable place among his essays in remembering the traditional orchestra—and, of course, transforming it. As in many works from *Allelujah I* onwards, a transformation of sound is secured by a transformation of seating: there are 'formations' of brass on either side of the platform (powerfully interlocutory at the great climax soon after example 75), and woodwind ensembles at front and rear (engaging in subtler dialogues across the main body of strings). A signature feature, found too in *Voci* (1984) and Concerto II (1988–90), is the placing of a group of violins at the back, whence they can make striking penetrations, as they do answering the piano soloist in Concerto II. Whereas in the 1950s and 1960s Berio, like most composers, transformed the orchestra by radically changing its makeup, in the 1980s and 1990s a reconfiguring of standard resources—achieved by virtuosity of orchestration as well as by changing the platform layout—is enough. *Formazioni* is scored for a quite normal large orchestra; Berio subsequently made a demonstration of the lesson by revising *Epifanie* for more practical resources as *Epiphanies*.

However, the most startling display of his ability to find new sound worlds latent in the conventional, even classical orchestra is *Rendering* (1988–90), in which late Schubert sketches for a D major symphony are realized in Schubertian style and joined—with only a celesta added to the orchestra—by music that bends away from Schubert, or rather ripples out over the larger memory field available to Berio. Transcription and composition are not different activities: even the most mechanical arrangement will take on a trace of the arranger; even the most radical new departure will be in some measure a revision. For the transcriber-composer, self-transcription is a waiting fascination, pursued in the *Chemins* series and *Corale* (1980–81), on *Sequenza VIII* for violin. If in some of Berio's arrangements of other music his own voice is, nevertheless, rather quiet, these works are perhaps to be seen as balancing, and perhaps facilitating, the adventure going on at the same time in *Formazioni*.

Berio's own anxiety about his music of memory might have been that it could not forget, that it was committed to evolution, not revolution; and what may be his most powerful works came about when he engaged with that anxiety: in the middle movement of *Sinfonia*, in the finale of his opera *Un re in ascolto* (1979–84), and in the magnificent *Ofanim* (1988–92). This is the most important piece he produced with his Tempo Reale Audio Interactive Location System (TRAILS), developed at the Tempo Reale institute he founded in Florence in 1987 to carry on work begun at IRCAM. Just as *Formazioni* works with orchestral space, so *Ofanim* works with electronic space: with illusions of space contrived by electronic sound, and with moving sound through space. The work's title, meaning 'wheels' in Hebrew, alludes to the dramatic rotations engineered by TRAILS, over the heads of the audience and of the performers: antiphonal groups of singing children and instrumentalists, the former alternating between Ezekiel's fiery vision (of lightning, whirlwind, strange creatures, the voice of God, and, again, great wheels flying through the air), and the Song of Songs. All the while a solitary woman is crouched on the stage. When everyone else has stopped, she rises to sing, and what she sings is an unyielding lament, also taken from Ezekiel: 'Thy mother is like a vine in thy blood . . . and she appeared in her height in the multitude of her branches. But she was plucked up in fury, . . . and the east wind dried up her fruit.' We may want to think here of Berio remembering folk song, remembering Weill, remembering Monteverdi, remembering Verdi. Or it may seem that the music shames such a response—almost shames itself—by the directness of its force.

IRCAM and Boulez

The establishment of IRCAM in 1977 coincided with the peak of a period of creativity in computer sound synthesis and transformation, and on the crest of that wave, many of the leading practitioners, whether technician-composers or composer-technicians, went to Paris. Chowning was there. So was David Wessel (b. 1942), whose *Antony* (1977) was one of the first and finest pieces to use the technology developed at IRCAM by Giuseppe di Giugno—specifically the 4A, predecessor of the 4X that was crucial to much of the institute's production in the 1980s, including *Répons*. *Antony* neatly circumvents the problem of the artificial quality of synthesized sound by avoiding entries and exits (very slow fades are the rule) and by concerning itself with great clusters, out of which distinct pitches gradually coalesce and disappear.

Among the European composers at IRCAM in the early days were Berio and Globokar, and with such a range of talent it well might have seemed that anything could happen: Boulez's call to arms has already been noted. But in the event, as was perhaps inevitable, many of the more celebrated personnel departed, and IRCAM became another electronic music studio, if one that was unusually well financed, and unusually able, therefore, both to embark on grand projects and to present itself to the public: a concert hall was built into the place and a small orchestra established, the Ensemble InterContemporain. During the 1980s IRCAM dominated computer music in Europe—but not entirely: at City University in London, for example, Alejandro Viñao (b. 1951) and others did notable work, Viñao's *Son entero* for four voices and computer (1988) powerfully creating an electronic folk orchestra evocative of Cuba.

Partly because of IRCAM's public—even state—role, partly because it was set up as a rendezvous for experts in both conventional instruments and electronics, and partly because this was the way electronic music was going anyway, Boulez's institute quite quickly came to specialize not in small studies, such as had been characteristic of computer music, but in big concert pieces, usually with an instrumental soloist or ensemble performing with the 4X, Boulez's *Répons* (first performed in 1980) being the prototype.

Boulez had drastically curtailed his conducting activities to devote himself to IRCAM and composition, though he continued to work on revising old scores: new versions of *Le Visage nuptial, Improvisation sur Mallarmé III,* and *cummings ist der dichter* all appeared in the 1980s and, in the very year IRCAM opened for business, he began a grand amplification of *Notations,* developing each of the piano miniatures into a movement for immense orchestra. Even one of his IRCAM projects, *Dialogue de l'ombre double* (1982–85), was a return to the materials and the situation of *Domaines,* but with the clarinettist now reflected in the mirror of the machinery designed at IRCAM for live manipulation of sound by computer. *Répons* (1980–84), however, was new, and by design the justification for Boulez's new direction and resources, though it also went back to the basic principle of *Eclat/Multiples* in contrasting percussive with sustained sounds: six soloists placed around the audience, playing on clangorous instruments (two pianos, harp, cimbalom, xylophone plus glockenspiel, vibraphone) and electronically transformed, perform with and against a central twenty-four-piece ensemble. Like most of Boulez's works apart from the piano sonatas, *Répons* is emphatically not a repertory piece. It goes out on its own adventure, and its appearance, at the high noon of postmodernism, could be interpreted as a 'response' on behalf of the modernist challenge—a response enthusiastically endorsed by Jean-Jacques Nattiez.[23]

23. See the several essays on the piece collected in his *Le combat de Chronos et d'Orphée* (Paris, 1993), 159–217.

Certainly Boulez wanted to set himself at a distance from the kind of stylistic reference which, in its earlier guise as neoclassicism, he had been decrying since his student days. For example, in talking once about the rhythm of *Répons* he indicated that the two types long characteristic of his music—'chaotic and irregular' ('smooth time', as he often used to call it) and 'very regular rapid repeated notes' ('striated time')—are now joined by a third sort: 'Finally at the end there is a regularity, a kind of metre—but with much ornamentation. The ornamentation is in fact very irregular, but the metre itself is very regular.'[24] This he defended, in modernist form, as something netted into the basic substance of the piece: 'The harmony always gives this impression of something followed by its inverse; there is always a centre—an axis of symmetry. This symmetry of harmony corresponds in harmonic terms to a regular metre.' There is no question, he insisted, of stylistic pluralism. 'I accept and use the values I refused before . . . I feel now that there is no reason to exclude such things. But it is always necessary to use them according to the stylistic purpose of the piece.'

Yet such an interpretation raises problems. Modernism—and especially Boulez's modernism—had been defined not only by its explorations but by its refusals. If those refusals are reconsidered, even rescinded, the thrust away from convention begins to falter. Also, *Répons* is clearly the work of a composer with a history of his own. However special the work's apparatus, and however spectacularly that apparatus imposes itself (especially when, nearly seven minutes into the piece, the soloists at last enter with a grand arpeggio that is re-echoed both acoustically and electronically), there are obligations to particular ideas Boulez had already set in play (the harmonies of *Messagesquisse*, a piece for cellos derived from the six-note set Eb–A–C–B–E–D in honour of the patron Paul Sacher, as well as the timbral conflicts of *Eclat/Multiples*). And in relation to wider history—quite apart from the resurgence of metre—the music's mechanisms of transformation contrive an almost thematic continuity. Where in *Le Marteau sans maître* the harmonies had been too fleeting and often too noise-trapped to decipher, those of *Répons* are spaciously prolonged, and melodies, as in *Messagesquisse*, are reduced to rudimentary linear statements of those harmonies. Also, the electronic manipulations (repositioning sounds in space, changing timbres, transposing figures) seem largely decorative when the live possibilities are already so various. If, as Boulez's technical assistant Andrew Gerzso has aptly put it, 'the score is full of answers to answers to answers to create a never ending mirror-like effect',[25] so too are the scores of *Eclat/Multiples* and *Figures-Doubles-Prismes*.

24. Peter McCallum, 'An Interview with Pierre Boulez', *Musical Times*, 130 (1989), 8–10.

25. Andrew Gerzso, 'Reflections on *Répons*', *Contemporary Music Review*, 1/1 (1984), 23–34.

Nothing, however, need be read into the fact that *Répons* has remained incomplete, since that is the common condition of Boulez's works. There was a first performance at the 1981 Donaueschingen Festival, when the piece played for under twenty minutes; it then grew by stages to reach three quarters of an hour by 1984.[26] Boulez suggested it ought to be twice that size, hence big enough to occupy an entire concert, but there it stopped.

By now younger composers were coming to the studio in some numbers, among them Magnus Lindberg (b. 1958) and Kaija Saariaho (b. 1952) from Finland, Gérard Grisey (b. 1946) and Tristan Murail (b. 1947) from France, and Jonathan Harvey (b. 1939) from England. Harvey composed a purely electronic piece with the sounds of a bell and a treble voice, *Mortuos plango, vivos voco* (1980), and Barry Anderson (1935–87) produced electronic inserts for Birtwistle's *The Mask of Orpheus*, but the presence of a resident ensemble was more a spur and a stimulus to work with instrumentalists, while the facilities for sound analysis provided clues for new ways of thinking about orchestration,[27] so that IRCAM contributed to the development of spectral music.

By the later 1980s, having seemingly concluded that *Répons* would not grow any further, Boulez had set himself and his assistants to a new realization of '. . . *explosante-fixe* . . .', for transformed flute with the same orchestra, the difference between the electronic and the natural being again part of the point. By contrast, the IRCAM piece created by George Benjamin (b. 1960), *Antara* for two electronic keyboards and ensemble (1987), suggests how there need be no difference of creative approach or compositional effect between the synthesizer and the flute, which are, after all, simply machines of different ages. The work uses its electronic machines in order to—among other things—project into the concert hall a set of panpipes, while also stabilizing their sound and increasing their range. Panpipe sounds, digitally recorded and stored with their microtonal inflections, are sampled by a keyboard, which seems in the early part of the piece to be teaching new tunes, and new intonations, to the flutes and strings (see example 76): as in contemporary Ligeti, the music uses the interplay between different tuning systems, while the engagement of human sound and human touch avoids the endemic problems in recorded computer music of a mechanization of timbre and rhythm. (Of course, finger rhythm is different from breath rhythm, and the music takes note of that. If breath rhythm

26. See Dominique Jameux, *Pierre Boulez* (London, 1991), 358.

27. Three articles concerning Harvey's music are included in *Contemporary Music Review*, 1/1 (1984), an issue devoted to 'Musical Thought at IRCAM'. Saariaho's early pieces are considered, and copiously illustrated, in her 'Timbre and Harmony: Interpolations of Timbral Structures', *Contemporary Music Review*, 2/1 (1987), 93–133.

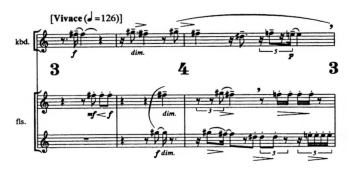

Example 76 George Benjamin, *Antara*

were wanted, it would be perfectly possible to use a synthesizer controlled by a blown device.)

In a better world, *Antara* might have been one overture to a new
future for the orchestra, as an assembly of normal instruments, of
normal instruments transformed—a technique adumbrated by Stockhausen in *Mixtur* and notably refined by Boulez, as well as by Saariaho
in her *Lichtbogen* for nonet (1985–86) and *Io* for chamber orchestra
(1986–87)—and of electronic instruments, producing together all kinds
of new possibilities of harmony, timbre, and rhythm. But other constraints, at a time when IRCAM's lavish funding was highly unusual,
were forcing orchestras into more conservative patterns.

22

Spectralisms

Spectral music—music whose composition is informed by the overtone spectra of sounds, especially instrumental sounds—is often associated with a group of composers who came to the forefront in Paris in the mid-1970s, among them Grisey, Murail, Michaël Levinas (b. 1949), and Hugues Dufourt (b. 1943).[1] That it happened when it did was partly because spectral composition depended on the digital analysis of spectra, which could then be reproduced by orchestral instruments, and depended, too, on the simulation of other techniques being used in computer music, notably ring modulation and frequency modulation (as introduced by Chowning). That it happened where it did was surely helped by the imminent opening of IRCAM as well as by a French tradition of timbre composition going back to Debussy and even to Rameau. Grisey, Levinas, and Murail all had a clear example in the work of their teacher Messiaen, whose harmonic practice had some-times been stimulated by a desire to render the sounds of splashing water or bird calls; *Chronochromie* provides many instances, in a score dating from a decade and a half before the first spectral works of the new generation. There were, however, intimations elsewhere. Some years before *Chronochromie* Stockhausen had tried to create artificial spectra with the orchestra of his *Spiel*, and Scelsi's intuitive work with slowly changing spectra went back further yet. Tuning to the harmonic

1. See Julian Anderson, 'A Provisional History of Spectral Music', *Contemporary Music Review*, 19 (2000), 81–113.

series—a powerful if not obligatory tool in spectral composition, most spectra being inharmonic—had been a feature of Partch's music since the 1930s and later of Young's, and had been brought to Europe by the early 1970s in works by Ligeti and Stockhausen (*Stimmung*). It was around the same time that Horatiu Radulescu (b. 1942), who had moved to Paris from Romania, and James Tenney began working with spectra. A lot of composers—some in groups, some independently, some learning from others—were listening as never before to the basic constituents of sound.

Radulescu and Tenney

Radulescu's first spectral composition, *Credo*, an hour-long piece for nine cellos performing the first forty-five harmonics of the instrument's lowest note, dates from 1969, the year he settled in Paris. The notion he developed of 'sound plasma'—'living sound that can only be comprehended from a global perspective, resembling the blue image of earth as viewed from outer space'[2]—is close to Scelsi's 'sphericity': sound is explored as a substance, into which the music delves, delving into itself, through gradual changes of colour and pitch. Rawness is implied. Ensembles of like instruments suited Radulescu's purposes in providing a malleable homogeneity together with the means to sound a large number of partials at the same time, as in the case of his *Byzantine Prayer* (1988), a memorial to Scelsi for forty flautists placed among the audience, or his Fourth Quartet (1976–87), in which the four players and their listeners are surrounded by eight recorded quartets. He also worked often with an instrument he had devised to suit his purposes: the 'sound icon', or grand piano lying on its side, so that the strings may be bowed, producing complexes of bowed tone and resonance depending on the tuning of the strings and the bowing technique. In *Clepsydra*, for sixteen sound icons placed around the audience (1982), the sound is characteristically tremulous with inner life while being broadly static, moving in a slow process from a dense mass to a single pitch (though one still with a rich spectrum of its own) and back again. Being centred on—or seeking its centre in—a single sound gave Radulescu's spectral works a meditative intensity, heightened by their allusion to chant, whether Orthodox or Tibetan Buddhist, in an emphasis on the deep bass, notably including that of Pierre-Yves Artaud's double-bass flute.

These dense humming and searing textures were, however, typical of only part of Radulescu's output. A different possibility is represented by his extraordinary *Das Andere* for solo viola (1984), whose title denotes, he said, with reference to the Romanian writer Mircea Eliade,

2. Note with Edition RZ 1007.

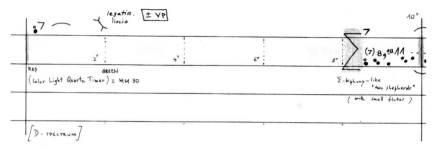

Example 77   Horatiu Radulescu, *Das Andere*

'the state in certain primitive religions where you confound yourself with your God'.[3] Requiring precision tuning and several special techniques, the piece works with two kinds of material: drones and melodies played on high harmonics of the four just-tuned strings, indicated in the score by the Greek letter Σ and sounding 'beautifully rough, primitive, and wild',[4] and low, gruff arpeggios. These two kinds of material start to interpenetrate as the play on harmonics slowly descends from the top two strings to the bottom two. The harmonics are notated throughout by number, as shown in example 77, from near the beginning. Heard from the A string here throughout is its seventh harmonic (flattened G two octaves above the treble staff), while from the D string come its seventh through eleventh harmonics (flattened C to G half-sharp). Since the A string's seventh harmonic is equivalent to the twenty-first harmonic of the D below the treble staff ($7 \times 3 = 21$), and since the D string's tenth and eleventh harmonics are equivalent to the twentieth and twenty-second harmonics of that same note ($10 \times 2 = 20$, $11 \times 2 = 22$), that low D will sound as a difference tone, a phenomenon much used by Radulescu as it was by Scelsi, conveying the sense of sound arising in a different sense spectrally, without being played, and also here adding to the 'beautifully rough' effect.

Tenney's first spectral venture[5] was *Clang* for chamber orchestra (1972), a harmonic process that performers could enter at will, playing one of the notes available at any particular juncture as the process moved from open octaves to complex dissonance and back again. *Spectral CANON for CONLON Nancarrow* (1972–74) he devised for a player piano tuned to the first twenty-four harmonics of the A below middle C, the notes arriving in order from the bottom and pulsing at rates

3. Preface to the score.
4. Ibid.
5. See Robert A. Wannamaker, 'The Spectral Music of James Tenney', *Contemporary Music Review*, 27 (2008), 91–130.

corresponding to their frequency ratios. Among his spectral works of the next decade or so, when he was also pursuing other lines of inquiry, his *Three Indigenous Songs* for a wind-percussion sextet (1979) are each modelled on the formant spectrum of a sung or spoken text.

Grisey

Rather than 'spectral' Grisey preferred to call the music in which he was interested 'liminal',[6] a music of thresholds: between timbre and harmony, in that chords were created as towers of partials that could potentially cohere as single sounds, and between what is sounded and what is heard, in that he was interested in combination tones and other effects taking place between source and ear. He made his first attempt at creating a spectrum with instruments in his orchestral piece *Dérives* (1973–74), but it was his next work that represented his creative threshold: *Périodes* for mixed septet (1974), which he wrote while studying sound at the Faculté des Sciences in Paris. Beginning with a D on viola enveloped by harmonics on the other instruments, it ends with a realization of the spectrum of a trombone playing a low E, with pitches adjusted to the nearest quarter tone or, in the case of the viola's slightly flattened D, eighth tone, as shown in example 78. This is, in Grisey's terms, 'the projection, into a dilated and artificial space, of the natural structure of sounds'.[7]

Dilation was necessary for a kind of music based not on notes but on sounds, and even more so on transitions between sounds: 'The real material', Grisey wrote, was not some motif, theme or series but 'the path the composer traces within the arborescence of possibilities stimulated by each aura'.[8] In his earliest theoretical statement, a lecture he gave at Darmstadt in 1978, he spoke of sounds as being not 'defined and permutable objects' but rather 'bunches of forces oriented in time', forces that are 'infinitely mobile and fluctuating; they are alive, like cells, with a birth and a death, and tend, above all, to a continuous transformation of their energy'.[9] To consider them thus was to find a third way, distinct equally from tonal hierarchy and serial egalitarianism with regard to pitch, respecting difference (with political implications accepted[10]). This view of sounds, strikingly echoing Lachenmann's vision of points along lines of force, led Grisey to work with smooth change or else with repetitions executing a gradual transformation, as at the start of *Périodes*, where the spectrum is altered little by little through a

6. See his *Écrits, ou L'Invention de la musique spectrale*, ed. Guy Lelong (Paris, 2008), 48–52.
7. Ibid., 92.
8. Ibid., 52.
9. Ibid., 30.
10. See ibid., 183.

Example 78 Gérard Grisey, *Périodes*

sequence of recurrences, taking the viola from its native habitat into increasingly alien environments.[11]

From an understanding of sound, therefore, came an understanding of rhythm. For Grisey it was important to keep in view the rudimentary periodic states of both: the harmonic series and pulsation. *Périodes* owes its title to the regular rhythm to which it returns from time to time, as at the end, a rhythm that is not metronomic but organic, close to the body's rhythms of heartbeat, breathing, walking, and so on. To this Grisey adds processes of progressively increasing or decreasing tension, for which he again finds corporeal corollaries in inhalation and exhalation. Conceived with the aid of contemporary technology for studying sound, *Périodes* nevertheless has an animal prowl to it.

The first performance took place in Rome, and was given by a new group Grisey, Murail, Dufourt, and Levinas had formed in Paris the year before: L'Itinéraire. (Scelsi was there, later recognized by Grisey as a forerunner.) For this same group Grisey went on to write *Partiels* for eighteen-piece ensemble (1976) as a follow-up to *Périodes*—literally, in that the new work begins where the old one is ending, enriching the spectrum, out of which come wonderful soundscapes, including a passage near the middle where woodwind soloists call out elemental phrases to one another like birds in a primeval forest. The two pieces may be performed separately, but Grisey, as always, favoured continuity; he may also have been taken with the idea he had discovered in *Partiels* of condensing just a few notes out of a spectrum and so deriving the means for melody, as in the woodwind-bird episode or an earlier one for solo strings. Hence the idea to incorporate *Périodes–Partiels* in a whole concert, beginning with a solo piece—*Prologue* for viola (1976), the central instrument of *Périodes*—and then roughly doubling the orchestra each time through *Modulations* (1976–77), written for the Ensemble InterContemporain, and *Transitoires* (1980–81), which had its first performance at the 1981 Venice Biennale as the conclusion to the

11. See ibid., 350.

whole eighty-minute unfolding, now given the global title *Les Espaces acoustiques*. With its large symphony orchestra, *Transitoires* can mount enormous spectra, up to the fifty-fifth harmonic,[12] creating a sense of vastness, of acoustic space indeed, within which events from earlier are reviewed, including the woodwind-birds of *Partiels* and the summoning bass strokes from the end of *Périodes*. At the end, when the orchestra has filtered away through scintillant and rougher sounds, the solo viola of *Prologue* is discovered once more alone. Grisey considered, however, that the process of growth and exploration could go on forever, and so he added *Épilogue* in 1985 to cut that process off with stentorian horns and disintegration. *Les Espaces acoustiques* thus reached its final form just a year before a composed concert by one of the composer's leading contemporaries, Ferneyhough's *Carceri d'invenzione*.

The excitement of the new work with spectra is transmitted also by Murail's *Gondwana* for orchestra (1980), with its recreated bell sounds introducing a realm of sumptuous timbre-harmonies not so far from Messiaen's. For Grisey, however, the fundamental discovery was one of time. By opening worlds of slowly changing sounds, exemplified in the Murail piece as well as in much of *Les Espaces acoustiques*, spectral composition made available a 'collective, dreamlike and cosmic time' as opposed to the 'individual and discursive time, that of language' to which Western music had generally been attached. *Prologue* was in language time, a recitative, but as point of departure for the 'acoustic spaces' that could now be explored.

While engaged on his major work, Grisey pushed that exploration in several directions. *Jour, contre-jour* for electric organ and ensemble (1978–79) was his most extreme venture into expanded time, a twenty-minute mapping of the sun's journey across the sky in slow, steady change, with shadowless noon marked by pure harmonics. Immediately afterwards came a work of similar length with no spectra at all, but playing with time and predictability by working with different pulse rates, slow and fast, single and counterpointed, solo or joined by the whole ensemble of six percussionists surrounding the audience: *Tempus ex machina* (1979). This became the first part of an hour-long composition, *Le Noir de l'étoile* (1989–90), where it prepares for the arrival of vibrations from a pulsar: star music with which the terrestrial musicians perform. In contact thus with objects far removed in space, Grisey's music could also, like that of Varèse or Xenakis, resonate with ancient times, not only in percussion drummings but also in the poetry of arhtyhmic and by implication incorporeal conveyance expressed in *Jour, contr-jour*, where the composer was thinking of the Egyptian Book of the Dead.

In 1982 Grisey and Murail both started working at IRCAM, where Murail produced a classic in what was becoming the house genre of

12. Ibid., 139.

music for ensemble with electronic adjunct: *Désintégrations* (1982–83), in which synthesized spectra, prerecorded, lead the ensemble through a fluorescent maze of colour-harmonies. Grisey's projects were both erotic: a revision of a piece for clarinet and trombone he had written in 1981, *Solo pour deux*, where the two instruments bend around each other and blend, notably when clarinet multiphonics fold into the trombone spectrum, and *Les Chants de l'amour* for twelve-voice choir and synthesized sound (1982–84). The latter, the first work he had done with vocal sound since 1970, is for the most part music for thirteen voices, the thirteenth being electronic, marvellously created with the assistance of Jean-Baptiste Barrière (b. 1958), director of musical research at IRCAM, who also collaborated with Saariaho (and married her). Grisey aptly describes this voice as 'at different times divine, monstrous, menacing, seductive';[13] it often sounds like an Easter Island statue come to life, though it can also be a small child, being taught by the human voices how to sing and how to feel.

It was a performance of *Désintégrations* in 1984 that persuaded Grisey it was time for him to 'add rupture and rapidity to the obsession with continuity and slowness of process.'[14] From that determination came *Épilogue* and also *Talea* for *Pierrot* quintet (1986), whose opening contrasts very fast with very slow scalar motion, and both with silence. *Presto* and *adagio* eventually fold into a pulsing harmonic spectrum, which initiates the second part of the piece, where tremolandos in the piano's bass prompt magical chords and melodies from the other instruments—'wild flowers, weeds', as the composer described them, generated by a 'machine for making freedom'.[15] The overall tempo of this later and longer section is, however, still slow, as is the case also of Grisey's next major work, *Le Temps et l'écume* (1988–89), for four percussionists, two synthesizers, and chamber orchestra. One may feel it also in works of the later 1980s by such different composers as Feldman and Nono that time was running down. Making liminal music move speedily would be a project for Grisey in the next decade.

Vivier

Many of the young composers drawn to Paris in the early 1980s by IRCAM found themselves learning as much from Grisey and Murail— not least Saariaho and Lindberg. Claude Vivier (1948–83) came for other reasons in 1981, by which time he had absorbed spectral thinking in parts of his *Orion* for orchestra (1979) and through it achieved his breakthrough in his next work: *Lonely Child* (1980), for soprano and chamber orchestra. Like Grisey (briefly), Vivier had studied with

13. Ibid., 148.
14. Ibid., 199.
15. Ibid., 151–52.

Example 79   Claude Vivier, *Lonely Child*

Stockhausen, whose technique of formula composition left its mark on his slow, solemn melodies, along with memories of plainsong from his Catholic upbringing and traces left from his more recent travels in Asia, including a spell on Bali. Asia also affected his sense of time. Where Grisey was adamant that his music executed 'western', directional time,[16] Vivier's temporality is more static or circular, more that of ritual than drama, a temporality he associated not only with the East but with a particularly homosexual consciousness.

Part prayer, part lullaby, part love song, *Lonely Child* is in several phases, each announced and punctuated by strokes on a large Japanese bowl gong, the rin (recalling Stockhausen's use of the sound in *Telemusik* and *Inori*), and each expanding the basic melody both horizontally and—in that the texture is repeatedly enriched with harmonies that become ever more complex until near the end—vertically. The melodic repetition is partly responsible for the sense of stasis, along with the slow tempo, the presence of drones, the parallel chords, and the immobile, glistening spectral harmonies in which everything comes to be draped. Example 79 shows the first vocal phrase, where, though the accompaniment is still relatively simple at this point (later the strings will be in seventeen parts, sometimes playing harmonics and continuous glissandos), the singer's line is characteristically supported below by a static single line—both parts being affirmed in octaves—and offset above by a halo of high violins. As Bob Gilmore has shown,[17] Vivier derived these spectral clouds by calculating the combination tones that would result from the vocal line and its support. In the first bar of the example the notes in question are A (440 Hz) and G (196 Hz), from which the composer calculated combination tones of 440 + 196 = 636 Hz (approximately a quarter-tone-flat E), 440 + 392 = 832 Hz (very nearly G♯) and so on.

16. Ibid., 41.
17. Bob Gilmore, 'On Claude Vivier's "Lonely Child"', *Tempo*, 61 (2007), 2–17.

Vivier's music demonstrates in an especially acute way the subjectivity already noted in work of this period by composers as diverse as Rihm, Kurtág, and Finnissy, for *Lonely Child* and succeeding works have an unparalleled immediacy, a sense of everything in the music working to communicate an intimate message, for which this unusual musical language was perfect conduit. Autobiography features in the texts of this and many of the composer's other vocal works: dreams and desires, the names of lovers. More than that, he often spoke of his creative drive as a search for purity, even redemption. During the next year and a half he developed his new style in several works, most of which had to do with a projected Marco Polo opera. It was then that he returned to Paris, where he renewed contact with Grisey, the influence surely now being reversed, for *Les Chants de l'amour* suggests the French composer had been listening to the Canadian's choral soundscapes. Meanwhile Vivier's music was becoming even more intensely personal, to the point where in his final work, *Glaubst du an die Unsterblichkeit der Seele?* (1983), he told with shocking uncanniness the story of his own death, at the hands of a young man he had picked up.

23

(Unholy?)
Minimalisms

Many of the original minimalists—Monk, Palestine, Riley, Young—went on as they had before, making music for themselves and close associates to perform. For others, unexpected success in the mid-1970s brought a change. *Einstein on the Beach* (1975–76), a production by the avant-garde director Robert Wilson with chants and dances by Glass, gained the latter a whole new level of attention. Commissions for further operas followed, including *Akhnaten* (1984), in which he wrote for the first time for a standard orchestra, and which in turn prompted works that, beginning with his Violin Concerto (1987), brought the heavy engines of his repetitive style into the regular concert hall.

Reich

Reich's breakthrough came at the same time with *Music for 18 Musicians* (1974–76), scored for pairs of clarinets and strings with four female voices around the central body of pianos and tuned percussion, and based on a sequence of chords performed at the start, after which an invention is played on each of the chords in turn, until the full sequence returns at the end. The rich chords, strong harmonic movement, and dynamic pulsations speak of a creative exhilaration that communicated itself widely, with important consequences for the composer. Unable to cope with demands for performances, he was obliged to publish his music and make it available to other ensembles. Also, he began to receive major commissions, which resulted in a sequence of large-scale works, up to *The Four Sections* (1987), for an orchestra including a characteristic tuned percussion group as a section along with woodwinds, brass, and strings. Such scores he interspersed with returns, in pieces that all have 'counterpoint' in the title, to the *Violin Phase* model of an instrumental soloist playing against a multitracked recording, albeit with the more complex patterning of his later music.

Though more complicated and multilayered than it was in the 1960s (the 1982 piece *Vermont Counterpoint*, for instance, is for flute plus ten recorded flutes), Reich's music did not lose its roots in repetition and process. If he, nevertheless, insisted that *Tehillim* 'is not composed of short repeating patterns' but rather of melodies whose 'flexible changing metres' (another departure) were dictated by the texts, because the melodies are composed of chains of motifs, and because they are frequently heard in strict unison canon, the effect is often of patterns circling at an insistent pulse. The grid of regular pulse is always there, but it can be more or less densely overlaid with conflicting rhythms: rhythms of different pace, as in the gamelanlike stratification of the orchestra in *The Four Sections*, where the strings are normally slow-moving and the tuned percussion rapid, or rhythms of different metre or alignment. 'Very often,' the composer noted, 'I'll find myself working in 12-beat phrases, which can divide up in very different ways; and that ambiguity as to whether you're in duple or triple time is, in fact, the rhythmic life-blood of much of my music.'[1] In rather the same way, on the melodic-harmonic plane, there may be uncertainty about which note is the tonic, and therefore about which mode the music is in: from *Tehillim* onwards the texture is often not only more complex but also more chromatic, allowing for suggestions of exotic modes as well as of Coplandesque pure diatonicism.

Sprung in rhythm and mode, Reich's music had always conveyed freshness too in its self-demonstrative character, its way of building itself from simple basic elements as it went along. *Tehillim* came from a realization that those elements were not freely invented, that they had histories in the composer's Jewish and U.S. heritages, and he began work by studying Hebrew, the Torah, and cantillation (the traditional Jewish ways of chanting sacred texts). The title is the Hebrew word for 'psalms', and a few verses from the book of Psalms provide the text for the entire thirty-minute composition. Reich notes in the score that his tuned tambourines without jingles may approximate the sound of the *tof* mentioned in the first verse he chooses from Psalm 150, and that his other small percussion instruments—maracas, crotales, and hands (clapped)—are similar to those that had a place throughout the Middle East in biblical times. So the essential sound of *Tehillim*—of voices with percussion—is archaeological.

1. Interview with Jonathan Cott included with Elektra Nonesuch 979 101.

Example 80   Steve Reich, *Different Trains*

What the voices sing, though, is not, and nor is what the percussion patter out. Reich remarks also that one of his reasons for deciding on psalm texts was the fact that the ancient tradition of psalm singing has been lost (except among Yemenite Jews). He was therefore free to invent his own melodies, and he made them in his own way, so that they keep up an ebullient mobility, rebounding between different modes and metres. They do so partly because of their self-similar structure, in which small groups of notes keep reappearing transposed or otherwise changed. The voices dance on, all the time singing the same things in different orders and perspectives, and gaining more rhythmic liveliness from jostling against the percussion.

In *Different Trains* for string quartet and recording (1988) Reich joined words to music in a different way, taking up a technique Scott Johnson (b. 1952) had introduced in his 1982 composition *John Somebody* for electric guitar and tape. Reich collected testimony about train journeys in the United States—from his governess, with whom he made transcontinental trips as a child, and from a retired porter—and also interviewed others who had been aboard trains taking Jews across Europe at the same time. He then notated excerpts as speech melodies, and produced a score in which these melodies are imitated by both recorded and live string quartets (four quartets all told in the first movement, three in the other two)—or rather, as shown in example 80, the speech melodies enter as if to musical prompting, and then the music can take them on by itself. In this case, the motif is first heard from a recorded cello, then repeated by the live viola, and at the second repetition doubled by the voice on tape. Filling alternate units of seven semiquavers, the motif progressively moves against the eight-semiquaver grid in a simple example of a Reichian rhythmic process; the next repetition will bring it back to the start of the bar, and then it will be extended. The tape component of the piece also includes train sounds (rattles of wheels and carriages that accord with the *moto perpetuo*, whistlings that similarly go with the sustained chords), so that the composition, besides being a description of train journeys, seems to enact one, as it shuttles along the tracks of repetition and shifts—across points made by metric or tonal modulation—from one speech melody to another. Its rigorous compositional process precludes sentimentality, but not poignancy and darkness. And, as Reich recognized at the time, it opened the way to a new kind of opera.

Andriessen

While Reich was putting together *Music for 18 Musicians* Andriessen was also moving towards a signal statement. In 1976, he stepped down from his position as pianist, composer, and arranger with De Volharding to concentrate on finishing a score he had been working on throughout his time with that rough and ready orchestra: *De Staat* (The Republic, 1972–76, see example 81), for an ensemble of oboes, brass, violas, electric guitars, electric bass, harps, and pianos, with episodes in which four female singers chant from Plato in the original Greek. The minimalist apparatus is still powerfully present, the score being essentially a sequence of choruses in which chords and motifs keep running round in circles, often at high speed, with distinct echoes at times of Reich and Rzewski especially. But there are reminiscences also of Stravinsky, in the incisive choral chanting and in how some of the chugging chords in regular rhythm call back to *The Rite of Spring*, while the brass-heavy sound and the scoring by ensembles sometimes bring a flavour of big-band jazz. Utterly distinctive, though, is the rendering of driving pulsation through deliberately coarse sound, a trait that came out of Andriessen's work with De Volharding and is instanced in the example. In that respect *De Staat*, though it marked a return to the concert hall for the

Example 81 Louis Andriessen, *De Staat*

composer (the first performance was given at the venerable Concert-gebouw in Amsterdam), refuses to behave properly. It is abrasive, intemperate, wilfully crude.

Its bite, however, may be directed at least as much inwardly as towards the Dutch musical establishment. By the time the work was first performed, in November 1976, Andriessen had been politically active for a decade, working alongside other Dutch composers, among them Reinbert de Leeuw (b. 1938), subsequently one of the great conductors of contemporary music, and Peter Schat (1935–2003). But though Dutch society had become more liberal, as had societies throughout the Western world, power remained where it was and the great institutions, including the Concertgebouw, were unshaken (as was also generally the case elsewhere). In a note for De Leeuw's 1990 recording of *De Staat*, Andriessen ruefully remarked, with reference to the words from Plato he had set in the piece: 'If only it were true that musical innovation represented a danger to the State!'[2] The acerbity of *De Staat* is the acerbity of that conclusion.

Andriessen's dilemma was that of the avant-garde composer throughout this period, politicized or not: whether to maintain a position outside the mainstream and thereby probably forfeit opportunities to work on a large scale and engage with internationally prominent performers (the position Andriessen had adopted hitherto, and to which Cardew and Rzewski, Denyer and Wolff, among others, held true) or to enter the approved culture and try to change things from within. Andriessen was evidently torn. While finishing *De Staat* he produced a piece for an ensemble of his students, *Hoketus* (1975–76), that maintained his kind of coarse minimalism, pulse-driven and heavily amplified, and was made for touring and unusual venues. Indebted as the piece is to Glass and Reich, it bespeaks a critical distance, which he expressed at the end of his programme note: 'What makes the piece differ from most minimal art compositions is that the harmonic material is not diatonic but chromatic, and that it radically abandons the tonal continuous sound-masses characteristic of most minimal art, with the inclusion of all accompanying cosmic nonsense.'[3] Whether or not the chromaticism was to have an effect on Reich, the resolute difference in Andriessen's music—the dirt, the urban quality—certainly excited U.S. composers of the coming generation, especially the three who, in New York in 1987, formed the downtown organization Bang on a Can: Michael Gordon (b. 1956), David Lang (b. 1957), and Julia Wolfe (b. 1958).

Long before this, though, concert life in Amsterdam was loosening up, in ways Andriessen's music profited from and encouraged. A converted church, Paradiso, had opened its doors in the revolutionary year of 1968 and become a centre for new and experimental music of all

2. Note with Elektra Nonesuch 9 79251-2.
3. Available at http://www.boosey.com.

kinds. There were also several groups in the city presenting twentieth-century music, notably the ASKO Ensemble (founded in 1965) and the Schönberg Ensemble (1974), as well as the revitalized Netherlands Wind Ensemble, for which Andriessen had written *De Staat*. But though the counterculture was thriving more abundantly in Amsterdam than anywhere else at the time, by the end of the 1970s the phrase was becoming a period term even there. Paradiso was more and more a jazz and rock club, while the ensembles, dependent on state support, necessarily took on the character of institutions.

Andriessen, drawn to big projects, was bound to move with the times. *De Tijd* (Time, 1979–81) withdraws, perhaps reluctantly, from the noisiness and pulsation of *De Staat* and *Hoketus* into the tense serenity of sustained chords from female voices and orchestral instruments, their attacks most often covered by clangs from an ensemble of pianos, harps, and bell-like percussion articulating a rhythmic machine. The effect is like that of watching the slow movement of a clock; time is stilled, too, in how the harmonies often suggest music from a century before—windows, as they sometimes seem, into Fauré's Requiem. Pulse comes roaring back in *De Snelheid* for three orchestral groups (1982–83), but to quite different effect than in *De Staat*, the sound now so much smoother with, as in *De Tijd*, a durational process placed in the foreground, events being pulled closer and closer together as the percussion pattering gets faster and faster.

If this was practical compromise, Andriessen managed to keep his musical ideals. His model for *De Snelheid* is much more the big band than the conventional orchestra, even though he wrote the piece to one of the few orchestral commissions he has accepted—from the San Francisco Symphony, which, under his compatriot Edo de Waart as music director, had become open to new music, engaging John Adams (b. 1947) as advisor. Moreover, his emphasis on overt process, at a time when Reich was moving in the opposite direction, is a gesture against the notion of the composer as dictator. Improvisation, as experience in Amsterdam and elsewhere had proved, could only lead to chaos when large numbers of musicians were involved, but inexorable process could also place composer and performers on a level, exacting its due from all concerned. Where that process was leading, of course, might be food for thought. *De Tijd* ends with its exquisite veils lifting to reveal a ticking time bomb.

24

Referencings

Music of reference, so startling around 1970 when it appeared in works by Berio, Holloway, or Schnittke, became almost the norm in the 1980s, partly defining that decade of springtime postmodernism. The masquerade might be mischievous, whimsical or unsettling, or all at once, as in the Fourth Symphony (1988) of Jonathan Lloyd (b. 1948), where out of the simplest material—rising scales—dreams and nightmares are conjured, or rudely present themselves, across a range from Debussy-like phrases to Latin rhythm to a recurrent cadential turn, as if the music were in auto-destruct mode from its beginning. There were also composers who, following Rochberg or Penderecki, wanted to play the game for real.

Kagel, et al.

In the face of a musical culture that, after three decades of avant-garde assault, was remaining impervious and even becoming more so, nervous laughter was an understandable response. It may be felt, for example, in the works of Poul Ruders (b. 1949), such as his *Bravour Studies* for solo cello on 'L'Homme armé' (1976), where the medieval tune is combined with modern transgressions (slapping the instrument, whistling or groaning while playing) within a musical world centred, by virtue of the medium, on Bach. More explicitly a musical comedian, H. K. Gruber (b. 1943) scored an immediate and lasting success with

Frankenstein!! (1976–77), intended for his own eldritch sprechgesang narration with orchestra. Setting poems by H. C. Artmann that ironically claim the innocence of childhood to speak of horrors and heroes, Gruber's sharply defined music stalks the history of Viennese music from Haydn to Schoenberg by way of Johann Strauss II.

To one whose music had long worn an ironic smile—Kagel—the postmodern comedy was no joking matter and Bach no merry model. Of course, the whole idea of writing an oratorio on the subject of the venerated composer, as Kagel did in his major work of this period, his *Sankt-Bach-Passion* (1981–85), is ridiculous, but Kagel typically took his outrageous task completely seriously, finding indeed a timeless story in that of the indignity and incomprehension meted out to the composer by his contemporaries. Running through the libretto, interspersed with adapted chorale texts, is an edited selection of documents relevant to Bach's life, chosen to present, in the more dramatic second half, moments of betrayal and suffering—though the work movingly stops just short of describing the composer's death. Bach's 'Passion' thus has somewhat the outlines of his own Passions, and those outlines are partly filled in by the dominance of tenor recitative as the narrative mode. Moreover, although Kagel ruled out quotations (he boldly sets forth on his own ricercare for the scene with Frederick the Great at Potsdam), the work is thoroughly infused with chorale-type phrasing, by no means only when chorale texts are being sung. The harmonies are smoky with dissonance and often chromatically falling in a spirit of depression or lament, but the homophony and the short, balanced gestures keep the chorale ideal almost constantly close, if not quite in reach.

There are lighter moments, as when Bach's complaint about 'so many incompetent boys' (the role of the composer is spoken) is illustrated by a boys' choir singing with raw tone and off-key. The work also has an undercurrent of dance music—a taste Kagel shared with his hero, except that his dances, as so often in his music, are of the twentieth century and move in the shadows. And beneath all this is another figure from musical history: not Bach but B–A–C–H, the four-note motif B♭–A–C–B. This, Kagel observed, 'has been a topos ever since Mozart, and one that I actually wanted to investigate thoroughly, for once. And so, as the serial composer I still am, I subjected B–A–C–H to a system of harmonic accompaniment formulae, from a minor second up to a major seventh. This way I came up with 6972 basic models, with which the piece is composed.'[1] Unusually sombre for this composer, the work is not only the grandest ever fantasia on B–A–C–H, but also a memorial—the more powerful for being inevitably and irremediably split with irony.

1. Note with Montaigne Naïve MO 782157.

Donatoni

Ebullient allusion was one of the tricks available to Donatoni, along with a technical sophistication and formal mastery often at the service of playfulness. Of the generation of Stockhausen, Boulez, Nono, and Berio, he produced his most spirited work when past the age of fifty, when the battles of postwar modernism were over (but not forgotten, for they are implicated in his playfulness, as in Ligeti's). He met Maderna in 1953, went to Darmstadt the next year, and abruptly turned from Italian neoclassicism to international modernism: 'Till I was thirty, I copied Bartók. After I met Maderna, I copied Boulez.'[2] 'Then', to continue this compact autobiography, 'I got interested in John Cage, had my negative period and so on.' This 'negative period', roughly coextensive with the 1960s, led him not only into indeterminacy but also into automatic procedures and the use of found material, as in *Etwas ruhiger im Ausdruck* (1967), which is scored for the quintet of *Pierrot lunaire*—a repeated fascination in Donatoni's instrumentation—but takes its material from another Schoenberg source: the eighth bar of the second of the Op. 23 piano pieces. 'There is something elusive in those few notes, something which evades what *must* happen and invites one to think about what *can* happen.'[3] Out of the invitation comes a chain of soft possibilities, leading up to Schoenberg's at the end.

It seems that then, gradually during the 1970s, Donatoni changed not his methods but their meaning. Quotation and mechanism, instead of being grim compulsions, became occasions for fun and brilliance; the ending of music—which was noticed most particularly by Italian critics and composers during this period—could be cause for carnival. From 1977 onwards Donatoni produced several new pieces each year, most of them for small ensembles or solo instruments—media answering his demands for clarity and for the projection of notes and motifs through canons and other strictly organized trajectories.

Example 82 shows a passage from *Still* for 'soprano leggero' with pairs of flutes, violins, and keyboards (1985), which looks to the little trio for the Three Boys in *The Magic Flute* for its text ('schweige still') and perhaps also for its musical elements: turn figures and single notes, chromatic neighbours and bright, high orchestration. Donatoni works these into a characteristic skein of miniature musical machines, where individual moments are highly determined but in their succession seem improvised. This is true even of the detail. For example, in the five-part canon—whose entries, as indicated, come at intervals of three demisemiquavers—the line flips unpreparedly from one diminished seventh (G♯–B–D) to another (C–E♭–F♯–A), and the soprano jostles her three-note path to the inevitable B♭. Typical also is the slightly wonky effect

2. Interview with Denise Faquelle, published with Adda 581 143.
3. Quoted in note with Etcetera KTC 1053.

Example 82   Franco Donatoni, *Still*

of patterns that do not quite fit together: the canon establishes a dotted-semiquaver pulse by its entries and its marcatos, and the soprano falls in with this, if irregularly (at least her motifs always begin and end on a pulse); but the piano tries to set up a quaver unit. In combining rigidity with whimsy, and in practising superb technical sophistication on cheerfully rudimentary ideas, Donatoni's post-1977 music suggests Nancarrow come alive on instruments.

Bolcom and Adams

A master of pastiche, who had by the early 1970s proved he could master anything from Viennese classical style (*Commedia* for chamber orchestra, 1971) to the Joplinesque piano rag, Bolcom put it all together in *Songs of Innocence and of Experience*, settings for soloists, choirs, and orchestra of the whole of Blake's book, mostly done between 1973 and 1982. Playing for over two hours altogether, the collection thoroughly displays the composer's many voices, from country and western ('The Shepherd') to Milhaudesque rhythmic choral speech with percussion ('The Tyger'), from cabaret spot ('Nurse's Song') to intense and strenuous chorus ('Infant Sorrow'), from mid-twentieth-century opera ('Earth's Answer') to folksong ('My Pretty Rose Tree'), from Broadway melodrama ('The Little Black Boy') to chromatic coloratura ('The Angel'), in most cases the styles being mixed. The drama of contrast, coupled with the brevity of the numbers (many are under two minutes in length), keeps the show on the road. Also, the diversity has a precedent in the music of Ives, evoked not only in the simulation of vernacular models but also in the rather rare moments of high dissonance and the more frequent plenitudes of mixed strands. This is just one respect in which Blake's songbook enjoys a comprehensive U.S. embrace; there is also the overall exuberance.

That comes, too, in the work of Adams, who made the polished minimalism of his *Shaker Loops* for string septet (1978) the basis for a restoration of late Romantic harmony and gesture together with the zing of U.S. popular styles. His opera *Nixon in China* (1985–87) trawls

Example 83   John Adams, *Nixon in China*

these rich waters, and gains a touching quality from the imbalance between the great international events recalled onstage and the small homely music—an imbalance that might express the diminishment of heroism in the television age. Nixon, arriving at Beijing in the first scene, exults in having 'made history', while his music is ruthlessly commonplace. 'Trivial things are not for me', sings his wife Pat; but they are, in what she sings. These characters provide Adams with the opportunity, found also in some of his concert works of this period, to treat minimalism's deficit of meaning—so much made of so little—as an irony. Only Chou En-lai, in the aria that closes the opera, appears to perceive that irony while being contained in it, his music entering, as shown in example 83, over a Holstian ostinato.

Ligeti

Passionately opposed to any return to late Romantic rhetoric ('I hate neo-Expressionism and I can't stand the neo-Mahlerite and the neo-Bergian affectations'[4]), Ligeti found his own very precise and highly diverse means of musical reference in the 1980s. Having completed his opera *Le Grand Macabre* in 1977, he seems to have felt at a loss. Young composers, including a number of his pupils, were reversing what he and his generation had struggled to achieve; he was also having difficulties with the piano concerto he had set himself to write. By the time he got going again, with his Trio for violin, horn, and piano (1982), two sets of choruses (1983), and first book of piano études (1985), followed at last by the concerto (1985–88), his style had taken a great leap, facilitated by two great discoveries: 'first of all the complex polymetres of Conlon Nancarrow's Studies for Player Piano, and secondly the great diversity of non-European musical cultures',[5] among which he mentions Caribbean music, to which he was introduced in 1980 by a pupil,

4. Tünde Szitha: 'A Conversation with György Ligeti', *Hungarian Music Quarterly*, 3/1 (1992), 13–17.
5. György Ligeti, 'Ma position comme compositeur aujourd'hui', *Contrechamps*, 12–13 (1990), 8–9.

Roberto Sierra, and the choral polyphony of the Banda Linda people of the Central African Republic, which came to his notice in 1982–83. Beyond that, as he again acknowledged, he was led to complexity by the computer, used not as a tool but as a metaphor: 'It's a question of adopting a "generative" kind of compositional thinking, where basic principles function in the manner of genetic codes in the unfolding of "vegetal" musical forms. . . . A final scientific pursuit, whose engrossing results have a decisive effect on my musical conceptions, is the world of fractal geometry, developed by Benoît Mandelbrot, and quite particularly the graphic representation of complex limits.'[6]

The Horn Trio, which unashamedly repeats a Brahmsian model, is a kind of golem Brahms, made with great virtuosity, but with deliberately unsuitable materials. It goes on from the dislocated tonal harmony that had arrived in parts of *Le Grand Macabre* and then been considered, perhaps with some surprise, in the harpsichord pieces that had followed, a harmony in which simple consonances return, but not in the right order, producing a disturbing or comic effect of tilting. Further tilting comes in Ligeti's use of nontempered tunings, which in such earlier pieces as *Ramifications* and the Double Concerto had been introduced for rather broad effects of harmonic colour and fuzziness, but which now had a quite particular function in setting up rivalries and tensions with normal tuning. In the case of the trio, it is by recourse to the horn's natural overtones, slightly 'mistuned', that these effects are obtained.

Ligeti may have felt he had opened too many possibilities all at once, which would explain his subsequent concentration on the piano, in the first six études of 1985. Microtonal inflections were now ruled out, and the new possibilities of broken consonance and polymetre could be explored lucidly, without the confusion of different instrumental colours. The first étude, 'Désordre', offers, as Denys Bouliane has shown,[7] an exemplary demonstration of polymetric process, of synthesis from elements drawn out of different musical cultures, and of 'vegetal' growth from a set of ad hoc ideas and rules, most of which are stated or implicit in the opening bars, reproduced in example 84. The principal idea—(one might even say 'theme', except that it is an object which, in keeping with the 'generative' ideal, just goes on repeating itself in different circumstances, in circumstances it has helped make different)—is a melody in three segments, of four, four, and six bars, as indicated by the phrasing. Among the rules are the following. The melody keeps changing its mind about whether there are three-plus-five or five-plus-three quavers in each bar. Unused quaver beats are filled with scale patterns, so that the melody, initially going at a quick

6. Ibid.
7. Denys Bouliane, '"Six Etudes pour piano" de György Ligeti', *Contrechamps*, 12–13 (1990), 98–132.

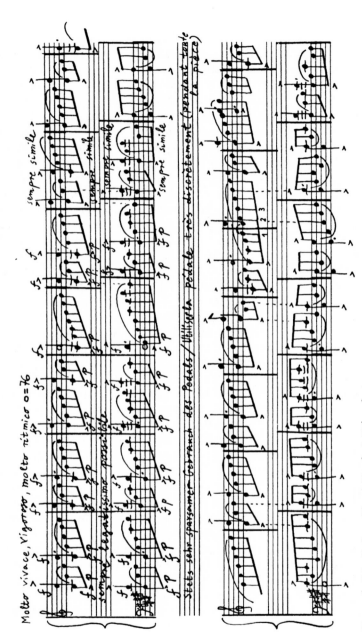

Example 84   György Ligeti, Etude 1 'Désordre'

but not immoderate pace, is placed in a hectic *moto perpetuo*. Where the right hand plays only on the white keys, the left plays only on the black. The left hand doubles the right, but because it is working in a five-note mode rather than a seven-note one, its intervals are larger. (Rider: This rule is subject to a lot of exceptions, which perhaps have to do with other aims Ligeti has for his harmony. For example, the interval between the two hands in the first segment of the melody is always a minor sixth, tritone, or major third, whereas in the second segment the minor third replaces the minor sixth. However, one of the sources of 'disorder' in the piece is the lack of agreement between harmony and rhythm: see the next rule.) The two hands slip out of synchrony in a manner that is at first organized—the right hand jumps a quaver every fourth bar—but later becomes more chaotic (as, indeed, so much in the music becomes more chaotic as it makes its journey upwards and offwards). The melody is repeated fourteen times, moving up a scale degree each time. From the fourth repetition to the tenth, a process of compression sets in, until by the tenth the notes of the melody are almost indistinguishable from those of the scalar infill.

Many of the features of this study—the withdrawal of figure into ground, the swirling but precisely mechanical activity, the intimations of processes that are never fully revealed or go astray (an essential point of difference from Reich)—can be traced back quite clearly to *Monument-Selbstportrait-Bewegung*, and even, a little less clearly, to *Continuum*. What is new is the retrieval of some sort of tonal harmony out of undifferentiated chromaticism, and the exactly analogous retrieval of some sort of metre out of undifferentiated pulsation. The harmonic retrieval is helped by the nature of the instrument, and by Bartók's example of a total chromaticism created by two hands playing on the piano in different modes. (In the seventh étude the hands play in meshing whole-tone modes.) But the retrieval is not assumed: it has to be wrested anew in each bar, as the music's disordered trajectory keeps changing the situation. Certainties about tonic or mode are perpetually having to be redefined. Is the right-hand melody in the Aeolian mode on A or the Locrian on B? Unable to make up its mind, it takes a step upwards. In just the same way—and this may be easier to appreciate in a short extract—certainties about accent or metre keep changing too, and the influence of Nancarrow is evident not just in the mad-machine sound world (which Ligeti had long had as his own) but in the liveliness and awkwardness of the polymetre and in the engineered acceleration. The music is in a marvellously organized confusion it has made inevitable, seemingly of itself, by its basic premises.

Of the twelve studies Ligeti originally planned, he ended up writing eighteen, all sharing the basic features of the first: 'generative' construction from simple elements, imprints from folk music, harmony and metre in states of bewilderment or veiling, and novel musical processes that come from the nature of the instrument, as in the third, 'Touches bloquées', where a *moto perpetuo* in the right hand moves over keys silently depressed by the left, so that gapped rhythms are made automatically. The titles of the pieces may, as in this case, be indications of how they were made, or they may be salutes to other musical cultures (the whole-tone piece has a Hungarian title chosen for its Indonesian sound: 'Galamb borong', meaning 'Melancholy Dove'), or they may be metaphors of effect: 'Désordre', 'Fanfares' for the fourth piece, a study in sixths, fifths and thirds, 'Vertige'. Not only the titles but the opalescent uncertainties of harmony and rhythm place the studies within the ambit of Debussy.

Ligeti's Piano Concerto is, in a sense, a set of five more studies with the addition of an orchestra, which made it possible for the composer to take up the matter of nontempered tunings again. In the odd-numbered movements the piano plays almost continuously, throwing up ideas that take on lives of their own in the orchestra, as if, in congenial substrates, they could express the genetic material contained within them. The piano here is the originating and directing machine, whereas in the second movement—and again in the startling fourth, which the composer has described as 'a fractal piece', 'a geometric vortex' in which 'the ever-decreasing rhythmical values produce the sensation of a kind of acceleration'[8]—it seems that both piano and orchestra are worked by a machine somehow existing elsewhere. The piece is wonderfully helter-skelter, as if it were conscious of itself as a contrivance, a seemingly ramshackle though in fact superbly composed assemblage whose diverse elements—Bartók, Nancarrow, Afro-Caribbean rhythm, fractal design—join to make something new.

8. Szitha, 'Conversation with Gyögy Ligeti,' 17.

1989

The breaching of the Berlin Wall in November 1989 marked out a year that saw notionally Marxist governments fall or move inevitably toward falling across Europe from Tirana to Moscow, and that also witnessed protests, violently subdued, in Tiananmen Square in Beijing. In December Presidents Bush of the U.S.A. and Gorbachev of the U.S.S.R. declared the Cold War officially over, without much doubt as to which side had come out on top. Bourgeois capitalism, its economy that of the marketplace, was now to be global.

Though experienced as revolution in many hitherto communist countries, the process was gradual, and had been in place since the mid-1970s, with the revocation of liberalism in the West and of hard-line socialism in the Soviet and Chinese blocs. The implications for music were manifold. In the most practical way, new music's historic dependence on the support of governments (whether directly or through broadcasting authorities) in Europe and Japan, or of universities in the United States, could no longer be guaranteed once the measure was the balance sheet. Meanwhile, conservatism and traditionalism, already well established, seemed to have the pace of events with them. As what had hitherto been 'music' came to be redefined as 'classical music', its history became not its motive force but its boundary. Countless composers, excited by the examples of Ligeti or Carter or

Boulez in their youth, moved on to write like Shostakovich;
popular musicians as esteemed as Paul McCartney (b. 1942)
started producing 'classical' scores to which the music of their
'classical' contemporaries (Ferneyhough, for example) had
little relevance.

Music also entered the marketplace directly as the compact disc provided a cheap and ready means of distribution.
Instead of creating scores that could be performed again and
again, composers found themselves in a world where the
recording, especially in the case of orchestral works, was the
endpoint. The consumer, increasingly, was not the performer
but the listener, and another aspect of market economies
entered the faculty of listening: individualism.

25

Towards Mode/Meme

Central to the continuing conservatism or consolidation of the 1980s and 1990s—that postmodern era already in the past—was a growth towards consonance, harmonic progression, and tonal stability, a development found not only in the music of composers who, like Bolcom, Rochberg, Penderecki, and Adams, were explicitly retrieving aspects of nineteenth-century tonality but also in that of contemporaries who held to the ideals expressed by the avant-garde since 1945. Lachenmann's move from a music of extreme techniques to one with room for familiar chords and gestures—albeit in new contexts—provides an example, and parallel tendencies may be observed continuing in the work of Berio and Holliger, of Birtwistle and Grisey. Saariaho's music evolved, through the pitch-centredness and cellular working of her cello concerto *Amers* (1992) and violin concerto *Graal théâtre* (1994), towards the style of modal melody couched within exquisite harmonic atmospheres that led her directly from an orchestral song cycle, *Chateau de l'âme* (1995), to her first opera, *L' Amour de loin* (2000). Parallelling Jacques Roubaud's approach in the book from which she took her title, she has the soloist in *Graal théâtre* sound medieval resonances within a late twentieth-century context, as example 85 may suggest.

More surprising, Finnissy, in his Seven Sacred Motets for unaccompanied voices (1991), extended his scope to include church music reaching back to medieval styles of decorated chant, often over a drone, and modal counterpoint. Goehr's search since the mid-1970s for a new harmonic soundness that would not limit range—a search he continued

Example 85   Kaija Saariaho, *Graal théâtre*

in works that included a creative recovery of Monteverdi's lost opera
Arianna (1994–95), at once imitating and updating the original composer—was now widely shared, with no embarrassment about retrogression. For almost any composer, music created in the 1990s is likely
to be less disjunct, less heterodox, and less challenging than work of
the 1960s or early 1970s—with the limit to be placed a little earlier
in the case of Stockhausen, whose technique of formula composition
was a kind of modality. The creeping influence of minimalism (itself, in
reverse, becoming ever more complex) may have had something to do
with this; so may a wish felt by many composers to fix themselves in
the soil of folk music, never mind ambitions for a place in orchestral
programming, which with rare exceptions (Ligeti's scores, in particular) resisted innovation even more firmly now than earlier. However,
the phenomenon was too widespread and too various in its manifestations to be regarded as anything other than a deep cultural shift.

Rootless Routes: Ligeti

Ligeti's return to the folk music of his youth, within a much wider world of reference and experience, had been evident in much of his work since the turning point of his Horn Trio (1982), though never yet so surprisingly as in the second movement of his Violin Concerto (1989–93), which the soloist begins alone, reaching back to the folk-style melody of another piece for lone soloist: the opening adagio of the Cello Sonata written forty years before. More than a quotation, this reuse reopens a question, for though the tune is openly diatonic and contained within the eminently singable span of an octave, it is now ambiguous in tonality and metre, a folk song in continuous search of home. It also calls to be understood within a vaster world than Ligeti could have realized in his twenties. The third of the subsequent variations has the melody on trumpet with trombone support beneath a wild high hocket for the solo violin with piccolo, and the next has the soloist playing in 4/4 against the 3/4 of the melody on horns producing natural harmonics. The composer's draft[1] is explicit about two of his sources for these inventions: Machaut and a more recent enthusiasm, pygmy music, characterized by the rhythmic independence of the polyphonic voices.

As for the just intonation, Ligeti could have found stimulus in Grisey's music as well as in that of Pacific cultures.[2] The concerto—his first instrumental work without a major keyboard component since *San Francisco Polyphony*, nearly twenty years before—offered opportunities to investigate further the acoustic and aesthetic effects of mixed tuning systems, tempered and untempered. According to his own account, he began by thinking about retuning a harp and a harpsichord, but realized he was 'entering a harmonic labyrinth so complicated that I was getting lost in it'.[3] He decided instead to have two instruments in the orchestra, a violin and a viola, tune their strings to natural harmonics played by the double bass and to have other natural harmonics sound directly into the score from brass instruments, multiplying the disparities of his Horn Trio and opening the way to those of his next and last orchestral work, the *Hamburgisches Konzert* with solo horn (1998–2002). Besides contributing to the strangeness and magic of these scores, 'mistuned' intervals opened the possibility of diatonic languages quite distinct from normal western tonality, an avenue Ligeti also ventured down in his Sonata for solo viola (1991–94).

Microtonally deviant modes afforded one means of creating a music that was, as he liked to say 'neither tonal nor atonal'; there were also

1. Reproduced in Richard Steinitz, *György Ligeti: Music of the Imagination* (London, 2003), 335.

2. See *»Träumen Sie in Farbe?«: György Ligeti im Gespräch mit Eckhard Roelcke* (Vienna, 2003), 195–96.

3. Ibid., 16.

the artificial modalities of melodies having the fractal quality of self-similarity on the small scale within a tonal chaos—that is, small motifs and significant intervals would recur at different pitch levels without the guidance of a scale repeating regularly in every octave, and certainly without any pull towards a tonic or modal final. The third movement of the Violin Concerto shows an instance, the soloist's melody throughout being built from three elements—a descent in chromatic, major-third, and whole-tone steps, a lift through a sixth or diminished seventh followed by a tritone fall, and a scalar rise—following on one another without any exact repetition or commitment to a particular scale. There need be no end to such a process. 'Caminantes, no hay caminos, hay que caminar.'

Further routes through fractal, fluctuating modalities are taken in the piano études Ligeti went on writing all this while. Etude 15 'White on White' (1995), which opens what he planned as his third book, unfolds almost entirely on the white keys, and though the largely scalar melodic motion of its slow first part—a strict canon disguised as a sequence of three-note chords—hints at European folk song, no tonal centre is established either melodically or harmonically. The much faster second part replays the wandering as stampede. 'Pour Irina' (1996–97), the next étude, is similar in its slow-fast form, the fast part going through three sections with gear changes in the ratios 2:3:4 (ending at around ten notes per second, close to physical limits), and similar, too, in its rootless modality. This time the first part draws from a six-note set C–Db–Eb–F–Gb–Bb (not a scale, since there is no starting or ending note), which yields a fluent blend of European and Indonesian flavours.

Another set, C–D–Eb–F–G–B, provides the point of departure for the seventeenth étude, 'À bout de souffle', and creates a much more chromatic world from the closeness of the two semitones. These are emphasized in the twist of melodic spiral, Eb–D–C–D–C–B, from which the piece seems constantly to be trying to escape, but which keeps appearing at the same or different levels around each new corner, as shown in example 86. Like the first section of 'White on White', the

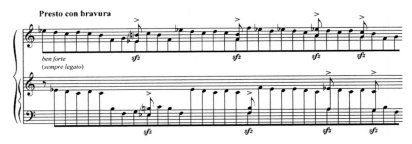

Example 86   György Ligeti, Etude 17 'À bout de souffle'

piece is, for most of its tearing length, a canon at the octave with the hands one beat apart. As in many of Ligeti's études, the modal and rhythmic aspects, touching on music from around the world but adrift from the regularities of tonal gravitation or metrical frame, are shreds of meaning in an incipient collapse. Whether the music's reaction to that state is desperate or ruminative becomes, as abrupt tempo changes often prove, largely a matter of speed.

Memory's Memorials: Berio and Kurtág

While Ligeti was travelling around the world of alternative musical cultures and tuning systems, Berio was sampling music nearer home. Always an adept arranger, he had accepted several invitations since the late 1970s to orchestrate existing music, including a Brahms sonata (*Opus 120 Nr. 1*, keeping the original solo part for clarinet or viola, 1984) and songs by Mahler (*Fünf Frühe Lieder*, 1986; *Sechs Frühe Lieder*, 1987) and Verdi (*Otto romanze*, 1991)—a body of work that culminated in completions not only of symphonic late Schubert, but also of Puccini's *Turandot* (2001) and of the unfinished contrapunctus from *The Art of Fugue* (2001). At the same time, traces of the great tradition were descending into his original compositions, or perhaps resurfacing there. This can be observed in his continuing *Sequenza* solos, which, from the violin piece (*VIII*, 1976–77) onwards, involve more fully formed gestures than had been the case before. For example, the accordion in *Sequenza XIII* (1995) keeps circling through certain harmonic regions and melodic traits, chief among the latter a fragment of a tune that starts out from descending fourths, E–B–F♯, the tone of virtuoso flamboyance characteristic of the earlier items in the series now replaced by one of fugitivity and loss.

This is the expressive condition of much of Berio's later music, and not least of his last two operas, *Outis* (1995–96) and *La cronaca del luogo* (1998–99), in which the drama turns increasingly from the allusiveness of the earlier such works that began as collaborations with Italo Calvino (*La vera storia* and *Un re in ascolto*) to a muteness betokening his growing absorption in the world of Celan. Music now is fathomless not so much because it is always susceptible to reinterpretation (the Ecoesque openness) as because what it should say is unsayable. Through the Norton Lectures he gave in 1993–94[4] runs the idea of the 'empty space', and his orchestral adagio *Continuo* (1989–91), revised as *Ekphrasis* (1996), is a voyage through such spaces. Once again the orchestra is reseated, with two groups of woodwinds and two of brass separated from a main group of clarinets, keyed instruments and strings, these projecting a long song that consistently floats through the echoes and shadows, interruptions and encouragements of the other groups. Rather

---

4. Published as *Remembering the Future* (Cambridge, Mass., 2006).

as in the third movement of Ligeti's Violin Concerto, though in a sombre key, the line keeps repeating its gestures in new contexts, seeking a stable habitation it will never find.

Besides setting lines by Celan in his two late operas, Berio took a phrase from the poet as epigraph for his last string quartet, *Notturno* (1993): '. . . You, the silenced word . . .', a phrase recalling the state of Moses at the end of Schoenberg's opera. The piece is close to silence quite directly in its dynamic level, often hovering between *p* and *ppp*, or even *pppp*, but it is so also in its faltering rhetoric. Its first figure, repeated several times, is a rising minor second that fades into note repetitions whose extreme quietness and haziness (the players are asked to alternate between strings, here and often later in the piece, to create a subtly tremulous sonority); even without the marking *molto lontano e parlando* one might imagine a mouth opening to speak but no word coming. When the viola eventually steps forward with a melody, arising out of an oscillating major third, it is shouted down by the first violin, and when this music returns, now with all the instruments becoming melodic voices, the marking is *come accompagnando*, as if the real song here were missing. An intense passage immediately after this filters away like water running through sand.

Within a world that has lost its way there remains one certainty. Continuing his *Játékok* all this while, Kurtág was occupied much more than before with *in memoriam* pieces, of which he produced eighteen in the 1990s (compared with seven in the 1980s). This may have been partly a matter of reaching an age at which mentors, senior colleagues, and elder friends are departing, but the importance of death to Kurtág is signalled also by the fact that the result of a residency with the Berlin Philharmonic—and his first work for standard orchestra since the 1950s—was an elegy, *Stele* (1994), scored for a Brucknerian complement including a quartet of Wagner tubas, to which he added only a characteristic group of keyed instruments. The work is a three-movement *symphonie funèbre*, made, like much of Ligeti's later music, with long-established elegiac figures. For example, the opening is in bold octave Gs, which through slow glissandos and vibratos weep away from confidence, and the rest of this adagio movement is made of frail offerings from different parts of the orchestra, with the lamenting image of a falling minor second ubiquitous. The second movement develops a fierce snarling into immense sonorities, and the finale—based on a *Játékok* piece of September 1993 written in memory of András Mihály, a composer and conductor who was a generous friend to Kurtág, as to many colleagues—recalls the music for the lake of tears in Bartók's *Bluebeard's Castle*. Through repetitions of what is essentially the same liquid musical event expressed as a sequence of polytonal chords, the work steps slowly on while keeping its gaze, always and unremittingly, in one place.

Remade Modes: Adès and Benjamin

For younger composers in the 1990s, Ligeti may have seemed the most encouraging signpost, pointing towards ways of achieving melodic definition and harmonic direction without restoring old-style tonality, or while doing so in an ungrounded manner, with a sense of the putative or playful. This was the period, for example, of the extraordinary youthful works of Thomas Adès (b. 1971), who recognized that Ligetian rhythmic-harmonic machines could be used to generate kinds of music less abstract than Ligeti's, absorbing ideas from or referring to anything from Renaissance polyphony to club music. Following Ligeti in his enthusiasm for Nancarrow, Adès often used polyrhythm to maintain two or more streams of activity and so ensure that no particular identity could quite take over (though some might threaten to). Typical, too, is a kind of scintillant or slippery tonality, supported by melodic lines that pick out concatenations of triads or by networks of widely spaced diatonic chords stepping in chromatic degrees. Such a world of variegated possibility could be home to figures of the most diverse kinds, and Adès showed other aspects of his inheritance—from Kurtág and Janáček, for instance—in devising compact and characterful images.

His string quartet *Arcadiana* (1994) contains several of these, ranging from a sultry tango to a summoning of 'Nimrod' from Elgar's 'Enigma' Variations, from a barcarolle to a fantasia largely in harmonics that whistles around and towards reminiscences of *The Magic Flute*. These and other musical states in Adès are always unstable, liable to vanish in a cloud of multicoloured dust; they are dream arcadias, provisional and uncertain asyla (to quote the title of his major symphonic work of this period, composed in 1997). Correspondingly, their harmony is often not a foundation but a superstructure, liable to totter or disintegrate but providing an atmosphere within and beneath which musical ideas can flourish, at least for the moment. *Arcadiana* starts out, as shown in example 87, from a characteristic harmonic aura of fifths on the steps of an augmented triad: C♯–G♯, F–C, A–E, providing a kernel of fifths, thirds, and minor seconds that provides material for everything that follows. Characteristic, too, is the repercussive setting of the fifths, and the subtle combination of colours, so that harmonies here are not so much asserted as proposed, interposed, hypothesized. And of course, the fifths come from the construction of the instruments, the first violin opening the last movement with an arpeggio of open strings to be played *molto espressivo* but also *quasi per accidente*.

In Benjamin's music, more than most, 1989 was a defining boundary. After an unproductive couple of years following *Antara* came *Upon Silence* (1989–90), setting a Yeats poem for mezzo-soprano with viol consort (or modern strings) in a style where modal tonalities are far more in the foreground than before in this composer's music, thanks in

Example 87   Thomas Adès, *Arcadiana*

part to a more scalar melodic style. As if released, Benjamin was now able to embark definitively on a long-considered orchestral project—*Sudden Time* (1989–93), a colourful fantasy at once strongly propelled and highly sophisticated—and other large scores, after which came reduction again to just two instruments in *Viola, Viola* (1997). The prompt here was a commission, but there was also the impetus of a wave of pieces that had discovered a new strength in the viola, pieces such as Grisey's *Prologue*, Schnittke's concerto of 1987, and Ligeti's sonata, and the further incentive of a new generation of outstanding players, including Yuri Bashmet and Nobuko Imai (who gave Benjamin's work its first performance), Tabea Zimmermann, Kim Kashkashian, and Garth Knox.

Viola, Viola is a plaiting of energetic impulses that, though modally diverse, combine to create a distinct harmonic tang having to do with

Example 88 George Benjamin, *Viola, Viola*

a general octatonic quality. As Benjamin observes, 'a larger array of instruments is suggested, each defined by motif, pace, dynamic and, above all, register'[5]—that is, in ways partly shown in example 88, from a crisis point about a third of the way through the ten-minute composition. For instance, the first viola's return to *fff* note pairs in the third bar easily sounds like an interruption from another instrument, and the subsequent emergence of a harmonic from behind the second viola's

5. Programme note printed in the score.

Example 88 (continued)

quasi-oriental ornamentation over a drone might give the impression
of ethereal violins in the distance. At least four of the work's basic elements are involved here: loud, staccato doubled notes, galloping upward runs, sforzando chords in sets of three, and decorated drones. The
first of these have hitherto been drawn from a partial octatonic collection (D–Eb–F–F♯–Ab), broken by the arrival of Bb, which lets in the sforzando chords, each bounded by a tritone plus an octave. These chords
had their origin in a triad stretched across a tenth at the beginning
(C–G–E), one of the flickers of traditional tonality to which the piece
does not betray its robust individuality; now they come from another
octatonic hexachord (Bb–B–D–E–F–G♯), made up of two examples of
what Benjamin calls 'the octatonic chord' and describes as a favourite
set,[6] that comprising a note plus its minor second and major third. One
may note also that the third of these chords has its outline picked up by
the second viola in the third bar, following a run that moves from one
octatonic scale (that of the sforzando chords) to another. The searing
fourteenth D–C♯ will, as is characteristic of the piece, carry the music
from one kind of urge or flow into another. Here all arrivals remain
provisional.

6. George Benjamin, *Les Règles du jeu: Entretiens avec Éric Denut* (Condé-sur-
Noireau, 2004), 95–96.

Pesson's Past and Pauset's

Berio's *Sinfonia* said it all: that time is fraying, but it is still 'our' time, the time of a collective 'we', whom the piece expects to share its memories of Mahler, Debussy, Strauss, and the rest, and even to share its attitudes to those memories. A generation later such things could not be presumed, and while many composers would not or could not keep an awareness of the past out of their work, for each the past would be different and the perspective different again. For Gérard Pesson (b. 1958) the image is archaeological: 'Music is the skeleton, and the few floating chords the brooch, belt, sword—residual signs of a life crumbled to dust.'[7] It is a sentiment that might have been echoed in the 1990s by Sciarrino or Lachenmann, two composers from whom Pesson took his bearings in treasuring the fragile and overlooked, though his music is more haunted than theirs: the 'residual signs' are present very often in metrical rhythm or overt gesture, sometimes in direct quotation, yet always brought into existence with a cool flair. What is remembered is individual, but not personal.

Pesson's biggest work of this period was a seventy-minute opera, *Forever Valley* (1999–2000), after the novel by Marie Redonnet, but even this is for chamber forces and most of his output is much more compact. His piano quartet *Mes Béatitudes* (1994–95), for example, is in ten sections averaging a minute and a half in length—stray reminiscences gathered together by a refrain of skidding in the high register, of whispered wisps, pulsing breathlessly, with the insistent rhythm of Wagner's Nibelungs emerging in the piano as the composition proceeds. Within that context the work includes a pantoum (a form, borrowed from Malay verse by way of Ravel's Piano Trio, that itself allows an assembly of varied fragments), a barcarolle founded on E♭ major chords in the piano and a 'Doux chant des morts' that quotes the second theme from the slow movement of Bruckner's Seventh Symphony, which the composer describes as 'one of the most beautiful melodies ever written'.[8] Quotations, allusions, and new ideas (unless all apparently new ideas are themselves veiled quotations or allusions) are brushed together as if being swept up from the floor of the composer's studio, and yet there is continuity, granted partly by the speed of the sweeping and partly by the presence of everything in the same dustpan. Pesson's form is, to be sure, more artful than he cares to admit (in, for instance, how the door is opened to the Bruckner theme), but the coherence of his music depends also on the hushed and exquisite instrumentation that conveys not only fragility but tenderness.

The past arrives not as floor-sweepings but as life at once present and distant in the music of Brice Pauset (b. 1965)—distant not only

---

7. *Cran d'arrêt du beau temps: Journal 1991–1998* (Paris, 2008), 183.
8. Note available at http://brahms.ircam.fr.

because Pauset is very conscious, as Pesson surely is, of standing now
long beyond the great ruptures of the mid-twentieth century but also
because his favoured historical territories are the early Renaissance
(from the ars subtilior to Ockeghem) and the Baroque, as if everything
between Bach and Webern had vanished, or remained only as a shadow
of itself. This must be somewhat a matter of taste, and perhaps also of
a desire to realize possibilities of sonority, articulation, and aura presented by period instruments, for though Pauset has pointed out that
the modern piano is also a period instrument, he has written for instruments more completely regarded as things of the past, such as the viola
d'amore, theorbo, and harpsichord that play in his *M for three singers
and two trios* (1996) alongside the more modern threesome of bass
flute, contrabass clarinet, and tuba (a Nono-like grouping he has used
in other scores). However, his inclination towards older music comes
as well from a distrust of the rhetoric that survived from Romanticism
into the modern era, and his affiliations in the nineteenth century
have been not with Pesson's beloved Bruckner (a distant beloved, no
doubt) but with composers whose music carries an uncertainty as to
the strength, singleness, and validity of the authorial voice: Schubert,
for whose A minor sonata he wrote the two framing movements of his
Kontra-Sonate (2000), intended specifically for Andreas Staier to play
on a Viennese piano of Schubert's time, and Schumann.

Several of Pauset's early works comprise sets of canons, a form suit-
ing him not only by virtue of its venerability, and not only in matching
the ruminative cast of his mind, but also in dividing music's voice. This
is not the canon as it was for Ockeghem or for Bach, however, but a
congruity that may have descended deeper into the music, virtually or
totally untraceable on its surface. As he has said, 'there [are] canonic
phenomena of a less direct nature, but also an integration of the forms
of a technique, in different parameters, different levels of organisation.'[9]
Worked with an intricacy worthy an admirer of Ferneyhough, Pauset's
counterpoint embeds and engenders a quiet lyricism of trailing suppo-
sitions, tight bursts of energy, and small defeats. His *Huit Canons* of 1998,
for oboe d'amore (a Baroque instrument also favoured by Ligeti) and an
expanded *Pierrot* group of flute, clarinet, piano, vibraphone, and string
trio, expresses all this in the shape of a chamber concerto—a genre almost inevitably raising questions of rhetoric in how the soloist will speak
to the ensemble and vice versa. Here the solo part does not emerge as
such until halfway through the second canon, where a 'denuding'[10]
creates an atmosphere of Webernian motivic polyphony out of which
the oboe d'amore's microtonally inflected line condenses. The relationship is followed in various phases through the continuous succession

9. 'Brice Pauset: Interview with Dan Warburton, January 8th 1997', http://
www.paristransatlantic.com.

10. See the composer's note, available at http://brahms.ircam.fr.

of canons, of which the seventh has the solo instrument alone until struck dumb by a single intervention from the ensemble, to be then crushed between the wheels of the massive, tutti finale, which, 'a chorale ruin in the form of a dead end, opens on to a coda in crumbling'.[11] The terms, after all, are not so different from Pesson's, for Pauset's struggle to engage with the past is undertaken in full knowledge of the colossal weight on the other side.

Traditions' Tracks: Around Zorn

The backwards gaze of the 1990s came partly from a longing for lost authenticity, an authenticity often felt to be still residing in non-western traditions or in traditions that had been preserved, albeit oppressively, from western anomie. Though there had been a Moscow avant-garde since the 1950s, its members had been trained in a musical culture dominated by Shostakovich, whose work went on being held up as a model in Beijing and Shanghai after the conservatories there had re-opened in 1978 following the Cultural Revolution. The Russian and Chinese composers who emigrated, as restraints slackened from the 1980s onwards, came from different generations: Schnittke and Gubaidulina were in their late fifties at the time they moved to Hamburg, in 1990 and 1992 respectively, whereas many of the new Chinese composers, including Chen Yi (b. 1953), Ge Gan-ru (b. 1954), Tan Dun (b. 1957), and Zhou Long (b. 1953), had still been in their twenties or early thirties when, a few years earlier, they left to complete their education in New York with Chou Wen-chung (b. 1923). Their emergence in the early 1990s was as new voices, whereas the Russians were fully mature by the time their music began to be known abroad anything but sporadically—from the late 1970s for Schnittke, who by then had two decades as a professional composer behind him.

Western responses to both groups, though, have been beset by similar conflicts and conundra. The music of Schnittke, Gubaidulina, and Ustvolskaya—and of other composers from the former Soviet Union, such as Giya Kancheli (b. 1935) and Tigran Mansurian (b. 1939)—is valued partly for what are perceived as national traits, having to do with a Russian tradition of art coming out of suffering and with local traditions in the cases of Kancheli (from Georgia) and Mansurian (from Armenia), whose music will often be at its strongest when the tradition is evoked as something broken or lost. That is not so with the Chinese composers, who commonly sought a liveness and presence in the Chinese elements (pentatony, the vocal delivery of Beijing opera, the use of gongs and drums as signalling instruments) they brought into Western-style music, along with a host of other influences to which young people in New York in the 1980s and 1990s would understandably

11. Ibid.

have been susceptible, from Hollywood film scores to Cage. Reborn Romanticism is often perceived differently if it is ex-Soviet, and orientalist eclecticism if it is Chinese.

An awareness of the dangers of stereotyping may be sensed in the work of other composers of the boom generation from the Far East, such as Toshio Hosokawa (b. 1955) and Unsuk Chin (b. 1961), both of whom, perhaps significantly, chose to finish their training in Germany with distinguished European composers: the former at Freiburg with Klaus Huber (b. 1924) and Ferneyhough, the latter at Hamburg with Ligeti. Hosokawa's absorption of lessons from the German-centred avant-garde appears to have preceded his reclaim of his Japanese heritage, as represented, for example, in the typical chords of the shō, while Chin, who has made her career wholly outside her native Korea, speaks in her music a mainstream Western-modernist language of high sophistication that can reflect a range of reference and colour, a language no more Asian than Ravel's, and perhaps less so. Similarly, even Hosokawa's more explicitly Japanese music, with its long, slowly modulating tones and preference for afloatness as a formal device, has parallels in the work of western composers—not least Chin's teacher. Chin and Hosokawa offer a reminder that even native languages have to be learned, and may equally be ignored.

If that is so, they may be learned and absorbed by anyone, as Cowell had proposed, and as many composers since the Renaissance had understood; authenticity inheres, if it does, in what is said, not in where it comes from. Hence the polyglot music of two other composers who came forward during this period: John Zorn (b. 1953) and Osvaldo Golijov (b. 1960). Zorn made his reputation in the late 1980s with two albums: one based on the film scores of Ennio Morricone (b. 1928), the second, *Spillane* (1987), of new, partly improvised tracks drawing on the full range of his musical experience. As he put it in his notes to the latter: 'I grew up in New York City as a media freak, watching movies and TV and buying hundreds of records. There's a lot of jazz in me, but there's also a lot of rock, a lot of classical, a lot of ethnic music, a lot of blues, a lot of movie soundtracks. I'm a mixture of all those things.'[12] Music and films in Japan, where he spent long periods around the time of *Spillane*, presented him with another 'vast, multifaceted culture that also steals . . . leeches upon other cultures, takes influences and mixes them in their own way'[13] (a Japan different from Hosokawa's). Soon, however, the mixture was tending to separate out a little. He went on working with improvising musicians, but his contact with the Kronos Quartet, involved on one track of *Spillane*, led to an invitation to write them a concert piece: hence *Cat O' Nine Tails* (1988), which chases from

---

12. Note with Nonesuch 9 79172-2.
13. William Duckworth, *Talking Music* (New York, 1995), 472.

one thing to another in the spirit of cartoon music, though over a wider range, from dark late Romantic progressions to bluegrass or tango, from hectic atonal counterpoint into a classical cadence.

Not just a metaphor, the cartoon score was a model. Zorn has said that the 'visual narrative' of such music—'all of a sudden this, all of a sudden that'[14]—provided him with a formal principle. *Cat O' Nine Tails* revealed him a virtuoso of comic timing (very little lasts longer than five seconds), and he created a similar zigzag, but through keyboard possibilities, in *Carny* for piano (1991). Yet though his music throve on the energy and the danger of humour, that was not its only mode; the jump cut could be ominous, startling or mysterious as well as funny. In *Aporias* (1994), described as 'requia for piano and orchestra', he composed a three-quarter-hour sequence of ten memorials to recently deceased heroes, including Elias Canetti and Marlene Dietrich, as well as Cage and Messiaen (remembered here without style imitation, though Messiaen's is one of the many languages Zorn has mastered). Now the leaps across gulfs of genre expose discontinuity as the human condition.

While discovering himself as a 'classical' composer (or rediscovering, since there were notated pieces from before), Zorn continued to work in the fields of jazz, experimental improvisation, and film music, and in 1995 he founded a record label, Tzadik, not only to handle his own bewildering productivity but also to release or rerelease music by members of his classical pantheon, including Babbitt, Brown, Feldman, and Wolff. His own notated music during this period remained overwhelmingly instrumental, perhaps from an uncertainty about how the narrative of a text could fit with the quick changes and reverses of his musical style. He was far from immune, however, to the power of language, as of music and film, and several of his pieces—made on the small scale out of tributes to this or that in his vast record collection (13,000 items he estimated around 1990)—were conceived as homages to admired writers (Walter Benjamin, Artaud, Bataille) as well as directors (Godard), visual artists (Joseph Cornell), and composers (Berg).

The object of honour in *Shibboleth* for string trio, percussion and clavichord (1997) is Celan, whose name appears to be encoded in the initial gesture, where a viola lament is placed in the context of a first-inversion A minor triad (thus spelling C–E–A from the bass). A fascination with ciphers is one of Zorn's links with Berg, who could also be cited as a master of quasivisual narrative, often involving reference or composing by type. *Shibboleth* typically sounds like a score for an unseen film, and, also typically, very different shots are often generated from the same pitch material. For instance, the fifth and penultimate section, 'etwas wie Nacht' (the section titles come from Celan poems),

14. Ibid., 471.

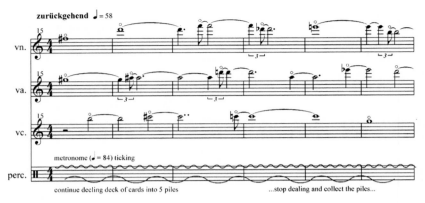

Example 89　John Zorn, *Shibboleth*

begins with a sequence of notes already heard as a clavichord melody in even values, as a violin melody exactly matching this and as a hocket for strings, a sequence now heard, with very small adjustments, in sustained high string harmonics. (Zorn mentions that the shibboleth in Judges 12 was a password whose pronunciation distinguished the Ephraimites from the Israelites, and also that the word was the title of a Celan poem, besides being used by Derrida in his essay on the poet, 'Shibboleth for Paul Celan'.[15]) The strings play with practice mutes, *pp* throughout, and are accompanied at this point by the percussionist with a pack of cards, as shown in example 89, which may be compared in its combination of standard and nonstandard categories of sound with Wolpe's Oboe Quartet (example 17).

This short passage exemplifies several qualities of Zorn's music, besides his eagerness to recycle even his own material. One is his skill with arresting and multireferential images, alluding in this case to the cardsharp as a sinister figure in movie history and perhaps also to the card games of Stravinsky (in *Histoire du soldat, Jeu de cartes,* and *The Rake's Progress*). Another is his alert attention to other music, with Kagel and Ligeti perhaps invoked here. Yet another is that the music is made for recording. The dynamic level is low not only for the strings but also for the keyboard player, the clavichord being again a practice instrument, and for the percussionist. Where Berio's Celan chamber piece seems to be made for a recital hall, in which it would have to be not so much heard as overheard, Zorn's presumes a close attention to quietness by way of microphones. In that respect his classical music is not so different from his nonclassical, being made to be put together by chosen musicians in the studio. What makes it classical is the deep subtext of history it incorporates in its notation, its references, and the training it expects of its performers.

15. Note with Tzadik TZ 8035.

These are features, too, of Golijov's music, with the difference that conventional performing media and venues are still implied, as might be expected from a composer who sought a lengthier academic training, in his native Argentina, in Israel (1983–86), and in the United States, where he settled. His discourse is similarly more conventional, maintaining a particular style or mélange for a whole movement, though there is the same open acceptance of idioms from all over. To a basic language of Piazzolla mixed with klezmer and regularized for the concert hall with Bartók and Stravinsky, he brought strains from a variety of Jewish sources in the chamber works with which he began his public career: *Yiddishbbuk* for string quartet (1992) and the clarinet quintet *The Dreams and Prayers of Isaac the Blind* (1994). An extension to Afro-Cuban drumming, plainsong, Brazilian percussion, and flamenco brought forth the exuberance of *La Pasión según San Marcos* for solo singers and dancers with choir and orchestra (2000). As Golijov's music may suggest, and Zorn's still more so, relevance, as well as authenticity, is established not by deeds of ownership but by the immediacy with which music from a given source has been made to speak again.

26

Towards the
Strange Self

Romanticism was not only a style but also an expressive attitude, valuing individual experience, and its postmodern resurgence, reaching an apogee in the 1990s, brought both aspects back to the fore, the subjectivity as well as the rhetoric, scale, means, and forms. But this would often be a warier subjectivity than before. Perhaps subjectivity is by definition bound to be self-aware, but the subjectivity of the late twentieth century involved extremes and hesitations, ironies and puzzles bespeaking uncertainty as to the nature of what was at once its object of interest and its source. Composers turned increasingly not only to writers who spoke of and from marginal or fragmented states, Hölderlin and Wölfli now joined by Robert Walser, but also to those whose inward gaze lit upon mirrors and blank walls: Kafka, Celan, Beckett. Opera became again a prime vehicle for such investigations, leading at the end of the century (also of the millennium) to an extraordinary succession of works.

Act I: Schneewittchen

Walser's play with the characters of the Snow White story gave Holliger the ideal substrate for an opera of profound mistrust, an opera he composed in 1997–98. The story itself is over; what remains is for the characters to consider it (which is why it must be a story the audience can be counted upon as already knowing). These characters are by no means neutral observers, for they have been participants in the story, and they may now have reason to falsify, deny, exaggerate, or ridicule what the story relates. In doing so, they have no compunction in contradicting themselves even within a single sentence, because they know they are not responsible for themselves, being characters. The moral ground has slipped away; they dangle in the air, and exert themselves with furious motions of hatred, animal lust, jealousy, belligerence, and sarcasm—motions that are fully operatic emotions—because the only alternative is silence and death. It is an Alice-in-Wonderland world, except that there is no Alice as stable point, for though Snow White is more dependable than the thoroughly carnal, murderous, and deceitful Queen and the impotent Prince, who are the other two major figures, she is equally adrift.

As a setting of an existing dramatic work, Holliger's opera falls in with a tradition going back to *Pelléas et Mélisande*—a tradition liberally stocked in the second half of the twentieth century, especially within the German-speaking region. But where *Literaturoper* commonly profits from the drama it consumes, from its psychological plot and psychological characters, Walser's fairy-tale play offers a collapsing assembly of shifting levels. Its guiding force is not representation but misrepresentation, not will but whim. And this perfectly suits music that, like Holliger's, loves to multiply its meaning and focus, music where form is not the bedrock but something crystallizing out in the surface, as canons do as frequently here as in the *Scardanelli-Zyklus*.

The text, governed by the iambic tetrameter and having a folk-ballad register, is set with due respect for its conscious crudity (especially in the Queen's part) but mostly in short phrases erratic in contour, with Marie's lullaby from *Wozzeck* a model for the role of Snow White.[1] The effect, however, is very different from that of expressionist opera (a genre with which *Literaturoper* is almost coextensive), partly because wide intervals and *fortissimos* do not necessarily imply emotional extremity (for we can never be sure these characters are being true to themselves—indeed, that they have notions of 'truth' or 'themselves'), partly because the whole tone of the piece can switch in an instant from (playful) savagery to (savage) playfulness, and partly because the orchestra does not reinforce the vocal gestures except—and very often —ironically. It is essential to the bewildering, bewitching groundlessness of the opera that the orchestra is no solid foundation. Instead it puts forward a variegated succession of ensembles, determined to some extent by who is singing at the time (Snow White, being drawn again and again to themes of death, snow, and her glass coffin, is often accompanied by high, shimmering sounds, notably those of glass harmonica and celesta with solo violin) and by mood, but projecting also a musical superabundance, a flourishing of invention that starts out

---

1. See Roman Brotbeck, 'On Heinz Holliger's Opera "Snow White"', published with the recording on ECM 1715/16.

from something in the vocal line (a rhythm, an image, a pun) to spin away into the gravitationless outer space where all this appears to be happening.

Events there can still exert immense power, as when the Queen has the Huntsman re-enact the killing of Snow White. Just before the deed is done, while the Huntsman holds his dagger raised, the brass together with percussion and wailing woodwind express alarm, and the composer, by ludicrously extending the moment, at once intensifies and undercuts it, in a tactic typical of the piece. The alarm music is cut off abruptly by a whip crack, and the Queen invites everyone to go out into the garden, pictured in music that starts out from a rising arpeggio in the harp—an about-turn of musical atmosphere that is again here the norm.

Perhaps the most poignant moment comes in the next scene, where the Huntsman asks Snow White if she believes he meant to kill her. It might be tempting to say that her 'Yes and yet no' expresses uncertainty, except that the opera, certainly by this late point, has made us cautious about interpreting motivation. These characters, whose displayed behaviour is so inconsistent and often outrageous, are totally opaque as to their inner lives, and we can do no more than try to stay with Snow White as she sings that she is tired of 'no' and that 'yes' is beautiful. So 'yes' will be her answer, extraordinarily reinforced at this point, shown in example 90. We may have forgotten—she may have forgotten—quite what the question was. She may be more involved in playing with words, even when it comes to tossing contraries about, as would not be unusual for this opera, where meaning comes from meaning lost, suspended in doubt, bifurcated or betrayed, all with the fine precision of Holliger's writing and his consciousness of multiple reference points, structural and historical. She may also be seizing the moment of this 'yes' to assert for once her independence, which the orchestra reassuringly echoes back to her—though many other explanations are possible, musical and dramatic. The triad is a destination as ambivalent as Snow White's response; it might be right or wrong, or it might be the right answer to the wrong question. It might also be a golden sun shining out into an empty universe.

Entr'acte: Kurtág's Beckett

Beckett's plays, along with Bornemisza again (his Hungarian version of the *Elektra* of Sophocles), were subjects Kurtág was considering when, in the 1980s and 1990s, he thought he might write an opera, and though what surfaced from the obvious affiliation was a pair of concert works—*Samuel Beckett: What is the Word* for contralto, voices, and ensembles (1990–91) and . . . *pas à pas—Nulle part* . . . for baritone with string trio and percussion (1993–98)—these are dramatic productions of their texts, to be delivered by soloists who are, as much as when

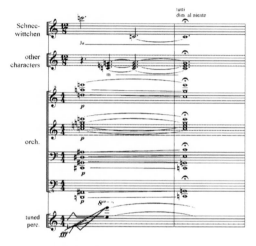

Example 90   Heinz Holliger, *Schneewittchen*

singing opera, in character. The singing persona, hardly more than a vague and transparent convention in most song literature, is here the figure on stage.

   That almost defines the vocal style, almost denuded of overt lyricism (only one of the twenty-nine vocal segments in *... pas à pas ...* has this in its extended phrases) to project the words, often one by one, through sung tones. It was a style Kurtág had developed before, notably in some of his *Kafka-Fragmente*, and to which he was now driven further not only by Beckett but also by meeting the actress Ildikó Monyók, who had lost her powers of speech as a result of a car accident and was learning to speak again through learning to sing. This kind of therapy—someone playing a note on a piano and so eliciting a sung word from the patient, then another—reminded Kurtág of the late Beckett piece 'What is the Word', which deals with faltering articulacy, and which he thereupon set in Hungarian for Monyók to perform with upright piano; she would thus have to take on the character of herself in making her former treatment into a performance. The pianist plays a note and looks to the singer to respond; the piano is a help, giving the singer her note, but it is also (as help sometimes is in a medical context) a scourge, driving the singer on in search of the right word, a quest that can never be ended, only abandoned. In the larger version that followed, the singer and pianist onstage are joined—heckled—by groups around the auditorium (as in . . . *quasi una fantasia* . . .), including a group of singers who shadow the soloist in English. Seeming to correct, mock and impel her, they add another layer of theatre to the drama of the struggle to enunciate.

All this is replayed in . . . *pas à pas* . . . as subtext to a sequence of brief statements from among Beckett's poems and translations of aphorisms by Sébastien Chamfort. Here the singer has no trouble finding the *mot juste*, except that the words, whose piecemeal setting respects and even intensifies the lostness they have on the page, are nearly always drawing attention to what lies around them: the silence of what is unsaid and unsayable. This silence is not mitigated by the instrumentalists, since their parts, like that of the pianist in *What is the Word*, are built on the singer's, to support and to force on—and, like those of the offstage singers in the larger version of the earlier work, to imitate (even vocally at some points), counter, and, more rarely, sympathize. As observers, these ensembles in both compositions partly occupy the unsettling position the audience has in witnessing an ordeal.

Act II. Luci mie traditrici

This is again an old story, that of Gesualdo's murder of his wife and her lover, and an older story in its concern with infidelity and revenge. Once again, too, the characters have some inkling of this. Based on a seventeenth-century drama, most of Sciarrino's chamber opera (1996–98, see example 91) plays out between the husband (baritone) and wife (soprano); just two of the work's eight scenes involve the wife and her lover (contralto or countertenor), who vanishes halfway through. The central couple know where the action is going, and their expressive resources, which one may imagine once to have been vivid, are now etiolated. They sing almost entirely in short, quiet phrases, giving full voice only very briefly in the final scene, much of which is contrastingly whispered. Also, wherever they are in the opera, they keep going over the same ground, repeating a few melodic formulae.

As the composer observes, without false modesty, the work is 'an opera in the full sense of the term', in that 'its power rests in expression through song, in the creation of a vocal style'[2]—a new style fashioned just for this piece, for these dramatic figures and for their dialogues, at

2. Salvatore Sciarrino, *Carte da suono (1981–2001)*, ed. Dario Oliveri (Rome, 2001), 108.

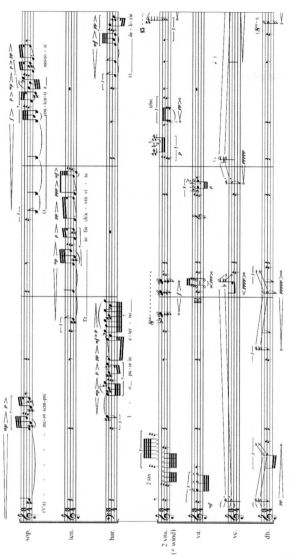

Example 91   Salvatore Sciarrino, *Luci mie traditrici*

once highly charged and tentative, close and remote. The conditions of the love duet, where characters customarily keep singing the same thing to each other, have bled out into the entire seventy-minute piece, but with the material grown fragile through overuse. Example 91 shows some of this simultaneously manic and passive imitation from the second scene, which features the wife and husband with an unseen servant. The accompaniment is unusually light but otherwise typical; the wind instruments very rarely produce normal tone (tongue clicks from the saxophones are heard here, breath noises from the trombone) and the strings play harmonics throughout. Only in the first of three intermezzos—arrangements of a lament by Claude Le Jeune that is sung unaccompanied as prologue—is the orchestral sound regular, fading in the other two as if 'marked by the wounds of time'.[3] If not lost in some kind of collapsed and oozing love duet, the body of an opera that has itself been murdered in flagrante delicto, it could be that the characters are still rehearsing their roles, trying ideas out in different situations and guarding their voices for an opera that is yet to come. Singers and instrumentalists, whose flickers, breath tones, and harmonics are at a low but very present, bodily present, level, seem to be engaged in what is either the shuddering remnant of an opera or the tentative beginning.

The prominence of Gesualdo as a topic at the end of the century—treated in Schnittke's eponymous opera (1994) and in *Carlo* for string orchestra with sampler (1997) by Brett Dean (b. 1961) as well as the Sciarrino work—may have something to do with Stravinsky's example but perhaps more with the extremity of Gesualdo's own music and with the invitation his music and his life offer to press for correspondences, for traces, for loci of sensitivity that link the one with the other. This, too, may be what Sciarrino's characters and his orchestra are engaged in as they feel their way through darkness (for though the scenes march through the day from morning to night, the musical light is held at an exquisite minimum), as, surrounded by waiting chasms of suspicion and betrayal, they exchange what evidence they can of their faint selves.

Entr'acte: Birtwistle's Celan

With the century moving near its close and those with adult memory of its worst growing old, the scar did not fade, and at such a time the poetry of Celan became ever more necessary. It spoke to many composers —to composers as different as Berio and Zorn, as has been noted, and also to Kurtág, who made Celan's meditation on Hölderlin the destination of his own homage (*Hölderlin-Gesänge* 1993–97), as well as to others who had, like Holliger, come to the poet long before. Rihm, who had composed a set of four Celan songs in 1973 and written a memorial

3. Ibid.

to the poet in his violin concerto *Lichtzwang* of 1975–76, placed a Celan poem at the end of his oratorio *Deus Passus* (1999–2000); Peter Ruzicka (b. 1948) similarly began an engagement with Celan very young, in 1969, and in 1998–99 created a full-length opera on the subject of the poet.

Like none of these, Birtwistle was both newcomer and outsider, and the work he produced in response to Celan was unusual: *Pulse Shadows* (1989–96), a sequence of nine songs alternating with nine movements for string quartet. The long period of work, itself unusual for this composer, is explained by the gradual process of discovery. Birtwistle first set a Celan poem in 1989 to answer a commission from the Composers Ensemble, whose lineup comprised soprano with two clarinets and low string trio (viola, cello, double bass); he then added two more settings for this formation in 1992. Similarly, a single quartet movement of 1991 prompted another two in 1993. Only when these triptychs were finished did Birtwistle decide that they belonged together, and that their interaction could generate a further threefold increase.

The bonding is no less tight for coming partly after the fact. Indeed, it is essential to the hour-long composition that incongruities exist (as well as points of relation that are sometimes even motivic), between the two sets of pieces and the two ensembles, which are alike only in having a viola—and it must be a different viola, since at times the two groups overlap. Birtwistle's opposition of 'cantus' and 'continuum' is once more playing itself out, with the songs' natural emphasis on melody offset by the machinery of the quartet pieces, ruled by pulse and ostinato—particularly in the four 'frieze' movements,[4] where tempo is fixed almost to the end. The songs are not only more fluid, they also have a good deal of rhythmic independence among the parts. Of course, there are also places where one kind of music interferes in the other's domain, whether songlike lines breaking through the bars in the quartet movements or pulsed patterns fixing themselves into the songs (as pulse shadows, perhaps).

Birtwistle does not disdain using pulse as an image of clock time, notably in the song 'With Letter and Clock', most of which has a patter of roughly five-per-second pulsations. But there seems to be more than this to the separation and partial interpenetration of pulsed time and drift (to use a word from the beautiful song 'White and Light' that was the starting point). At the end of the song placed first, 'Thread suns' (also set by Rihm), come lines that sound like an apologia from the poet, and through him from the composer: 'there are/still songs to be sung on the other side/of mankind'. Again not resisting the obvious but

---

4. See an analysis of 'Frieze 4', a response to Celan's 'Todesfuge', in Arnold Whittall, 'The Mechanisms of Lament: Harrison Birtwistle's "Pulse Shadows"', *Music and Letters*, 80 (1999), 86–102.

making it an achievement, Birtwistle writes a luscious melisma for the word 'sung', over just a low, soft fourth from the clarinets. Then he introduces a little figure repeating at intervals of almost a second, a clockwork mechanism that the soprano avoids falling in with. From the song's point of view, pulsation seems to represent 'the other side of mankind'; this may be, however, where the song, where the singing persona, actually is.

While this project remained unfinished (though he may not yet have realized the fact) Birtwistle wrote an opera, *The Second Mrs Kong* (1993–94), in which all the characters are dead, dwelling in the 'World of Shadows'. Not least among them is Orpheus, after his failure to draw Eurydice out from that very world. What may be happening in *Pulse Shadows* is that the work of an esteemed poet is being felt for its sympathetic vibrations with the composer's own central subject. Simply by taking the poetry away from its original language and using Michael Hamburger's translations, Birtwistle removes it from the thrall of German expressionism and makes it amenable to his own lyrical style. He creates a dematerialized effect by the voice's lack of rhythmic body and its commonly high perch, around the top of the treble staff, with E a significant note as it frequently is in his music; four of the songs start out from that note, including three in succession, and in a fifth, 'Tenebrae', it is used for the repeated word 'Lord'. Though the voice is luminous in this elevated register, and illuminated further by how the instruments sway around it with the same notes or create a harmonic foil beneath, it may be the voice of one of the shadows, taken from one shadow world, that of Europe in the mid-twentieth century, to another, Orphic, and granted an exit, for the voice goes on, projecting a sustained, high A♭ with amplification, after the instruments have finished, to the word 'light'.

Act III: *Three Sisters*

What is a life? There was an encounter with Eötvös earlier as one of the founders of the New Music Studio in Budapest and as a performer in Stockhausen's group. Another version of this book might have pointed out how rare it was for a young musician to follow a double career on both sides of the Iron Curtain in the late 1960s, and gone on to note that Eötvös settled in Cologne, where he was associated in the early 1970s with the Feedback Studio, a composers' collective formed by other members and ex-members of the Stockhausen team, his somewhat Kagelian compositions of this period including *Radames* (1975), a mini-opera for four singers and four instrumentalists. The story could have been picked up in the 1980s, by which time he had virtually abandoned composition to become a leading conductor of new music, responsible for the world première of Stockhausen's *Donnerstag* and for developing the Ensemble InterContemporain as its first music director (1978–91). Now, in the 1990s, he was still conducting while concentrating on composition again, his output of that decade including a dozen concert pieces, most of them on a large scale, besides, in 1996–97, a full-length opera.

Whereas Holliger and Sciarrino chose to set rather obscure plays that either embodied or could be edited to embody (in the Sciarrino case) an unusual kind of dramatic narrative, Eötvös took one of the great classics of the theatre and, together with his co-librettist Claus H. Henneberg, created a new form by radical alteration. Instead of the four acts of the Chekhov original, progressing through time, the opera offers three 'sequences', or successions of episodes in which the same story is glimpsed through the eyes of one of the characters: the younger two sisters, Irina and Masha, and between them their brother Andrey. To situate these different viewpoints is one of the music's functions; for example, the orchestral sound in the Andrey sequence has by design a more male character, lower in register, rhythmically robuster. But, as in any opera, it is music's place as well to create the temporality in which the characters and their stories exist. Eötvös's piece has dialogue passages where time pushes forward emphatically, but it also has pools of slack time, where vocal motifs are copied and repeated or harmonically reflected within the echo chamber of the score, which is for two orchestras: an eighteen-piece group in the pit, similar in lineup to a standard new-music ensemble, and a larger ensemble behind the acting area. Music gives the characters identity and emotion, and yet it equally surely expresses—even contrives—their helpless passivity. The world of action lies elsewhere: in Moscow, and in a more directed time that the Prozorov siblings can only observe in others. Their condition, by implication, is not unique to them. Casting back to the last fin-de-siècle (Chekhov wrote the play in 1900), Eötvös created a work for another epoch when the calendar would shift but the human mind and body would not.

His piece belongs to its moment also in recognizing the new importance of countertenors on the operatic stage. The early music movement, and especially the growing appetite for Handel's operas since the 1970s, had brought forward a strong generation of such artists, and Eötvös provided roles for four, as the sisters and their sister-in-law (though women singers may alternatively be engaged). Links are formed with other species of theatre in which men assume female roles, notably kabuki, but the main effect of the cross-sex casting is to emphasize the distance from the naturalist particularities of the play, to present something universally human stranded.

Entr'acte: Kyburz's No-one

By no means was another Hungarian, Ligeti, the only composer to interest himself in generative procedures during a period, the 1980s, when

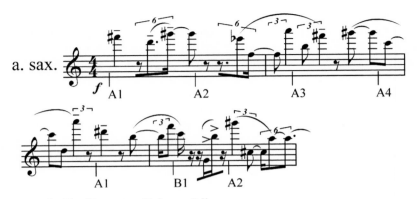

Example 92   Hanspeter Kyburz, *Cells*

computers were becoming familiar domestic items in the developed world. Hanspeter Kyburz (b. 1960) attended a conference on chaos theory in 1989 and began investigating the compositional possibilities of L-systems, named after Aristid Lindenmayer, who had elaborated them to provide models of plant growth. An L-system is based on an axiom with rules of transformation. For example, if we start with *a* and apply the rules *a→b* and *b→ab*, then a chain emerges: *a–b–ab–bab–abbab–bababbab–abbabbababbab*, etc. As this simple example shows, self-similar features start to reveal themselves, such as in this case *bab* and *abbab* (which is commoner than *abab*), their occurrences irregular and therefore unpredictable, unless one knows or divines the rules. Kyburz recognized how useful such systems could be when applied to sets of pitches or durations, engendering both pattern and process—and how useful computers could be in accomplishing the necessarily more complex transformations involved in working with musical motifs rather than a rudimentary pair of items.

From that understanding came *Cells* for saxophone and ensemble (1993–94), of which example 92 shows a sequence from the solo part. As Martin Supper has indicated,[5] the sequence is based on a three-note cell and on various rules, which include $A^1{\to}A^2$, $A^2{\to}A^3$, $A^3{\to}A^4$, $A^4{\to}A^1B^1$, $B^1{\to}B^2$ and $B^2{\to}B^3$. The chain splits whenever an A4 appears, whereupon Kyburz follows the two paths in alternation. Note that the second appearance of A^1 is a transposition of the first, down three semitones, with very little change of rhythmic shape, but, since this is the exception, there must be other rules in play, perhaps concerning how a cell is affected by what comes immediately before it. No doubt the composer also allows himself to intervene, in order to enhance or correct the system's image of natural growth and so attain that Carterian paradox of stable instrumental character in continuous flow.

5. Martin Supper, 'A Few Remarks on Algorithmic Composition', *Computer Music Journal*, 25 (2001), 48–53.

For music seemingly coursing of itself but bound by impenetrable rules, Kyburz found a literary analogue in an illustrated book that has defied attempts to decipher it for four centuries, a book on which he based his first acknowledged vocal work, *The Voynich Cipher Manuscript* (1995), devised for twenty-four singers and seventeen players split into vocal-instrumental groups around the audience. Written in an unknown script by an unknown author, the Voynich manuscript could be read— or unread—as a metaphor for contemporary music: a message is being conveyed, one seemingly of great sophistication and moment, but in an unfamiliar language. There is every evidence of communication going on, but this is more observed than received.

Since the Voynich text cannot be set (we do not know how it should sound, or even if it could sound at all, as it may be a sixteenth-century hoax), Kyburz created his own assemblage of numbers, Latin and English syllables, and so on, in the spirit of the original, and added poems Khlebnikov (a poet also noted by Nono) wrote in his 'futuristic-archaic "star language"'.[6] None of this, of course, imperils the sense of wonderful and abundant bafflement that is one of the score's most Voynichian aspects, along with the pleasures and virtues of bafflement: that meanings may be constantly in flux, the music spinning with references to choral chant, solo song, virtuoso instrumental study, or string chamber practice as music rains all around the hall.

Act IV. Das Mädchen mit den Schwefelhölzern

Holliger, Sciarrino, and Eötvös had all been writing dramatic works since the 1970s, and had all moved, in keeping with the moderating current of the time, from compact experimental music-theatre to full-length opera. Lachenmann had none of that background, and indeed had written no vocal music of any kind for well over two decades when, in 1990, he set out to compose an opera on Hans Christian Andersen's story 'The Little Match Girl', a work he finished six years later. To keep faith with his earlier music (and to do otherwise would have been unthinkable for a composer of such moral conviction) he would be bound to remake the genre, just as he had remade the string quartet, the piano concerto, and other types. His opera duly has no singing characters, its pair of sopranos being as integrated with the orchestra as its pair of pianos, and though it follows the story in outline—though, too, its composer describes it as 'music with scenes'—there are no actions or situations that have to be represented onstage. The story is told by voices from within the chorus, often susurrant, the challenge of the tale exacerbated by the quasi-secrecy with which it has to be divulged, as something almost unspeakable, for in the very act of making it the subject of an opera, engaging large forces in complex activity for two

6. Note by Kyburz with Col Legno WWE 3CD 31898.

hours, Lachenmann lifts it out of the realm of children's literature and makes it an accusatory parable, while keeping much of its delicate, touching quality intact. Tracking the story, but in no ordinary way dramatizing the events, the work offers no illusion, no illusions, and in its vast vacancy brings reality into the theatre through the medium of music: not only the reality of which the original story tells but also that of the world outside, to which the story provides a mirror, and that of music itself, firmly maintaining an existence under hostile circumstances.

By no means is the contact with the outer world just a matter of description and sound effects, even though Lachenmann finds a poetry of cold in his extreme but here predominantly pitched sonorities (quiet and sustained string harmonics, breath tones, chinks in the highest register of the piano) and comes up with the required richness and surprise for the girl's visions: a Ligetian soundscape of bulging, glowing sounds happening one upon another for the domestic stove she imagines, for instance. Reality is exposed also, and much more, in the transparency of the score to the situation beyond the theatre, in the invitations offered to listen not only to the music but through it, to the story and to what that story has to say, when told in so acute a way, about the world. Perhaps this was in Lachenmann's mind when he said, in connection with his „. . . *zwei Gefühle* . . ." for ensemble with narration (1991–92), a scene from the opera that can be performed separately as a concert piece, that 'the attentive perception of immediate sound, and of the connections at work therein, is connected to internal images and sensations that in no way distract from the process of attention but rather remain inseparably linked to it and even lend it a particular characteristic intensity'.[7] A more conventional operatic narration could not have anything like the same force, either as music or as political statement.

There are ironies here, of course. Lachenmann's opera benefited from the state patronage that has fostered much of the music considered in this book, especially that from Germany. As an instance of government-funded social criticism it is in a precarious position, but it seems conscious of—seems to exist in—that very precariousness. It claims the right to speak within a major forum, the opera house, and to speak otherwise than does the standard repertory performed there. In declining linear narrative and theatrical imagery it refuses to behave appropriately, and yet there is nothing rude or banal about its inappropriateness. Indeed, only by offering a musical experience of astonishing range, freshness, and grace can it insist, as it does, on the independence and freedom of music, exactly as it insists on the imperilled life of its unseen, unheard but omnipresent heroine. In providing no easy

---

7. Helmut Lachenmann, *Musik als existentielle Erfahrung*, ed. Josef Häusler (Wiesbaden, 1996; 2004), 402.

explanation for what is heard, it asks its audience to listen alertly. A story is being told. But that story is not comfortably, comfortingly enclosed within the theatre; it seems, rather, to be reverberating from beyond the building's walls, to be sensed within in wisps and shivers, or sometimes in more formidable shocks.

Narrative here is a vehicle that is, for once, not moving smoothly along familiar rails but is, rather, being pushed down a cobbled street, and the jolts and awkwardness in the storytelling are part of the point, exactly as they were in this composer's earlier works. They are essential to the drama and tension of the piece. But there are also the keenly dramatic moments any opera should have, including the opening of the penultimate scene, when Lachenmann's fearsome 'Ascension' for the full forces—at once an image of the match girl's rise to heaven and a protest at her death—gives way to the new sound of the shō, lightly accompanied, bringing forward another space, not necessarily in the hereafter but perhaps ideally to be found in this world, a promise. This might be the answer to another of the work's crises, when members of the chorus, speaking, keep insisting against orchestral onslaughts on the word 'Ich'. It is in defence of the first person singular that this opera, whose heroine has been almost pressed out yet is everywhere to be felt and heard, makes its powerful voice heard.

27

Towards
Transcendence

It need be no surprise that with the return of the subjective came the return of the metaphysical, for the address in both is to the unfathomable beyond consciousness and will. Here again, the opening of borders with Eastern Europe and China may have played a part, in bringing into the musical commonwealth composers who felt no embarrassment in expressing themselves in religious terms. Growing up and working in an officially atheist state may have intensified that impulse in such composers as Gubaidulina, Pärt, and Ustvolskaya (of whom the last wrote nothing after the fall of the Soviet Union), and, too, in their young Chinese colleagues, who, whatever they learned in New York, were eager to place themselves also within an indigenous tradition going back centuries, if not millennia, a tradition in which music was by nature invocation. However, attitudes were changing, too, in the West. Continuing developments in minimalism, electronics, and spectral music were bringing many composers closer to the substance of their art—to considering not only what could be done with sound but what sound itself could do, in realms beyond the physical. The drive to retrieve past ways of musical thinking had the same effect. There were composers who had made clear their spiritual aims from long before, whether those aims were Christian (Messiaen and Tavener, as well as many from the former Soviet Union), Jewish, Buddhist, or more esoteric (Scelsi, Stockhausen, and Radulescu), but by the 1990s higher purposes were becoming quite normal.

Lachenmann, ends one of his essays by quoting Beethoven's remark that 'whatever is to touch the heart must come from above' and adding the postscript: 'This only leaves the question: where is "above" . . . ?'[1]

Gubaidulina and Christ

When, in 1995, the International Bach Academy of Stuttgart determined to commission settings of the four Passion stories for the millennial year of 2000—also the 250th anniversary of Bach's death—Gubaidulina was an obvious choice (more so than Golijov, who took on St Mark for this occasion, the other two composers involved being Rihm and Tan). Not only had she been dealing explicitly with Christian themes from long before—even when living in the Soviet Union, her *In croce* for cello and organ having been introduced in Kazan in 1979—but Bach and the B–A–C–H motif had been reference points in other works of hers besides *Offertorium*. The resulting St John Passion for soloists, choir, orchestra and organ (1999-2000) is a work very different from Pärt's of eighteen years earlier: big and overwhelmingly dark, the gospel narrative (much of which is chanted by a solo bass, answered by two choral groups and other soloists, with a powerful atmosphere of Russian liturgical music) intercut with scenes from the same author's Revelation.

As in her earlier works, Gubaidulina draws on a standard musical imagery of pain, shock, and glory as transmitted through Shostakovich. So far, so traditional—except that the traditions being addressed here, of sacred oratorio and Romantic expressivity, are broken ones. The work seems to be hammering at the door of plausibility, questioning itself, in all its magniloquence and drama. Piled against loss of meaning, its gestures exert themselves with maximal force. There is a demand to be heard. But by whom? The adherence to Russian culture, symphonic and sacred, and to Russian languages, vernacular and ecclesiastical, makes the work a visitor in the Germany of its première. Its otherness it shares with much of the music of the holy minimalists, who often chose texts in Church Slavonic, Greek, or Latin, languages remote from the general run of Western audiences and thereby granting any settings a kind of automatic transcendence, making them speak from another place, another time. However, Gubaidulina's Passion lacks the confident serenity that comes, in Pärt or Tavener, from also blanking out the entire post-Renaissance Western experience. That experience is still there, and Gubaidulina vigorously takes hold of it, while knowing that she takes hold of a ghost.

---

1. 'Philosophy of Composition—is there such a thing?', in Peter Dejans, ed., *Identity and Difference: Essays, on Music, Language and Time* (Leuven, 2004), 69.

Example 93   Sofia Gubaidulina, *Now Always Snow*

The Passion is unusual among Gubaidulina's works in its scale—
she is one of very few leading composers in the last quarter of the twentieth century not to have written an opera—but not in its subject matter, for her way of inserting a determined symbolism extends even into
her purely instrumental works. *Two Paths* (1999), her concerto for two
violas, carries the subtitle 'A Dedication to Mary and Martha,' making
it a double portrait of the sisters Jesus visited in Bethany, and her extraordinary Fourth Quartet (1993) has the musicians on stage accompanied by two recorded images of themselves as well as by colored
lighting in an investigation of 'how the "real" arises from the "unreal"'.[2]

Such thinking is inescapable in her comparatively few vocal works
of this period, which include one of her most remarkable compositions,
Now Always Snow (1993, see example 93), setting poems by her contemporary Gennady Aigi for choir and ensemble. Aigi's fragmented in-
cantations squeeze out a voice through a space between Russian mod-

2. Note available at http://www.sikorski.de.

ernism and the Orthodox liturgy, a space in which Gubaidulina is at home. The repetition of sounds, words, and images is answered by, in the first movement, a hovering around G♯ with the recurring motif of a rising minor second followed by a rising major third—a motif that will recur in the last movement on the word that first prompted it, *tishina* (silence), and that, quiet and tonally ambiguous, conveys the cold light of the poetry. Little used in this first movement, the ensemble takes over for the second, making the work a cross-genre hybrid of a kind that may suit such an adamantly individual composer better than the schemes of oratorio and concerto. Playing and copying single melodic intervals, the instruments seem to be trying to find the divine candor that was the voices' in the opening movement. Each of the subsequent movements is different again: a contralto song moving through choral-instrumental shadows, a wordless and clamorous meditation for the full forces coming after a spoken poem, and a finale that finds the ensemble almost silent again, a lone violin playing a line of lament connecting sporadic vocal interventions through most of the piece, as shown in the example. Now Gubaidulina's appeal to an old vocabulary of pathos—magically transformed as the violin's closing high note is taken over by bowed flexatones offstage—sounds like a breakthrough.

Haas and Darkness

Gubaidulina's reinvention of Scriabin's colour organ in her Fourth Quartet (and also in her choral-orchestral *Alleluia* of 1990) was parallelled a little later in the work of Georg Friedrich Haas (b. 1953). The twenty-four scenes of his short opera *Nacht* (1996), another product of the period's fascination with Hölderlin, are distinguished by differently coloured lighting, partly for the practical reason of swiftly indicating particular dramatic spheres (blue is used, for example, for scenes involving Susette Gontard, carmine-red for those extracted from the poet's tragedy *Der Tod des Empedokles*), partly to honour ancestors, including the Scriabin follower Ivan Vishnegradsky (1893–1979). Little known until he was in his forties, Haas represented a new and international generation of spectral composers, and Vishnegradsky interested him as a predecessor in microtonal composition—though not only in that, for Haas also identified with the Russian as an artist coming forward at a time of world change: the Russian Revolution then, the forfeit or relinquishment of revolutionary ideals now. What was implicit in Nono's Hölderlin quartet is now voiced, the letter about bidding farewell to hope being sung by Gontard and the poet in octaves with almost no accompaniment.

Highly productive once he had made his delayed start, Haas in the remaining four years of the century produced two quartets and various orchestral works, investigating, like Grisey, how music could move under its own power through spectral-microtonal figures and fields.

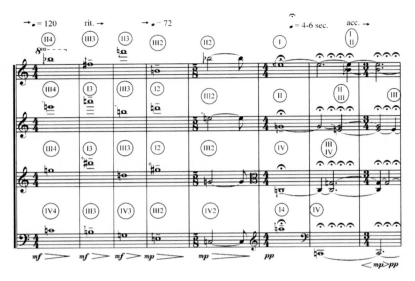

Example 94   Georg Friedrich Haas, String Quartet No. 1

His First Quartet (1997) has the players tune their instruments so that they can play four chords, each consisting of the fundamental plus the third, fifth, and seventh partials in a harmonic series (the lowest has the cello's fourth string tuned to its regular C, with the viola's third string at G in just intonation, only two cents away from its normal tuning, the second violin's third string at a lowered E and the first violin's second string at a lowered B♭). The four chords are microtonally separated to make possible a range not only of harmonies but also of beat effects and combination tones, as well as frustrated unisons recalling Scelsi, the overall iridescence enhanced by having the musicians play harmonics through most of the piece. But after twenty minutes of dazzling in the upper air, with all four instruments on the treble staff or far above it, producing harmonics up to the sixteenth, the quartet alights on some extraordinary spectral harmonies suggesting resonances from the deep bass. Example 94 shows the approach to and beginning of this passage. The notation indicates which string is to be played and which harmonic, so that chords of odd-numbered partials march down to one on the viola's flattened low C, beneath which the cello enters an octave below.

Haas's most spectacular achievement of this period was *in vain* for small orchestra (2000), where the colours of *Nacht* are replaced by the basic elements of light and darkness, the musicians performing some sections under blackout conditions. Quite apart from the effect on the concert experience for the audience, this changes the game for the performers, who cannot see each other, or the conductor, or, indeed, their parts, so that their music must be relatively easy to memorize and depend only on aural cues. For example, the lights first start to dim as the downward ripples of the opening are infiltrated by nontempered pitches, which become part of a slowly changing chordal mass during the phase of complete darkness. There are magical spectral chords later in this work, some complex, others of a simplicity recalling older harmonic practice (for example, the fourth, fifth, and sixth harmonics together come close to a major triad in root position) and even suggesting memories playing across these lustrous surfaces, though never distinct, of the Vienna-centred tradition to which the composer belongs: Schubert, Mahler, Ligeti. Even more radical, his third quartet, '*In iij. Noct.*' (2001), is played in total darkness throughout, the score comprising guidelines for harmonies, gestures, and textures of various sorts on which the players, seated at the far corners of the hall, will agree or not after one of them has issued a prescribed aural invitation. The moments include overtone chords such as appear in example 94, as well as a quotation from Gesualdo's tenebrae responsory *Eram quasi agnus*, another instance of the age's fascination with this dour figure.

Notes Haas wrote in connection with his Hölderlin opera seem germane to the artificial nights of these later works: 'For me the concept of night is not connected with any Romantic ideas but with hopelessness and the loss of a grip on reality, with the plunging of the soul into darkness, and with the loss of utopias. I am constantly asking myself what right I have to withdraw into my quiet little house to compose . . . while all around me things are happening which are different in scale yet not in principle from what has been happening in, for example, Bosnia or Ruanda.'[3] Haas's self-questioning would have been echoed by innumerable other composers aware in the 1990s that the world was becoming a darker place.

Harvey and the Goddess

Trained as a boy chorister, Harvey has gone back repeatedly to the British cathedral tradition, as in his unaccompanied *Missa brevis* (1995). Great balancer of contraries, though, he has drawn also on texts and subjects from Indian spirituality, and has often sought to bring West and East together. Such a goal is explicit in another work of 1995, *Soleil noir/Chitra* for nine instruments and electronics, an encounter between 'Europe, with its fascination with darkness, melancholy and madness' and 'India, with its radiance, its naivety, its nostalgia for the divine presence and its mysteriously inviting profundity'.[4] From a rich dialogue of dance (flute-led, high, irregular in rhythm) with death-knell (brass-loud, low, pulsating) comes, as so often in Harvey, a strange union—of

3. Note with recording of his String Quartets Nos. 1–2, edition zeitklang 19017.

4. Note available at htttp://www.fabermusic.com.

shining dark, of grave dance, of a world where spirit and body, East and West, are one.

Soleil noir/Chitra is typical of his music in another balance it strives for, between instrumental (or vocal) sound and electronic, a balance— or, more, an arena of dialogue—he had been investigating since adding a synthesizer to the orchestra in his orchestral piece *Inner Light 3* (1975). Besides several return visits to IRCAM, his experience was to include work at the BBC studios on the electrified symphonic piece *Madonna of Winter and Spring* (1986) and at Stanford during his time there (1995– 2000) alongside Mathews and Chowning. Like Stockhausen, on whom he wrote a book,[5] he found in the electronic domain—of music unper- formed and invisible—the sense of another dimension. Writing of what was, with *Mortuos plango*, one of his first IRCAM compositions, *Bhakti* for fifteen-piece ensemble and recorded electronic sound (1982), he interpreted the latter as 'reaching beyond the instrumental scale to a more universal dimension'.[6] Similarly, the entry of synthesized sound towards the end of the song cycle *White as Jasmine* (1999) opens a new vista, of dense, brilliant tone corresponding to the poem's imagery of light. Such effects depend, of course, on the presence of an instrumen- tal-vocal domain that the electronic can exceed, and Harvey is careful to maintain that duality. His one important composition for electronic means alone, *Mortuos plango*, is rooted in recordings of identifiable sounds, and in his many concert works with computer technology the electronic sound is keyed into what the performers produce. There has to be connection—timbral, rhythmic, harmonic, melodic—for the be- yond to manifest itself.

By no means, however, is electronic intervention a necessary con- dition. For Harvey—as for many of us, perhaps most—music by its nature 'possesses a unique, mysterious capacity to speak of what lies beyond or beneath the everyday'.[7] He has tried to find words for that 'what' in terms of encountering not the old 'patriarchal God' but 'a Goddess in all her unpredictability: fluid, instinctual, affirming what is' or of entering a 'state of liberation, of emptiness, of healing'.[8] But words may not help. Like Messiaen, whose *Eclairs sur l'Au-delà* also dates from this period late in the millennium, Harvey was offering an experience of dazzlement—that is, of music suddenly overreaching any attempt to contain it with explanation. The overwhelming can be achieved electronically, but just as well by a sonority astonishing in its context, whether because it is quite new (the spectral harmonies of Harvey's orchestra) or old but unexpected (the major chords that loom

5. Jonathan Harvey, *The Music of Stockhausen* (London, 1974).

6. Note available at http://www.fabermusic.com.

7. Jonathan Harvey, Music and Inspiration, ed. Michael Downes (London, 1999), 128.

8. Ibid., 163, 166.

up in *White as Jasmine*). It can, again as in Messiaen, be a matter of time, whether of changelessness foreshadowing eternity, of driving cosmic dance or of a bewilderingly rapid pulse, which for both composers may be modelled on that of birdsong. At earlier times in his life Harvey had profited from advanced serialism (after a year, 1969–70, he spent at Princeton) as well as from a notion of harmony built in symmetrical intervals around a midpoint, and none of this was quite lost. By the 1990s, however, he was coming back to agree with Messiaen—and with Grisey, and, more broadly, with the age in general—on the fundamental importance of the harmonic spectrum and of pulse, in whatever new realms of sound.

Grisey and Rebirth

With his view of sounds as living beings, Grisey might well have felt music could speak of birth and death from its own experience. *L'Icône paradoxale* (1992–94), his first work for large forces since *Les Espaces acoustiques*, is music of birth, prompted at once by an image of pregnancy —Piero della Francesca's 'Madonna del parto'—and by the cultural rebirth to which Piero contributed, the title of the work coming from an essay by Yves Bonnefoy. Considering himself to be living through, and participating in, another paradigm shift, Grisey found a pre-echo in the Renaissance, and particularly in the work of Piero, who based his art on measure and the study of perception, and who even left a manual describing his techniques—a predecessor who shared that 'dream, always renewed, of an art-science'.[9] Grisey set extracts from Piero's theoretical text in his piece, which is for soprano and mezzo-soprano accompanied by a small ensemble and a further orchestra; the painter's name is also set, and its phonemes provide the principal spectra, by analogy with the procedure in *Les Chants de l'amour*.

L'Icône paradoxale picks up from the drama of *Épilogue*, echoing its eruptive horns and gaining great power in its middle part from rising scales, microtonally inflected, to which the singers hold against lightning-bolt descents from tuned percussion and other instruments. Not only do such conjunctions bring about a characteristic fusion of speeds, they also reproduce in musical terms Piero's art of intersecting lines. At the same time, the exploration of scales seems to be working toward a new kind of melody, a supposition reinforced by one of the goals for spectral music Grisey outlined in his last theoretical article: 'Establishment of new scales and—eventually—reinvention of melody.'[10] Steps toward this are taken soon in some passages where two-note and three-note melodies have Vivier-like spectral coronas and again in the work's

9. Gérard Grisey, *Écrits, ou L'Invention de la musique spectrale*, ed. Guy Lelong (Paris, 2008), 122.

10. Ibid., 123.

beautiful slow coda, where the singers, hitherto bound together or imitating one another, are at last in dialogue.

Grisey's next work, *Vortex Temporum* (1994–96), also ends in a new place. Its starting point is a little flurry taken from the dawn scene in Ravel's *Daphnis et Chloé*, a figure so short and elementary it barely speaks as a quotation, consisting of little more than a diminished triad (G–B♭–C♯) arpeggiated up and down. Being a basic musical bit was what suited it to the processes of repetition, transformation, and extension through which it creates a forty-minute span for quintet (flute, clarinet, and string trio) with solo piano, but there was the further advantage from Grisey's point of view that its shape is roughly sinusoidal, so that it mimics on the level of motif what is happening within the sound several hundred times faster. It also lends itself to music in which the endlessly manipulable diminished seventh chord is the central harmony. The work sets its chosen shape whirling in a musical space where the piano is tuned a quarter-tone flat, which not only enlarges the harmonic possibilities but also makes the piano sound more inharmonic. Much of this 'vortex of times' is fast, but the central movement achieves an effect of almost unrelieved descent for the piano's chords stepping slowly down through the even more slowly changing light projected by the quintet. And the piece ends once more with slow pulsations from the piano, accompanied now only by sounds as of breathing.

Vortex Temporum was given its first performance by one of the leading new-music groups, the Freiburg-based ensemble recherche, at one of the most prestigious festivals, the Days for New Chamber Music in the German town of Witten, a couple of months before the composer's fiftieth birthday. As he was aware, spectral music was by now spreading to a younger generation of composers, including Haas and Marc-André Dalbavie (b. 1961); he is less likely to have known of the quite independent work with spectra being undertaken in Edinburgh by Paul Keenan (1956–2001), who based his *Palimpsest* for soprano, ensemble, and electronic sound (1992–95) on analyses of trombone multiphonics.[11] Solitariness—observant and marvelling rather than melancholic—seems to be written into this work, in much of which the texture is thinned to a single line maintaining a long, slow melodic unfolding through whatever bursts and breaks occur. Instruments may rest for long periods: the clarinet is not heard until the forty-five-minute piece is more than half over. Without any appeal to the drama of ritual, the work gives the impression its performers are engaged in something vast, under the sky of the remarkably subtle and individual electronic sound.

Grisey, who had no use for electronics during this period, moved on to investigate another threshold in *Quatre chants pour franchir le seuil*

11. See notes by the composer on the Web site devoted to his work, http://www.cloudscapes.demon.co.uk.

Example 95 Gérard Grisey, *Quatre chants pour franchir le seuil*

for soprano and ensemble (1996–98), setting poems on death from diverse times and places: modern France and ancient Egypt, Greece, and Babylonia. Boundaries are touched in many ways: for example, in the striking coalescence of vocal and instrumental sound as steady unison crescendos ring out from soprano and trumpet at the repeated word 'ange' in the first song. The work also renews venerable musical images of death, such as descending scales and figures, weight in the bass (the ensemble has three treble-register instruments around the soprano but includes two tubas, cello, and double bass with predominantly low saxophones and clarinets in the larger group behind), interrupted phrases and, for the close, a lullaby. Once again Grisey ends a score at a turning point, as if at a border indeed, the soprano extending her voice over a rocking accompaniment as shown in example 95.

The fact that Grisey died soon after writing this music, and before it had been performed, has given it's near-death aura a sombre veracity. However, Grisey had set out on another project (for mezzo-soprano and double bass, after a Beckett poem), and there is no reason to interpret his lullaby as an endpoint rather than as another threshold, towards the 'reinvention of melody' he was hoping would be spectral music's gift to the world.

Riehm and Reality

For a composer whose effort has been to uncover present reality, independently of personal expression or even coherent stylistic development, transcendence might seem a step too far. Reality needs continuously to be refound because in some respects it is continuously changing; what is real at one time—total serialism in 1951, say—may cease to be so. And the urgency of the search has only become more intense with the array of alternative, factitious realities increasingly available.

Riehm's *Hawking* (1998), for piano, percussion and six other players distributed around the auditorium, was prompted by a picture of the astrophysicist Stephen Hawking seen against a photograph of the night sky, an image of an exceedingly frail human being penetrating the profound secrets of physical reality. Hence the scoring for a pianist as protagonist in communication (if so it be) with the distant and widely separated players on woodwinds and strings. However, the Hawking portrait was more than a cue for an effective sound drama; it also presented a challenge to the composer's sense of mission. Riehm does not embrace the marginal effects of Lachenmann or Sciarrino, but his writing has an implacable otherness that is also an insistent directness—a character suggestive of Ustvolskaya. The questions that are being asked appear quite simple, unmistakeble. But answers are not forthcoming, or yield themselves only reluctantly. It is as if reality now is so deeply hidden that a huge effort, a transcendent effort must be made even to seek it.

2001

A new millennium might have signalled change without
the brutal reinforcement provided by the attacks on New
York and Washington on September 11, 2001, by agents of
Al-Qaeda. An assault against the United States was swiftly
interpreted as a threat to the entire Western world, from an
enemy having no national territory that could be invaded
in return, no government to which appeals could be made,
no representation on international councils, no framework
of law. Where the many wars of the 1990s had mostly
been civil—in central Africa, Algeria, Chechnya, and the
former Yugoslavia, the Gulf War of 1990–91 being the main
exception—the new conflict of the twenty-first century went
beyond all boundaries and seemed, as retaliatory actions in
Afghanistan and Iraq dragged on, potentially endless. Confidence that bourgeois capitalism could be exported as the way
of the future (as it had been in the 1990s throughout much of
central and eastern Europe) evaporated in the face of these
stalemates and setbacks. Its supportability even at home, in
North America, Western Europe, and the Far East, began to
seem uncertain as concerns grew over dislocations of the
earth's climate and as deep faults in banking and finance
began to reveal themselves.

The developing heterogeneity of music could now
seem the symptom of an impending cultural swerve on the

scale of the Renaissance, so many arrows pointing towards so many potential futures. Many of those futures would depend on the rapid rise of the Internet, which in the first years of the century became, especially for younger composers, the main channel of communication. For more traditional means—symphony orchestras, music publishers—a continuing relevance to new music looked less certain. Twenty-first-century music might be smaller, and more nimble in its diffusion. It might also, as postmodernism became a historical phenomenon, be tighter and more serious.

28

Towards Change?

Music's move into a new century—the first new century that modernism had encountered—brought no immediate disruption. Indeed, a listener might have great difficulty in identifying, on internal evidence alone, an unknown piece as belonging to the first decade of the twenty-first century rather than the last decade of the twentieth, or even the last decade but one, possibly two. For such a degree of stasis, universally observable, one might have to go back to the first half of the eighteenth century, a period perhaps similar (and unlike intervening ages) in its social stability. No less remarkably, this stasis survived a fundamental shift in the means of disseminating music, from disc to download. Vastly more music became available, in many cases free of charge, with barely a quiver in its nature.

Similarly unaltering was the larger musical culture, within which contemporary work was by now restricted to a small, ring-fenced realm. For example, the 2010–11 subscription concerts of the Los Angeles Philharmonic offered fourteen pieces by living composers—quite a high tally for a major orchestra, if representing no more than 20% of the season's repertory in terms of duration. Of those fourteen, however, eleven were being given in world or local premières: new music, in what had become a widespread phenomenon, would have to be 'new' to squeeze in. Again like many symphony orchestras, the L.A. Philharmonic presented a contemporary-music series, devoted almost exclusively to living composers and less dominated by premières, but given in a smaller venue by a smaller ensemble. Visitors to most of the Western world's concert halls, and listeners to most of the Western world's radio stations, would easily gain the impression that the classical tradition ended where this book begins, save for occasional spurts.

So mightily present, the past easily continued to seep into new music, and qualities of retrospection, reinspection, retrieval, recuperation or recycling earlier found in Ligeti and Berio, Rihm and Riehm, Schnebel and Goehr, Adams and Saariaho, or Pesson and Pauset became inescapeable, contributing to the stationary feel of music in the new century—the new millennium. From one point of view, music was becoming more realistic, more attuned to its audience's habits of listening. However, the example drawn from the L.A. Philharmonic's programming suggests that its realism was rather bleakly rewarded. One might rather see the fate of new music now as to be sidelined, stifled and deprived of its antecedents, only in relation to which would understanding be possible. Lachenmann, for example, found the outlook grim in writing that the 'all-suffocating barbarism diagnosed by [Karl] Kraus[1] was not overcome through the two world wars—on the contrary, it came to infiltrate all areas of life in a fatally harmless guise: as a culture of "fun" whose universal, cheapened availability gives rise to a rapid devaluation of all that has been precious to us as artistic experience. We are thus today once again faced with the task of bringing art "to safety" . . . , discarding false securities, and doing this with reference to an innovatively-oriented work-ideal that subjects our experience of music to constant dialectical renewal.'[2] It is, in Lachenmann's view, the removal of art to the sphere of entertainment that compromises comprehension—of old music, one may say, as well as new. The need then becomes to reclaim, to draw back works of art, to place them, with new ones, in a vessel that will convey them safely to the future—a domain of which so much is said, and so little hoped, in the present age.

We live in unusual times. The subject matter of this book remains virtually unknown to a very large proportion even of people for whom the experience of Western classical music is a regular necessity, let alone the vast majority of others. Composers—still heirs to a nineteenth-century ideal of music's universality, despite the chastening of recent decades—find themselves writing only for specialized ensembles, specialized festivals, specialized audiences. It is a reality Lachenmann reflects in the torn, pressured extremity of his music, excoriates in his outbursts of protest, and fights in his flares of beauty. Music from the Renaissance to the Romantic era was driven by a tug of forces involving the composer's desires and inclinations (what might be called in one age 'taste', in another 'self expression'), the nature of the musical language and the expectations of the audience. In the labyrinth of contemporary music, however, no Ariadne's thread of common practice is

1. Viennese cultural critic, contemporary of Schoenberg.
2. 'Philosophy of Composition—is there such a thing?', 55–56.

to be found, while the audience has similarly lost whatever unanimity it might have had. With certainty gone about means and destination, 'taste' easily becomes a mirage and 'self expression' shadow boxing.

For the aspiring composer, the enquiring listener or the despairing critic, the abundance of avenues is at once overwhelming and unsettling. Yet it may also be illusory, for each of today's many musical languages implies all the others, and is implied in them. Just as the early atonal works of Schoenberg, Berg and Webern called to be understood against a background of Austro-German diatonic symphonism, so the hurtling flux of shreds and spangles in Lachenmann's large-ensemble piece *Concertini* (2004-5), for example, presents itself in opposition to—and to that extent depends on—the conservative musical world into which it was born. It may even draw near to or refer to that world, with whatever shadows of irony, for *Concertini* is more ebullient, more humorous and certainly less noise-oriented than its composer's earlier works for a comparable formation. In a passage bringing forward the strings, two-thirds of the way through the forty-minute single movement, an older kind of music is trying to break through, or perhaps is being striven for, in a scrupulous and necessarily hazardous act of salvage, as might be suggested by example 96.

Example 96 Helmut Lachenmann, *Concertini*

At such a point a thread of connection is offered to music coming from a very different background and motivated by very different aesthetic principles. Writing at much the same time as Lachenmann, Steven Stucky (b. 1949), expressed an alternative attitude to history, both in his music and in his essays, writing, for instance, that: 'One kind of artist is always striving to annihilate the past, to make the world anew in each new work, and so to triumph over the dead weight of routine. I am the other kind. I am the kind who only sees his way forward by standing on the shoulders of those who have cleared the path ahead. . . . I sometimes talk about my Household Gods, those founders of the great twentieth-century musical traditions I still depend on: Debussy, Stravinsky, Bartók, Sibelius, Ravel, Berg, and many others. Their DNA is still in my musical genes, as it is in the genes of so many of the composer colleagues and friends of my own day to whom I feel closest musically.'[3]

This is not a difference between old, tradition-bound, pessimistic Europe and a New World springing with optimism and opportunity, for Stucky goes on to mention several Europeans among his like-minded friends (Knussen, Benjamin, Lindberg) and it would not be hard to find U.S. composers—Babbitt, for one—sharing Lachenmann's sense of disaffection and urgency. The central differences concern the nature of the modernist project, whether that remains unfinished business or has largely been accomplished, and beyond that the whole state of Western culture.

Yet the antithesis can be overemphasized, for just as Lachenmann's *Concertini* touches close at times to familiar musical tropes, so Stucky's almost exactly contemporary Second Concerto for Orchestra (2003) may edge into strange and dangerous territory. Its big central movement is a slow set of variations, music whose poignancy is intensified by a sense of striving for something that can never be reached, as most powerfully in the climactic section for—again—strings, excerpted in Example 97, before the final dissolution. Stucky in this work accepts many of the conventions Lachenmann in *Concertini* questions: the makeup of the orchestra, a functional harmony, symphonic continuity, a familiar language of expression. But something is being glimpsed on the other side, as it is conversely in the Lachenmann work. Both scores speak, one may say, of a certain frustration and bewilderment that composers of all sorts may feel at being marginalized.

The stability of new music—the fact that there has been no major innovation since the developments in computer sound synthesis, noise composition, new complexity, spectral music, and minimalism in the 1970s—may also have something to do with the greying of the avant-garde. In a heartening display of longevity, almost all the composers

---

3. 'Coming Home: On Writing a Second Concerto for Orchestra', available at www.stevenstucky.com.

Example 97   Steven Stucky, Second Concerto for Orchestra

who were young in the 1950s and 1960s remained active into the first decade of the twenty-first century and in many cases beyond, working on well past the age of seventy (Berio, Stockhausen, Lucier, Gubaidulina, Kagel, Goehr, Penderecki, Birtwistle, Davies, Pärt, Lachenmann, Reich, Glass, Riehm, Silvestrov, Harvey, Holliger, Andriessen), eighty (Babbitt, Boulez, Kurtág, Henze, Schnebel) and even, in the astonishing case of Carter, one hundred. What was remarkable in Stravinsky is now the norm—and that comparison also points up how little the septuagenarian and octogenarian composers of the twenty-first century have been affected by colleagues more than forty years their junior, as

Stravinsky was in his time. The histories entailed in, say, Birtwistle's Orpheus scene *The Corridor* (2008), Kurtág's homage to his Romanian birth and to Bartók in his *Colindă-Baladă* for choir and instruments (2006–8) or Gubaidulina's violin concerto *In tempus praesens* (2007) stretch back richly through the half-century of these composers' creative lives, whereas the epoch-making works of the 1950s, most of them written by musicians still in their twenties, were much less deeply rooted, and perhaps therefore able to point in new directions, more forwards than back.

Older composers may feel no closer kinship with the great past than do their younger colleagues, but the weight of their own achievements —and the sense they would probably wish to feel of the artistic life as a progress—could contribute to a rising valuation of continuity, spilling over from the output as a whole into the individual work. Boulez provides an example, in how his *Dérive 2* for eleven players (1988–2006) moves as a single sweep through well over half an hour, the basic shapes not so different from those of works he completed sixty years earlier but now participating in kaleidoscopic movement through fixed or fleeting harmonies. Even more surprising was Kurtág's arrival, after a lifetime of fragments, at the single twenty-minute-plus span of his . . . *concertante* . . . for orchestra with violin and viola soloists (2002–3).

The reach of continuity extends, however, far beyond such senior figures, though continuity in the twenty-first century will tend to be, as in these works by Boulez and Kurtág, or those already mentioned by Lachenmann and Stucky, uncertain, liable to wear thin, aware of the dangers (or delights) of familiar paths, subject to sudden slippage or escape. There may also be, more in the music of younger composers than of those who took part in the post-war revolution, a stronger wish for continuity and connectedness with music of the past. As several composers found in earlier decades, the Middle Ages and Renaissance seem, through a loop in time, only a step away, a step taken by, among others, Holliger in Machaut transcriptions for four voices and a trio of violas (2001–9), Isabel Mundry (b. 1963) in a set of Dufay arrangements for ensemble (2003–4) and Ferneyhough in *Dum transisset I-IV* for string quartet (2007), after Christopher Tye. But more recent music, aesthetically more distant as it might seem, has been brought near in, for example, Haas's *Sieben Klangräume* (2005), devised to be performed in the context of Mozart's Requiem and scored for the same forces with the addition of percussion, or Pesson's *Wunderblock (Nebenstück II)* (also 2005), in which the composer rescores the first movement of Bruckner's Sixth Symphony with the wisps and fairy dust of his own orchestral manner. Haas's intense score exposes—gives voice to—the lacunae in the original work, while Pesson's reworking puts forward unexpected Brucknerian affiliations, notably with the fairground organs suggested by the prominent place given an accordion, the effect at once comic and touching.

Such adventures increasingly seem like reactions to a landscape that, for the moment, will not change. The past is not moving on but staying there, and so leaving very little space for the present—which makes it all the more encouraging that so many composers are eager to project themselves into this straitened space. Where action in the decade or so after 1945 was in the hands of rather few, their successors two generations later have become legion, all contributing to a present that becomes increasingly unknowable as the past, too, goes on increasing, with the continuous recovery of music that had stayed silent through many decades, even centuries.

It should not be surprising that a composer took the matter of history, the weight of time, as the subject for an opera, as Ferneyhough did in his *Shadowtime* (1999–2004). The work places itself in a multidimensional borderland: between France and Spain, where Walter Benjamin—from whose thought the opera derives—is travelling on his last journey; between this world and the next; between present and past; between chronological time and eternal simultaneity; between words and music; between philosophy and poetry; between both and absurdity; between theatre and concert. Moments with singing characters are few, and confined to two of the seven scenes, one (the first) involving an overlay of events from different parts of Benjamin's life, the other (the fifth) a parade of bizarre colloquies with contemporary, historical, and mythic beings. The second scene, *Les Froissements d'ailes de Gabriel*, is purely instrumental, a concerto for guitar and ensemble in the form of a jostle of splinters. Paradoxically, though, this is the one scene that keeps a strong dramatic image in imaginary view, that of the angel of history, as described in Benjamin's essay 'On the Concept of History': 'His face is turned toward the past. Where a chain of events appears before *us*, *he* sees one single catastrophe, which keeps piling wreckage upon wreckage and hurls it at his feet. The angel would like to stay, awaken the dead, and make whole what has been smashed. But a storm is blowing from Paradise and has got caught in his wings; it is so strong that the angel can no longer close them.'[4] The entrapped feathers are there in the guitar part, stable in sonority but swept this way and that by the ideas hurtling through.

We meet the angel again in the sixth and seventh scenes, movingly in the latter, *Stelae for Failed Time (Solo for Melancholia as the Angel of History)*, scored for chorus (this is largely a choral opera) with electronic sound. Where the vocal writing in earlier scenes, notably the fifth, is often wildly angular, here the singers fold over one another in long, lyrical lines sticky with time, evoking passing memories of traditional opera and at the same time giving the present work a lament-coda. At

4. Walter Benjamin, *Selected Writings*, trans. Harry Zohn, 4 (Cambridge, Mass., 2003), 392–93, quoted in Charles Bernstein, *Shadowtime* (København and Los Angeles, 2005), 60–61.

the end, when the voices on stage have all stopped, the loudspeakers go on with the composer's voice in several channels, speaking in an invented language. The gesture perhaps recalls not so much the close of the end of the *Carceri d'invenzione* cycle as that of Stockhausen's *Hymnen*, though the effect is to project not the creating spirit but the frail residue left when the work has gone its way.

There are also connections with Stockhausen's *Licht*, in how solo singers—the mainstay of opera as it was known—appear only infrequently, and in how the scenes may be given as independent concert pieces. More generally, *Shadowtime* suggests an ambition on music's part to return to the alliance with word and action from which it began to be riven in the Renaissance. It is an ambition countered by Ferneyhough's subsequent works, which include his Sixth Quartet (2010) and *Chronos-Aion* for ensemble (2007–8), but not by Stockhausen's that came similarly in the wake of his vastly larger operatic project, *Licht*. Having completed that undertaking in 2003, Stockhausen went on to *Klang*, a sequence of pieces mostly for soloists or small groups (the exception is the electronic *Cosmic Pulses*) in which there is often a theatrical component.

Music's reintegration with drama occurs also, but quite differently, in the work of Heiner Goebbels (b. 1952), work that has consisted mostly since the late 1980s of full-length theatre compositions he both scores and directs.[5] Aspects of spoken theatre, opera, concert and ballet are not so much fused as brought into a provocative balance of tensions: texts, taken from nondramatic sources, will tend to challenge one another, in message, language, and register, and the same is true of musical styles. In the closing scenes of *Landschaft mit entfernten Verwandten* (Landscape with Distant Relatives, 2002) words from Gertrude Stein's *Wars I Have Seen*, spoken over cool jazz, are followed by another Stein extract accompanied by a soft regular beat that might suggest respiration or a distant march, then by a cowboy song ('Out where the West begins', an example of found material), by an interleaving of more Stein (on travelling by train) with Henri Michaux (on not travelling, but finding volcanoes in the city) over a drift from the cowboy ensemble that develops into another song, 'Freight Train', and finally by a solemn bell sound that is taken up and coloured by the instrumental ensemble while a Poussin letter is quoted, remarking on the basic natures of vision and of painting.

Though this ultimate moment might seem a gesture toward wholeness, embracing—or consciously failing to embrace—everything that has gone before, Goebbels is more interested in presenting his audience with disparities, with evidences that engage the thinking of the

5. Some impression of his works' spectacular visual character may be gained from the many photographs posted on his Web site: http://www.heiner goebbels.com.

spectator (at the original show) or listener (to the recording that ensued). Hence the relevance of Stein, whose 1943 memoir relates banal day-to-day events in the same tone as the progress of the war and crosscuts cynicism with idealism, and also of Poussin's landscapes, in which the eye is free to travel from a mountain contour to the shape of a tree to whatever human story may be unfolding in part of the picture, for both Stein and Poussin similarly offer multiple foci and undetermined relationships. The Stein book is germane, too, as a document on war, for *Landschaft* was created as the U.S.-led invasion of Afghanistan was proceeding, so that, for instance, the choice of 'Out where the West begins' is hardly innocent. Nevertheless, the work takes no position, but rather presents a sequence of abutting, interpenetrating, and sometimes conflicting surfaces to help members of the audience define their positions, or at least their prejudices. Music, to have a place in this enterprise, will have to be flagged with pre-existing meanings, to abandon the post-1945 dreams of creating new intrinsic meaning. Yet the style wars (if only those) of the early twenty-first century are less heated than of yore; Goebbels has commented with knowledge and sympathy on Lachenmann, and his *Landschaft mit entfernten Verwandten*, like the latter's *Concertini*, was written for the Ensemble Modern.

Creating works for particular performers and for a particular run of performances, rather than scores designed to live on indefinitely, Goebbels behaves like an eighteenth-century composer, and he is by no means alone in circumventing the Romantic notion of the enduring masterpiece. It is a notion, in any event, hard to sustain in a world where almost all new music is over once the experience of a few performances has been sealed into a recording. Perhaps the most realistic response is to create pieces that, imagined for a specific time and place, look for no continuing life, as Peter Ablinger (b. 1954), among others, has done. His *Landschaftsoper Ulrichsberg* (2009) involved events and installations in the Austrian town and vicinity—a suggested walk with fourteen stations for listening, an archive of recordings made by inhabitants, a grand final concert—and survives only as model or stimulus. Other Ablinger projects are more adaptable. His *Orte* (2001), for example, proposes performances in three spaces within walking distance. The resonant properties of each are to be measured in advance, and the distinctive formants discovered to be played or sung by the musicians for twenty minutes or so, audience and performers then moving on to the next.

There is a clear connection here with the room-exploring work undertaken three or four decades earlier by Lucier, who has himself gone on imagining not so much finished works as conditions under which sound may display itself. A beautiful example is his *Ever Present* (2003), where, through just over a quarter of an hour, two electronic sources slowly bend apart from unison in opposite directions and then rejoin, while three instrumentalists, on flute, alto saxophone, and piano, make gentle interventions that produce beat effects with the gradually changing electronic frequencies. Ablinger, too, is interested in sound as exhibitive, in offering not something to be heard but an occasion for hearing—or not hearing. (This might be a definition of experimental music.) His *Fallstudie* (2004–8) is a museum piece: a video recording of someone pushing a glass across a table is repeated as a loop until a visitor sits in the only available chair, whereupon the projection shows the glass being advanced toward the edge of the table and falling off, at which point the show stops. Scarcely less dramatic is his *Deus cantando* (2009), where a recording of a boy reading the Declaration of the International Environmental Court is computer analysed and fed into a piano, whose sounds sometimes come uncannily near projecting the words.[6]

Whereas music in the work of Goebbels and Ablinger (or Kagel and Aperghis) rejoins theatre, spectacle, or carnival, it remains a realm of essentially sonic discovery in that of many composers of their generation or younger, composers for whom, as for Lachenmann, the task of modernism to confront each new status quo goes on (until, perhaps, there has been a change in society so fundamental as to engender and be hospitable to a wholly new and presently unimaginable music). As Rebecca Saunders (b. 1967) put it: 'The need to continually open ones ears to new ways of perceiving sound and music remains always important.'[7] And she is true to her word in such a piece as *Stirrings Still* (2006), where three woodwinds keep circling through a very soft, dislocated chorale of tones estranged by their microtonal tunings and character as harmonics. Like other British musicians uncomfortable with native habits of compromise (Ferneyhough, Dillon, Barrett, and Dench among them), Saunders looked for opportunities abroad, studying with Rihm, settling in Berlin, a city favoured by other composers including Ablinger, and working with such groups as Ensemble Modern and musikFabrik, as well as with the receptive German radio stations and festivals.

Many composers have, like Saunders, formed long-term relationships with ensembles, none more so than Beat Furrer (b. 1954), who founded Klangforum Wien and has written for it extensively through a quarter-century while also welcoming other conductors and composers. Indeed, the group has helped promote, among others, a whole third (or fourth) Viennese school, a disparate collectivity whose other members include Haas and Klaus Lang (b. 1971). Where a work of Lang's will move calmly through sequences of recurring harmonies rather in the manner of Cage's String Quartet in Four Parts, pursuing a course to which it alone has the key, Furrer's music is expressively hot, immedi-

---

6. A recording is available on his Web site: http://ablinger.mur.at.

7. Interview on the Ensemble Modern Web site: http://www.ensemble -modern.com.

ate, and investigative. Like Lachenmann and Sciarrino, two key figures of this period, he achieves something that is at once abstract, contrary to the codes and languages by which we are used to understanding musical expression, and forcefully direct. Radical reinvention sharpens communication.

So it does in the several dramatic works of this prolific composer (that quality he shares with Haas), notably *FAMA* (2004–5), named after Rumour in Ovid's *Metamorphoses*, who lives in a house where 'millions both of troths and lies run gadding every-where'.[8] To represent this murmurous dwelling Furrer had an enclosure built inside the auditorium for the public, listening to the performers in the space beyond: an ensemble of twenty-two instrumentalists with eight singers and an actress, enacting the victim of rumour. Since the walls and roof of the enclosure could slide open, and since the musicians could move, a great variety of acoustical and visual relationships with the audience became possible, on the part of a performing ensemble ranging from a turbulent vocal-orchestral tutti to a duet for actress and bass flute speaking and whispering to one another.

Furrer's concert works are often just as dramatic, even down to the appropriation of vocal gestures in how instruments or ensembles project themselves: shouting, screaming, whistling. His writing for orchestra, hallucinogenic in its sharp brightness, may owe something to Ligeti and Grisey, to name two others who have remained key figures, though deceased; certainly his Piano Concerto (2007) places itself in lineage after Ligeti's. Cast in one movement with a central slow—frozen —section, its main activity for the soloist is a hobbling ascent, against resonances and distractions from the orchestra, which includes an echo-piano. Ascent is constantly being undermined by turning in circles, whether at the level of ostinato or of longer slips back to earlier times, and in this struggle to move on, to escape from mere repetition, from being stuck in the treacle of the past, the piece speaks for an objective Furrer shares with many of his contemporaries.

For example, Mark André (b. 1964), a pupil of Lachenmann, has pushed on with his teacher's search for new sounds not so much for their own sake as for the new attitudes to performance and listening they bring about. In his *durch* for soprano saxophone, percussion, and piano (2004–5), all the instruments are to a degree denatured, or renatured. Not only is the piano partly prepared with pieces of bread and rubber, amplified at times and occasionally played on the strings, but the pedalling is notated in detail; moreover, the part consists almost entirely of single sounds, each requiring its particular care. The same is true of the other parts, the saxophonist often being asked to play into a gong, tam tam or suspended sheet of aluminium foil, quite apart from producing a range of finger slaps and other effects. Example 98

8. Arthur Golding translation.

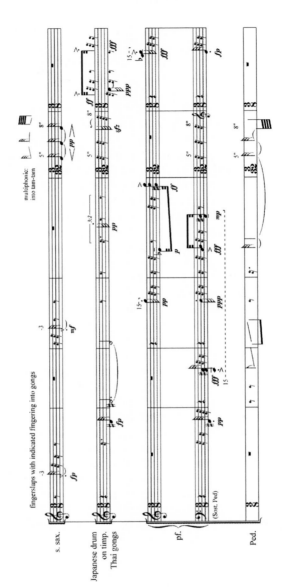

Example 98   Mark André, *durch*

may indicate how André tries to prescribe sounds—and not least resonances—with great exactitude, and also how the progress of his music
is a kind of stuttering coming-into-being alleviated by luminous moments of recognition, as here when the saxophone, playing into the
tam-tam, accords with the piano's controlled reverberation. As André
acknowledges in his note on the piece,[9] he could not have created
the score without the sympathetic and exploratory collaboration of the
original performers: Marcus Weiss, Christian Dierstein, and Yukiko Sug-
awara (Lachenmann's wife, and a noted performer of his music). Just
as a composer in an electronic studio will need to work with professional programmers, a piece like *durch* draws on the expertise of relevant
experts—though with the difference that the score provides the means
for its recreation, by performers willing to enter into its difficulties and
its spirit. The title, meaning 'through', comes from Luther's translation
of the Bible (a frequent source for André), in this case from a passage
in Luke 13: 'Strive thus, that you enter through the narrow gate, for
many, I tell you, are drawn there, as if to enter, but will not be able to'
(vs. 24). With reference to this, André asks his listeners to understand
that 'the search by way of the basic materials and the composed spaces
refers directly and explicitly to the question of the presence or disappear-
ance of the track'.[10] One is left to wonder whether the delicate, hushed
rustlings at the close represent the track found or irretrievably lost.

André's music extends the principle, inherited from Lachenmann,
from Cage and even from Debussy, that a musical composition is not
made of sound but is the sound itself. The same may be said of the work
of another Lachenmann pupil, Pierluigi Billone (b. 1960), who studied
with Sciarrino as well and inherited from both teachers a desire to explore further what instruments, and instrumentalists, are capable of. In
his *1+1=1* for two bass clarinets (2006) the players project long, soft,
slowly bending notes, meeting one another in beat effects (they are to
station themselves far apart, but close enough for acoustic interaction)
and drawing away again, around more excited passages where multiphonics may suggest the instruments speaking, quite apart from still
other sections in which vocal sounds are part of the musical action. The
work's duration of over an hour—it is intended to be a stand-alone
event—goes beyond not only the norms of concert life but also those of
listening. It is, in many respects, unprecedented. But it also conveys the
impression, like so much innovatory music of the period (Birtwistle's,
notably), of having come from a remote, forgotten culture.

There may be no less sense of newness, though, in music whose
affiliations are far more identifiable, as in much that has followed from
minimalism. In its salting of repetition with caprice, the music of Donnacha Dennehy (b. 1970) descends from Reich's while also having

9. Available at http://www.ricordi.de.
10. Ibid.

Example 99   Donnacha Dennehy, *Elastic Harmonic*

links with Glass and the Bang on a Can composers. Many of his works
are scored for small ensemble and have an urban feel, in terms of pulse,
amplification, and the use of recorded sounds, but not so his one-
movement violin concerto *Elastic Harmonic* (2005), which picks up from
Vivier in the dense restedness of its harmony and layered construction. As shown in example 99, the soloist spins and wheels over much
slower movement in the orchestra, within which, for much of the
time, two chords are alternating, the timing of the pull back and forth
constantly varying (hence the title) and so lending a disconcerting unpredictability to what is eminently predictable. Sonorities, too, are finely
obfuscated, both by the doublings and by the use of a group of 'prepared violins' having paper clips attached to their strings. Orchestral
conventions are stretched but not broken; the new emerges from within
the old's warm embedding.

There are a myriad other ways in which the known and the unknown meet in the multifarious music of the early twenty-first century, and many of them intersect in *Schnee*, a work of 2006–8 by Hans
Abrahamsen (b. 1952) that seems to stand for the era also in its poetry
of winter: of whiteness, crystal form, quietude, and expectation. Subtitled 'Canons for Nine Instruments', it is laid out for mirroring ensembles of piano plus trio (strings on the left, woodwinds on the right)
with a percussionist at rear centre stage. There are five pairs of canons,
each pair distinct in character and duration (they get incrementally
shorter, from nine minutes per canon down to one), but all based on
the melody at the start, which is in a white-note pentatonic mode:
A–C–D–E–F–A. Further iciness comes from the use of the extreme treble, especially in the first canon, where everything is in the piano's top
octave. At such an altitude there would be no certainty about modal
resting place even were it not that the music is conceived in circular
form, one phrase leading into the altered next, around a larger circle

Example 100   Hans Abrahamsen, *Schnee*

that restores the original form at the end. And then there is the larger circle still of the whole hour-long work.

Abrahamsen had made his reputation in the late 1970s and early 1980s with instrumental miniatures that took a distinctively hesitant and tender approach to the period's Romantic restoration, vigilant of Ligeti as well as Schumann. He was then virtually silent for over a decade, through the heyday of postmodernism, until the new century. During this time, aside from a very few small pieces, he worked on arrangements, including instrumentations of seven canons by Bach, of which he has said that, depending on the point of view, 'the music stands still, or moves forwards or backwards'.[11] This is perhaps even more true of his own *Schnee*, where the perpetual variety within repetition—repetition of motif, of phrase, of section, of whole canon (since

11. Note with the recording of *Schnee*, appropriately on Winter & Winter 910, 159–52.

each has its double)—creates unusual effects of mobile stillness. Links with Ligeti are maintained, in the self-similarity and the use of microtonal intonation to instil mist or dazzle, after each of three short 'intermezzos' made for retuning. Other currents in the music come from minimalism and from Lachenmann (guirolike sounds made by skittering the fingernails over the keyboard without depressing any keys), a rare combination enjoined by a work that is, for all its delicacy, absolutely certain.

If Bach is in the background, Mozart makes appearances in the detail of the fourth pair of canons, which borrow the sleigh bells from his 'Sleighride' German Dance, K. 605 No. 3 (as the composer mentions) and end with a twinkle from Papageno (as he does not). Yet the work is unlike anything else. It is also remarkable for its absence of rhetoric, how nothing seems to be pushing here but the music itself, nothing speaking but the music alone. The start of the final canon, shown in example 100, may indicate some of the forces, regularities, and symmetries with which the music is so manifoldly girded, the second piano (in a transposition of the mode) being in rhythmic canon with the first, to which the woodwinds add a canonic voice in long notes while the second piano is shadowed by the harmonics in the strings, both they and the woodwinds, with their microtonal displacements, adding shimmer to what is already shimmering. This is the end but not the destination, rather the prelude to the beginning.

It is tempting to scrutinize any composition from this complex period—during which nearly all the composers active in the 1970s, 1980s, and 1990s remained active, in addition to the senior figures already mentioned—for evidence of the future. The currents are many in contemporary music but the water at the moment looks calm, certainly by comparison with the foam and rush of the decades after 1945. However, a river may appear equally smooth in a lowland valley and at the approach to a cataract.

Resources

This list is centred on, but not limited to, books and Web sites available in English.

1. General

Monographs, Anthologies, and Directories

Battcock, Gregory, ed. *Breaking the Sound Barrier: A Critical Anthology of the New Music.* New York: Dutton, 1981.

Cage, John, and Alison Knowles. *Notations.* New York: Something Else, 1969.

Cooper, Martin, ed. *The New Oxford History of Music, 10: The Modern Age 1890–1960.* London and New York: Oxford University Press, 1974.

Davies, Hugh, ed. *Répertoire international des musiques électroacoustiques/International Electronic Music Catalog.* Cambridge, Mass.: MIT Press, 1968.

Emmerson, Simon. *Living Electronic Music.* Farnham, Surrey: Ashgate, 2007.

Gann, Kyle. *American Music in the Twentieth Century.* New York: Schirmer, 1997; London: Prentice Hall, 1997.

Griffiths, Paul. *The Substance of Things Heard: Writings about Music.* Rochester, N.Y.: University of Rochester Press, 2005.

Heintze, James, ed. *Perspectives on American Music since 1950.* New York: Routledge, 1999.

Hodeir, André. *Since Debussy.* London: Secker & Warburg, 1961; New York: Grove, 1961.

Johnson, Tom. *The Voice of New Music: New York City 1972–1982.* Eindhoven: Het Apollohuis, 1989.

Karkoschka, Erhard. *Das Schriftbild der neuen Musik.* Celle: Moeck, 1966.

Kolleritsch, Otto, ed. *Zur 'Neuen Einfachkeit' in der Musik.* Vienna: Universal, 1981.

Lang, Paul Henry, and Nathan Broder, eds. *Contemporary Music in Europe.* New York: G. Schirmer, 1965.

Marger, Brigitte, and Simone Benmussa, eds. *La Musique en projet.* Paris: Gallimard, 1975.

Mellers, Wilfrid. *Caliban Reborn.* London: Gollancz, 1967; New York: Harper & Row, 1967.

Mertens, Wim. *American Minimal Music.* London: Kahn & Averill, 1983; 2nd ed. 1998; New York: Alexander Broude, 1983.

Morgan, Robert P. *Twentieth-century Music: A History of Musical Style in Modern Europe and America.* New York: Norton, 1991.

Nyman, Michael. *Experimental Music: Cage and Beyond.* London: Studio Vista, 1974; 2nd ed. Cambridge and New York: Cambridge University Press, 1999.

Potter, Keith. *Four Musical Minimalists: La Monte Young, Terry Riley, Steve Reich, Philip Glass.* Cambridge and New York: Cambridge University Press, 2002.

Rahn, John, ed. *Perspectives on Musical Aesthetics.* New York: Norton, 1994.

Schick, Steven. *The Percussionist's Art: Same Bed, Different Dreams.* Rochester, N.Y.: University of Rochester Press, 2006.

Schwartz, Elliott, and Daniel Godfrey. *Music since 1945: Issues, Materials, and Literature.* New York: Schirmer, 1993; Toronto: Maxwell Macmillan, 1993.

Schwarz, K. Robert. *Minimalists.* London: Phaidon, 1996.

Smith Brindle, Reginald. *The New Music.* London and New York: Oxford University Press, 1975; 2nd ed. 1987.

Vinton, Jon, ed. *Dictionary of Twentieth-Century Music.* London: Thames and Hudson, 1974.

Watkins, Glenn. *Pyramids at the Louvre: Music, Culture, and Collage from Stravinsky to the Postmodernists.* Cambridge, Mass.: Belknap Press, 1994.

Whittall, Arnold. *Music since the First World War.* London: Dent, 1977; 2nd ed. Oxford and New York: Oxford University Press, 1995.

———. *Musical Composition in the Twentieth Century.* Oxford and New York: Oxford University Press, 1999.

———. *Exploring Twentieth-Century Music: Tradition and Innovation.* Cambridge and New York: Cambridge University Press, 2003.

Collections of Interviews

Duckworth, William. *Talking Music: Conversations with John Cage, Philip Glass, Laurie Anderson, and Five Generations of American Experimental Composers.* New York: Schirmer, 1995; London: Prentice-Hall, 1995; repr. New York: Da Capo, 1999.

Dufallo, Richard. *Trackings: Composers Speak.* New York: Oxford University Press, 1989.

Ford, Andrew. *Composer to Composer: Conversations about Contemporary Music.* London, Quartet, 1994.

Gagne, Cole, and Tracy, Caras. *Soundpieces: Interviews with American Composers.* Metuchen, N.Y.: Scarecrow, 1982.

Griffiths, Paul. *New Sounds, New Personalities.* London: Faber, 1985.

Schwartz, Elliott, and Barney Childs, eds. *Contemporary Composers on Contemporary Music.* New York: Holt, Rinehart & Winston, 1967.

Strickland, Edward. *American Composers: Dialogues on Contemporary Music.* Bloomington and Indianapolis: Indiana University Press, 1991.

Stürzbecher, Ursula. *Werkstattgespräche mit Komponisten.* Cologne: Gerig, 1971.

Zimmermann, Walter. *Desert Plants: Conversations with 25 American Composers.* Vancouver: A.R.C. Publications, 1976.

Publishers' Web sites

Boosey & Hawkes: http://www.boosey.com
Breitkopf & Härtel: http://www.breitkopf.com
Chester Novello: http://www.chesternovello.com
Donemus: http://www.donemus.nl
Durand/Salabert/Eschig: http://www.durand-salabert-eschig.com
Faber Music: http://www.fabermusic.com
Peters Edition: http://www.editionpeters.com
Ricordi: www.http://ricordi.it
Ricordi London: http://www.ricordi.co.uk
Ricordi München: http://www.ricordi.de
G. Schirmer: http://www.schirmer.com
Schott: http://www.schott-music.com
Sikorski: http://www.sikorski.de
United Music Publishers: http://www.ump.co.uk
Universal Edition: http://www.universaledition.com
Wilhelm Hansen: http://www.ewh.dk

Other Web Sites

Art of the States: http://www.artofthestates.org
British Music Information Centre: http://www.bmic.co.uk
Finnish Music Information Centre: http://www.fimic.fi
IRCAM: http://www.ircam.fr
IRCAM documentation: http://brahms.ircam.fr
The Living Composers Project: http://www.composers21.com
Music Information Center Austria: http://www.mica.at
Musique Contemporaine: http://www.musiquecontemporaine.fr
New Music Box (American Music Center): http://www.newmusicbox.org
Sequenza 21: http://www.sequenza21.com

2. Specific

Peter Ablinger

http://ablinger.mur.at

John Adams

Adams, John. *Hallelujah Junction: Composing an American Life.* New York: Farrar,
   Straus and Giroux, 2008.
May, Thomas. *The John Adams Reader.* Portland, Oreg.: Amadeus, 2006.
http://www.earbox.com

Louis Andriessen

Adlington, Robert. *Louis Andriessen: De Staat.* Aldershot: Ashgate, 2004.
Andriessen, Louis. *The Art of Stealing Time.* Edited by Mirjam Zegers. Todmor-
   den, Lancs.: Arc Music, 2002.
Everett, Yayoi Uno. *The Music of Louis Andriessen.* Cambridge and New York:
   Cambridge University Press, 2006.
Trochimczyk, Maja, ed. *The Music of Louis Andriessen.* New York: Routledge, 2002.

Milton Babbitt

Perspectives of New Music, 14/2 – 15/1. 1976.
Babbitt, Milton. *Words about Music.* Edited by Stephen Dembski and Joseph N.
   Straus. Madison: University of Wisconsin Press, 1987.
Mead, Andrew. *An Introduction to the Music of Milton Babbitt.* Princeton: Prince-
   ton University Press, 1994.
Peles, Stephen, et al., eds. *The Collected Essays of Milton Babbitt.* Princeton, N.J.:
   Princeton University Press, 2003.

Jean Barraqué

Entretemps, 5. Paris, 1987.
Musik-Konzepte, 82. Munich: text+kritik, 1993.
Griffiths, Paul. *The Sea on Fire: Jean Barraqué.* Rochester, N.Y.: University of
   Rochester Press, 2003.

George Benjamin

Benjamin, George. *Les Règles du jeu: Entretiens avec Eric Denut.* Condé-sur-
   Noireau: Musica Falsa, 2004.
Nieminen, Risto. *George Benjamin.* London: Faber, 1996.

Luciano Berio

Contrechamps, 1. Paris: L'Age d'Homme, 1983.
Musik-Konzepte, 128. Munich: text+kritik, 2005.
Berio, Luciano. *Remembering the Future.* Cambridge, Mass.: Harvard University
   Press, 2006.
Dalmonte, Rosanna, and Bálint András Varga. *Luciano Berio: Two Interviews.*
   London: Boyars, 1985.
Hall, George, ed. *BBC Berio Festival at the Barbican.* London: BBC Concerts, 1990.
Osmond-Smith, David. *Playing on Words: A Guide to Luciano Berio's* Sinfonia.
   London: Royal Musical Association, 1985.
———. *Berio.* Oxford and New York: Oxford University Press, 1991.

Stoianova, Ivanka, et al. *Luciano Berio: Chemins en musique* [= *Revue musicale*, 375-7]. Paris: Richard-Masse, 1985.

Harrison Birtwistle

BBC Birtwistle Festival. London: BBC Concerts, 1988.
Adlington, Robert. *The Music of Harrison Birtwistle*. Cambridge and New York: Cambridge University Press, 2006.
Cross, Jonathan. *Harrison Birtwistle: Man, Mind, Music*. London: Faber, 2000; Ithaca, N.Y.: Cornell University Press, 2000.
———. *Harrison Birtwistle: The Mask of Orpheus*, Farnham: Ashgate, 2009.
Hall, Michael. *Harrison Birtwistle*. London: Robson, 1984.
———. *Harrison Birtwistle in Recent Years*. London: Robson, 1998.

Pierre Boulez

Boulez at the Barbican. London: BBC Concerts, 1989.
Musik-Konzepte, 89–90. Munich: text+kritik, 1995.
———. 96. Munich: text+kritik, 1997.
Aguila, Jésus. *Le Domaine Musical: Pierre Boulez et vingt ans de création contemporaine*. Paris: Fayard, 1992.
Boulez, Pierre. *Boulez on Music Today*. London: Faber, 1971.
———. *Conversations with Célestin Deliège*. London: Eulenburg, 1977.
———. *Orientations*. London: Faber, 1986.
———. *Stocktakings from an Apprenticeship*. Oxford: Clarendon and New York: Oxford University Press, 1991.
Glock, William, ed. *Pierre Boulez: A Symposium*. London: Eulenburg, 1986.
Goléa, Antoine. *Rencontres avec Pierre Boulez*. Paris: Juillard, 1958.
Griffiths, Paul. *Boulez*. London: Oxford University Press, 1978.
Häusler, Josef, ed. *Pierre Boulez: Eine Festschrift zum 60. Geburtstag am 26. März 1985*. Vienna: Universal, 1985.
Jameux, Dominique. *Pierre Boulez*. London: Faber, 1991.
Koblyakov, Lev. *Pierre Boulez: A World of Harmony*. Chur and New York: Harwood, 1990.
Nattiez, Jean-Jacques, ed. *The Boulez-Cage Correspondence*. Cambridge and New York: Cambridge University Press, 1993.
Peyser, Joan. *Boulez*. New York: Schirmer, 1976; London: Cassell, 1977.
Stacey, Peter F. *Boulez and the Modern Concept*. Aldershot: Scolar, 1987.

Earle Brown

http://www.earle-brown.org

Gavin Bryars

http://www.gavinbryars.com

John Cage

John Cage. New York, Peters, 1962.
Musik-Konzepte, Sonderband John Cage I. Munich: text+kritik, 1978.

————. Sonderband John Cage II. Munich: text+kritik, 1990.

Rolywholyover: A Circus. New York: Rizzoli, and Los Angeles: Museum of Contemporary Art, 1993.

Cage, John. *Silence: Lectures and Writings*. Middletown, Conn.: Wesleyan University Press, 1961; London: Calder & Boyars, 1968.

————. *A Year from Monday: New Lectures and Writings*. Middletown, Conn.: Wesleyan University Press, 1967; London: Calder & Boyars, 1968.

————. *M: Writings '67–'72*. Middletown, Conn.: Wesleyan University Press, 1973; London: Calder & Boyars, 1973, repr. Marion Boyars, 1998.

————. *Empty Words: Writings '73–'78*. Middletown, Conn.: Wesleyan University Press, 1979; London, Marion Boyars, 1980.

————. *Themes & Variations*. Barrytown, N.Y.: Station Hill, 1982.

————. *X: Writings '79–'82*. Middletown, Conn.: Wesleyan University Press, 1983; London, Marion Boyars, 1987.

————. *I-VI*. Cambridge, Mass.: Harvard University Press, 1990.

————. *Composition in Retrospect*. Cambridge, Mass.: Exact Change, 1993.

Cage, John and Daniel Charles. *For the Birds*. Boston, Mass. and London: Marion Boyars, 1981.

Fleming, Richard, and William Duckworth eds. *John Cage at Seventy-Five*. Lewisburg, Penn.: Bucknell University Press, 1989.

Griffiths, Paul. *Cage*. London: Oxford University Press, 1981.

Kostelanetz, Richard, ed. *John Cage*. New York: Praeger, 1970; London, Allen Lane, 1971; rev. New York: Da Capo, 1991.

Nattiez, Jean-Jacques, ed. *The Boulez-Cage Correspondence*. Cambridge and New York: Cambridge University Press, 1993.

Nicholls, David. *John Cage*. Urbana: University of Illinois Press, 2007.

————, ed. *The Cambridge Companion to John Cage*. Cambridge and New York: Cambridge University Press, 2002.

Perloff, Marjorie, and Charles Junkerman. *John Cage: Composed in America*. Chicago: University of Chicago Press, 1994.

Pritchett, James. *The Music of John Cage*. Cambridge and New York: Cambridge University Press, 1993.

Revill, David. *The Roaring Silence: John Cage: A Life*. London: Bloomsbury, 1992.
http://www.johncage.info

Cornelius Cardew

Cardew, Cornelius. *Stockhausen Serves Imperialism, and Other Articles*. London: Latimer New Dimensions, 1974.

————, ed. *Scratch Music*. London: Latimer New Dimensions, 1972.

Prevost, Edwin, ed. *Cornelius Cardew: A Reader*. Harlow: Copula, 2006.

Tilbury, John, *Cornelius Cardew: A Life Unifinished*. Harlow: Copula, 2008.

Elliott Carter

Bernard, Jonathan W., ed. *Elliott Carter: Collected Essays and Lectures: 1937–1995*. Rochester, N.Y.: University of Rochester Press, 1997.

Edwards, Allen. *Flawed Words and Stubborn Sounds: A Conversation with Elliott Carter*. New York: Norton, 1971.

Link, John F. *Elliott Carter: A Guide to Research*. New York and London: Garland, 2000.

Meyer, Felix, and Anne C. Shreffler, eds. *Elliott Carter: A Centennial Portrait in Letters and Documents*. Woodbridge: Boydell, 2008.

Ponthus, Marc, and Susan Tang, eds. *Elliott Carter: A Centennial Celebration*. Hillsdale, N.Y.: Pendragon, 2008.

Schiff, David. *The Music of Elliott Carter*. London: Eulenburg, 1983; 2nd ed. Faber, 1998.

Peter Maxwell Davies

Bayliss, Colin. *The Music of Sir Peter Maxwell Davies: An Annotated Catalogue*. Beverley: Highgate, 1991.

Gloag, Kenneth, and Nicholas Jones, eds. *Peter Maxwell Davies Studies*. Cambridge and New York: Cambridge University Press, 2009.

Griffiths, Paul. *Peter Maxwell Davies*. London: Robson, 1981.

Pruslin, Stephen, ed. *Peter Maxwell Davies: Studies from Two Decades*. London: Boosey & Hawkes, 1979.

Seabrook, Mike. *Max: The Life and Music of Peter Maxwell Davies*. London: Gollancz, 1994.

http://www.maxopus.com

Donnacha Dennehy

http://www.donnachadennehy.com

Frank Denyer

http://www.frankdenyer.eu

Péter Eötvös

http://www.eotvospeter.com

Franco Evangelisti

Musik-Konzepte, 43–44. Munich: text+kritik, 1985.

Morton Feldman

Musik-Konzepte, 48–49. Munich: text+kritik, 1986.

DeLio, Thomas, ed. *The Music of Morton Feldman*. New York: Routledge, 1996.

Feldman, Morton. *Essays*. Edited by Walter Zimmermann. Kerpen: Beginner, 1985.

Friedman, B. H., ed., *Give My Regards to Eighth Street: Collected Writings of Morton Feldman*. Cambridge, Mass.: Exact Change, 2000.

Mörchen, Raoul, ed. *Morton Feldman in Middelburg: Words on Music*. Cologne: MusikTexte, 2008.

Villars, Chris, ed. *Morton Feldman Says: Selected Interviews and Lectures 1964–1987.* London: Hyphen, 2006. www.cnvill.net/mfhome.htm

Brian Ferneyhough

Contrechamps, 8. Paris: L'Age d'Homme, 1988.
Musik-Konzepte, 140. Munich: text+kritik, 2008.
Ferneyhough, Brian. *Collected Writings.* Edited by James Boros and Richard Toop. Amsterdam: Harwood, 1995.

Michael Finnissy

Fox, Christopher, et al. *Uncommon Ground: The Music of Michael Finnissy.* Aldershot: Ashgate, 1997.

Heiner Goebbels

http://www.heinergoebbels.com

Alexander Goehr

Music Analysis, 9/2–3. 1992)
Latham, Alison, ed. *Sing, Ariel: Essays and Thoughts for Alexander Goehr's Seventieth Birthday.* Aldershot: Ashgate, 2003.
Puffett, Derrick, ed. *Finding the Key: Selected Writings of Alexander Goehr.* London: Faber, 1998.

Henryk Górecki

Thomas, Adrian. *Górecki.* Oxford: Clarendon Press, 1997.

Sofia Gubaidulina

Kurtz, Michael. *Sofia Gubaidulina: A Biography.* Bloomington: Indiana University Press, 2007.

Jonathan Harvey

Downes, Michael. *Jonathan Harvey: Song Offerings and White as Jasmine.* Farnham, Surrey: Ashgate, 2009.
Harvey, Jonathan. *In Quest of Spirit: Thoughts on Music.* Berkeley, Calif., and London: University of California Press, 1999.
———. *Music and Inspiration.* Edited by Michael Downes. London: Faber, 1999.
Whittall, Arnold. *Jonathan Harvey.* London: Faber, 1999.
http://www.vivosvoco.com

Hans Werner Henze

Musik-Konzepte, 132. Munich: text+kritik, 2006.
Henze, Hans Werner. *Music and Politics.* London: Faber, 1982.

————. *Bohemian Fifths*. London: Faber, 1998.

Rickards, Guy. *Hindemith, Hartmann and Henze*. London: Phaidon, 1995.

Heinz Holliger

Albèra, Philippe, ed. *Heinz Holliger: Entretiens, textes, écrits sur son oeuvre*. Geneva: Contrechamps, 1996.

Landau, Annette, ed. *Heinz Holliger: Komponist, Oboist, Dirigent*. Bern: Zytglogge, 1996.

Mauricio Kagel

Musik-Konzepte, 124. Munich: text+kritik, 2004.

Musique en jeu, 27. Paris, 1977.

Heile, Björn. *The Music of Mauricio Kagel*. Aldershot: Ashgate, 2006.

Kagel, Mauricio. *Worte über Musik*. Munich: Piper, 1991.

Klüppelholz, Werner. *Mauricio Kagel 1970–1980*. Cologne: DuMont, 1981.

————, ed. *Kagel . . . /1991*. Cologne: DuMont, 1991.

Schnebel, Dieter. *Mauricio Kagel: Musik, Theater, Film*. Cologne: DuMont, 1970.

http://www.mauricio-kagel.com

György Kurtág

Contrechamps, 12–13. Paris: L'Age d'Homme, 1990.

Albèra, Philippe, ed. *György Kurtág: Entretiens, textes, écrits sur son oeuvre*. Geneva: Contrechamps, 1995.

Beckles Willson, Rachel. *Ligeti, Kurtág, and Hungarian Music During the Cold War*. Cambridge and New York: Cambridge University Press, 2007.

Spangemacher, Friedrich, ed. *György Kurtág*. Bonn: Boosey & Hawkes, 1989.

Varga, Bálint András. *György Kurtág: Three Interviews and Ligeti Homages*. Rochester, N.Y.: University of Rochester Press, 2009.

Helmut Lachenmann

Musik-Konzepte, 61–62. Munich: text+kritik, 1988.

————, 146. Munich: text+kritik, 2009.

Lachenmann, Helmut. *Musik als existentielle Erfahrung*. Edited by Josef Häusler. Wiesbaden: Breitkopf & Härtel, 1996; 2nd ed. 2004.

György Ligeti

Ligeti in Conversation. London: Eulenburg, 1983.

Beckles Willson, Rachel. *Ligeti, Kurtág, and Hungarian Music During the Cold War*. Cambridge and New York: Cambridge University Press, 2007.

Griffiths, Paul. *György Ligeti*. London: Robson, 1983; 2nd ed. 1997.

Michel, Pierre. *György Ligeti: Compositeur d'aujourd'hui*. Paris: Minerve, 1985.

Nordwall, Ove. *György Ligeti: Eine Monographie*. Mainz: Schott, 1971.

Sabbe, Hermann. *György Ligeti* [= *Musik-Konzepte*, 53]. Munich: text+kritik, 1987.

Steinitz, Richard., *György Ligeti: Music of the Imagination*. London: Faber, 2003.
Toop, Richard. *György Ligeti*. London: Phaidon, 1999.

Witold Lutosławski

Musik-Konzepte, 71–3. Munich: text+kritik, 1991.
Rae, Charles Bodman. *The Music of Lutosławski*. London: Faber, 1994.
Skowron, Zbigniew, ed. *Lutosławski on Music*. Lanham, Md.: Scarecrow, 2007.
Stucky, Steven. *Lutosławski and his Music*. Cambridge and New York: Cambridge University Press, 1971.
Varga, Bálint András. *Lutosławski Profile*. London: Chester, 1976.

Alvin Lucier

Lucier, Alvin. *Reflections: Interviews, Scores, Writings*. Cologne: MusikTexte, 1995; 2nd ed. 2005.
Ottmann, Klaus, ed. *Alvin Lucier*. Middletown, Conn.: Wesleyan University Press, 1988.
http://alucier.web.wesleyan.edu

Olivier Messiaen

Musik-Konzepte, 28. Munich: text+kritik, 1982.
Dingle, Christopher. *The Life of Messiaen*. Cambridge and New York: Cambridge University Press, 2007.
Goléa, Antoine. *Rencontres avec Olivier Messiaen*. Paris: Julliard, 1960.
Griffiths, Paul. *Olivier Messiaen and the Music of Time*. London: Faber, 1985.
Hill, Peter, ed. *The Messiaen Companion*. London: Faber, 1995.
Hill, Peter and Nigel Simeone. *Messiaen*. New Haven and London: Yale University Press, 2005.
Maas, Sander van. *The Reinvention of Religious Music: Olivier Messiaen's Breakthrough Toward the Beyond*. New York: Fordham University Press, 2009.
Nichols, Roger. *Messiaen*. London: Oxford University Press, 1975; 2nd ed. 1986.
Samuel, Claude. *Olivier Messiaen: Music and Color*. Portland, Oreg.: Amadeus, 1994.
Sherlaw Johnson, Robert. *Olivier Messiaen*. London: Dent, 1975.
Sholl, Robert, ed. *Messiaen Studies*. Cambridge and New York: Cambridge University Press, 2007.

Conlon Nancarrow

Gann, Kyle. *The Music of Conlon Nancarrow*. Cambridge and New York: Cambridge University Press, 1995.

Luigi Nono

Contemporary Music Review, 18. 1999.
Contrechamps, special number. Paris: L'Age d'Homme, 1987.
Musik-Konzepte, 20. Munich: text+kritik, 1981.
Feneyrou, Laurent, ed. *Luigi Nono: Ecrits*. Paris: Christian Bourgois, 1993.

Häusler, Josef, ed. *Brennpunkt Nono.* Salzburg: Residenz, 1993.

Stenzl, Jürg, ed. *Luigi Nono: Texte, Studien zu seiner Musik.* Zurich: Atlantis, 1975.

http://www.luiginono.it

Pauline Oliveros

Gunden, Heidi von. *The Music of Pauline Oliveros.* Metuchen, N.J.: Scarecrow, 1983.

Mockus, Martha. *Sounding Out: Pauline Oliveros and Lesbian Musicality.* New York: Routledge, 2008.

http://www.paulineoliveros.us

Arvo Pärt

Hillier, Paul, *Arvo Pärt.* Oxford and New York: Oxford University Press, 1997.

http://www.arvopart.info

Harry Partch

Partch, Harry. *Genesis of a Music.* New York: Da Capo, 1974.

———. *Bitter Music.* ed. Thomas McGeary. Urbana: University of Illinois Press, 1991.

Krzysztof Penderecki

Schwinger, Wolfram. *Krzysztof Penderecki: His Life and Works.* London: Schott, 1989.

Gérard Pesson

Pesson, Gérard. *Cran d'arrêt du beau temps: Journal 1991–1998.* Paris: Van Dieren, 2008.

Henri Pousseur

Musik-Konzepte, 69. Munich: text+kritik, 1990.

Pousseur, Henri. *Fragments théoriques sur la musique experimentale*: i. Brussels: Institut de Sociologie, Université Libre de Bruxelles, 1970), ii. 1972.

———. *Musique/Sémantique/Société.* Tournai: Casterman, 1972.

Steve Reich

Reich, Steve. *Writings about Music.* Halifax, Nova Scotia: Press of the Nova Scotia College of Art and Design, 1974)

———. *Writings on Music, 1965–2000.* Edited by Paul Hillier. Oxford and New York: Oxford University Press, 2002.

http://www.stevereich.com

Rolf Riehm

http://www.rolf-riehm.de

Wolfgang Rihm

Musik-Konzepte, Sonderband. Munich: text+kritik, 2004.
Rexroth, Dieter, ed. *Der Komponist Wolfgang Rihm*. Mainz: Schott, 1985.
Rihm, Wolfgang. *ausgesprochen: Gesammelte Schriften, Reden und Gespräche*. Winterthur: Amadeus, 1992.
———. *Offene Enden: Denkbewegungen um und durch Musik*. Edited by Ulrich Mosch. Munich: Hanser, 2002.
Storch, Wolfgang, ed. *Wolfgang Rihm*. Düsseldorf, 2000.

Frederic Rzewski

Rzewski, Frederic. *Nonsequiturs: Writings and Lectures*. Cologne: MusikTexte, 2007.

Kaija Saariaho

Moisala, Pirkko. *Kaija Saariaho*. Bloomington: University of Illinois Press, 2009.
http://www.saariaho.org

Giacinto Scelsi

Musik-Konzepte, 31. Munich: text+kritik, 1983.
Angermann, Klaus, ed. *Giancinto Scelsi: In Innern des Tons*. Hofheim: Wolke, 1993.

Salvatore Sciarrino

Giuliani, Roberto. *Salvatore Sciarrino: Catalogo delle opere*. Milan: Ricordi, 1999.
Sciarrino, Salvatore. *Le figure della musica: Da Beethoven a oggi*. Milan: Ricordi, 1998.
———. *Carte da suono, 1981–2001*. Edited by Dario Oliveri. Rome: CIDIM and Palermo: Novecento, 2001.

Alfred Schnittke

Ivashkin, Alexander, *Alfred Schnittke*. London: Phaidon, 1996.
———, ed. *A Schnittke Reader*. Bloomington: Indiana University Press, 2002.

Arnold Schoenberg

Ringer, Alexander L. *Arnold Schoenberg: The Composer as Jew*. Oxford: Clarendon and New York: Oxford University Press, 1976.
Stuckenschmidt, H. H. *Schoenberg: His Life, World and Work*. London: John Calder, 1977.

Dmitry Shostakovich

Norris, Christopher, ed. *Shostakovich: The Man and his Music*. London: Lawrence and Wishart, 1982.
Wilson, Elizabeth. *Shostakovich: A Life Remembered*. London: Faber, 1994.

Karlheinz Stockhausen

Contrechamps, 9. Paris: L'Age d'Homme, 1988.

Karlheinz Stockhausen: Music and Machines (1954–1970). London: BBC, 1985 (programme book with notes by Richard Toop).

Musik-Konzepte, 19. Munich: text+kritik, 1981.

Conen, Hermann. *Formel-Komposition: Zu Karlheinz Stockhausens Musik der siebziger Jahre*. Mainz: Schott, 1991.

Cott, Jonathan. *Stockhausen: Conversations with the Composer*. London: Robson, 1974.

Harvey, Jonathan. *The Music of Stockhausen*. London: Faber, 1974.

Heikinheimo, Seppo. *The Electronic Music of Karlheinz Stockhausen* [= *Acta musicologica fennica*, 6]. Helsinki: Suomen Musiikkitieteellinen Seura, 1972.

Henck, Herbert. *Karlheinz Stockhausen's Klavierstück X: A Contribution toward Understanding Serial Technique*. Cologne: Neuland, 1980.

Kurtz, Michael. *Stockhausen: A Biography*. London: Faber, 1992.

Maconie, Robin. *The Works of Karlheinz Stockhausen*. London: Oxford University Press, 1976; 2nd ed. 1990.

———, ed. *Stockhausen on Music: Lectures and Interviews*. London: Marion Boyars, 1989.

———. *Other Planets: The Music of Karlheinz Stockhausen*. Lanham, Md.: Scarecrow, 2005.

Nevill, Tim, ed. *Towards a Cosmic Music: Texts by Karlheinz Stockhausen*. London: Element, 1989.

Stockhausen, Karlheinz. *Texte*, i. Cologne: DuMont, 1963; ii. 1964; iii. 1971; iv. 1978; v. 1989; vi. 1989.

Tannenbaum, Mya. *Conversations with Stockhausen*. Oxford: Clarendon and New York: Oxford University Press, 1987.

Wörner, K. H. *Stockhausen: Life and Work*. London: Faber, 1973.

http://www.stockhausen.org

Igor Stravinsky

Andriessen, Louis and Elmer Schönberger. *The Apollonian Clockwork: On Stravinsky*. Oxford: Oxford University Press, 1989.

Boretz, Benjamin and Edward T. Cone, eds. *Perspectives on Schoenberg and Stravinsky*. Princeton: Princeton University Press, 1968.

Walsh, Stephen. *The Music of Stravinsky*. London: Routledge, 1988.

———. *Stravinsky: The Second Exile: France and America 1934–1971*. London: Jonathan Cape, 2006; New York: Knopf, 2006.

Steven Stucky

http://www.stevenstucky.com

Tōru Takemitsu

Burt, Peter. *The Music of Tōru Takemitsu*. Cambridge and New York: Cambridge University Press, 2001.

Takemitsu. Tōru, *Confronting Silence: Selected Writings*. Edited by Yoshiko Kakudo and Glenn Glasow. Berkeley, Calif.: Fallen Leaf, 1995.

John Tavener

Haydon, Geoffrey. *John Tavener: Glimpses of Paradise*. London: Gollancz, 1995.
Tavener, John. *The Music of Silence: A Composer's Testament*. Edited by Brian Keeble. London: Faber, 1999.

James Tenney

Contemporary Music Review, 27/1. 2008.
Polansky, Larry. *The Early Works of James Tenney* (= *Soundings*, 13. 1983; available online at www.frogpeak.org).

Galina Ustvolskaya

Musik-Konzepte, 143. Munich: text+kritik, 2009.

Edgard Varèse

Bernard, Jonathan. *The Music of Edgard Varèse*. New Haven and London: Yale University Press, 1987.
Charbonnier, Georges. *Entretiens avec Edgard Varèse*. Paris: Belfond, 1970.
MacDonald, Malcolm. *Varèse: Astronomer in Sound*. London: Kahn & Averill, 2003.

Christian Wolff

Wolff, Christian. *Cues: Writings and Conversations*. Edited by Gisela Gronemeyer und Reinhard Oehlschlägel. Cologne: MusikTexte, 1998.

Stefan Wolpe

Clarkson, Austin, ed. *On the Music of Stefan Wolpe: Essays and Recollections*. Hillsdale, N.Y.: Pendragon, 2003.
http://www.wolpe.org

Hugh Wood

Venn, Edward. *The Music of Hugh Wood*. Aldershot: Ashgate, 2008.
Wood, Hugh. *Staking Out the Territory, and Other Writings on Music*. London: Plumbago, 2007.

Iannis Xenakis

Musik-Konzepte, 54-5. Munich: text+kritik, 1987.
Harley, James. *Xenakis: His Life in Music*. New York: Routledge, 2004.
Matossian, Nouritza. *Xenakis*. London: Kahn & Averill, 1986.
Varga, Bálint András. *Conversations with Xenakis*. London: Faber, 1996.
Xenakis, Iannis. *Formalized Music: Thought and Mathematics in Composition*. Bloomington: Indiana University Press, 1971; 2nd ed. Stuyvesant, N.Y.: Pendragon, 1992.
———. *Music and Architecture: Architectural Projects, Texts, and Realizations*. Edited by Sharon Kanach. Hillsdale, N.Y.: Pendragon, 2008.
http://www.iannis-xenakis.org

La Monte Young

Duckworth, William, and Richard Fleming. *Sound and Light: La Monte Young and Marian Zazeela.* Lewisburg, Penn.: Bucknell University Press, 1996.
http://melafoundation.org

Bernd Alois Zimmermann

Contrechamps, 5. Paris: L'Age d'Homme, 1985.
Musik-Konzepte, Sonderband. Munich: text+kritik, 2005.
Zimmermann, Bernd Alois. *Intervall und Zeit: Aufsätze und Schriften zum Werk.* Mainz: Schott, 1974.

John Zorn

http://www.hipsroadedition.com

Index

CPSIA information can be obtained at www.ICGtesting.com
Printed in the USA
BVOW04s1335120115

382822BV00001B/1/P